# A PASSION TO SERVE

Here is a riveting account of Atlanta's recent history in matters of faith, race, and justice, written by Sherry Frank, herself an important history-maker and highly regarded bridge-builder in the city. Atlanta would not be Atlanta without her. Frank's generosity of spirit, unflinching honesty, and recollection of fascinating details make this book a real page turner. I couldn't put it down.

—**Reverend Dr. Joanna M. Adams**
**Presbyterian Pastor and Community Leader**

Sherry Frank is the epitome of a bridge builder. Her commitment, passion and dedication, leading her to celebrate similarities and respect differences, are reflected in her memoirs. She articulates the need for the betterment of our society.

Sherry is a strong supporter of good causes and a pillar of social action. Her wisdom, intelligence, and strategic thinking are the seeds for improvement and growth. She weaves relationships and walks the walk. A role model whom I admire and love deeply, Sherry is the figure to follow whenever we are ready to create a better world.

—**Rabbi Dr. Analia Bortz, M.D.**
**Congregation Or Hadash, Atlanta, Georgia**

*A Passion to Serve: Memoirs of a Jewish Activist* compellingly summarizes the legacy of Sherry Frank. She was an early advocate for women's issues. She challenged those who resisted interfaith experiences and fought against those who opposed racial/cultural diversity. This transparent, well-conceived and written book will encourage its reader to pursue a fuller life.

—**Reverend Dr. Gerald L. Durley**
**Pastor Emeritus, Providence Missionary Baptist Church**

Sherry Frank has been a close friend since childhood, and that makes me especially proud that she has written such an eloquent, moving memoir that demonstrates how during the course of her remarkable career, she has been an inspiration to those who wish to become leaders in both the Jewish and broader American communities. As both a volunteer at the National Council of Jewish Women, and particularly as the head for a quarter of a century of the southeast region of the American Jewish Committee based in Atlanta, she was the crucial bridge between the Jewish and African-American communities, working on an astonishing array of important issues with national and international implications. Her excellent book takes us through an important period in our country's history, when religious, civil rights, and Jewish leaders found common ground, and provides important lessons in our polarized and divisive times.

—**Ambassador Stuart E. Eizenstat**
**Chief White House Domestic Policy Adviser to President Jimmy Carter;**
**U.S.Ambassador to European Union;**
**Deputy Secretary of the Treasury; and**
**Special Representative for Holocaust-Era Issues in the Clinton Administration**

Sherry is the perfect mix of prime mover and raconteur. She has a fifty year track record of seeking out pivotal moments of history and entering the fray, mobilizing cohorts to follow her lead and superb intuition and savvy. She is a sincere friend to the great and small, and a storyteller par excellence. This book may be Sherry's memoirs, but it captures the social justice history of our generation.

—**Lois Frank**
**Past National President, Jewish Council for Public Affairs,**
**and National Board Member, American Jewish Committee**
**and MAZON: A Jewish Response to Hunger**

Sherry Frank has demonstrated commitment to and skill for connecting people and organizations across the metro Atlanta region for the common good. Her stories document how the city and its people have faced the challenges of the time by overcoming obstacles and seizing opportunities to grow with grace and dedication to expanded human rights for all. Sherry opens her heart to others and welcomes them into her vast network of colleagues who honor the past while forging a better future.

—**Shirley Franklin**
**Mayor of Atlanta, 2002-2010**

Readers of this book are in for a rare treat. Sherry Frank offers a ringside view of fifty years of American and Jewish history. She was on the front lines as a superb ambassador and tenacious advocate for civil rights, interfaith cooperation, Israel's well-being and Jewish security. What a powerful legacy she leaves, and what a compelling story she tells!

—**David Harris**
**CEO, American Jewish Committee**

This book tells the story of a central figure in the last half of the 20th century's struggle to gain respect for human dignity. Sherry Frank was a bridge between the Jewish and African-American communities when their collaboration created a moral force for good. I met her there on the front lines of change, and we have been friends ever since. This is her story about what happened and how it happened in the fight for social justice in America that changed this country forever.

**—The Honorable John Lewis**
**U.S. Representative for Georgia's 5th District**

What a joy for me to know that my friend, Sherry Frank, has written her memoir. Her work covers an extraordinary life that has touched so many in so many different ways. Sherry Frank's life offers the reader a record of what one modern Jewish woman can attain through her endeavors to bring to bear the prophetic teachings of our faith to the diverse world she has encountered. The broad range of topics she touches upon in her book reflects the diversity of her interests and the passion for these causes that has motivated her life. And what Sherry Frank's life manifests most of all, is the goodness of her heart coupled with the strength of her conviction that each of us, to the best of our abilities. is here to make the world a better place.

**—Alvin M. Sugarman**
**Rabbi Emeritus, The Temple, Atlanta, Georgia**

# A PASSION TO SERVE

# A PASSION TO SERVE

## MEMOIRS OF A JEWISH ACTIVIST

SHERRY Z. FRANK

**BOOK**LOGIX˙
Alpharetta, GA

The author has tried to recreate events, locations, and conversations from her memories of them. The author has made every effort to give credit to the source of any images, quotes, or other material contained within and obtain permissions when feasible.

ISBN: 978-1-63183-486-8 - Paperback
eISBN: 978-1-63183-435-6 - ePub
eISBN: 978-1-63183-436-3 - mobi

Library of Congress Control Number: 2019903990

10 9 8 7 6 5 4 3 2                                           040419

⊗ This paper meets the requirements of ANSI/NISO Z39.48-1992 (Permanence of Paper)

Author photograph by Eric Bern Studio

# CONTENTS

# INTRODUCTION AND ACKNOWLEDGMENTS

"May you live in interesting times," supposedly a Chinese curse, is used ironically, because those "interesting" times are historically filled with challenges, conflict and strife. I have been blessed/cursed to live in those times. Since my young adulthood, I have been actively involved in the critical social and political issues of the day. I have seen my life unfold into a series of adventures that sometimes involved risk, but most often yielded reward.

Wanting my eleven grandchildren to know about the complex times I lived in and the significant work I was devoted to, I decided to write my memoirs, documenting the activities and accomplishments of which I am most proud and the friends and partners with whom I collaborated over the decades.

I was truly fortunate to be first a leader in the National Council of Jewish Women (NCJW) and later a Jewish professional in the American Jewish Committee (AJC). Through these organizations, I embraced the feminist movement, defended Zionism, battled anti-Semitism and discrimination, and continued the fight for civil and human rights. I witnessed the fall of the Berlin Wall, the release of Anatoly Shcharansky from the former Soviet Union and Nelson Mandela from South Africa, and the liberation of Ethiopian Jews. I played a role in the establishment of a genetic screening center at Emory University, the creation of the Atlanta Jewish Film Festival and the formation of a new synagogue, Congregation Or Hadash. I helped initiate the Atlanta Black/Jewish Coalition as well as ACCESS, AJC's young leadership group, and expanded the Jewish oral history program. Through speeches, marches and lobbying, I was able to provide leadership and voice to a wide array of social justice issues within the United States and internationally.

When I began volunteering in the community in the late 1960s, the definitions were narrow: ethnic diversity was viewed as black and white, and interfaith diversity included only Catholics, Protestants and Jews. In the ensuing fifty years, I had a front row seat to Atlanta's changes through its extraordinarily rapid demographic growth. Today we live in an international city that embraces representatives of all world religions and ethnic identities. I thought it was important to write chapters on this growth and our responses to it.

My work took me to countries around the world to build bridges of understanding with people of multiple faiths, document significant events, to walk in sacred places and to observe an historic trial. I will forever be grateful for the opportunity to travel to England, Germany, the former Soviet Union, South Africa, Turkey, Jordan and, more than ten times, to Israel.

Driven by a strong Jewish identity and pride in my community involvement, I decided to make a link in this memoir between the Hebrew word, *Chai*, which means both life and the number "18." I chose to write eighteen chapters, each quite different, as was my life's work. Some chapters are very personally about me and my family; others are more historic, providing the timeline and development of the wide array of areas that I was involved with and places I traveled. The Appendix contains lists of various programs and specific advocacy topics to provide additional background information regarding the subjects that I followed.

The book can be read straight through or by choosing chapters that beckon the reader. I have no favorite. Each one tells a story that formed a piece of the history I have been so lucky to be a part of.

So how and when did I start off on this journey to chronicle my last fifty years of communal endeavors? It began in 2009 when a fortuitous occasion served as my catalyst. My friend, Diana Silverman, and I were rooming together in Washington, D.C., having gone there to celebrate our mutual friend Fran Eizenstat's 65th birthday at a party given by her husband, Stuart. I shared with Diana my desire to write my memoirs, and she told me (modestly) that she really enjoyed editing and had edited all of her late husband, Dr. Mark Silverman's, books. That turned out to be the incentive I needed. Diana and I had worked together for years in the National Council of Jewish Women and shared a strong commitment to community and family. I felt sure we could collaborate successfully.

I took a few years off trying to find time to work on the book in earnest. Then we began our research in the NCJW offices, reviewing scrapbooks filled with bulletins from 1970-2006. We pulled the files marked Tay-Sachs, Soviet Jewry, Women's Issues, and my personal one, Sherry Frank. I am deeply indebted to the staff over the decades who kept such impeccable in-depth and up-to-date records.

We next turned to the American Jewish Committee office. When I began to serve as the Southeast Area Director, I asked our national archivist to come to Atlanta to teach me how to create a comprehensive filing system. That was one of the smartest things I ever did, because it led to an easily accessible reservoir of materials. I was able to access information quickly from meticulously numbered and dated archive boxes. Diana was a dedicated partner as we spent months patiently reviewing twenty-five years of AJC files and my work in the community.

I am often reminded of Atlanta Chapter Past President, Candy Berman's, advice: "tell stories." As I began to fill every chapter with material from press releases, newspaper articles, letters, reports and descriptions of programs and activities, I found myself telling one story after another. Words cannot express the sheer joy I experienced in reviewing so many materials, reliving the events they brought to mind and then writing about them with pen and paper. (I still think best writing on a legal pad rather than on the computer.)

I discovered a number of things I had not expected to write about when I started this project. It was especially meaningful to share brief personal reflections about my parents. My children never knew my father, and my grandchildren knew neither of my parents. In addition, I was able to retrieve the memories of five women who had passed away with whom I shared a unique relationship. I wrote about the support the Jewish community received time and again from non-Jewish leaders, clergy, politicians, media and civic activists, for causes central to our Jewish agenda. Special among these were my personal connection to Congressman John Lewis; my advocacy and professional work in countless interfaith and social justice areas with my dear friend, the Reverend Dr. Joanna Adams; and my trusted and close relationship with one of the members of my Black/Jewish Sisters Group, Ingrid Saunders Jones, former Senior Vice President of Global Community Connections for The Coca-Cola Company and Chair of The Coca-Cola Foundation.

I worked with outstanding lay leaders and an impressive list of Atlanta Chapter presidents. Although I focused attention on the outstanding women presidents I worked with -- Elaine Alexander, Lois Frank, Candy Berman, and Elise Eplan -- I am equally grateful for the men who served as presidents and enabled us to reach new heights. This blue-ribbon list included Tom Asher, Larry Lowenstein, Joel Goldberg, Marvin Weintraub, Steve Selig, Richard Cohen, Arnold Sidman, Buck Goldstein, Lewis Kravitz and Kent Alexander.

My decades of work in the interreligious community were strengthened by the unwavering support and engagement AJC received from three exceptional Atlanta rabbis. I was blessed to have learned from and partnered with Rabbi Arnold Goodman, Ahavath Achim Synagogue; Rabbi Alvin Sugarman, The Temple; and Rabbi Ron Segal, Temple Sinai.

We always had a small but very dedicated and talented staff working for AJC. They each contributed to our work and enhanced the sense of teamwork and collaboration we maintained in our office. I am particularly grateful for the service given by April Levine, Jean Saul and Pam Rosenthal. Staci Brill was our first Development

Director, and she took us to a totally new level of campaign achievement. Ronnie van Gelder was not only my invaluable and gifted colleague, but she became my best friend. Judy Marx was one of the smartest people I ever worked with, and she patiently led me, albeit reluctantly on my part, into the world of technology. Sunny Stern was a gentle soul, beloved by everyone, who worked with us for nine years until she passed away.

For over twenty years, Lillian Troop and Dale Shields kept our office running, my endless memos, letters, reports and speeches typed and filed, and our membership records updated. They were caring friends to our members, informed communicators with our community partners, and my personal supporters in challenging times. So much more than efficient staff, they were truly devoted to the mission of AJC.

It was a privilege being associated for over twenty-five years with the national staff of the AJC. Our distinguished Executive Director, David Harris, inspired me and led us brilliantly to become a major player in the world of global advocacy. My national colleagues were the best in their respective fields and were held in the highest esteem. They shared their expertise with us and generously supported our local work.

As I concluded writing each chapter, I turned to Betsy Turner to type my convoluted handwritten notes that were complicated by a plethora of attachments interspersed throughout the pages. Betsy is a bright, young Presbyterian minister whom I met through Joanna Adams. She went far beyond her role as typist, and with each chapter returned, she appended thoughtful questions and comments that enabled me to clarify and expand on many of the stories I had written.

Diana received drafts of chapters as they were updated and typed. With great skill and wisdom, she edited each one to ensure that it read smoothly and accurately conveyed my thoughts. We spent long hours reviewing every word, while reflecting on so many shared and fond community memories. Diana's contribution to my memoirs was extraordinary, and I treasure the deepened friendship it has fostered. My talented friends, Jeanney Kutner, Deborah Payne, and Ronnie van Gelder, agreed to review these lengthy chapters for clarification. I am sincerely appreciative of the hours they spent and the guidance they gave me.

I have been blessed with a loving family who have added so much joy to my life. In the most difficult times, they have offered me unconditional love and support. They listened to me talk about my memoirs for years as I labored over the research and reported to them on my progress. I appreciate the interest and encouragement I always receive from my brother, Neil Zimmerman, my cousins Lois Frank, Lynn Goodman, Helen and Frank Hahn, and my sisters-in-law Sherry Zimmerman and Helene Grablowsky.

My children, Jacque and Tom Friedland, Laura Barnard, Jake and Kendall Frank and Drew and Jana Frank, have made me so proud of their dedication to family, career accomplishments and commitment to community service. Most of all, they have given me the greatest gift of all, eleven wonderful grandchildren: Michael, David and Elliott Friedland; Eliana, Whitney, Peri and Danielle Barnard; Bode and Miriam Frank; Jordan and Peyton Frank

This memoir is dedicated to each of them with love and affection.

With my adult children (L-R) Jacque Friedland, Drew
Frank, Sherry Frank, Jacob Frank, Laura Barnard, 2003

With my grandchildren -(L-R) Miriam Frank, Elliott Friedland,
David Friedland, Bode Frank, Michael Friedland, Danielle
Barnard, Whitney Barnard, Jordan Frank, Eliana Barnard,
Peyton Frank, Peri Barnard, Sherry Frank seated, 2017

AJC Atlanta
Staff: standing,
Judy Marx, Dale
Shields, Lillian
Troop - seated,
Sherry Frank

Sherry Frank with David
Harris, CEO, American
Jewish Committee, 2017

# WOMEN'S ISSUES

MY MOTHER, MYSELF, MY KEHILLAH (COMMUNITY)

---

*Doing for others is the rent we pay for living in this world.*

—Marian Wright Edelman

## MY MOTHER, ESTHER HOROWITZ ZIMMERMAN

It would be nearly impossible to write my memoirs without including memories of my mother and the impact she had on my life. We shared a birthday, November 11, and she told me that when I was born, my father said, "Now I know you will always have a friend." Nothing could have been truer. My mother was my closest friend, greatest critic and most ardent supporter. On our mutual birthdays, my dad sent my mother red roses and me a bouquet of sweetheart roses. My mother was a gracious hostess who loved to entertain, which she did beautifully, and to this day I relish the opportunity to host meetings, meals and holidays at my house, frequently using her china and elegant serving pieces.

When I went through my divorce and began working full time, my mother often stepped in to drive a carpool, take a sick grandchild to the doctor and make a pot of chicken soup, of course. She spent the

1

night at my house when I worked late or left town, and my children adored her. Her family was her pride and joy, and our extended family loved her as well. My friends also had a special connection to my mom and even today will speak of her with warm affection.

On April 2, 1954, my dad died of a heart attack at the too young age of 47; my only living grandparent, my mother's mother, Bertha Horowitz, died the next year on May 13; my mother's only brother, Henry Harris, died of a heart attack in October, 1957. In a few short years, my mother had become a widow and a working woman raising two young children without the strong support of her immediate family. Still, she faced tragedy with strength and resolve, never letting on if she was down or feeling uncertain.

We were extremely close in those early years, my mother, Neil and I. In our adult years, my brother was a generous and devoted son to my mother and my personal rock when I went through my divorce and challenging financial times. I held onto a brief note Neil sent me shortly after our mom passed away.

> *She was truly a remarkable person*
> *so much love,*
> *so many strong feelings,*
> *there's a certain emptiness now,*
> *I do miss her.*

At mom's funeral on February 5, 1990, Rabbi Arnold Goodman read the following poem I had written for my mother's 50th birthday in 1965 that expressed my heartfelt love and admiration for her.

> **A Tribute**
> *A woman walks across life's path*
> *Misfortune haunts her way*
> *The woman turns her back on wrath*
> *Goes steadfast through each day.*

*Two small children are hers to raise*
*And this is her life's goal*
*Never asking for any praise*
*She works with all her soul*

*Insurance courses she will take*
*To carry on dad's work*
*Never taking a single break*
*Her duties not to shirk*

*She only wanted everything*
*For her daughter and her son*
*And all the joys that she could bring*
*She gave them, barring none*

*And in her home she always shined*
*For here she took great pride*
*A hostess lovely and refined*
*Good judgment by her side*

*Stephens and a wedding for one*
*Two granddaughters also*
*North Carolina for her son*
*Where did these past years go*

*And on a birthday such as this*
*The natural thing to do*
*Is just glance back and reminisce*
*And see what's come of you*

*You've gained love and respect and more*
*You're an inspiration*
*Loyal friends, admirers galore*
*Join our admiration*

*We're proud to know you, proud to be*
*Among a special few*
*Who love you dearly and agree*
*God's light should shine on you.*

I combed through countless speeches in writing these memoirs. My daughter Jacque's speech on May 12, 1994, when I received AJC's Selig Distinguished Service Award, is at the top of my list of favorites. It is especially meaningful because she concluded it with verses from my birthday poem for my mother, indicating that these same sentiments reflected her feelings towards me.

*Last summer I attended the annual retreat for UJA's (United Jewish Appeal) young women's leadership cabinet. The focus of the opening session was the importance of identifying our role models – specifically our female role models. We were directed to answer the question: Who were the women that influenced our lives and why?*

*This was a very easy task for me. Without a moment's hesitation, without a single doubt – I could identify my mother as my role model and my hero. Everything about the way I live my life – communally, Jewishly, and in relationship to my family and friends – is a direct result of my mother's influence on my life.*

*I know I don't need to provide a lengthy explanation to any of you on why my mom is our hero – but I would like to just share a few of my memories of growing up with a mom like Sherry.*

*Some of my very earliest memories are of playing at the NCJW's Thrift Shop. I remember tagging clothes with my sister, Laura, and mom in the crowded space behind the shop and helping set up for the big annual Bargainata sale.*

*I also remember NCJW mailings! This was before the day of computer-sorted mailing labels. Mom would bring home mailings to be labeled and sorted – all over the family room floor, we would have piles – 30327, 30328, 30329, 30330 and the piles went on and on and on!*

*I remember marching with mom and Laura in front of the Fox Theatre for Soviet Jewry, and I remember our first adopted Russian family and their two daughters, Tanya and Bella. Because of your example mom, so many special people have become part of our lives – Sasha and Dmitri, Victoria and Ilya, and Victoria and Gennady.*

*I remember mom's political activities with Barbara Asher, Andrew Young, Wyche Fowler, and, of course, John Lewis. The whole family became involved for John!*

*At this point I must diverge for just one minute to tell a very special story that happened last year at the Young Leadership Cabinet Retreat. For those of you unfamiliar with Cabinet, it is a group of 300 women from throughout the United States who participate in leadership roles in their respective Jewish communities. Our guest speaker for the opening night of Retreat was Congressman Lewis. After an engrossing speech in which Congressman Lewis shared his story and his experiences during the Civil Rights movement and his trip to Israel with the Black Congressional Caucus, he opened the floor to questions. The first woman asked, how can we make a difference in our individual communities with Black-Jewish relations? Congressman Lewis' response was to immediately identify the efforts of my mother in Atlanta and the work of the American Jewish Committee. I cannot tell you how proud I was to be sitting in the audience at this UJA conference in Chicago – glowing in the success stories of my mom and AJC in Atlanta.*

*And interwoven with all of mom's communal and political activities has always been an uncompromising sense of the importance of family, and the role of Judaism in our family. As I explain to my friends in San Francisco – my mom created a Jewishness that was one of celebration. Our calendar was set from one family and holiday celebration to the next.*

*I remember growing up with family Shabbat – mom did not answer the phones on Friday night. We lit candles and said the prayers and were not allowed out to the high school football games* until after Shabbat dinner was over (and not rushed to be over!). I cannot count the sheets of construction paper that went to create colorful chains to decorate our sukkahs on Windy Ridge, in Memphis, and now on Abernathy Road. I know many of you have joined in mom's Sukkot celebrations.

A couple of years ago my sister and I were talking about how we would raise our kids – of course this was somewhat of a hypothetical conversation – we both responded instantly that we hope to raise our kids just like mom raised us.

While each of us kids – Andrew, Jacob, Laura, and me – each grew up with different experiences and have different memories, we all grew up with a wonderful sense of love, support, and encouragement that mom provided us and a true sense of strength and independence.

When my mother was installed as president of NCJW in 1973, she thanked her mother, her strongest supporter and dearest friend. When Sunny Stern called me and asked me to speak on behalf of the family in paying tribute to mom, I wanted to somehow make my grandmother Esther a part of the evening as she was always such a part of our lives.

For grandma's fiftieth birthday, mom composed a special poem for her. I would like to close with a portion of this poem that is applicable to our mom, Sherry, as it was to her mother, Esther.

You've gained love and respect and more
You're an inspiration
Loyal friends, admirers galore
Join our admiration

We're proud to know you, proud to be
Among a special few
Who love you dearly and agree
God's light should shine on you.

I have always felt an immense sense of Jewish continuity whenever I see girls and boys celebrate their *bat* or *bar mitzvahs*. My children, Jacque, Laura, Jacob, and Drew, all observed this important passage in their lives at the Ahavath Achim Synagogue. What especially impressed me over the years, however, was when I saw grown men and women who had not had a *bar* or *bat mitzvah* study Torah and participate in this ceremony. When I told my children I was studying for my own *bat mitzvah* and would share this day with my close friend, Jeanney Kutner, it was somewhat laughable because we would be chanting Torah and Haftorah in spite of not being able to carry a tune. (I thought Jeanney's voice was as bad as mine.)

We studied with Rabbi Marvin Richardson, learning our Torah portions from tapes and printed booklets. The first time we went onto the *bimah* for a practice, only days before our special day, Rabbi Richardson opened the ark, placed the Torah on the table and opened it to the section we had studied. We both teared up immediately, and it surprised him to see us react so emotionally; we were simply in awe of seeing the sacred scroll for the first time. There is still something special beyond words when women have an experience once unavailable to them.

On December 10, 1988, coinciding with *Shabbat* and *Hanukkah*, we celebrated our *b'not mitzvah* at the Ahavath Achim Synagogue. Jeanney's husband, Dr. Steve Kutner, gave us a wonderful party with latkes, *Hanukkah* candles, songs and more. My daughter Jacque, now a working woman, told me how strange it was to tell her boss she needed a day off to attend her mother's *bat mitzvah*. The loudest laugh came when my kids informed me that compared to my voice, Jeanney's is really good.

When friends asked if I would like to have a *tallit* (prayer shawl) and said they would be pleased to give me one as a gift, I said "thanks but no thanks," as very few women were wearing them in my synagogue at that time, and I was not ready to be a pioneer.

Two years later, as the Gulf War was approaching, tourism in Israel was at an all time low. Shops were closing and trips to Israel were being cancelled. On November 29, 1990, AJC initiated "Mission Undaunted," and twenty Atlanta Chapter members joined AJC members from all over the United States for an amazing trip to Israel. One night, the stores in the Cardo, that ancient colonnaded street near the Western Wall, were opened for our buses of AJC tourists. I thought as we traveled in the Old City of Jerusalem, "I must spend some money tonight."

Visiting the shops, I decided *this* was the moment for me to buy a *tallit*. As a feminist, I wanted my *tallit* to be both a Jewish and a woman's statement. Those requirements were fulfilled in the beautiful pink one I found. When I bought it, the store stitched my Hebrew name, *Shanah Leba*, on the matching bag. After I returned from Israel, I put away my new *tallit* and only wore it for the first time in February. Months later, Janice Alper, Director of the Jewish Education Services, came up to me at synagogue and asked "What's your story?" I was stumped by her question. She went on to say that every woman who wears a *tallit* has a story, and again she asked what mine was. I couldn't help tearing up while I told her how and where I bought my *tallit*, and that I had held onto it until my mother's death. I wore my beautiful Israeli *tallit* for the first time when I said *Kaddish*, the mourner's prayer, for my mom.

When my daughter, Laura, gave birth to my first grandchild, Eliana, she named her for my mother, Esther. At her *Simchat Bat* (baby naming), Eliana was wrapped in my pink *tallit*, blessed, and given her Hebrew name. To this day, every time I put this *tallit* across my shoulders I think of my mother and feel God's presence wrapped around me.

The idea of women's stories linked to their wearing a *tallit* came alive once more in a personal way for me. A few days before my daughter Jacque was married, she said she wanted to buy a *tallit*. We selected a unique white and navy one, and on December 31, 1996, she and Tom were wrapped in it under the *chuppah* (wedding canopy) when they received their wedding blessings.

I now have three *tallitot*, each with its own story. My second one was a gift Rabbi Arnold Goodman and Dr. Richard Cohen bought for me while on Atlanta Chapter's Rabbinical Trip to Israel. Funds from its purchase supported the Women of the Wall, an Israeli organization fighting for women's rights to pray at the *Kotel* (Western Wall), read aloud from Torah scrolls and wear religious garments. The four corners of the *tallit* include the names of the matriarchs Sarah, Rebekah, Rachel and Leah.

My most recent *tallit* was designed and exquisitely handmade by Rosanne Kauss. It was a gift from my synagogue when I completed my term as President of Congregation Or Hadash. Its four corners bear important symbols of our congregation – our rabbis; hammer and bricks for building our *shul*; the dancing *aleph*, our logo; and musical notes on a Torah. I wear each *tallit* at different times throughout the year and love reflecting on the stories they tell and memories they hold.

## HONORS

Serving the community has given my life untold personal satisfaction and pride. I never sought recognition – I just relished the work, the people and the causes I championed. Still, along the way, I received four honors that were especially meaningful and touched me deeply. I hope I accepted them with humility; they truly energized me to work harder to make this world a bit more just, inclusive and closer to Dr. Martin Luther King, Jr.'s, dream of the Beloved Community.

When few women received wide public recognition for their work, I was honored by Atlanta Israel Bonds on June 15, 1978, with the Golda Meir Tribute Medallion at the Israel Independence Celebration. Our guest speaker was Ruth Gruber, distinguished author, foreign correspondent, and lecturer. The event observed Golda Meir's 80th birthday and Israel's 30th anniversary. This rang all my bells: women, Israel, scholarship, service and philanthropy.

The YWCA has had a significant impact on the lives of women and girls in our community for decades. It draws the most influential and talented women to its leadership and its projects. It was wonderful to be included in the YWCA Academy of Women Achievers in May, 1988.

In 2003, the Atlanta History Center hosted an exhibit, "Enterprising Women: 250 Years of American Business." As a complement to this impressive national exhibit, an additional exhibit was created to recognize "outstanding women who have contributed significantly to the local community." Fifty women were featured in categories including Arts and Communications, Business, Community Activism, Education and Public Service, Law and Medicine, Leadership, and Philanthropy. It was gratifying to be listed in Leadership in the company of amazing Atlanta innovators and women who were genuine change agents.

After retiring, I continued to be involved in the community and especially the issues of social justice that were near and dear to me throughout my life. I was invited to early planning meetings for the National Center for Civil and Human Rights. Attending the groundbreaking ceremony, supporting the women's campaign and being at the Opening Celebration was satisfaction enough, as Atlanta welcomed visitors to this new and important institution. But it was a tremendous rush to receive a letter from the Honorable Shirley Franklin, Board Chair and former Mayor of Atlanta, inviting me to receive the Center's Power to Inspire Award on May 5, 2016.

Service to community is a true privilege and honor. My cup runneth over with gratitude for these years of service, and I am humbled beyond words for the recognition I received along the way.

I sometimes wonder if I was born or made a feminist; it seems that women's issues have been in the forefront of my special interests and attention all my life. I was able to express my feminist bent most fully in my days with NCJW, and later at AJC. In doing the research for these memoirs, I loved reading the NCJW bulletins from the 1970s and 1980s and reviewing AJC flyers and reports with the details about how we advocated for and developed programs on women's issues. I have highlighted some of these in the chapters on Politics and Advocacy and Israel and the U.N. There is a compilation of additional programs in the Appendix.

Women have made enormous strides since I began my volunteer work over fifty years ago. An example of this was the election of Leah Sears-Collins to the Supreme Court of Georgia. Her warm letter recognizing my part in her campaign appears in the Appendix.

Sadly, there is still much to do to gain full equality for women in employment, political office and in our civic and religious institutions. Battles still loom large to protect women's reproductive rights, and advocacy, education, and coalition building remain a priority. NCJW continues to play a leadership role in these pressing challenges.

## WOMEN LEADERS

Equality for women has many dimensions, encompassing home, community, and the workplace. I have been engaged most directly on the challenges and successes we face within our Jewish communal organizations. In the late 1980s and early 1990s, when my children were students at The Epstein School, I watched with pride as young women assumed top leadership roles. Lynne Halpern and Lois Kuniansky were trendsetters, each rising to serve as President of The Epstein School when most schools, congregations and organizations were led by men. They surely benefitted from the leaders serving before them, and received special support from their husbands, Jack Halpern and David Kuniansky. I loved working with them and was deeply touched to receive a personal handwritten letter from Lois on June 8, 1990.

*Dear Sherry,*

*I wanted you to know how much I appreciate you allowing us the privilege of honoring you last night at the Founders Dinner. Having you as our honoree was like a dream come true for our school. I, being totally objective, think it was our finest dinner ever, and I attribute a tremendous part of that to you. Your work, your style, your passions, your life make you the type of person people enjoy knowing. And I feel so fortunate to be the President when The Epstein School became the lucky institution to honor you. I am, fondly,*

*Lois*

In the mid 1980s, when we were evaluating the strengths and weaknesses of AJC's Atlanta Chapter, several people listed as assets the significant role that women were playing in our organization. I worked with many talented and devoted civic leaders who generously served as chapter presidents, but I particularly want to share some personal reflections on the four extraordinary women who served in this capacity and co-chaired my retirement event.

Elaine Alexander was President from 1989-1991 and brought her wisdom and important connections to the general community to AJC along with her advocacy on women's issues and all things political. In my early days at AJC, Elaine sternly told me that if I stay on the sidelines and serve, rather than take my seat at the table and set the agenda, I would never be taken seriously. As the first woman to serve as Southeast Area Director, I heeded Elaine's sage advice and it served me well. After her retirement as co-director of

Leadership Atlanta, Elaine printed up a clever business card that included her current profession. I asked her to make me a similar one if and when I ever retired. True to her promise, Elaine made business cards for me that read "Sherry Frank - Grandmother, etc." and included my address, phone number, and email.

My cousin-by-marriage, Lois Frank, was President from 1993-1995. From our earliest married days, Lois and I have had a special bond and a strong commitment to Black-Jewish relations. Her passion for social justice and human rights has no equal. In addition to our AJC connection, we have shared family, holidays, synagogue, serving on the national board of MAZON: A Jewish Response to Hunger, and worked together on a City of Atlanta Task Force to honor Congressman John Lewis.

Candy Berman was President from 1997-1999. She was the most hands-on leader I have ever worked with and was the go-to person for interviewing potential staff members. Her limitless creativity and interest in all aspects of membership and fundraising were invaluable. Candy left an indelible mark on our leadership development program, endowed with the Berman Family name, and was instrumental in helping us organize and implement our first Atlanta Jewish Film Festival.

Elise Eplan was President from 2003-2005. *L'dor v'dor* – from one generation to the next – we must pass on the mantle of leadership. Elise was an early officer in ACCESS and our first member to serve as both ACCESS Chair and Atlanta Chapter President. She brought her keen intellect, knowledge about community, and talent for strategic planning to our work as we approached a new decade.

All of these outstanding women also served on AJC's National Board of Governors. And in the years since my retirement, other exceptional women continue to serve in these capacities.

I experienced the natural bond that draws women to one another over my years in NCJW, in my *Rosh Hodesh* group at the Ahavath Achim Synagogue, and in the early years when we created

Congregation Or Hadash. Our first five presidents at Or Hadash were all women: Gita Berman, Lynn Epstein, Abby Friedman, me, and Betsy Edelman. It was as though we were giving birth to a new baby, nurturing it from toddler to adolescence. When Fred Wachter became our congregation president, he joked that he better get it right, or we would never let another man serve as president. He got it more than right, served for three years and guided us into our new building.

Today women hold top leadership positions in our schools, synagogues, organizations and agencies. I never take this for granted and am always mindful of those trailblazers who opened doors for all the women in leadership today, including those in paid positions as well as volunteer roles. I remember only too well the men running these organizations and agencies when I took over at AJC. They talked while I spoke and didn't take me seriously, but given some time, they realized I was a force to be reckoned with. I wonder at times, when I am particularly outspoken at meetings, if this assertiveness (not aggressiveness!) harkens back to the days when I was not fully heard.

## BLACK/JEWISH SISTERS

In 1992, as a result of the 10th anniversary of the Atlanta Black/Jewish Coalition, the Black/Jewish Sisters Group was formed; it remains my longest lasting and most meaningful women's group. It was comprised of six African-American women and six Jewish women. The original Black sisters were Veronica Biggins, Nancy Boxill, Johnnetta Cole, Myrtle Davis, Shirley Franklin and Ingrid Saunders Jones. (Sharon Campbell participated for a very brief time.) I was one of the Jewish sisters along with Elaine Alexander, Barbara Asher, Dianne Harnell Cohen, Lois Frank, and Judith Taylor.

For over twenty years, we have laughed and cried together, experienced happy and sad times, celebrated December holiday dinners with gift giving, and attended civic and cultural events. We have shared weddings, political victories, community honors and reached out to one another at times of illness and death. We learned from one another as we discussed and debated the most challenging issues of our times.

Together we traveled to Israel, Harlem and Washington, D.C. In Israel we met with Jewish, Arab and Palestinian women, toured the country and engaged in exciting and, at times, heated discussions during home hospitality. We toured Harlem, went to the Schomburg Center for Research in Black Culture, and had lunch with activists at Sylvia's, a Harlem institution. In Washington, we had a private tour of the U.S. Holocaust Memorial Museum.

One gift of dialogue is learning about one another's culture and traditions. This was evidenced in the discussions that followed Barbara Asher's death and the different views the Jewish and Black sisters held regarding inviting a new member to join our group. Our African-American sisters were surprised that we would even raise the issue so soon after she died, but the Jewish sisters turned this into a learning opportunity with the following letter sent on January 23, 1996.

*Dear Sisters,*

*In the spirit of fostering deeper understanding of our common-alities and our differences, we Jewish sisters want to share some insight into the Jewish responses to death. This issue arises because of the sudden and sad death of our sister, Barbara.*

*Jewish tradition has specific rituals to follow when death occurs. We show honor and respect through specific burial and mourning procedures. Following burials, there is a seven-day period of mourn-ing, referred to as* Shiva. *Family members refrain from work and usual activities during this week. Prayers are said each evening and friends of the deceased person frequently show their respect by visiting at the home where the family is observing* Shiva. *At the end* of this week, there is a tradition of walking outside and around the Shiva house to symbolize the return to the everyday world.

During the 30 days following the death of a family member, there is an extended period of mourning. It comes from the Bible's reference that following Aaron's death, "the children of Aaron mourned for 30 days." This period, referred to as Shloshim, is sometimes concluded with a prayer service. Traditional Jews recite Kaddish, the mourner's prayer, for eleven months following the death of a parent, while resuming their normal activities.

In mid-December, there were services, widely publicized in Israel and in many U.S. cities, to mark the end of Shloshim following Israeli Prime Minister Yitzhak Rabin's death. Activities in Israel then resumed and Leah Rabin accompanied Prime Minister Shimon Peres to the U.S. for his meetings with the President and Congress.

Jewish tradition prescribes a fixed time for mourning and for the rhythms of life to continue. We are reminded that death is a part of God's plan for the universe... one generation goes, and another generation comes, as one season follows another. We remember the deceased, but we are guided to move ahead with life.

Within this framework for Jewish tradition, we Jewish sisters feel it is time to cherish Barbara Asher's memory and to move forward and consider inviting another Jewish sister to join in our very special Black/Jewish Women's Dialogue Group. We are conscious that African-American tradition may see this matter differently, and therefore, we need to dialogue about it. We look forward to discussing this when we are together on February 11th. Warm regards,

Elaine Alexander, Dianne Harnell Cohen,
Lois Frank, Sherry Frank, Judith Taylor

Following church services at Hillside Chapel and Truth Center with Dr. Barbara King, our Sisters enjoyed a home-cooked lunch at Shirley Franklin's house. After discussing a list of candidates, we invited Spring Asher to join our group. Spring often said this was one of her sister-in-law Barbara's best gifts to her. Years later, Dr. Johnnetta Cole, speaking on cultural diversity at a forum on Faith, Feminism and Philanthropy, cited this as an example of how differing traditions honor individuals who have passed away.

From the beginning of our Sisters' Group, Ingrid Saunders Jones, former Senior Vice President for The Coca-Cola Company, and I developed a unique bond. We coordinated most of the Group's activities, and, for nearly twenty years, Ingrid and Nancy Boxill co-hosted our holiday dinner.

A native Atlantan, I grew up hearing jingles on the radio and TV describing Atlanta as "The Coca-Cola town." In my role at AJC, I became even more aware and appreciative of The Coca-Cola Company and its impact on our community and world. I was included at their corporate table at significant community events, and The Coca-Cola Company generously supported numerous AJC projects from the Atlanta Jewish Film Festival to our Centennial Celebration and my retirement event.

In the spirit of our annual holiday gift-giving, Mark Taylor surprised us with a special gift after we admired one of his wife Judith's beautiful pins. It was stunning, brushed silver and shaped like a mask. I saved his note, dated September 6, 1995.

*Dear 'Sister-in-law' Sherry,*

*It seems safe to assume that the twelve of you are a sisterhood that will never adopt a sorority pin. This, then, is an instead-of pin, one of twelve, all different as they must be, and made especially for you by J. Cotter in Vail, Colorado.*
*With much affection and sincere admiration,*
*Sincerely,*
*Mark*

Participating in the Sisters Group was, and continues to be, especially gratifying. There is a unique connection and a comfort we feel when we encounter one another at civic and political events. At times I have sought professional advice regarding ways to interpret and respond appropriately and with sensitivity to specific community issues. Although two sisters moved out of town, our communication with them has continued. Together we have shared more than two decades of life, work and community. While we meet less frequently, we still refuse to let a year go by without at least one opportunity to break bread and share views with one another.

## FAITH, FEMINISM AND PHILANTHROPY

Divisions occur in many community sectors, and so it was among a diverse group of feminists. In 2005, I worked on a unique program to help bring our women's community together. I co-signed, along with Reverend Dr. Joanna Adams, Jane Fonda, Ingrid Saunders Jones, and Saleemah Abdul-Ghafur, an Atlanta Women's Foundation invitation for an Afternoon of Tea and Conversation on Sunday, February 20. The featured guest speaker was Helen Lakelly Hunt, feminist, activist, founder of The Sister Fund and Author of *Faith and Feminism: A Holy Alliance*. This event was the "soft" launch of a three-year grant-making and public education effort administered by The Atlanta Women's Foundation.

*The Faith, Feminism and Philanthropy Initiative*
*The Atlanta Women's Foundation (AWF) launched its three-year Faith, Feminism and Philanthropy collaborative initiative with Atlanta's feminist and faith-based communities. Generously funded through a $600,000 grant from the Ruth Ray Hunt Memorial Fund of the Communities Foundation of Texas and the Dallas Women's Foundation, this grant-making, education and advocacy, and philanthropic initiative seeks to create a space for open and healing conversations between secular feminists and women of faith about the issues that bind us and those that divide us.*

AWF's initiative has three distinct, but interrelated components:

**Grant-making** – Funds were given to four programs with historical ties to the faith-based community that supported the needs of Atlanta's women and girls, including Black Church and Domestic Violence Institute, Genesis Shelter, Trinity House, and the YWCA of Greater Atlanta.

**Collaboration and Conversation** – A conference was held bringing secular feminists and women of faith together to discuss issues that divide us and explore ways to work collaboratively. Over the next two years, additional forums were held that addressed the topics of religion, social justice and the women's movement. Dr. Laurie Patton, Chair, Religion Department, Emory University, and Dr. Layli Maparyan, Associate Professor of Women's Studies and Associated Faculty of African-American Studies, Georgia State University, were outstanding participants and generously contributed their insights and expertise to our deliberations.

**Philanthropy** – A $100,000 grant was designated for use as a catalyst to fund and increase philanthropy of secular feminists and women of faith.

This was a rich bonding experience for the three of us who were co-leaders of the program: Reverend Dr. Joanna Adams, a Christian; Saleemah Abdul-Ghafur, a Muslim; and me, a Jewish representative. We deepened our knowledge of each other's religion and traditions and widened our circle to include others from our faith communities.

We traveled to California for a conference with participants from the four other communities involved in this grant. Expert speakers addressed us from the three religious communities on the issues of faith, feminism and philanthropy.

In the final sessions in Atlanta, we were successful in expanding the number of women donating to new and worthy women's causes, at the same time increasing mutual understanding and respect and serving community needs. We had a strong supportive team shepherding this unique project. Deborah Richardson, Executive Director of The Atlanta Women's Foundation, secured the grant and gave sustained guidance and superb leadership to this project.

Polly Simpson was the Chair of the Board of the Foundation, and Joanna served as overall Project Chair.

For me, every worthy endeavor is a learning experience, and this project was no exception. I learned new words to add to my feminist vocabulary. "Womanist" and "womanism" are populist and poetic synonyms for black feminists and black feminism. "Womanist" was coined in 1983 by Alice Walker in her book *In Search of Our Mother's Garden: Womanist Prose*, and is viewed as giving visibility to the experience of African-American women and other women of color. I like the sound of this expanded expression of feminism, just as I love when Dr. Johnnetta Cole talks about her "sheroes" rather than her heroes. I also feel a deep connection to the word *Shechinah*, the Hebrew word meaning dwelling, that refers as well to the presence of God. The *Shechinah* is the feminine aspect of Divinity. Words have great power, and I like being open to new expressions of women's power and authority in both secular and religious terms.

My family: Jack, Esther, Sherry, and Neil Zimmerman, 1951

My mother, Esther Zimmerman, with her grandchildren Jacob, Jacque, Laura, and Drew

My brother, Neil Zimmerman, and me, 2016

Black/Jewish Sisters Group in Harlem (L - R) Johnnetta Cole, Barbara Asher, Lois Frank, Myrtle Davis, Elaine Alexander, Veronica Biggins, Dianne Harnell Cohen, Sherry Frank, Ingrid Saunders Jones, Judith Taylor, 1995

Black/Jewish Sisters Group Holiday Dinner (L - R) seated: Johnnetta Cole, Judith Taylor, Ingrid Saunders Jones, Veronica Biggins, Nancy Boxill, standing: Elaine Alexander, Shirley Franklin, Sherry Frank, Dianne Harnell Cohen, Spring Asher, Myrtle Davis

# SYNAGOGUES

*The world is sustained by three things: Torah, service to God, and acts of lovingkindness.*

—Pirkei Avot

As far back as I can remember, Judaism has always been front and center in my life and a major part of my identity. My earliest memories include lighting candles on *Shabbat*, celebrating holidays with family, my mother and grandmother changing dishes for Passover, and being with family and friends at synagogue.

Congregation Shearith Israel was my first religious home, and its rabbi, Sydney Mossman, was important to me in my early years. He helped me through my father's death when I was only eleven years old, and I turned to him for guidance during my teen years when writing speeches for youth group activities. My father's family were all members of this synagogue, and many of the early presidents were Zimmermans, my family name.

The first time I participated in the *Yizkor* service (a Jewish memorial service recited for deceased loved ones on certain holy days) for my father, I felt alone and frightened. All the non-mourners had left the sanctuary, and the grief was palpable. Rabbi Mossman gave a powerful sermon that has stayed with me my whole life. He related his story of going up and down the halls at a hospital, visiting with people who had been injured in World War II. One of his favorite patients was a jovial man at the end of the hall who always greeted him warmly. The rabbi didn't know what his physical problem was, because he was always in bed and looked so healthy. One day he saw the man walking down the hall and realized he only had one leg. The man fell, but when the rabbi rushed to help him up, he pushed the rabbi aside and said, "It's not the leg I've lost, but the leg I have that will lift me up and keep me going." I tell this story often, because it summarizes the philosophy I've adopted throughout my life and shows the inspiration and strength I have received from my rabbis.

My family belonged to Ahavath Achim Synagogue as well, as did most of my childhood friends. My brother, Neil, and I attended, graduated from and were confirmed at their religious school; however, in those years it was uncommon for girls to have a *bat mitzvah*, and I was no exception.

Harry Epstein, Ahavath Achim's Senior Rabbi, was an important figure to me. In my early adult years, I was inspired by him and greatly admired his wife, Reva. They were both highly educated, and Rabbi Epstein was a brilliant speaker. He married my in-laws, Maurice and Mickey Frank, and my husband, Leonard, and me. On February 6, 1990, shortly after my mother passed away, I received a beautiful letter from Rabbi Epstein. He added a handwritten note at the end that touched me deeply. It said: "Having a daughter such as you is the greatest tribute to your mother. God comfort you."

These were years when synagogue life was more formal, and traditional family roles were not challenged.By the late 1970s, women's roles in the world had changed, and the synagogues reflected this as well. Upon Rabbi Epstein's retirement in 1982, Rabbi Arnold Goodman became Senior Rabbi at Ahavath Achim. He had served as President of the Rabbinical Assembly, the international association of Conservative rabbis, and was an advocate in the Conservative

Movement for women's full inclusion and ordination. He was a community activist, and I quickly became close to him and his wife Rae. Rabbi Goodman was an outstanding teacher and preacher, and I gained insight and inspiration from his sermons and classes. Services were much more interesting to me, and I became a regular *Shabbat* attendee, along with the crowds that grew each year.

Rabbi Goodman was one of my most important mentors throughout my years at AJC. We worked closely together on a wide array of interfaith, international and political issues during his 20 years at the synagogue. I was thrilled that he received AJC's Selig Distinguished Service Award in 1993, and I was honored to speak at the Ahavath Achim tribute dinner for him upon his retirement in 2002.

I was an active board member at Ahavath Achim, and, at Rabbi Goodman's suggestion, I chaired the Social Action Committee, involving the congregation more directly toward community service projects. In 1991, again with the rabbi's encouragement, I started a *Rosh Hodesh* group. Similar women's study groups, centered around the holiday of the first day of the new month, were being formed around the country. Rae Goodman was an active participant and gracious hostess for our meetings and many other congregational events in their home. Our group grew quickly and represented women of all ages.

For nearly ten years, we met monthly, studying new books on women's issues and new interpretations of biblical stories. My favorite books were *Standing Again at Sinai: Judaism from a Feminist Perspective* by Judith Plaskow, *Deborah, Golda, and Me: Being Female and Jewish in America* by Letty Cottin Pogrebin, and *How to Run a Traditional Jewish Household* by Blu Greenberg.

Our *Rosh Hodesh* group always tried to be imaginative in its programming. In 1992, we hosted our first annual women's Seder at the home of Phyllis Franco. In 1994, Emory University professor, Dr. Deborah Lipstadt, joined me in leading the Seder and shared insights with us about both Passover during the Holocaust and the women's role in the Exodus story. In honor of her daughter Gabrielle's *bat mitzvah*, Marjorie Tiven donated beautiful Judaic artwork for our *Haggadah* cover, beginning an annual tradition that was repeated for many years. Some years we asked participants to share a Passover memory or reflect on a woman who influenced them, and once we asked everyone to bring to the table the story of a person dear in their memories.

In 1992, we marked Black History Month by studying with prominent African-American minister Reverend Dr. Cynthia Hale and the female members of her church, Ray of Hope Christian Church. We discussed "A Mistress, A Maid, and No Mercy: Hagar and Sarah" and "Blessed Be the Tie That Binds: Naomi and Ruth" from the book *Just a Sister Away: A Womanist Vision of Women's Relationships in the Bible* by Renita Weems. To enrich our study, we attended Sunday services at their church and hosted them at Ahavath Achim for additional discussion.

1994 was a year for innovation and action. We gathered in Lois Frank's home for a *Tu B'Shevat* Seder, using a *Haggadah* that focused on environmental issues, and we began a wonderful tradition of celebrating *Sukkot* together. I loved hosting the group in my *sukkah*, as well as seeing other members' *sukkot*. In a statement explaining the tradition, we said:

> *The Women's* Rosh Hodesh *group of Ahavath Achim Synagogue has started a* Sukkot *ritual of welcoming babies born to group members during the previous years. We have adapted the* Sukkot *tradition of* ushpizin *– symbolic guests. When we say "This is the chair of the* ushpizin*," our honored guests are the mother and newborn baby.*
>
> *We eat in and enjoy the* Sukkah *setting. The young baby is brought to our meeting, and each of us gives the baby a gift we've written or selected from a text. They might be poems, emotionally touching readings or photographs. They may be personal and*

*sentimental, or clever and original. It's a time of warmth and shar-*
*ing, mothering and nurturing and bonding with one another. It is as*
*unique a season of joy in our group as* Sukkot *is in our tradition.*

On the cover we listed the new babies born within our group and their mothers' and grandmothers' names. Every year we read a piece of liturgy I was inspired to write especially for this occasion.

Not only did we study, observe holidays and celebrate happy times over the years, but we also shared times of sadness and loss. We came together for a brief memorial service on August 7, 1995, to remember Matthew Ben Blumenthal, beloved son of synagogue leaders Elaine and Jerry Blumenthal, who passed away at age twenty-four from Muscular Dystrophy. We each lit a candle as we reflected on a personal memory of Matthew.

Beginning in 1994, and in following years, we advocated for change on the issue of *agunot*, a term that describes a Jewish wom-an who is "anchored" or "chained" to a recalcitrant husband who refuses to give her a *gett*, a divorce document in Jewish religious law. Jewish divorce continues to be an unresolved issue and was dramatically depicted in an award-winning Israeli film screened at the Atlanta Jewish Film Festival in 2015, "Gett: The Trial of Viviane Amsalem."

As an Ahavath Achim board member over the years, I partic-ipated in the decisions to hire rabbis and other staff members. I worked late at AJC one Friday afternoon and had to push myself to attend *Shabbat* evening services when two young Argentinian rabbis, a husband and wife, were in Atlanta for the weekend, being interviewed to join our congregation. Totally exhausted from a dif-ficult week, I was surprised at how moving and spiritually uplifting I found the voices of Rabbis Analia Bortz and Mario Karpuj. Their music awakened something inside of me, and I was hooked! To this day, I can unexpectedly find my eyes filled with tears watching them, listening to them, and learning from them.

Their distinctive energy, music, spirituality and warmth was contagious and they immediately attracted a large group of followers. Three years later, as their contract at Ahavath Achim was ending, a group of us began to talk about how we could keep them in Atlanta. This became my next challenge. I was determined to see if there was interest in creating a new synagogue. Sandy Springs had no Conservative synagogues, and the Jewish community was growing rapidly. There were already several Jewish day schools in the area.

I made innumerable phone calls to people I knew and to others suggested to me whom I didn't know, and a meeting date was set at the home of fellow Argentinians, Rosie and Dr. Arnoldo Fiedotin, who had become close adopted family to Analia and Mario. On a cold night in December, 2002, eighteen interested people met to discuss the feasibility of starting a new synagogue with Analia and Mario as our spiritual leaders. Time was not on our side, as the rabbis were already interviewing for positions across the country. But that incredible first meeting energized everyone to roll up their sleeves and go to work.

We solicited small donations to pay for a series of ads in the *Atlanta Jewish Times* inviting interested individuals to gatherings in homes to hear about our plans to establish an egalitarian Conservative synagogue in Sandy Springs. Over the next three months, the initial group of eighteen continued holding planning meetings at the Fiedotins' and at the same time wrote by-laws and a mission statement, drafted a budget and grew our list of potential members. On March 23, 2003, our application was accepted, and we became an approved member of the United Synagogue of Conservative Judaism.

To everyone's surprise, once we became "official," graduating rabbinical students applied to serve our congregation. Emory University professor Dr. Kenneth Stein, a key member of our organizing team, systematically held phone interviews with all of the candidates and scheduled face-to-face interviews with Analia and Mario. During a group interview, they were asked what their dream synagogue would be like. Paraphrasing a bit, Analia said a kosher heart is a kosher home, and she looked forward to shared *Shabbat* dinners in our new home. Mario, loving music, said he looked forward to leading a congregation that would enthusiastically join in with new melodies to familiar prayers.

An excited group gathered in my living room, only five months after planning began, when we made the official call to ask Analia and Mario if they would be the rabbis of our synagogue, to be called Or Hadash, meaning "new light." This name had special significance, as Analia and Mario served Congregation Or Hadash in Buenos Aires while they were rabbinical students. Their daughter, Tami, was named in their last days in that synagogue.

It is hard to overemphasize how difficult and unsettling it is building something from scratch. There is no history to build on, no blueprint, no rules to follow or experiences to give you a sense of security and belonging. It is all wide open, a blank book in which to write each new chapter. At once this was both daunting and exhilarating.

Our rabbis must have felt all of this when they said yes to a reduced salary, no synagogue home, and a guarantee of a possible two years with money promised for only one year. I recently asked Analia and Mario "what made you say yes and take the risk?" Analia said it was all about trust, as she had total trust in the people working on this. Mario thought it was all about community. He knew from the beginning that the one we were creating would be unusual and especially caring.

There were monumental decisions to make with this amazing "start up." From the beginning, I would guide the organizational issues, and Dr. Steve Wertheim would handle the financial matters. Privacy regarding money and donors was and continues to be a unique part of our ethos.

Our rabbis' love of hospitality and music continued as their home became our office, a gathering place for festivals and study and countless *Shabbat* dinners, *Havdallah* celebrations, and more. We are part of a wonderful Jewish community and were welcomed with amazing generosity by Atlanta area congregations and schools who lent us ritual objects, meeting space, and furniture. From the sounds of the first tambourines I bought at Marshalls, to our members' band performing at services, music is a defining feature of our synagogue.

There were moments that took my breath away and continue to give me pride as I reflect on our first thirteen years:

- Record crowds attending information meetings at Ruth and Mark Hackner's home
- August 1, 2003, when we held our first *Servicio de Shabbat*, Friday night service, at Sandy Springs United Methodist Church and over 300 people attended
- Running out of free tickets for our first High Holiday Services at the Hebrew Academy (now Atlanta Jewish Academy) and the sense of joy as the Torah was carried all through the aisles and into the balcony
- Sending *bar* and *bat mitzvah* invitations without an address, knowing that somehow we would be able to secure a place for prayer
- High Holidays with 1,000 people at the Marcus Jewish Community Center of Atlanta, with Analia and Mario holding hands while singing *Kol Nidre*, children crowding the floor in front of the *bimah* to hear the Shofar and the ark kept open during *Neilah* for people to come up to the *bimah* and stand in front of the open ark to offer their personal prayers
- Elatedly phoning Analia and Mario at the Weber School, insisting they get in my car, and driving them to the place that would hopefully be our future home
- Hosting the Jewish world's top scholars at our *Shabbatons*
- Traveling to Israel and Argentina and doing service projects in Honduras
- Building our own space for offices and sanctuary at the

Weber School and demonstrating how well two Jewish organizations can live and work together

There were occasions when our leadership showed extraordinary trust and faith in what we hoped to accomplish. At a tenuous time in the housing market, our board, apprised of the potential purchase of property for our permanent home, kept the secret for months, assuring that we did not lose the opportunity to close the sale.

I kept the historic email that I wrote as President and sent to members on March 29, 2010.

> Ma nishtanah halayla hazeh? *How is this night different from all other nights?*
>
> *I am thrilled to tell you that this will be a memorable Passover for Congregation Or Hadash. Today we signed a contract on a wonderful property that will be a future home for our congregation.*
>
> *As you sit around your* Seder *table and tell the story of the journey of Jewish people from slavery to freedom, we will soon begin to write our story about our journey from the Weber School to 7475 Trowbridge Road. This is the site of the former Tom Jumper Chevrolet Service Center, just off Roswell Road, and is 1.8 miles north of our current location.*
>
> *We want to tell you all the details and answer your questions about costs, design, timeline, fundraising and more. This is an exciting and historic time for our community and we want you to share in this moment with our board, rabbis and staff. Please join us for a Congregation Town Hall Meeting on Sunday, April 18, 2010, 4:30.p.m. in our Sanctuary.*
>
> *Thank you for your continued support. I look forward to writing the next chapter in our history with you.*
>
> Pesach Kasher v'Sameach!

I spoke about this exciting time in the life of our synagogue in my President's message on the eve of *Rosh Hashanah*, September 9, 2010. Part of my speech included the following:

> Shanah Tova. *I am so honored to be able to welcome each of you, our members, guests and families from near and far.*
>
> *We are all familiar with the story of creation, how God created the world in six days. Each day God looked at what he had created and said, "It is good." On the seventh day, we are taught, God rested.*
>
> *For six years we have created our own small world within Congregation Or Hadash. Each year as we added new members, programs,* Tikkun Olam *projects, our own New Light Band, staff and more, we paused and said, "It was good."*
>
> *Yet somehow in this past year, our seventh year, we did not rest. Instead, I think we said what we have created is so good, let's share it more widely, expand our programs more demographically, and dream more ambitiously. Now, as we conclude our seventh year and pause only momentarily, I think we can all say, "It was good."*
>
> - *We grew to over 360 families.*
> - *We have a full time Executive Director and Religious School/Youth Director.*
> - *We have a* Havurah *for families with young children and one for young adults.*
> - *Our Men's Club is thriving, and we have started a Sisterhood.*
> - *Our rabbis have signed a 10-year contract in our midst at a Town Hall Meeting.*
> - *We are buying property for a permanent home and have launched a capital campaign.*
>
> *Looking through the 2010-2011 Calendar of Events tells the whole story that time does not permit me to cover today. I think*

*you will agree. We can look at our seventh year and together let us say, "It was good."*

*This year we will have the privilege of building for future generations, literally, as we break ground on our own permanent* Beit Midrash, *our house of prayer, learning and celebration. Please join with us on this historic journey. We are embarking on a voluntary capital campaign and not a mandatory building fund or assessment. You will be invited to participate in a personal and tangible way to express your love for and commitment to Congregation Or Hadash.*

*On October 3, we will have a Time to Shine Capital Campaign Kick-off Celebration to share all the details of this undertaking with you. You will meet our extraordinary architects and begin to share in the vision of our new home. In the weeks after October 3, you will be asked to make a generous pledge, payable over five years. I hope you will be inspired by this significant moment in our synagogue's history and will make a very meaningful gift.*

*I am especially proud to tell you that our rabbis made their own very generous pledge to this campaign. We also have 100% Board participation. Over the summer, in a quiet preliminary campaign, we are now at a point when I can tell you with great delight that we have raised almost $2,500,000.*

*We can look at these past seven years and truly say, "It was good." As we come together for our eighth High Holidays, we are on a shared and holy journey and I have every confidence that it will continue to be very good.*

Shanah Tova.

We hired Coxe Curry and Associates to guide our capital campaign, confident that we could raise the money necessary to build our synagogue. A brochure describing this campaign, called "Time to Shine" had these words in the opening paragraphs:

*When Congregation Or Hadash was founded in 2003, it brought a new light to the north Atlanta suburbs. It offered us a new way to worship, a deeply moving spiritual experience. It gave us new insight on what it means to live a rich and fulfilling Jewish life. And it continues to inspire us with new hope for the future.*

*All of us – members and friends of Congregation Or Hadash – help to keep the light alive by adding our own sparks to the flame as it burns ever brighter. Together we celebrate the joys of Judaism in a warm and welcoming environment. We sing and dance, we pray and reflect, we study and learn, and we reach out to serve others. We believe that a caring community is a holy community... and that's what we have created in the heart of Sandy Springs.*

Honoring our tradition of inclusion and equality for all members, there were no naming opportunities associated with this campaign. We have maintained a strong sense of fiscal responsibility and were determined to build only what we could raise the funds to cover. Over four million dollars was raised in this totally voluntary campaign. As planned, when our construction loan came due in the Spring of 2018, we were able to pay it off.

Our rabbis believe that the noise children make in the sanctuary is joyful, and the sound of children wandering around the aisles, being held by strangers or, at times, the rabbis themselves while they are speaking or praying, is quite the norm. One of our "*bar mitzvah,*" thirteenth year, activities and innovations included the creation of a "prayground" inside our sanctuary. Young children now have their own carpet and toys to keep them busy while family members participate in the services.

One never knows what to expect at Or Hadash. On any *Shabbat,* babies could be named, converts could be welcomed, new members from every continent could be introduced, gay or straight couples could have an *aufruf* (pre-marriage blessing), Holocaust survivors could tell their stories, women could read Torah for the first time in their lives, and young children crowd the *bimah* to chant Hebrew blessings as familiar to them as nursery rhymes. At *kiddush*, rabbis are hugging kids and calling everyone by name. The word "community" is inadequate to describe the enormous sense of friendship and family that permeates Or Hadash.

Analia and Mario are actively involved in organizations and agencies throughout Atlanta and have glowing reputations. They are exemplary role models for all of us in their relationship to each other, family, friends, work and community. Their love of Israel has made Zionism an important part of our synagogue's adult learning, religious school, and activism. For years we celebrated Israel's Independence Day with a festival, food and camels (yes, real camels,) drawing a large outside attendance to our synagogue. Their frequent trips to Israel allow them to bring spirit and new insights back to the congregation.

For me personally, my journey to fill my life with a meaningful sense of tradition, enhanced by music, spirit, friends, and learning, is fulfilled here with Analia and Mario and my Or Hadash family. I celebrated my 70th birthday at the synagogue, suggesting that rather than giving me a gift, friends and family make a donation to purchase items for our soon-to-be built kitchen. I hope to continue celebrating milestone birthdays, helping in my small way to add to the synagogue's wish list. While I am blessed to have wonderful children, grandchildren and family, I feel that in a special way, Analia and Mario are part of my extended *mishpocha* (family).

Rabbi Dr. Analia Bortz, Sherry Frank, Rabbi Mario Karpuj, 2016

# NATIONAL COUNCIL OF JEWISH WOMEN AND TAY-SACHS SCREENINGS

## ORGANIZATIONAL BEGINNINGS

*Never doubt that a small group of thoughtful, committed people can change the world. Indeed it is the only thing that ever has.*

—Margaret Mead

When I grew up in Atlanta in the 1950s and 1960s, the Jewish community was very divided by congregational affiliations and, to a lesser degree, geography, between Jews from Eastern Europe and those of German descent. The more well-to-do, primarily Reform, German Jews came to Atlanta in the mid 1800s, whereas the Conservative and Orthodox Eastern European Jewish immigrants arrived in the late 1800s, coming from a very different culture, economic and educational level. As an activist teenager, I was involved in B'nai Brith Youth Organization (BBYO), as were most of my friends who went to Morningside Elementary School and Grady High School. Nearly all of us belonged to Ahavath Achim Synagogue or Congregation Shearith Israel. Girls growing up in northwest Atlanta were most often members of The Temple and participated in Reform-sponsored youth groups.

For young marrieds, these divisions continued. Conservative Jewish women were more likely to be active in Hadassah and B'nai

Brith Women, and Reform Jewish women gravitated toward the National Council of Jewish Women (NCJW).

In 1964, pregnant with my second child, I moved with my family to Plainfield, New Jersey. In an effort to meet people, I inquired about Jewish organizations active in the area and was directed toward NCJW, the place to be for young marrieds interested in community service, advocacy and education. Instantly, I had found my organizational home, new friends, meaningful programs and projects, and impressive leaders. I was on the fast track to being president of our section (chapter) when I joined members from all over New Jersey attending NCJW's Biennial Convention in Atlanta from April 9-13, 1967. I traveled there with my daughters Jacque, age five, and Laura, age three, who would be spending special time with grandparents and family while I immersed myself in the convention. I didn't know it at the time, but later that year our family would move back to Atlanta.

The convention's theme of "One Woman Can Make a Difference" inspired my dedication to NCJW. I often reflect on how relevant that theme continues to be today.When NCJW was founded in 1893 by Hannah Greenbaum Solomon, it was the first national association of Jewish women. Hannah Solomon famously asked, "Who is this woman? Who has become such an old subject? She is the woman who dares to go into the world and do what her convictions demand."

In *American Jewish Women* of 1880-1920 she is quoted as saying "women's sphere is the whole wide world." In 1895, two years after the founding of the national organization, the Atlanta Section was established with close ties to The Temple and to Rabbi David Marx, who was instrumental in its creation. Its initial priorities of community service, education, social action, human rights, women's and children's issues, resettling new Americans, Israel and Judaism remain relevant to this day.

I connected with NCJW's Atlanta Section shortly after relocating back home to Atlanta. I knew very few members, but quickly became active and moved up the ladder to serve as president in 1973. At the time, this didn't seem remarkable to me, but later I would find the traditional divisions of Reform and Conservative Jews in our community were still alive and well. Conservative Jews were much more involved with internal Jewish issues and more public in their advocacy. Reform Jews, while involved in Jewish issues, were very active in the interfaith community and in service projects in the inner city. They were often more "behind the scenes" in their public advocacy. It was pointed out on more than one occasion that I was the first Atlanta Section president who was not a member of The Temple.

My deep ties to Israel, support for Soviet Jewry, commitment to intergroup understanding and interest in lifelong Jewish study were nurtured in my early years in NCJW. For this foundational awareness, I will forever be indebted to this organization.

In 1973, the mass departure of Jews from the Soviet Union began with 35,000 leaving that oppressive regime. The Jewish community was galvanized to respond to this exodus by actively involving established national organizations and creating new ones to meet unmet needs. All of the major women's organizations came together to link December 10, Human Rights Day, with the struggle to free Soviet Jews. The goal was to have a different organization chair the program every year. Already active on this issue, I jumped right in and volunteered NCJW to coordinate our community observance in 1973.

At the time, Soviet Jews serving in prison were facing very severe existences, and it was critical to bring attention to this struggle, so we designed a program aimed at securing media attention. We set up a soup kitchen in a downtown city park and made large pots of watered-down potato soup to demonstrate the inadequate food given to prisoners. Interestingly, it was the food editor of the *Atlanta Journal-Constitution* who wrote an article about this event, providing excellent exposure. We received additional coverage when Max Cleland, Georgia State Senator and disabled veteran of the Vietnam

War, read a resolution passed by the Georgia Senate, the first of its kind in the United States, supporting the plight of Soviet Jews.

While most of our members were extremely proud of this innovative and successful program, a few of our older members were quite the opposite. In fact, they were appalled that NCJW would be so publicly outspoken; a few even inquired if their life membership could be revoked. While this was little known to most folks and never inhibited my personal or our Section's efforts, it was, in its time, another reminder of the early divisions in our Jewish community.

During this period of activism on behalf of Soviet Jewry, we became increasingly involved in resettling those arriving in Atlanta. Hannah Entell, long-serving chairperson of NCJW's Service to New Americans Committee, was often recognized for her excellent work over the decades serving refugees primarily from Europe. But these new Russian émigrés were vastly different, coming from life in a communist country with little Jewish background or knowledge. New co-chairs and initiatives were put in place for these new Americans. I have written about this in detail in my chapter on Soviet and Ethiopian Jewry.

I served as NCJW president from May, 1973 to May, 1975. Each month, I wrote a president's message in our newsletter titled "Frankly Speaking." On August 16, 1973, part of my message included:

*Dear Friends,*

*There are many exciting experiences that I have had as President of the Atlanta Section. Attending the Nashville Presidents' Institute was a highlight of this past summer.*

*A gift was made to the National Organization by the Nashville Section. This donation was followed by an anonymous gift. The National Board matched those gifts and thus began the NCJW Nashville Presidents' Institute.*

*More than 300 NCJW community leaders from around the country enrolled at the Graduate School of Management at*

*Vanderbilt University, Nashville, Tennessee, for a week-long training program in management skills especially designed by the University for NCJW.*

*The primary educational objective of the Presidents' Institute was to produce managers of change for purposive organizations. We worked on skills in delegating authority, motivating people, utilizing volunteer resources, training future leadership, understanding the value of planning, dealing with opposition, and much more.*

*At the graduation ceremony the following quote was given: "Talking is to know, Teaching is to know and grow, training is to know, grow, and do."*

Marilyn Shubin, Susie Elson, Barbara Asher and I participated in NCJW's Presidents' Institute, and I have continued to benefit from the management skills I gained that summer.

As president of Atlanta Section, I went to Israel for the first time as a participant in NCJW's 2nd Summit Conference. From November 6-13, 1974, we traveled around the country and saw first-hand important NCJW projects. The NCJW Research Institute for Innovation in Education is the major project in Israel undertaken by NCJW. Organized in 1968, the Institute became a permanent unit in The Hebrew University School of Education in 1971. I shared my trip experience in a speech I gave to our members.

*The Hebrew University High School, truly the house that Council built, continues today to be one of Israel's finest high schools. Our ship-a-box warehouse, stocked from floor to ceiling with toys, school materials and clothes, is a thrill to see. The entire inventory is turned every six weeks, thanks to sections' support. Thirty thousand kids receive our items, with 275 social welfare agencies using our varied supplies. Toy and game libraries are springing up all over Israel in community centers, schools and even laundromats, and they too are using our ship-a-box items.*

*Almost half of Israel's school children are now considered disadvantaged. It has been said:*

*If you want to plan for 1 year – plant rice.*

*If you want to plan for 10 years – plant trees.*

*If you want to plan for 100 years – educate a man.*

*Due to the significance of its projects, it's now considered the "research arm" of Israel's Ministry of Education, with several completed projects on their way to being integrated into the school system. As I stood on top of Mt. Scopus, the highest spot overlooking Jerusalem, on the beautiful modern campus of the Hebrew University of Jerusalem, I saw Elly Marvin, then National President, pull the curtain and uncover the engraving which reads, "The National Council of Jewish Women Institute for Innovation in Education."*

*In Israel I learned that there is no word in Hebrew for "disadvantaged;" instead they use the term "needs nourishment." How significant that is.*

My President's Message in January, 1975, highlighted some special aspects of my Israel experience.

*There are many memories that I will cherish of my term as President of the Atlanta Section, but none as precious as ten days I spent as a delegate at the NCJW Second Summit Conference in Israel.*

*My eyes welled up with tears at the first sight of Israel from the window of the plane, and they never dried until we were on our way home. Even now, as I write this article, my heart is full of excitement and sadness, of stronger commitment and a deep sense of pride.*

*From early morning till late at night we were busy. We began our Summit at the Dan Hotel in Tel Aviv. Avraham Harman, President of Hebrew University, spoke to us at our opening dinner.*

*We spent an unforgettable day with the CHEN (Women's Army). We watched the girls drill, toured their base and spoke with Colonel Ruth Muskall and other officers. The beautiful young faces and the strength and dedication of these girls is impossible to describe.*

*We arrived in Jerusalem as Kissinger was leaving, in time to usher in the* Shabbat *at the Western Wall. There were few moments as moving as the sight of the young Orthodox boys, arms locked together, dancing as they approached the Wall. As I looked up at the rooftops all around, there were soldiers with guns. The harsh reality of the soldiers above, amidst the joy of these young people immersed in the spirit of their tradition below, seemed to capture Israel all at one moment. I think I will see that picture in my mind every Sabbath for the rest of my life.*

*The President of Israel and Mrs. Katzir hosted a reception at their home for us at which time Mrs. Katzir was made an NCJW Honorary Life Member.*

*We gathered for our closing banquet at the Knesset, where the Prime Minister of Israel, Yitzhak Rabin, addressed our delegates. Inside the beautiful Knesset, against the backdrop of the magnificent Chagall tapestries, we brought to a close a milestone occasion in the history of our organization. I will always cherish the memories of those ten days in Israel spent with 150 delegates from across the United States at our Second NCJW Summit Conference in Israel.*

In those exciting and issue-filled days of the 1970s, our agenda included support for Israel, childcare, the Equal Rights Amendment (ERA), abortion rights, Title IX (the 1972 education amendment prohibiting sex discrimination), juvenile justice, constitutional rights, and needs of the elderly. We met to study NCJW's syllabus entitled "The Jewish Experience" which was created for university-level adult education. I loved helping to create the fundraiser, Bargainata, our popular used clothing sale, that thrived for decades.

Atlanta Section owned a two-story Victorian house on Piedmont Avenue that bustled with the activities of our NCJW volunteers, staff and service projects, the Golden Age Employment Service and the Information and Referral Service. Volunteer Atlanta was created in this special hub of volunteerism. I went to the office as though it was a paid job, making connections and learning skills that would enable me to be an effective professional for decades to come.

I had the unique experience of chairing the Atlanta Organizing Committee when our Section hosted the International Council of Jewish Women's (ICJW) Triennial Convention from May 17-23, 1978. 157 delegates and 268 visitors from twenty ICJW affiliates representing every continent were in attendance. Atlanta NCJW members volunteered in droves to offer exceptional "Southern hospitality" to such a varied audience. It was extraordinary to see women from Jewish communities as far away as India sitting down together to discuss common social themes.

From 1978-1982, I served on NCJW's National Board, both an honor and a growth experience. I had the additional privilege to serve for two terms on the U.S. Commission for UNESCO as NCJW's NGO (non-governmental organization) representative. I framed my formal letters of appointment, first issued in 1978 and signed by Secretary of State Cyrus Vance, and reissued in 1982, signed by Secretary of State Alexander Haig. This was the genesis of my awareness of the anti-Israel bias of the UN and its affiliated organizations, and it jump-started my involvement in responding to it.

The 1970s were also a time when our Jewish community was growing with new arrivals from Canada, Israel and South Africa. I opened my home for lunch or brunch with these new Americans, so many of whom came with a history of service in their home communities, certain that they would be able to make a contribution to NCJW. I continue to enjoy personal ties to these women whom I have often worked with over the years in communal endeavors.

Conventions were always a highlight of our NCJW activities; they were a source of new programming and new relationships. One year, I participated in a panel to discuss the topic of "Displaced Homemakers." This was a new term for women experiencing divorce, single parenting, financial and credit struggles, relocation and employment challenges. One of the panelists, Ronnie van Gelder, a Section President in South Florida, would later move to Atlanta and become AJC's Assistant Area Director from 1984-1988. That NCJW connection has led to a lifelong friendship. Today our lives are intertwined with family, community involvement, and she is my cherished confidant, mentor, and best friend.

Throughout my tenure at AJC, I continued to work with NCJW on varied projects, advocacy on women's issues and interfaith programs. For many years, I served as moderator of an annual NCJW Interfaith Women's Luncheon. In my introduction for the event on March 28, 2006, which was focused on "the stranger" in our faith tradition, I read aloud a poem I had written for that occasion.

### The Stranger

*Who is the stranger in our midst?*
*Surely it's someone God has kissed.*
*Aren't each of us born with the spark of the divine*
*Yet some of us haven't had our little light shine.*

*Is the stranger near or are they far away?*
*Is it the frail elderly bent with the winter's day?*
*Are they abused or homeless, cast aside*
*Removed of dignity and all their pride?*

*Are they suffering masses we cannot see?*
*Yet the media tells us about their tragedy.*
*Are they victims of drugs, gangs or war*
*Or immigrants living behind a closed door?*

*While we may not do all that we should*
*I believe each of us deep inside is good.*
*We find courage and wisdom when we open the pages*
*And turn to the guidance of our traditions' best sages.*

*We're called on, each one, in a unique way*
*To embrace different faiths and do more than just pray.*
*Honoring, respecting, caring and seeing*
*Acknowledging the stranger is a human being.*

*Who is the stranger in our midst?*
*Surely it's someone God has kissed.*
*Aren't each of us born with the spark of the divine*
*Yet some of us haven't had our little light shine.*

It gave me tremendous satisfaction when, in 2017, I went back to my organizational roots, reconnecting with NCJW to lead a monthly study group. Using an old and familiar title, we call this "Frankly Speaking" and added the phrase "Looking at the News Through a Jewish Lens." During Passover, I was delighted to lead a Women's Seder for NCJW. Sandy Abrams and I hosted this event, made even more special by the participation of two of my grandchildren, Peri and Danielle Barnard. We used the *haggadah* my daughter, Jacque, had produced for her Toronto Women's Seder that I attended only a few weeks earlier.

In April, 1978, when I installed the NCJW officers serving with my dear friend, Diana Silverman, in her second year as section president, I quoted remarks made by Shirley Leviton, past national president, who said:

*The volunteer is neither unpaid nor underpaid – but simply paid in a different coin. I am paid in achievement as I witness the success of programs my efforts have helped fund. I am paid in personal involvement in the lives of others (a precious commodity in our impersonal world). I am paid in faith in the future, as I see that an investment in human welfare today will affect the lives of children still unborn.*

I, too, feel I have been paid in a different coin from my decades of work with NCJW. The world has changed dramatically over these forty-five years. Yet, NCJW, in its 125th anniversary year, continues to confront the urgent economic and social needs of children, women and families.

Things have come full circle. Now, late in 2018, I am once again serving as NCJW Atlanta Section president. I hope I can add new energy and leadership to this organization that has enhanced my life in countless ways.

## TAY-SACHS

In the early 1970s, new research findings were being published on Tay-Sachs disease, an inherited metabolic disorder. This fatal disease is rare in the general population but more common in the Ashkenazi Jewish population. While no cure has been discovered to date, at that time strides were made in accumulating the knowledge that could lead to control of Tay-Sachs disease through its prevention. Such promising research prompted NCJW sections around the country to coordinate screenings in their cities. The Atlanta Section participated in this new program which would be decades ahead of its time in awakening the community to the field of genetic counseling.

An article in the Section newsletter provided the following background.

The Atlanta Section is actively preparing for three community-wide screenings for Tay-Sachs disease to be held in May. Utilizing the experience of other Council sections throughout the country, Council volunteers have been active since last spring in laying a foundation for this important program. A community wide advisory committee, medical committee and eight NCJW task forces are assuming responsibility for the planning and implementation of this program, working in close cooperation with the Emory University School of Medicine.

A brochure was developed which described Tay-Sachs.

> *Tay-Sachs is an inherited disorder caused by the absence of a vital enzyme, resulting in destruction of the nervous system. It is always fatal; to date, there is no cure.*
>
> *A Tay-Sachs baby develops normally for the first few months. Then a relentless deterioration of mental and physical abilities begins. Blind, paralyzed, unable to swallow, the child loses contact with its world. Death is inevitable, usually by age five.*

NCJW committees provided support in the areas of publicity, volunteers, material development and a speakers bureau. We worked in close cooperation with the Emory University School of Medicine, Division of Medical Genetics, and received invaluable aid and support from our Community-wide Advisory Committee and the Medical Advisory Committee. Gordon Sugarman served as Chairperson of the Community-wide Advisory Committee, which included rabbis and community leaders. Drs. Nanette Wenger and Samuel Poliakoff served as Co-Chairpersons of the Medical Advisory Committee.

At this early stage in the disease's detection, few places had the machine for testing locally. Sections coordinating Tay-Sachs screenings around the country were sending their blood samples to a laboratory in the northeast for analysis. This presented a significant roadblock for us in Atlanta. Our challenge was the requirement that we establish a testing center at Emory's School of Medicine if we were to have a doctor willing to provide an amniocentesis for high-risk couples identified in the screenings.

I was president of the Atlanta Section. Fran Eizenstat was vice president and brought her keen insight and leadership in overseeing this community service project. Fran briefed her husband, Stuart, on our problem. An activist with significant political connections, Stuart contacted Georgia Governor Jimmy Carter and requested State Emergency Health Funds for this project. This was truly a case of "it's who you know," because NCJW received the funding requested, and we were able to provide Emory University with the equipment required to test for Tay-Sachs disease. The State of Georgia, March of Dimes, and United Way of Metropolitan Atlanta all contributed funds for the screenings, as well as to purchase medical machinery to maintain a permanent Tay-Sachs testing facility at Emory University School of Medicine.

Tay-Sachs screenings were held on May 4, 13, and 18, 1975, at the Atlanta Jewish Community Center. The October, 1978, *NCJW Bulletin*, reported highlights of this project.

In May of 1975, a comprehensive Tay-Sachs Disease Prevention Program was initiated in Atlanta. Spearheaded by the Atlanta Section NCJW, this program was operated and co-sponsored with the Division of Medical Genetics of Emory University's Department of Pediatrics. Results of that screening are now available as the tremendous amount of meticulous follow-ups has been completed.

In three days of clinic operation, a total of twenty-three hours, blood specimens and biographic data were collected from 2,330 participants.

Funding for equipment to establish a laboratory facility to assess blood specimens was provided through the Atlanta Section NCJW.

This cooperative effort between Atlanta Section and Emory University to provide a continuing disease prevention program is the first volunteer organization/medical facility liaison of its kind in the Atlanta area. Hundreds of hours of planning and gathering of resources preceded this effort. The clinics were almost totally staffed by trained volunteers. NCJW and its hundreds of volunteers who worked to make this project the success it was and is, can take a great pride in this accomplishment.

In 1983, when Beth Sugarman was Atlanta Section president, and Terry Epstein was vice president, NCJW once again organized a series of Tay-Sachs screenings under new lay leadership. Dr. Michael Wolfson chaired the Community Advisory Committee. On February 10, as NCJW was once again partnering with the Emory University School of Medicine, Department of Pediatrics, Beth and Terry received a letter from Dr. Louis J. Elsas.

*Dear Beth and Terry,*

*Thank you for your letter of February 3, 1983, requesting an updated estimate of laboratory expenses to be incurred for mass screenings of from 2,000-3,000 persons for the Tay-Sachs disease carrier state.*

*Volunteerism is a by-word for success of such a mass screening. Our success seven years ago can easily be surpassed and the professional members of my division will all volunteer clinical, organizational, and laboratory expertise.*

*I encourage you to find the capital outlay to upgrade this laboratory equipment and enable the Atlanta area to continue a leadership role in preventing heritable disorders more frequent in the Jewish population.*
*Sincerely,*
*Louis J. Elsas, III, M.D.*
*Professor of Pediatrics*
*Director, Division of Medical Genetics*

On February 17, NCJW submitted a request to Georgia Governor Joe Frank Harris for support.

> We are requesting $5,000 in emergency funds to be used for a Community Tay-Sachs Screening. The screening will be a follow up to one held eight years ago. It will also serve to expand and upgrade the permanent testing lab at the Emory University School of Medicine, Division of Medical Genetics. We received $5,000 in Emergency Funds from former Governor Jimmy Carter for our 1975 screening. We hope to have support for this important preventative measure once again.

It listed other sources of support for this project that included grants from the Atlanta Metropolitan Foundation, March of Dimes, an endowment gift from the Atlanta Jewish Federation, and donations from those screened. The request also included a rationale for planning a second Tay-Sachs screening.

- *Atlanta is a mobile community. Thousands of Jewish singles and families have moved to Atlanta since the 1975 screening.*
- *Atlanta colleges and universities have a large number of Jewish students who are not familiar with genetics and/or Tay-Sachs Disease.*
- *Many people who were not 18 years old at the time of the last screening are now eligible to be tested.*
- *In the past eight years, Tay-Sachs disease has been discovered in families that are not Jewish. Through the screening and upgraded testing lab a broader number of individuals can be involved in this program.*
- *Through the funds raised from screening we can purchase the badly needed equipment to upgrade the Tay-Sachs Testing Lab at Emory University.*
- *The need for another screening has been substantiated, and the NCJW has the expertise to meet this need that no one else is filling.*

Dr. Wolfson wrote to area rabbis on July 1 asking them to encourage participation in the screenings in their sermons and newsletters and offered to provide information about Tay-Sachs disease to all couples contemplating marriage.

> *You will have the opportunity to have a simple blood test in order to determine if you are a Tay-Sachs carrier. Please do not eliminate yourself from this testing program because your family is complete; if you are a carrier, your children may be carriers, and it is important for them to be aware of this fact.*
>
> *We hope that you will take advantage of the easy accessibility of this test – select a time and date convenient for you and plan to come. We cannot cure Tay-Sachs disease, but we can prevent it.*

In September, *The Southern Israelite* published an article titled "A piece of the future."

> Would you like to buy a piece of the future? Well, the Atlanta Section of the National Council of Jewish Women is providing an opportunity to do just that.
>
> NCJW's upcoming mass screening shows that they are "looking ahead to the future," states Joanie Shubin, overall chairwoman of the project.
>
> Although Tay-Sachs is incurable – it does not have to happen. A simple blood test can make the difference between a beautiful family and a nightmare. "It's terribly unfortunate for affected people who weren't screened – what they go through..." Shubin says sadly, adding, "You want the future for your children to be the best and brightest – and then something like this has to happen."
>
> The test can provide peace of mind for the future. As Shubin says, "The future of Judaism lies in the future of our children."

NCJW made multiple contributions to this city through the Tay-Sachs screenings. It brought early and sustained awareness to the importance of genetic counseling and testing. It created and enhanced the lab facility and capacity at the Emory University School of Medicine. It had a personal impact on individuals identified as carriers and surely saved some families from the tragedy of having a child born with Tay-Sachs disease. Finally, it galvanized the community, rabbis, doctors, nurses, lay leaders, media and young adults in a unique way and for a significant purpose. Today, the number of Jewish and other genetic diseases that have been identified has grown greatly as has the acceptance in the community for the need and importance of education and testing.

NCJW leaders (L-R) Luci Sunshine, Joyce Shlesinger, Barbie Levy and Lila Hertz

Advocating for children
(L-R) Gloria Frisch, Sugar
Eisenberg and Luci Sunshine

Supporting the Equal Rights Amendment (L-R) Beth Sugarman,
Rosalyn Carter, Linda Hallenberg and Susan Feinberg

Supporting the Equal Rights Amendment (L-R) Sherry Frank,
Roz Cohen, Jeanney Kutner and Betty Talmadge

Working at Bargainata (L-R) Holly
Strelzik and Rebecca Atkinson

Past National Board Members (L-R)
Sherry Frank and Susie Elson

Lobbying and political action (L-R) Luci Sunshine, (unidentified), Fran
Travis, Congressman John Lewis, Margie Steiner and Holly Strelzik

# Politics and Advocacy

---

*Fight for the things you care about, but do it in
a way that will lead others to join you.*

—Ruth Bader Ginsberg

I think I must have inherited my zeal for politics from my father, for it has run through my veins since I was a young child. My dad, Jack Zimmerman, who died of a heart attack when I was eleven years old, was not a man who sat idly by. His 1954 obituary in the *Atlanta Journal-Constitution* reported that he was the owner of Allied Insurance Agency, was on Governor Herman Talmadge's staff, and was on the Board of Directors of Georgia Casualty Insurance Company and General Assurance Corporation. (Leading the Board of Directors of these companies were Austin Dilbeck and Dan Dominey, well known Atlanta community leaders. The companies they started in 1937 were acquired in 1974 by J. Mack Robinson.) He was on the Board of Directors of a number of organizations, including Masons, Shriners, B'nai Brith, and the Progressive Club, and was a member of Congregation Shearith Israel and Ahavath Achim Synagogue.

I regret that I have only a few precious, tangible reminders of my father.  One of these is a letter he wrote to Adolph Rosenberg, Editor of *The Southern Israelite,* on Friday, June 25, 1948, that I kept framed on my desk for many years.

*Dear Abe,*

*It has come to my attention that you are taking an active part in the planning of an Old Age Home for the Jewish people of this city and state. It is my opinion that this is a most urgent necessity for the aged and ill people of this area. I personally know of about a dozen age Jewish people staying in homes which are old houses that would be fire traps and a calamity in case of fire. Also, we may not feel that serving non-Kosher food is important, but after visiting one of these homes myself, I left with the feeling that of all the pain these good people are suffering, the worst was the fact that, after so many years of living by what they had been taught, in their last years they had to eat non-Kosher food.*

*Feeling as I do about this matter, I am enclosing my check in the amount of $200 for this year's contribution and would like to pledge myself as a life member at $200 a year to this worthy cause and to offer my services as a collector, solicitor, or in any other capacity in which I may serve this needy cause.*

*I also wish to take this opportunity of placing at your disposal my office, my girls, my phones, and anything else that will be of help to you in saving a dollar for this magnificent undertaking. I write the above in all sincerity as I have seen the plight of these unfortunate people, for I have my own mother in one of these homes, and I feel very deeply about this cause.*

*Looking forward to having the pleasure of working with you or with the committee in this splendid undertaking.*
*Yours very truly,*
*Jack Zimmerman*

It often strikes me that my dad would have been so gratified if he could have seen the fine William Breman Jewish Home that his early efforts supported and that, decades later, provided a home for his wife, my mother, during the last months of her life. I also like to think that his passion for community service and philanthropy is one of the gifts I inherited from him.

Jack Zimmerman was an active and supportive community member. His civic-minded and politically connected friends were frequent guests in our home before and after his death. One friend, Jack Cravey, Georgia State Comptroller, likely helped my mother, Esther Zimmerman, expedite her studies and acquisition of an insurance license and take over Dad's business.

Our family was one of the first in our neighborhood to get a television in the early 1950s. I have warm memories of sitting in our den watching *The Howdy Doody Show* in black and white. This popular puppet show first aired on December 27, 1947, when I was five years old. Children today, with all their electronics, would most likely have a hard time imagining when there were only a few channels and family gathered around one TV set to watch such innocent fare.

When the 1952 presidential election season aired on television, my entire Morningside Elementary School class crowded around the TV in our house to watch Dwight D. Eisenhower and Adlai Stevenson II make their campaign speeches. All these years later, I still remember how excited I was when I went down the street to see the election materials at the home of my neighbor and close friend, Peggy Alterman Shulman, whose parents, Roz and Max Alterman, were hosting an election night party. When President Dwight D. Eisenhower won a landslide victory on November 4, he reversed Democratic wins since 1932.

Throughout my teens, I not only followed politics, but I also ran for offices in my youth group, B'nai Brith Youth Organization, and as a freshman at Stephens College. I was always interested in the news and involved in social action.

When I moved to Plainfield, New Jersey in 1964 as a young

married, it seemed that everyone I met was involved in National Council of Jewish Women (NCJW), and I soon became actively engaged in its community service projects and expanded my knowledge about and advocacy on a wide array of contemporary issues.

By the early 1970s, I was back in Atlanta and fully engaged in political and social justice issues in NCJW, the Atlanta Jewish Federation, and the community at large. I demonstrated to "Save the Fox" in the tumultuous time when ticket sales declined and investors wanted to redevelop the property for commercial use. A successful grassroots campaign took root, securing a 150,000 signature petition from the Atlanta community. On May 17, 1974, the Atlanta Fox Theatre was placed on the National Register of Historic Places.

I was by no means the only young person in my group who was keenly interested in politics. My childhood classmate was Stuart Eizenstat, who became President Carter's Chief Domestic Policy Advisor and President Clinton's Deputy Secretary of the Treasury, Under Secretary of State for Economic, Business and Agricultural Affairs, and Ambassador to the European Union. Early in his political career he was actively engaged in Andrew Young's second run for Congress. Young lost in 1970 but was victorious in 1972. On more than one occasion, I sat on the floor in Fran and Stuart Eizenstat's home, listening to Andy Young speak about running for office. His wife Jean and young toddler, Bo, were with us in these earlier and much more personal campaign events.

On election day, I volunteered to help get out the vote and was assigned to Techwood Homes, the first public housing development in the country. From 7:00 a.m. until the polls closed at 7:00 p.m., I drove total strangers to the polls, my car festooned with a big Andrew Young sign. I rang doorbells and waited at bus stops to drive people all over areas I had never been before. I went to headquarters to anxiously await the polling reports and cheered when news of my precinct came in, and the historic victory was confirmed.

I was hooked that day by the thrill and satisfaction of working together, across race and religion, to elect progressive people to political office. My husband, Leonard, and I hosted a fundraising event in our home for Atlanta City Councilman Wyche Fowler when he ran for City Council President. I was an avid supporter of Wyche as he continued his successful political career as a U.S. Congressman from 1977 to 1985 and a U.S. Senator from 1986 to 1992. During the Clinton administration, from 1996 to 2001, he served as U.S. Ambassador to Saudi Arabia.

When working for a 501(c)(3) non-profit organization, it is important to stay focused on issues and not partisan politics. Although I was very careful to stay away from publicly being involved in political campaigns while I was on staff at AJC, I did maintain private personal relationships with some elected officials. It was our practice at AJC to send copies of our political correspondence to our national colleagues. I always followed this rule, with the exception of one letter I received from Wyche on June 10, 1981, congratulating me on my appointment as AJC's Southeast Area Director:

*Dear Sherry,*

*I was pleased to learn of your new responsibilities with the American Jewish Committee. [handwritten] (WAS I EVER! WONDERFUL!)*

*I am certain that the close working relationship I have enjoyed with the Committee will continue under your guidance, but I hope your new position will not prevent you from future campaign work. Remember 1982 is fast approaching!*

*Please let me know if I can be of assistance to you or the Committee.*

*Sincerely,*

*Wyche Fowler, Jr.*

*Member of Congress*

I did share with my colleagues my December 1, 1986, letter to the newly elected Senator Fowler.

*Dear Wyche,*

*I still get a thrill thinking about your broad smile on election night.*

*What a stunning victory you won. Needless to say, the best man won and Georgia's representation in Washington is greatly enhanced by your role as our Senator.*

*The day before the election I received the National Council of Jewish Women's quarterly Journal. The enclosed page comes from that publication and mentions your receiving the Roz Cohen Award. Roz would have been so proud of your victory.*

*Good luck Wyche. It will be an honor to call you Senator. I plan to be in Washington to see you and John Lewis sworn in to your well-deserved new offices.*

*Warm Regards,*

*Sherry Frank*

*Southeast Area Director*

I also sent my colleagues my January 6, 1988, letter from Congressman John Lewis.

*Dear Sherry,*

*One year ago today, I took the oath of office to represent the people of the Fifth Congressional District of Georgia as a freshman member of the historic One Hundredth Congress.*

*As I reflect on my first year in Congress, I must tell you that each day as I walk into the Capitol to cast my vote, speak on the House floor, or meet with a group of concerned citizens, I feel blessed. I also feel humbled, yet challenged by the multitude of issues I face as your United States Congressman.*

*I am in Washington because of you. Here and in my local office, my staff and I are continuously available to serve you. I have set aside the third Friday of every month to meet with any citizen to hear their opinions, concerns, or grievances on any matter, and no one needs an appointment. I would especially welcome your reflections on issues that concern you. Please feel free to call on me at any time.*

*I want to thank you for all your help and support, and I look forward to our continued partnership.*

*Best wishes to you and your family for a healthy, peaceful, and prosperous New Year.*
*Sincerely,*
*John Lewis*
*Member of Congress*

*P.S. [handwritten] Sherry, I value your friendship and support.*
*-John*

Few Jews have served in the Georgia General Assembly; however, in the 1980s and 1990s, there were successful campaigns to elect Cathey Steinberg, Doug Teeper, and Ron Slotin. We worked closely with them on key public policy issues at the state level. Parenthetically, those were not easy times, especially for Cathey. She faced challenges as a Jew, a woman, and a New Yorker. Following are some of the significant issues we addressed.

## SEPARATION OF CHURCH AND STATE

My love for politics was nurtured throughout my 25 years at AJC. Our domestic agenda was full of important issues that lent themselves to superb bridge-building initiatives. First among these was supporting a variety of attacks on the separation of church and state. In the early 1980s, the Moral Majority was a strong movement in our country. Founded by the Baptist minister Jerry Falwell, it espoused a highly conservative agenda that supported prayer in schools and laws against abortion. (There was a bumper sticker that pointed out that "The Moral Majority is neither moral nor the majority.") In this climate, challenges to religious liberty were surfacing in state legislatures. Bert Levy, AJC's Vice President of Interreligious Affairs, and Bill Gralnick, AJC's Southeast Area Director, were actively involved in this work. The Georgia Committee for Religious Liberty was the driving force in opposing these initiatives, particularly the proposed creationism statute.

The Reverend Joanna Adams, Associate Minister of Central Presbyterian Church, wrote to Larry Lowenstein, AJC Chapter President, on November 13, 1981.

> *Dear Mr. Lowenstein,*
>
> *Please accept the deepest appreciation the Georgia Committee for Religious Liberty has to offer! We are so gratified that the Atlanta Chapter of the American Jewish Committee believes in the vitally important work of our committee. In these difficult days in Georgia, your generous grant to us will enable us to be more effective in supporting the principle of separation of church and state in our state.*
>
> *It is always a pleasure to work with Bert Levy, by the way, and we were delighted to have Sherry Frank and April Levine in attendance at our meeting yesterday. I look forward to our continued partnership as we work toward common goals in the days to come. Sincerely yours,*
>
> *The Rev. Joanna Adams*
> *President, Georgia Committee for Religious Liberty*

A press release on February 22, 1982, announced that Reverend Adams would speak for the committee on the steps of the State Capitol in support of State Representative Ben Barron Ross, Chair of the House Education Committee.

The group also voiced its strong disapproval of the proposed creationism statute. According to the clergy committee's president, the Rev. Joanna Adams, "we are a Bible-believing group. We all accept the Genesis account of Creation which affirms God's action in causing to be all that there is. We just don't think this ought to be taught in our public schools. To do so breaks down the separation of church and state. But more fundamentally, this is a subject that is too important to be left with public school teachers. It should be taught in the home and in the context of a community of faith."

The Committee also noted the recent Arkansas court case on dual-treatment legislation. Rev. Adams observed that total costs in that case approached 1.5 million dollars. "For people whose mission it is to preach good news to the poor, feed the hungry, visit the sick and imprisoned and to free the oppressed, it is a sad development to devote so much money on imposing our narrow doctrines on the general public instead of living out our primary mandate."

The Committee concluded with a call for other legislators to support Rep. Ross in his decision to keep this bill from reaching the floor of the House, claiming that "the State of Georgia, our religious institutions and especially our children will be the better for it."

On March 18, AJC, the National Conference of Christians and Jews and the Georgia Committee for Religious Liberty co-sponsored a community forum entitled "Separation of Church and State – A Constitutional Guarantee in Jeopardy." Sam Rabinove, National Director of AJC's Discrimination and Legal Department, joined with State Representative Ben Barron Ross and Reverend Joanna Adams as the speakers.

In the end, righteous Christian leaders, many in large churches and led by Reverend Adams, kept creation science out of the schools in Georgia. We owe her a debt of gratitude for her steadfast leadership. Among the many benefits I reaped from our working together was our long-standing and very special friendship.

## EQUAL RIGHTS AMENDMENT

Few issues were more galvanizing than the Equal Rights Amendment (ERA). It passed Congress in March, 1972 and was sent to the states for ratification. We had a decade to secure thirty-eight states to support the Amendment, but when 1982 arrived, only thirty-five states were in support.

In Georgia, as the vote drew closer, organizations and prominent women went into high gear building support for this issue. Atlanta First Lady, Jean Young, lent her voice and active support to the effort. Marlene Rinzler, AJC'S Women's Issues Committee Chair, hosted a December Sunday morning fundraiser at her home to underwrite an ad campaign for the ERA Georgia. AJC and NCJW co-sponsored this high-powered event along with honorary hosts former U.S. First Lady Rosalyn Carter, Jean Young and Betty Talmadge (wife of Senator Herman). However, when we woke up that morning, the entire town was covered in snow. It seemed unlikely that anyone could get to the program. But that day, we discovered that it really paid to know people in high places, and thanks to Mayor Andrew Young, the roads were cleared by the time the event took place, and an exciting gathering of women activists made their voices heard.

It was a sad day in Georgia in 1982, when I sat in the balcony of the State Capitol witnessing the ERA go down in defeat. I think about that moment when, teary eyed, I said to myself, you can't always win, but you must always fight the good fight. I have learned that some issues require decades of diligence, as progress is often achieved in frustratingly small increments. In 2018, support for the ERA has resurfaced among some members of Congress with the hope to extend the date for passage.

## Voting Rights

Some of my earliest advocacy work focused on the renewal of the Voting Rights Act. At the suggestion of Hyman Bookbinder (Bookie), AJC's beloved Washington Representative, we organized a 1982 meeting of African-American and Jewish leaders. This effort was so well received that it led to the creation of the Atlanta Black/Jewish Coalition in Support of the Voting Rights Act, which is covered in the chapter on Black/Jewish Relations. My personal involvement with this Coalition led to a close and life-long relationship with John Lewis, a civil rights legend who played a major role in the voting rights issue.

The Coalition provided the vehicle for us to raise our voices on numerous public policy issues, and we responded to new initiatives to suppress voting in our country, including opposing the 2005 Voter ID Bill. It is unfortunate that the assault on this basic constitutional right faces ongoing challenges with each passing year. I have a deep continuing interest in this and have registered people to vote and driven people to the polls on election day.

Since 2017, I have led a monthly NCJW study group on current events. I continue to raise concerns about voting rights. We discuss the gerrymandering cases going to the Supreme Court and steps to make voting more secure, including Georgia's debate over returning to the use of paper ballots. I highlight the increasing concern over voter suppression and purging of electoral rolls and have advocated for laws that allow election-day voter registration, early voting days and expanded poll locations.

## Georgia Flag

The subject of the Georgia flag was high on our agenda throughout the 1990s and into the 2000s. On February 19, 1993, an ad in the *Atlanta Jewish Times* cogently summarized this issue and the Jewish community's strong support for changing the flag. The ad was signed by representatives of AJC, ADL, NCJW, the Atlanta Rabbinical Association, and the Atlanta Jewish Federation. It endorsed Governor Zell Miller's proposal to restore the State Flag of Georgia to its pre-1956 form. The full-page ad provided a brief history of Georgia's state flag.

- *The first flag of Georgia, adopted in 1799, had the State Seal, with its three pillars of "Wisdom, Justice, and Moderation" supporting the arch of the Constitution, centered on a field of blue.*
- *Based on the National Flag of the Confederacy (popularly known as the "Stars and Bars"), Georgia's second flag was adopted in 1879 by the legislature to honor those Georgians who had given their lives to the South in the War Between the States.*
- *Georgia's third flag unified the state's first and second flags when, in 1905, the legislature added the state seal. This is the flag that Governor Zell Miller has proposed be restored as the official flag of Georgia.*
- *The fourth flag replaced the red and white bars of the Stars and Bars with the star-spangled cross of the Confederate Battle Flag. Adopted in 1956, this flag was the physical manifestation of the legislature's contempt for federally-mandated racial desegregation and the civil rights movement.*

My statement at a press conference at the Georgia State Capitol on July 17, 1996, also highlighted the issue.

*Symbols matter. For years we have looked at the five bright rings that are the symbol of the 1996 Centennial Olympic Games. They represent a symbol of unity – of fairness – of inclusion*

*– of pride. Leaders and athletes from all over the world will be in Atlanta participating in this uplifting spirit that the Olympics represent. These guests look to Atlanta as a city that stands for unity, fairness, inclusion, and pride.*

*Symbols do matter. They often speak louder than words. Think of the horrific images conjured up by these symbols: a burning cross, a swastika, and yes, the Georgia flag – the stars and bars.*

*The Georgia flag is a symbol of the divisions that still exist, regrettably in our society. The bigots and hate-mongers who use this flag as their symbol of defiance, desecrate the memory of the men and women who served and died under this battle flag 130 years ago. This flag certainly has its place in history. In 1956, when the Confederate battle emblem was added to the Georgia flag, it dramatically changed what our State Flag stood for and it is now an undeniable representation of racism, segregation, hate, and bigotry. This flag is a festering wound that will not heal. It is a disgrace to see it fly in front of buildings in the great city that the entire world will see in the coming weeks.*

*There is simply no denying that today this flag is used as a badge of honor for hate groups of all kinds – Ku Klux Klan, Skinheads, Neo-Nazis, Militias, etc.*

*I'm proud to speak for the American Jewish Committee and acknowledge the support of the Anti-Defamation League, the Atlanta Jewish Federation Community Relations Committee, and the National Council of Jewish Women in this battle to change the Georgia flag.*

*Jews have learned through history that toxic words and toxic symbols lead to toxic views and toxic actions. Symbols often do speak louder than words. This is true for the Georgia Flag. It is a symbol of shame, not a symbol of honor. It should be removed forever as the Flag of Georgia.*

In the mid-1990s, I was an active leader in the "Coalition to

Change the Georgia Flag." Participating organizations included Common Cause of Georgia, National Rainbow Coalition, Georgia Civil Rights Network, Southern Christian Leadership Conference, and the Martin Luther King, Jr., Center for Nonviolent Social Change. We expressed our views through a variety of actions and in communication with elected officials. There were demonstrations at venues during the Atlanta Olympics. We wrote to companies that flew the Georgia flag and asked them to remove it, and when, or if, they did, we supported them. In our July 29, 1994, letter to Michael Leven, President of Holiday Inn Worldwide, Americas Division, we wrote:

> *Dear Michael,*
>
> *Bravo! We were so proud to follow the news coverage that you and Holiday Inn received for taking down the racist flags from your hotels.*
>
> *The AJC, Atlanta Chapter, has continued to join with community groups in fighting for a change in our state flag. With leadership like you have demonstrated, perhaps a victory will be closer at hand.*
>
> *Warm regards,*
>
> *Lois Frank*            *Sherry Frank*
> *President, Atlanta Chapter*     *Southeast Area Director*
>
> *P.S. We still look forward to your having the time to join our Board of Trustees.*

The current State Flag of Georgia was adopted on May 8, 2003. Finally, Georgia had a flag we could all be proud of. Although it is not the one that Cecil Alexander designed that was so enthusiastically embraced in 2001, it was nevertheless an acceptable compromise. When Congressman John Lewis was first elected, he would not display the state flag at his office door. Today, he is proud to have the current one welcoming visitors to his office in Washington, D.C.

Some pundits say that Governor Barnes' courageous support for changing the flag and opposing tenure for teachers cost him a second term. He remains a close friend to the Jewish community and an admired political leader.

For a number of years (2000-2006), AJC hired lobbyist Linda Smith Lowe to follow our key issues at the Georgia General Assembly and inform and advise us on action being considered. In January 2001 and 2002, we hosted breakfasts for members of the legislature to inform them of our priorities. Excerpts from my report on the first breakfast follow.

*The grits were hot, and the bagels were fresh. The sun would soon rise over the Georgia Capitol with the post-1956 Georgia flag flying for the final day. The gold dome of the Capitol was shining as a group of nearly 40 State Representatives and Senators and 25 American Jewish Committee, Atlanta Chapter, members checked in at AJC's first Legislative Breakfast, "Grits with a Side of Politics." Packets filled with materials on public policy issues were distributed.*

*Enthusiasm was high as legislators and advocates congratulated one another on the flag victory the prior day in the Senate. Cecil Alexander, AJC Past President and creator of the new flag, arrived with TV, radio, and print media focusing all of their attention on him.*

*I reviewed priority issues on AJC's Domestic Policy agenda, stressing the fact that the Jewish community is multi-faceted and our issues are numerous and diverse. These include: improvements in public education, changing the Georgia State Flag, free exercise of religion and the separation of church and state, violence prevention, welfare reform as it pertains to non-citizens who are lawfully present in the U.S.*

At the close of the Georgia General Assembly in 2003, I reported on our work on a great number of important topics: the state flag, charitable choice, immigration, voting rights, hate crimes and discrimination. We continued to follow issues related to separation of church and state, religious liberty, abortion rights, racial profiling, and bills pertaining to gun violence and anti-terrorism.

My tenure at AJC began with work on the renewal of the Voting Rights Act; it concluded with addressing new challenges in the same area – particularly the voter ID issue. As my years at AJC came to a close, less attention was directed to the domestic agenda as challenges in the international arena were taking precedent. AJC's work, in which I was involved for 25 years, intensified on support for Israel, responding to global anti-Semitism, extremism, and terrorist threats abroad. My personal commitment to social justice, advocacy and political action continues through my involvement in AJC, NCJW, various civic organizations and my synagogue.

My dad, Jack Haynes
Zimmerman, c. 1935

Sherry Frank and Stuart Eizenstat,
Henry Grady High School prom, 1960

Stuart Eizenstat greeting newly elected Senator Wyche
Fowler and Congressman John Lewis, 1987

Reverend Dr. Joanna
Adams addresses
the AJC Board

Supporting the Equal Rights Amendment (L-R) Georgia State Representative
Cathey Steinberg, Atlanta First Lady Jean Young, Marlene Rinzler, 1981

# INTERRELIGIOUS AFFAIRS

LOVE THY NEIGHBOR AS THYSELF

---

*We forfeit the right to worship God when we humiliate the image of God in other people.*

—Rabbi Abraham Joshua Heschel

## INTRODUCTION

The South is known as the Bible Belt for good reason. For a great many, religion plays a defining role in their lives, impacting much of the civic and political arena. During my tenure at AJC, I participated in events sponsored by various religious-based organizations, while being an active player in efforts to bring the interfaith community together.

The Christian Council of Metropolitan Atlanta (CCMA) was a strong umbrella organization that provided a network for communication, advocacy and community service. It initiated projects that are still operating, including the Atlanta Interfaith Broadcasters and the Airport Interfaith Chaplaincy. It was actively engaged in immigration and refugee resettlement work and was the leading voice in responding to the homeless crisis.

From 1979-1981, when the tragic specter of Atlanta's murdered and missing children had everyone on edge, the annual CCMA Prayer Breakfast provided an important opportunity for the community to come together. AJC's National Director of Interreligious Affairs, Rabbi Marc Tanenbaum, and The Honorable Andrew Young were the keynote speakers for the 1980 Breakfast. I vividly remember the rabbi relating a chilling Holocaust story of Nazi soldiers tossing Jewish children up in the air to shoot like pigeons. He asked an emotion-filled audience, "could anyone doubt that the Jewish community shares your pain and horror when our innocent children are callously murdered?"

The Council began to diminish in strength in the 1980s and closed up shop in the early 2000s as several religious organizations were going through transition, hastened by the terrorist attack on September 11, 2001 (9/11). Soon after, Christian leaders created the Regional Council of Churches.

Another group, Concerned Black Clergy, was a compelling voice for the black community throughout my years at AJC. Nationally prominent black clergy would frequently be guest preachers at Atlanta churches on Sunday and stay over for the regularly scheduled Monday morning Concerned Black Clergy breakfast meeting at Paschal's Restaurant and Hotel. It is hard to do justice in describing the energy and intensity of these meetings, especially when they took place during election time. It was awesome to witness the proposal of the Black Slate (candidate recommendations) and the organized "get out the vote" efforts, utilizing countless church buses and volunteers.

I loved attending these meetings, which were open to activists of different faiths and races. On occasion, I was invited to speak on a specific issue. In the mid 1990s, when black churches were being burned across the South, I spoke at a Concerned Black Clergy press conference where I described the feeling of fear and vulnerability I experienced as a young teen in 1958 when The Temple was bombed.

The Jewish community's clergy were connected through their

own organization, the Atlanta Rabbinical Association. Additional interfaith coalitions brought together clergy from designated areas of Metro Atlanta, including, among others, Sandy Springs, Cobb County, and the in-town congregations.

Atlanta is home to the important seminaries Candler School of Theology at Emory University, Columbia Theological Seminary, and the Interdenominational Theological Center (ITC). I worked with each of them, and they, in turn, added to our effective interfaith work. The Atlanta community is also endowed with exceptional clergy and faculty within the Departments of Religion at Emory University, Spelman College, and Morehouse College. These gifted scholars participated outside their college campuses and brought their expertise and support to numerous community-based initiatives.

In the 1990s, several new interfaith organizations were created. One of the most consequential was the Georgia Human Relations Commission's Interfaith Coalition of Metropolitan Atlanta, under the leadership of Executive Director Joy Berry and Chairman Paula Lawton-Bevington. Additionally, effective coalition work took place in partnership with Reverend David Key of the Georgia Interfaith Alliance. In 1999, through a joint effort of Andrew Young, former Atlanta Mayor and Ambassador to the U.N., and retired Emory University President, Dr. James Laney, Faith in the City was created. Doug Gatlin was its Executive Director and actively worked with us on our interfaith programming.

The tragic terrorist attacks of 9/11 led to an expansion of my relationships within Atlanta's Muslim community. Our years of engagement with a wide array of religious leaders bore fruit when we all came together to support the Muslim community at this critical time. The Faith Alliance of Metro Atlanta (FAMA) was born out of this historic event.

The "go to" person for interfaith and interracial outreach for the Christian community was Jan Swanson, who directly participated in virtually every sustained program we did. I was deeply involved and made lifelong friends, while building AJC's credibility as a central player in interfaith relations.

The 1980s and 1990s were formative years for Atlanta as its population increased exponentially, bringing more religious diversity than ever to our city. Not only was I personally involved in interfaith coalitions, but AJC was also a leader in this area through programs we initiated and hosted. The staff and lay leadership brought important advocacy and education to our members and the Jewish community at large. While the list of our interfaith activities is extensive, I have chosen to highlight a number of my favorites and the most significant ones in order to provide important historical information about the organizations that provided leadership in this area.

## GEORGIA HUMAN RELATIONS COMMISSION, INTERFAITH COALITION OF METROPOLITAN ATLANTA AND THE GEORGIA INTERFAITH ALLIANCE

On June 6, 1991, I received a letter from State of Georgia Governor Zell Miller confirming "The Human Relations Commission has informed me of your willingness to serve on the steering committee to organize the Interfaith Coalition. The Coalition has the potential for promoting and increasing understanding and cooperation among our many cultures. In lending your leadership, you are providing a valuable service to the state." On October 30, Governor Miller issued a proclamation recognizing Human Rights Week on December 9-13.

By the spring of 1992, a steering committee was actively planning events for the Interfaith Coalition of Metropolitan Atlanta. Rabbi Philip Kranz of Temple Sinai, Rabbi Julie Schwartz of Temple Emanu-El, Dr. Laurie Patton, Chair of the Emory University Department of Religion, and I were the four Jewish members of this twenty-member steering committee. For the following decade, the Coalition's work was guided by Paula Lawton-Bevington, Chairman, and Joy Berry, Executive Director, of the Georgia Human Relations Commission.

Our early programs included an anti-hate campaign, a youth leadership training program, and regularly scheduled luncheon meetings to discuss issues such as race relations and religious pluralism. The Coalition launched an ambitious project titled "Common Threads: Faith Perspectives on Social Justice." It compiled a sixty-one page document, and a thirteen-segment television program that exemplified interfaith dialogue at its best. The show ran on Atlanta Interfaith Broadcasters, Inc. Jean Saul, AJC's Assistant Area Director, was featured as a host for one session.

The National Interfaith Alliance was established in July, 1994, to celebrate religious freedom and offer faith-based voices an alternative to the radical religious right. On December 24, 1995, Reverend David Key and Jean Saul sent an invitation to join the Georgia Interfaith Alliance.

*Dear Friend,*

*Religious leaders and lay persons throughout the Metro Atlanta area have joined together over the increasing concerns that face us in local, state and federal politics. With greater frequency in each year's election and political debate – accusations, intolerance and the misuse of religious language have created an environment hostile to the free exchange of ideas.*

*Sincerely,*

*Reverend David Key*      *Jean Saul*

*Georgia Baptist Minister*      *American Jewish Committee*

Advocacy was the driving force of this coalition. At the opening session of the Georgia General Assembly on January 16, 1996, we spoke out for separation of church and state at a press conference on the steps of the State Capitol. Following the press conference, members gathered across the street at Central Presbyterian Church for lunch and a panel discussion on "Religious Pluralism and the Secular State."

When political campaigns heated up in the fall, the Georgia Interfaith Alliance distributed a "Candidate Pledge of Civility" signed by over seventy individuals running for federal, state, and local offices. It called on candidates to "affirm the positive role that religion plays in the democratic process... repudiate the use of religion as a weapon to demonize those whose religious or political beliefs are different from mine... repudiate any campaign tactics and refuse any campaign contributions from organizations and individuals who practice or advocate exclusion or intolerance."

Programs, advocacy, and bridge-building continued throughout the decade with increased clergy and lay participation in these key coalitions.

## JOHN ROCKER

As the 1990s ended, a firestorm erupted over racist comments made by Atlanta Braves pitcher, John Rocker. The December, 1999, edition of *Sports Illustrated*, quoted Rocker, who made offensive comments about New York and the many non-English speaking foreigners found walking around Times Square. In the article, he questioned how these people even got into the United States and went on to say he would retire before playing ball for a New York team. Adding to his insults, he made disparaging comments about the diversity of people one might encounter riding the train to the ballpark.

Reaction to his comments was strong and immediate, and an explosion of media attention followed these comments and the many responses to them, including those from New York City Mayor Rudy Giuliani and Atlanta Mayor Bill Campbell. On December 23, national Korean and Chinese organizations issued statements of condemnation and called for punitive measures.

AJC issued a press release supporting those who spoke out.

The American Jewish Committee (AJC), Atlanta Chapter, applauds the leadership demonstrated by our city over the tasteless and offensive remarks of Braves player John Rocker. Once again, Atlanta stands tall in its repudiation of bigotry. From Mayor Bill Campbell to Braves General Manager, John Schuerholz to star pitcher Tom Glavine, Atlantans are, at every level, stating in unequivocal terms that we will not tolerate the denigration of any minority group. Braves teammates have made it clear that there is no room on their team for the views expressed by John Rocker.

All the hard work, which goes on daily, to bring religious, ethnic, and diverse groups together sets Atlanta apart from many other cities. Today in Atlanta there are no apologies to be made, but rather a chorus to be heard of unabashed denunciations of John Rocker for derogatory comments about single mothers, new immigrants, African-Americans, gays, and those who have yet to learn to speak our common English language.

It is said that you cannot understand another person until you have walked a mile in his/her shoes. Perhaps John Rocker needs to walk in the shoes of some new immigrants trying to make it in America, or a gay person confronting discrimination, or a single mother trying to balance work, family, and personal needs. Sensitivity training can help those who truly want to learn.

In a letter to Braves President Stan Kasten, the AJC Atlanta Chapter is offering to assist in setting up a positive program for this misguided young man.

CONGRATULATIONS ATLANTA, you've stepped up to the plate once again.

On December 22, 1999, a contrite Rocker had issued a personal statement in which he took responsibility for his unacceptable remarks, blaming them partially on his competitive zeal. Claiming not to be a racist, he noted that everyone makes mistakes and said his comments were not what he believed in his heart. He acknowledged that he should not have made them and further expressed his intention to learn from the experience.

After thanking city leaders who made public statements repudiating Rocker's words, AJC sought a way to use this incident to reinforce respect for diversity in Atlanta. Instead of reacting directly to the Rocker comments, we chose to respond to the entire episode by focusing on the inherent unity of our city. In light of the upcoming New Year, New Century, and New Millennium, we drafted, in cooperation with the Georgia Human Relations Commission, the following declaration:

*Declaration of Respect: Commitment to Pluralism*

*In this first week of a new century, we come together as representatives of the diverse communities in Georgia to affirm our commitment to transcend mere tolerance of our differences and to achieve a genuine appreciation of the beauty of our interwoven cultural and religious tapestry.*

*In this first week of a new century, we acknowledge that building bridges of human solidarity and strengthening relations between all religious, racial and ethnic groups is not a luxury, but rather an absolute necessity in order for us to live in peace and justice.*

*In this first week of a new century, we dedicate ourselves to ensure that those whose voices are muffled by oppression and poverty are heard.*

*In this first week of a new century, we vow to welcome immigrants and other newcomers to our midst, and to be inclusive of them in our community activities.*

*In this first week of a new century, we celebrate the spark of the*

*Divine in each of us that renews our religious spirit and brings us to new levels of understanding.*

*In this first week of a new century, we dedicate ourselves to combating bigotry, stereotyping and hatred and to speaking out when anyone or any group is spoken of or treated in a disparaging way.*

*In this first week of a new century, we sign this Declaration of Respect with hope and faith that by celebrating our diversity, Georgia will continue to flourish.*

We invited a large number of religious and ethnic leaders to join us in signing the Declaration on Friday January 7, 2000, at the Georgia State Capitol, South Wing Rotunda.

The program, titled "The First Week of a New Century: A Time for Renewal and Commitment," listed the following speakers:

- *Roy E. Barnes, Governor State of Georgia*
- *Joy Berry, Georgia Human Relations Commission*
- *Reverend Gerald Durley, Concerned Black Clergy*
- *Cantor Nancy Kassel, Temple Beth Tikvah*
- *Sherry Frank, American Jewish Committee*
- *Subash Razdan, National Federation of Indian-American Associations*
- *Swami Yogeshananda, Minister, The Eternal Quest*
- *Pat Upshaw, Leadership Atlanta*
- *Steve Choi, Asian-American Coalition*
- *Reverend David Jenkins, Christian Council of Metropolitan Atlanta*
- *Harry Knox, Georgia Equality Project*
- *Jeffrey Tapia, Latin American Association*
- *Rabbi Brett Isserow, Interfaith Coalition of Metropolitan Atlanta*
- *Imam Plemon El-Amin, Atlanta Masjid of Al-Islam*

On January 11, 2000, Ambassador Andrew Young wrote an article in the *Atlanta Constitution* regarding the behavior of baseball's John Rocker. He said Rocker could learn from the teachings of Martin Luther King, Jr., and reflect on the experiences of Jackie Robinson and Hank Aaron, who kept their cool despite vicious taunting, ugly race-baiting and indignities of segregation during their baseball careers. "They were prepared by generations of training from their elders in tolerance and restraint. There were religious and political reasons for their self-discipline. They carried the hopes and prayers of the race and nation. Success had to be earned on and off the field, and they were never allowed to forget that." Young wrote that Rocker is still young enough to change and learn. "When he absorbs those lessons, he can throw 100-mile-per-hour strikes with a smile, and we'll all win."

On January 18, Buck Goldstein and I wrote to the Honorable Andrew Young.

> *Dear Andy,*
>
> *You continue to be a source of inspiration and wise counsel for our community. How fortunate we have been to have you in our midst.*
>
> *We wanted you to know how much we agreed with your sentiments as expressed in your* Atlanta Constitution *article, January 11, 2000, "Rocker Has Chance for Redemption." We can always count on you to take the high road and find a way to build community. Thanks for being so special.*
>
> *Sincerely,*
>
> *Buck Goldstein                    Sherry Frank*
> *President, Atlanta Chapter        Southeast Area Director*

We framed the Declaration of Respect, signed by the speakers and other leaders in attendance, and presented it to Governor Roy Barnes. On February 2, I received a letter from him thanking us for organizing the press conference and for his gift and expressing his wish that we continue this important work.

## FAITH ALLIANCE OF METRO ATLANTA (FAMA)

The world changed dramatically after 9/11, and there was a new urgency for the faith community to come together in a stronger, more unified and sustained way. Nearly sixty individuals responded to a letter from Rabbi Brett Isserow, The Temple, and Reverend Dr. Joanna Adams, Trinity Presbyterian Church, inviting interested individuals to a November 13, 2001, luncheon at The Temple. On January 22, 2002, a steering committee met to approve a statement of purpose. I helped draft it with Doug Gatlin from Faith and the City and Reverend Budd Friend-Jones from Central Congregational Church.

By July, the newly formed Faith Alliance of Metro Atlanta (FAMA) was actively engaged in programming. Candidates for Governor, Lieutenant Governor, United States Senate, and Atlanta area congressional offices, were asked to sign a "Commitment to Fair Campaign Practices." It called on them to "affirm the religious diversity of this country and steadfastly support the separation of church and state... conduct their campaign without appeal to prejudice, discrimination or scapegoating based on race, religion, class, gender, marital status, national origin, ethnicity, sexual orientation, disability, immigrant status or age." At the same time, we were urging people to exercise their right to vote. In August, 2002, we released our Mission Statement and Goals.

*Mission:*

*To promote understanding, respect, prayer, interaction, and unity among the diverse faiths in the greater Atlanta region, and to advance the influence and voices of the faith communities for the common good*

*Goals:*

- *Communal Prayer - To foster interfaith and multi-faith occasions for prayer, meditation, and celebration among the region's religious communities*
- *Education on Religion – To encourage and provide opportunities for learning about the rituals of prayer, worship, and meditation, and about the values and beliefs of the region's varied religious traditions*
- *Dialogue – To organize and promote thoughtful multi-faith and interfaith dialogue concerning important issues of the day*
- *Cooperation and Networking – To stimulate and foster cooperation between people and groups actively engaged in religious and interreligious work*
- *Advocacy and Action – To be a unified and/or coordinated, ethical force for justice and the common good*

The strength of the new coalition was evidenced at our first large community event, an interfaith service held on September 11, 2002, commemorating the prior year's terrorist attack. After a year of planning, aided by Reverend Dr. Joanna Adams, Reverend Dr. P.C. (Buddy) Ennis, and Reverend Jane Fahey, all of Trinity Presbyterian Church, this became Atlanta's most religiously inclusive service. With the dramatic entrance of a large number of robed clergy, a huge audience, and extensive security inside and outside of the church, FAMA and interfaith relations were on the map in Atlanta. We repeated this commemorative service for several years and moved on to create new and substantial ongoing projects that responded to community faith-based challenges.

FAMA quickly evolved into a multi-faceted alliance, creating significant and enduring programs. One of these was our outreach to high school students. Peace By Piece, developed in 2003, was FAMA's response to the reality that prejudice and hate begin in childhood. It employed techniques in experiential education to bring youth of differing faiths together for the purpose of building trust, understanding, and ultimately, peace. Bart Cohen served as the project director of this program, which is still ongoing, with the partnership of The Weber School, a trans-denominational Jewish high school, Marist, a Roman Catholic school, and the W.D. Mohammed School for Muslim students. Programs involved students within their own schools and in retreat settings.

AJC was the central address for FAMA, with meeting space, lunches, support staff and warm hospitality generously provided through the years. FAMA continued to develop programs after my retirement. It still provides an important forum for clergy and lay leaders across the religious landscape to come together for education, advocacy and worship.

## WORLD PILGRIMS

In 9/11's aftermath, Wayne Smith, the founder of Friendship Force, reached out to Jan Swanson. Her work bringing black and white folks together for shared overnight weekend experiences encouraged him to develop more sustained interaction among Jews, Christians, and Muslims. Wayne understood the value of travel and time spent with people beyond the usual community meetings of engagement. It provided a way for people to gain shared first-hand insight into the sacred spaces, religious history, and ritual practice of people of different faiths.

From October 20-29, 2002, with Jan, Imam Plemon El-Amin, and Wayne at the helm, we tested this premise when forty-five Christians, Jews, and Muslims went to Turkey. I was given the privilege of participating in this life-changing experience. We learned about the country and the religious history and traditions of our three faiths. We prayed, explored, and developed lifelong relationships. In 2004, the destination was Spain and Morocco, and in 2005, Jerusalem.

As of this writing in 2018, twenty-seven World Pilgrimages have taken place producing nearly five hundred alumni. Each participant has felt the intimate impact of this experience, and it has provided new insight into religion, its teachings, history, clergy, and followers. Deep and lasting personal relationships have been nurtured while traveling and sustained when we returned home to our individual and extended communities. Jan Swanson's tireless efforts in organizing these pilgrimages, and the continuing work back at home, have contributed immeasurably to the experience. Imam Plemon El-Amin has shared his expertise about travel and knowledge of the world in nearly every pilgrimage. He has led us through inspiring reflections about our day's learnings and interactions.

From the first, the program was designed to encourage maximum bonding between participants. Each individual received a blank "dance card," numbered for each day of travel, to be completed at a briefing before we left. We were asked to enter a different person's name on each day on the card. This became who we spent that entire day with at meals, as well as in reflection and meaningful conversation. Roommates changed during each trip, allowing for additional opportunities to enhance relationships. At the end of our 2002 World Pilgrimage to Turkey, we adopted a resolution that continues to speak to the mission of this amazing program declaring to our communities that we have found hope, trust, and an abundance of common ground.

As I write these memoirs, World Pilgrims continues to bring clergy and people of faith together for travel, learning, exceptional bonding and new relationships. After I retired, I chose to participate in a second World Pilgrimage, this one to Canada, and a third, when we went to Morocco and Spain. In Canada, we spent time at Niagara Falls, and since our daily reflections included an exploration of water in our faith traditions, this visit was all the more meaningful. We spent a truly magical evening with my daughter, Jacque, and her family at their home in Toronto and shared the beauty of welcoming Shabbat. Each pilgrimage included an interface with another culture where all three Abrahamic faiths are practiced. It also closed with the opportunity to make a financial contribution to a site we visited that was in need of support. In Morocco, our donations to the Hilltop Shepherds' Village enabled them, for the first time, to provide water and sewers to their community.

An active alumni network is central to the success of this program, bringing new friends together on a regular basis once they return back home. Atlanta's interfaith community has been dramatically strengthened and our organizations enhanced by the sustained personal relationships developed by pilgrimage participants.

## PRESBYTERIAN CHURCH (U.S.A.)

Rabbi A. James (Jim) Rudin, AJC's Director of Interreligious Affairs, guided me through some of the thorny challenges of interfaith understanding. He helped me understand the significant and historic ties that Presbyterians have to the Middle East. This is summarized in an article published by the *Jewish Telegraphic Agency (JTA)* on May 11, 2006.

*Presbyterian Divestment has deep historical roots*
*by Rachel Pomerance*

The Presbyterians' Palestinian sympathies can be traced back to the 19th century. Mainline American Protestant churches at that time specialized in certain regions, and the Presbyterians focused on Palestine.

In, fact, universities like Bir Zeit in the West Bank and the American University in Beirut were founded by Presbyterians, according to Rabbi A. James Rudin, senior interreligious adviser for the American Jewish Committee.

As Presbyterians and their Protestant brethren began to

identify with Palestinian Christians and Arab Muslims, they looked askance at Israel and Zionism. Many of the movement's leaders voiced disdain for the creation of the Jewish state upon its birth. Antipathy towards Israel hardened as visitors to the region met with Palestinian Christians rather than Jews or Israelis, said Rudin, who led a Protestant-Jewish mission to Lebanon, Jordan and Israel in 1974.

The 2004 resolution seeking divestment from companies that do business in Israel isn't the first time Protestants have proposed divesting from Israel. But it never gained steam or came to a vote in any denomination until 2004, he said. Talk of divestment surfaced among Protestant leadership in the 1980s, comparing Israel's actions to that of the apartheid government in South Africa.

Several bodies of the United Methodist Church, for example, have passed resolutions to limit or monitor U.S. and other government's aid to Israel based on the Jewish state's presence in the West Bank or its settlement activity. But the wave of divestment activity among the mainline churches marks a new era. That it returned was due to the Palestinian uprising, the growing U.S.-Israel alliance and the fact that divestment helped bring down the South African government, Rudin believes.

My involvement with the Presbyterian Church (U.S.A.), its clergy, and its declarations against Israel began with Israel's 1982 Lebanon War. I could write chapters on AJC's work in this area alone. Various positions taken by the denomination's General Assembly were often under discussion at their conferences, and they regularly released statements throughout my twenty-five years at AJC. We responded to forums sponsored by several Presbyterian churches in Atlanta where the dialogue was especially acrimonious and critical of Israel. Hostile statements often came from the Reverend Fahed

Abu-Akel, a Palestinian Christian and Presbyterian minister. In 2009, he was elected Moderator of the Presbyterian Church (U.S.A.). As a leader in the Presbytery, he led the charge for many of the national statements against Israel and in support of BDS (boycott, divestment, and sanctions).

I first became aware of the conflict this was causing within the Presbyterian Church when David Harris, AJC's CEO, visited Atlanta during the Lebanon War. In addition to speaking to Chapter members, he insisted that meetings be scheduled with community clergy. We invited Presbyterian minister, Reverend Dr. Joanna Adams, to one of them. At that meeting, she tearily shared with David the pain she was feeling as criticism of Israel spilled over into anti-Semitism. The Jewish community, locally and nationally, knows no better ally than Joanna. Our deep and personal friendship has strengthened over the decades as we shared struggles over the Presbyterians' often one-sided criticism of Israel. There were deep divisions within the Church, and while many members in the pews did not agree with the positions taken by the General Assembly, votes were close and reflected the differing opinions of the membership.

Strong bonds among Presbyterians and Jews have existed for many years in Atlanta and continue today. Even in the darkest times of Presbyterian-Jewish relations, there were moments of light, fostering understanding and friendship. In 2004, Temple Sinai Rabbi Ron Segal, an AJC Chapter Vice President, and Joanna Adams of Morningside Presbyterian Church agreed to co-chair a Presbyterian-Jewish clergy dialogue group. These meetings, tense and honest as they were, brought about small yet meaningful developments. Letters to the Editor signed by the group acknowledged the pain experienced by Israel when terrorist attacks occurred. Programs sponsored by their churches usually included balanced and pro-Israel speakers. One of the participating ministers left Atlanta to take a new parish, but his name continued to appear on pro-Israel statements, a direct impact of these open and heartfelt dialogues.

Community relations require long-term and sustained involvement and communications. Participants in the AJC-initiated dialogue group showed that necessary dedication and seriousness of purpose. In addition to Rabbi Segal, the Jewish participants were Rabbi Ilan Feldman, Congregation Beth Jacob; Rabbi Philip Kranz, Temple Sinai; Rabbi Shalom Lewis, Congregation Etz Chaim; Rabbi Hillel Norry, Congregation Shearith Israel; Rabbi Jeffrey Salkin, The Temple; Rabbi Neil Sandler, Ahavath Achim Synagogue; Rabbi Scott Saulson, Jewish Family & Career Services; and Rabbi Julie Schwartz, Temple Emanu-El. The Presbyterian participants, along with Reverend Adams, were Reverend Dr. Gary Charles, Central Presbyterian Church; Reverend Joe Clifford, Alpharetta Presbyterian Church; Reverend Steve Goyer, Covenant Presbyterian Church; Reverend Dr. Scott Black Johnson, Trinity Presbyterian Church; Reverend Dr. D. Scott Weimer, North Avenue Presbyterian Church; Reverend Dr. George B. Wirth, First Presbyterian Church Atlanta; and Reverend Dr. Ed Albright, Presbytery of Greater Atlanta.

Of special note was George Wirth, who, along with Joanna Adams, has been tireless in the defense of Israel and has fought numerous times against the anti-Israel national statements of the Presbyterian Church (U.S.A.). As far back as 1982, I had my work cut out for me responding to the Presbyterians. In addition, there was no shortage of other Christian denominations critical of Israel. Sadly, that continues today in 2018 as I write these memoirs.

For seven years after we retired, Joanna and I worked together as coordinators of "Reclaiming the Center," a study program on text and contemporary issues developed by the Institute for Christian-Jewish Studies (ICJS) in Baltimore, Maryland. Clergy and members of The Temple and First Presbyterian Church participated in the first four-year project. Classes led by ICJS scholars and clergy from the sponsoring congregations engaged hundreds of Christians and Jews. In the second four-year project, we moved from in-town Atlanta to Sandy Springs. Over one hundred participants were involved from the six congregations of Temple Sinai, Congregation Or Hadash, Congregation B'nai Torah, Sandy Springs Christian Church, Holy Innocents' Episcopal Church, and Mount Vernon Presbyterian Church.

The group experience of learning together and developing relationships fostered understanding of our different faiths as well as to the challenges facing Israel. Reverend Dr. Joe. B. Martin, Mount Vernon Presbyterian Church, candidly acknowledged that insofar as troubling statements on Israel by the Presbyterian Church (U.S.A.) were concerned, this program had a positive impact on him and his relationships with his rabbinical friends in Sandy Springs.

One of the great joys of my work with ICJS was getting to know their founder and scholar, Reverend Dr. Christopher Leighton. For decades, he was a strong voice within the Presbyterian Church (U.S.A.) for a balanced approach toward Israel. After Dr. Leighton retired as Executive Director, he continued to serve as Protestant Scholar. He will long be admired for his brilliant writings and teachings and his steadfast commitment to strengthening ties between Christians and Jews. In our last four years with ICJS, the Muslim community became a part of their mission. Today the agency is known as the Institute for Islamic, Christian, and Jewish Studies.

AJC–ITC SEMINARIANS CONFERENCES

There is power in the pulpit. Clergy of all faiths have the ability to influence their members in ways large and small, personally and communally. I embraced AJC's idea of bringing rabbinical students from different seminaries to Atlanta for conferences with students from the Interdenominational Theological Center (ITC). The Protestant participants are students in the consortium of six predominantly African-American denominational Christian seminaries that make up ITC. It is located on the Atlanta University Center campus and attracts students from all over the world.

I was engaged in planning and participating in three AJC-sponsored Seminarians Conferences, each one different and enhanced by the experiences and recommendations of prior seminary conferences. Intensive dialogue, study, and worship were central components of the 1986, 1989, and 1992 conferences. The first conference included an evening of spiritual music that was open to the community at which the ITC Chorus and the Shirim Chorale of Atlanta performed. Conservative, Reform, and Reconstructionist rabbinical students came from seminaries in New York, Cincinnati, and Philadelphia. They were housed on the ITC campus, which added to the experience of bridge-building.

The planning in itself provided both learning and relationship-building. Dr. David R. Blumenthal, Emory University Professor of Judaic Studies, was a valuable member of our committee, as was legendary ITC President, Dr. James Costen, whose views were especially important as we developed our program.

A striking episode occurred while we were screening a large number of films on slavery and the Holocaust with our committee in order to select the most appropriate ones for our session on suffering. While we did not want to get into comparing victimhood, we wanted our participants to have an authentic opportunity to learn about the pain and hardships each community had experienced. At one point, we saw a beautiful film about righteous Christians' response to the Holocaust and saving Jews. The Jewish members of the planning committee were delighted – we had found the perfect film! Dr. Costen's immediate reaction has remained with me. Slapping his hand firmly on the table, he said, "Absolutely not." He insisted that what is possibly the students' first discussion of the Holocaust should not be about the few who saved Jews, but the enormous scope of this historic tragedy. In the end, we showed "Night and Fog," and later viewed "Slavery and Slave Resistance."

In addition to a session on *Suffering: Holocaust and Slavery,* other forums topics were *Facing our Mutual Histories, Redemption: Liberation and Zionism,* and *Understanding and Interpreting Scripture.*

The most revealing and emotional sessions were almost always the ones in which participants introduced themselves and shared a personal item with the group. Many rabbinical students brought ritual objects that had unique meaning to them...perhaps a grandparent's *tallit* or *Shabbat* candle sticks that survived the Holocaust. It quickly became obvious that the black students didn't have much in the way of similar memorabilia. I came to understand that in the days of slavery, families were often separated, the gathering place or church was modest and moved frequently, and the African-American tradition is not filled with ritual objects as is the Jewish tradition.

Our sessions always included the weekly Christian chapel service for all students at ITC. The rabbinical students were in awe of the spirit, singing, and preaching. One said, in jest, "I would feel fulfilled if I ever gave one sermon stirring enough to be interrupted by so many *Amens.*"

Each conference included a bus ride to The Temple for a morning service and Torah reading. In those sessions, it was especially heartwarming to see the enormous respect and interest the Christian students had in the Jewish ritual objects, Torah, *tallit, tefillin,* and sanctuary.

The rabbinical students loved attending ITC classes, particularly Homiletics. We left each concluding session on "Next Steps" wishing we could meet more often, have funding to travel to Israel and Africa together, and continue to develop closer ties. I have often thought that working with seminaries and influencing future clergy are two of the most important investments we can make in Christian-Jewish relations. Over the years, I had the opportunity to work with Candler School of Theology and Columbia Theological Seminary, bringing AJC scholars to their campuses. It seems to me that the yearning to do more is simply a part of the human spirit.

In November, 1992, the *Atlanta Journal-Constitution* printed an article by Gayle White titled "Religion Students Sign Covenant;

Blacks, Jews Pledge Cultural Understanding." It quoted me as saying, "I was struck by the real honesty of the participants and the special privilege it is to watch people studying for the ministry talk about God. I also feel a real sense of pride in the American Jewish Committee's recognition of the important role the church plays in the black community and the synagogue in the Jewish community as a strong basis of community building." In the same article, Dr. James Costen, president of ITC, called the conference "an eye-opening experience for both the Jewish participants and the black participants enrolled here at ITC." Stereotypes were "literally smashed," he said, as students "came to a new appreciation of how much they have in common." Students came to "appreciate their differences" rather than letting their differences divide them, he said.

## MINISTERS' MANIFESTO

At the height of the struggle for civil rights in America, Atlanta was one of the bright spots. While we had our challenges with the issues of segregation and integration, our civic and religious leaders and elected officials kept the city from the violence occurring around the country. One defining achievement was the 1957 Ministers' Manifesto. I had been unaware of how important this was until I was invited to serve on the Christian Council of Metropolitan Atlanta's Planning Committee for the Commemorative 35th Anniversary Conference.

Over the months of planning this conference, I gathered knowledge about that period of history, the response to the Ministers' Manifesto, and the distance we have yet to travel in race relations and human relations. Important milestones included:

- May 17, 1954 – In *Brown v Board of Education*, the Supreme Court ruled segregation in the public schools unconstitutional.
- November 2, 1957 – The Sunday edition of the *Atlanta*

*Journal-Constitution* carried the text of what came to be called the Ministers' Manifesto. It was signed by 80 white, male, Christian ministers.

- Dr. Benjamin Mays, President of Morehouse College, criticized the ministers for taking three and a half years to come out with a weak and inconclusive statement on segregation in the public schools.
- Friday, *Shabbat*, November 8, 1957 – Rabbi Jacob Rothschild, The Temple, delivered a sermon titled "Eighty Who Dared – A Salute to My Christian Colleagues." He said, "Judaism and Christianity have always shared a passionate belief in and concern for justice for all."
- Sunday, November 10, 1957 – The Atlanta papers reported a response from the city's black clergy. They accepted the overture for communications between responsible leaders of both races. In response, an informal dinner group of black and white Christian clergy was formed.
- November 12, 1957 – An editorial in the *Atlanta Constitution* said "All over America these simple principles [of the 80 ministers] are being reprinted or repeated."
- November 23, 1958 – A second statement, signed by 310 white clergy, including Catholics and Jews, was released.
- On October 27-28, 1992, over one hundred twenty-five progressive leaders of various faiths and races attended the conference titled "Race, Religion, and Reconciliation." Its mission was stated in the flyer for the meeting.

*A major social movement was well underway in the United States by October, 1957. The crisis centered on the Supreme Court ruling that public schools must be integrated. President Dwight D. Eisenhower had ordered Federal troops into Little Rock, Arkansas, and it was clear that similar action could soon follow in other cities.*

*Mr. Ralph McGill, then editor of the* Atlanta Constitution, *could see the need for immediate and decisive action, both to keep the peace, and to begin moving toward racial justice. The faith community, in McGill's mind, had to play a central role in this action.*

*The result was a document that became known as THE ATLANTA MINISTERS' MANIFESTO. This document was drafted by a group of eight pastors, and endorsed by 80 Atlanta ministers. Then the MANIFESTO was published in the combined issue of the Atlanta Journal-Constitution for Sunday, November 3, 1957.*

*In the days and weeks that followed, this Manifesto was hailed as a small but critical step toward justice and reconciliation. As we approach the 35th Anniversary of the publication of THE ATLANTA MINISTERS' MANIFESTO, we consider again the role of the faith community in the pursuit of justice.*

The conference had sessions on freedom of speech, obeying the law, public schools, race relations, communications, and faith in God. One of its goals was to develop a new statement, reflecting the challenges of our times.

A twenty-person committee worked to write a new Manifesto. Conference participant, Rabbi Alvin Sugarman, The Temple, advocated for pursuing a strong action-oriented Manifesto for the 1990s. He said, "Anyone can put words on paper. But they are only worthwhile if they lead to specific, concrete change. It's a long journey between words and deeds."

Gayle White, religion writer for the *Atlanta Journal-Constitution*, wrote an article dated October, 31, 1992, titled "35 Years Later, Issues For Second 'Manifesto' Are Less Clear."

Thirty-five years ago when 80 white, male, Christian ministers signed a 'manifesto' calling on the community of faith to act with justice and good will, the goal was plain – to integrate Atlanta's public schools without mayhem.

This week, when 125 religious leaders of various faiths, races and genders gathered to commemorate that document and lay the framework for a new one, the issues were much less clear.

"Leaders were called together in the '50s because of the integration crisis," said Sherry Frank, Southeast Director of the American Jewish Committee. "I think we're called today because of a moral and economic crisis. There's also a motivation, somehow, because of a time clock ticking for the Olympics. We know we're in trouble. The greatness of Atlanta is that we'll admit it and grapple with it."

An updated "Manifesto of Faith" was released on March 10, 1993. It was a long and broadly-based document. Highlights included:

- Affirm that all mankind in its magnificent diversity is created by God.
- Affirm that we are called by God to be partners in the shaping of the Beloved Community.
- Affirm the integrity of religious diversity.
- Affirm the equality and worth of all persons regardless of gender.
- Recognize the relationship between our tolerance of sexism and the abusive treatment of women.
- Affirm that all people, regardless of sexual orientation are created in the image of God.

It went on to express sensitivity to those with mental and physical challenges, call for protecting the earth's resources, acknowledge our worldwide economic interconnectedness, and support immigration laws that are just and fair for all ethnic groups.

Over twenty years later, motivated in part by increased anti-Muslim rhetoric, religious intolerance and a call for more community engagement, a strong interfaith statement was once again needed. Tom Glenn and the Glenn Foundation were the driving force, along with key Christian and other faith clergy, in creating a new Atlanta Interfaith Manifesto. On Sunday, September 25, 2016, the *Atlanta Journal-Constitution* published a full page ad titled *Atlanta Interfaith Manifesto, a statement denouncing religious bigotry and calling for interfaith understanding.*

Signed by over seventy influential leaders, it called on the community to endorse the Atlanta Manifesto by learning more about interfaith opportunities and the organizations around Atlanta that support it. When I added my name to this list, I felt as if I was part of history in the making. At the time of this writing, there are over seven hundred endorsers of the 2016 Manifesto and a website gathering more signatures every day.

## HIS HOLINESS THE DALAI LAMA OF TIBET

Early in 1995, we learned that His Holiness the Dalai Lama of Tibet would be traveling to Atlanta to speak at Emory University. In addition to speaking on campus to students and faculty, the Dalai Lama asked to address a diverse group of interfaith leaders. I received a call requesting my assistance with this event, as AJC was recognized as the agency most able to coordinate such a gathering.

Plans developed rapidly through numerous meetings, and an impressive list of co-sponsors joined AJC for this historic event. On August 15, an invitation was sent to religious leaders over the signatures of Rabbi Alvin M. Sugarman, The Temple; S. Stephen Selig, III, President, The Temple; and Arnold Sidman, President, Atlanta Chapter, AJC.

An AJC press release on August 23, announced the interfaith forum and breakfast with His Holiness.

*Interreligious Groups Welcome His Holiness The Dalai Lama of Tibet to Atlanta,* September 4-6, 1995

The Dalai Lama, the exiled leader of the Tibetan people

will make an historic visit to the United States with stops in Atlanta, Houston, Boston and Washington, D.C. The purpose of the U.S. visit is to meet with key U.S. policymakers, business leaders, students, Chinese residing in America and the public-at-large.

While in Atlanta, a group of interreligious organizations will host an interfaith breakfast for His Holiness on Wednesday morning, September 6, 8:00 a.m., at The Temple on Peachtree Street. This event is for clergy and religious leaders by invitation only. Co-sponsors of this interfaith gathering are: The American Jewish Committee, The Catholic Archdiocese of Atlanta, Concerned Black Clergy, Christian Council of Metropolitan Atlanta, The Interfaith Coalition of Metro Atlanta, The Temple, The Atlanta Rabbinical Association, and the Department of Religion, Emory University.

It was no surprise that this remarkable morning was well attended. Follow-up articles appeared in the *Atlanta Journal-Constitution* and *Atlanta Jewish Times*.

September 6, 1995 *Atlanta Journal-Constitution*
*Dalai Lama urges religious unity*
*by Gayle White and Mark Silk*

Speaking to 600 religious leaders from around Metro Atlanta, the Dalai Lama today called upon people of all faiths to follow their own religions as a way of fostering harmony among different religious communities.

Each religious institution, he said, has great potential to foster "the spirit of patience, tolerance and forgiveness" among people.

The religious leader spoke at an interfaith breakfast at The Temple on Peachtree Street sponsored by the American

Jewish Committee, Christian Council of Metropolitan Atlanta, Concerned Black Clergy and other groups. He outlined steps to promote greater interfaith harmony.

The leader of Tibetan Buddhism said one thing people of different groups could do is make pilgrimages to holy sites of other religions, just as he had journeyed to Jerusalem and Lourdes, France, where a sighting of the Virgin Mary was reported.

"I do get some kind of extraordinary experience" at these places, he said.

In the *Atlanta Jewish Times*, Neil Rubin wrote:

The Dalai Lama, that most famous of Buddhist monks, is the last guy I'd expect to see behind a lectern with the Hebrew words "Shema Yisrael" emblazoned on it.

But there he was last week in the sanctuary of The Temple, with some 600 representatives of Atlanta's religious community gathered by the American Jewish Committee.

The scene itself: The simple bringing together of these people – with their kippot, turbans, clerical collars, and Buddhist robes – was inspiring.

Prior to his introduction by Rabbi Alvin Sugarman, the deep voice of an African-American singer stirred us all. "In this very room," he movingly intoned, "there's quite enough love for all of us… There's quite enough hope to chase away anything. Oh God, oh thou God, is in this very room." And then the Dalai Lama arose. All eyes riveted on the exotic red-robed figure. "Religious friends," he began, "I'm extremely happy to be with you here today."

The Dalai Lama spoke to us in generalities. His words were not enough. The wise Tibetan monk knew that. He also understood that before the world can be improved,

> people must understand the common bonds that all of God's creations share – and that faith and its expressions are a comprehensive framework in which to do so.

## THE CHALLENGE OF INTERFAITH PRAYER

Late in the afternoon of July 29, 1999, a mass murder occurred across the street from our AJC office; shots were fired at our building as well. Earlier in the day, a man had killed his wife and children, then traveled to the Buckhead offices of All-Tech Investment Group, Inc., and Momentum Securities, Inc., where he killed nine people and wounded thirteen. The dead represented a cross section of world religions – Christian, Jew, Muslim, and Hindu.

Quickly after the news broke, there was a lockdown of all the buildings in the area, and we were instructed to stay away from the windows. Every TV channel was covering the crisis, and our phones rang off the hooks as worried family and friends called to inquire about our safety. It was hours before the police could determine that there was a single shooter and that he had killed himself. We were glued to our television until word came that we were safe and could leave the building to go home. It wasn't until a SWAT team, guns out and aimed, escorted us from the building that we began to truly feel the impact of the day.

Several days later, on August 4, an interfaith memorial service was organized at Peachtree Road United Methodist Church. Senior minister Reverend Don Harp, Mayor Bill Campbell, and the mayor's staff organized the service. Candles were lit for each victim and their respective clergy participated in the service. Family members sat together in a reserved section. The week of *Shiva* was still being observed for Charles Allen Tanenbaum, President of Congregation Or VeShalom, the Jewish leader who was killed.

With the best of intentions, the service, titled "Service of Hope and Remembrance for the City of Atlanta," proved to be more divisive than healing. The printed program had a cross and shield on the cover, and the liturgical pieces included "Jesus as Lord." The service began with Christian clergy marching in with large crosses.

We wrote a letter to the minister expressing our concern.

*Dear Reverend Harp,*

*It was with these dual feelings of personal uneasiness and communal devastation that we attended the Service of Hope and Remembrance for the City of Atlanta hosted by your Church. We walked in looking for spiritual solace and for community connection. We knew that people of many different faiths and backgrounds shared our need for closure and were expecting a service that spoke to us in a common language of hope, healing and peace.*

*From the moment we entered the Church and were handed a printed program, we realized that this was not an Interfaith Service, as we had hoped and expected. Despite the tremendous religious and ethnic diversity of the grieving families, the service, in structure and content, was a Christian one. The processional with the Crosses, the printed prayers and the choir's hymns were exclusive to the Christian faith. As Jews seeking to connect to all of Atlanta, we were very uncomfortable.*

*Please know that we appreciate your congregation's warm hospitality. Your sermon and the Mayor's opening remarks were meaningful and inclusive of all people of faith. We are grateful for the inclusion of those who spoke from different faith traditions on behalf of the bereaved families.*

*We are writing to you in hopes that, in the future, when we gather as Atlantans of faith, we do so with increased sensitivity to all religions and backgrounds. The American Jewish Committee has a long history of working to strengthen intergroup and interfaith relations in Atlanta. We continue to offer our help in this important work.*

*Sincerely,*

*Sherry Frank*      *Judy Marx*

*Area Director*      *Assistant Area Director*


Reverend Harp's response proved to be frustratingly unsatisfactory. While he acknowledged that his letter probably sounded offensive, in his opinion every effort had been made to make this service acceptable to the community. Since he had received a great deal of criticism from the Christian community, he indicated that he would only do services for his own congregation in the future, suggesting that others plan interfaith services, and that perhaps next time one might be held at a synagogue and would demonstrate how to make it more inclusive. He questioned whether a service for multiple faith communities could truly be comfortable for its diverse attendees. Concluding with an apology for any discomfort we might have felt, he added "it is a Christian church, and I make no apologies for that."

There were conflicting views from the Jewish Federation staff and lay leaders regarding the service and the criticism we expressed. Mayor Bill Campbell, who had long standing and close ties with the Jewish community, was frustrated with the critical responses. In a letter, Campbell acknowledged, "Unfortunately, while we had the best intentions with respect to the interfaith service, we are not perfect."

In the end, we were all left with the question, "Can we come together as a community in a meaningful way for interfaith prayer?" Dianne Harnell Cohen and I were quoted in an article by Bill Nigut in the *Atlanta Jewish Times* on September 3, 1999, responding to this question.

Frank said, "There are times when people of faith should come together." For Frank, the services held for years during King Week were an outstanding expression of unity formed out of diversity.

Dianne Harnell Cohen, an aide to Gov. Roy Barnes,

who got high marks for her work in an interfaith service on Barnes' inauguration day, believes such services can work, albeit only with careful planning. "I do think they are hard to put together," she said. "After all, religion is very personal to everyone."

But Cohen believes there are huge rewards. "Interfaith services offer an authentic window into the way each of us talks to God... whether it's chanting Hebrew, reading from the Koran, or singing in Latin."

Bill Nigut concluded his article saying, "The real problem with the service at Peachtree Road United Methodist Church was that it was mislabeled. It was a genuine expression of grief and a moving plea for comfort. But it wasn't, as promised, expressed in a language that could be shared by all the people who gathered in the church that day." After years of working in this interfaith arena, I was really stung by this event.

On September 8, I attended an inspiring, and in many ways therapeutic, gathering of interfaith leaders. Titled "Atlanta 2000: Faith in a Good City," it was sponsored by the Christian Council of Metropolitan Atlanta and the Interdenominational Theological Center. The program was designed as an interfaith conversation with Archbishop Desmond Tutu. A panel of distinguished clergy including Rabbi Alvin Sugarman, The Temple; Reverend Dr. Joanna Adams, Morningside Presbyterian Church; Reverend Dr. Joseph Roberts, Ebenezer Baptist Church; and Imam Plemon El-Amin, Atlanta Masjid of Al-Islam; and corporate leaders including Ann Cramer, IBM; Ingrid Saunders Jones, The Coca Cola Company; and Alicia Philipp, Community Foundation for Greater Atlanta; followed the Archbishop's speech with questions they posed to him.

I had been in touch with most of these clergy after the disappointing memorial service and the letter I received from Reverend

Don Harp. I felt that some of my concerns were reflected in the questions posed.

As Archbishop Tutu spoke, I unexpectedly felt my tears flowing as I heard his words of morality, inclusion, and godliness. I was moved to write down his statements.

- "God didn't make us all of one color or the same."
- "Like an orchestra, it's impoverished if missing a violin or cello. We would be impoverished if we strike only white notes on a keyboard, but if you want music, strike both the black and white notes."

His most profound observation, shaking many in the audience, was: "God is not Christian. We constrict God with narrow labels."

With regard to the importance of interfaith work, he said:

- "Don't pretend you are what you are not. Each one must not be wishy-washy. Relax in the goodness of God. Find the central themes of every faith – love, goodness, caring, compassion of God."
- "People of faith are in the majority. We must use this power."

I felt this program was transformative for many of us. It is possible that it even played a role in the work done after 9/11 to bring harmony to the interfaith community in new ways of unity and inclusive models of prayer.

SEPTEMBER 11, 2001

The deaths of President John F. Kennedy, Robert Kennedy, and the Reverend Dr. Martin Luther King, Jr., are three moments in history that are forever held in our minds. All who are old enough also remember clearly where we were when we first learned the horrible news of the terrorist attack on America on September 11, 2001.

I arrived at the AJC office early that morning, because ACCESS had scheduled its Annual Entrepreneurs' event for that evening. Refreshments had been prepared, and a large attendance was expected. Of course, by mid-morning, meetings were cancelled, and fear seized us as, in shock and disbelief, we stayed glued to the television.

Within twenty-four hours of the attack, every mosque in Atlanta had received threats. We quickly made plans to bring our communities together. By Thursday night, September 13, an "Interfaith Memorial Service of Healing and Reflection" was scheduled at Northside United Methodist Church. Sponsors of the service included Ahavath Achim Synagogue, Atlanta Masjid of Al-Islam, Northside United Methodist Church, and Trinity Presbyterian Church. The press release stated the following:

> In reaction to Tuesday's tragedy, Atlanta area faith communities will gather for a memorial service of healing and reflection. Members of all religious backgrounds are invited to join with the community in sorrow and to offer prayers for peace in our world. Leading members of Atlanta's clergy including Reverend Joanna Adams, Rabbi Arnold Goodman, Imam Plemon El-Amin, and Reverend Gil Watson will be participating in this unifying worship service.

The following day, Friday, September 14, I participated in a press conference at the Atlanta Masjid of Al-Islam, convened by the Imams of Metro Atlanta. A large crowd assembled outside of the Masjid, and press coverage was extensive. I spoke on behalf of the Jewish community, standing with our Muslim friends at this moment in history when they were feeling especially insecure. I was warmly embraced by the Muslim women who, I sensed, were proud to see a woman among the people speaking.

I spoke about the vulnerability the Jewish community felt in 1958 when The Temple was bombed. I recalled speaking about that feeling on another occasion during my time at AJC when there was a series of burnings of black churches in the south. Concerned Black Clergy held a press conference, and I shared the feeling of my faith community when our sacred spaces are under attack.

The Faith Alliance of Metro Atlanta (FAMA) was born out of the terrorist attack of 9/11. Its mission was dedicated to understanding, cooperation, dialogue, and respect among the people and faith traditions in our city. The anniversary of 9/11 continued to be a time to come together for prayer, bonding, and spiritual healing, and it was meaningful for me to work with FAMA in convening these events.

In the first couple of years, our commemorative service was held at Ebenezer Baptist Church. Governors, mayors, clergy, and lay leaders from every part of Atlanta's faith community participated in these events. In words, songs, musical instruments, and meditation, we experienced the presence of God in our midst.

In 2002, Governor Roy Barnes, Mayor Shirley Franklin, and the Reverend Dr. Joseph Roberts all participated in the observance. In 2003, Governor Sonny Purdue attended, and Mayor Franklin and Reverend Roberts were there again as well. The featured guest speaker was the Reverend Dr. Robert M. Franklin, Presidential Distinguished Professor of Social Ethics, Emory University. Atlanta's slogan, "A City Too Busy To Hate," played out in an especially meaningful way as our interfaith activities expanded and participation increased.

## THE PASSION OF THE CHRIST

For months prior to the release of Mel Gibson's film "The Passion of the Christ," Jewish leaders were already critical of the movie as scripts and versions of the film had leaked out. The Anti-Defamation League's (ADL) National Director, Abraham Foxman, and Rabbi Marvin Hier, Dean of the Simon Wiesenthal Center, warned that the film would fan anti-Semitism and set back the dialogue between Jews and Christians for decades. Some people faulted both agencies for drawing increased attention to the film with their very public criticism.

Rabbi A. James (Jim) Rudin, AJC's Senior Interreligious Advisor, saw the film multiple times and noted changes being made in ensuing versions. In a January 23, 2004, *New York Times* article he lamented the change made from an earlier version he had seen which had omitted, then later re-inserted, a verse from Matthew. He noted that even the most notorious Passion Plays do not include this incendiary verse, which is known as the blood libel, placing collective guilt and the charge of deicide against the Jews.

At AJC, we devoted a great deal of time and energy preparing for the release of this film, which opened in some two thousand theaters nationwide on February 25. Several local Jewish agencies and synagogues planned programs to discuss the film's anti-Semitism and violence.

Nationally, AJC produced "The Passion: A Resource Manual" and drafted a letter and short statement to distribute to local clergy and civic leaders. We developed a plan to help educate our Jewish community and to engage the interfaith community as well. Taking a leading role, we helped FAMA organize a screening and discussion of "The Passion of the Christ" on Thursday, February 26, at the Madstone Theater Parkside (LeFont Theater). Imam Plemon El-Amin welcomed a sold-out crowd of over 300 clergy, academicians, and civic leaders. Monsignor Henry Gracz, Catholic Shrine of the Immaculate Conception, presented the closing remarks. After the film's screening, I moderated a panel of three distinguished religious leaders -- Rabbi Phil Kranz, Temple Sinai; Dr. Kathleen M. O'Connor, Professor of Old Testament, Language, and Exegesis at Columbia Theological Seminary (Catholic); and Reverend Tina Pippin, Professor of Religious Studies, Agnes Scott College (Protestant).

Several clergy attending the screening expressed appreciation for the opportunity to see the film and learn from the panelists. They now understood, in ways they may not have before the screening, the sensitivity of the Jewish community and the film's potential for inflaming anti-Semitism. One minister was bringing his congregation to see the film that evening and told us he would be responding to it very differently as a result of this program.

In the weeks that followed, we brought Rabbi Rudin to Atlanta for two programs on March 3. He spoke at a lunch meeting at The Temple, hosted by FAMA on the topic "Moving Beyond 'The Passion of the Christ': How will it affect interfaith relations?" That evening, AJC, ACCESS, and Temple Sinai hosted Rabbi Rudin for a discussion of "A Jewish Understanding of Christian Anti-Semitism: A response to Mel Gibson's 'The Passion of the Christ'."

In order to help us understand Mel Gibson, Rabbi Rudin explained that this film's version of the death of Christ is a fundamentalist attack on Vatican Council II and liberalists. Mel Gibson respects the 15th and 16th century Pope Pius IV and no popes since. Rudin viewed this as a defining moment for Christian leaders: "Is Gibson's version of your most sacred story the one you want told? The decades of biblical study can be for naught if this story, as told by Gibson, goes unchallenged."

One of the most important outcomes of the discussions surrounding this film was summarized in a letter written to former Mayor Andrew Young and former Emory University President James Laney who were serving as co-chairmen of Faith in the City.

*Dear Andy and Jim,*

*We just read your opinion piece, "'Passion' Should Be Pulpit Teaching Tool," in the Atlanta Journal-Constitution, February 24, 2004. Your words touched our souls, and we are truly grateful for your vision and insight. We pray that "The Passion of the Christ" will be used as a teaching moment throughout our community and not a vehicle to inflame anti-Semitism.*

*It is gratifying that nearly 300 community leaders, clergy and*

*lay, will see this film and participate in an interfaith discussion in*
*a program hosted by the Faith Alliance of Metro Atlanta (FAMA)*
*on Thursday February 26, 2004.*

*We are going to make copies of your article to distribute at this*
*FAMA screening. Your wise advice should be taken seriously. It*
*will serve the community well as we try to build bridges of trust*
*and understanding in a diverse and challenged world.*

*Thank you for lifting up the prophetic voice at this important*
*moment.*

*Sincerely,*

*Elise Eplan*        *Sherry Frank*
*President, Atlanta Chapter*        *Executive Director*

This experience provided a valuable teaching moment for Jews and our interfaith community. It illustrated the effectiveness of AJC's leadership in a controversial situation. I have learned from it that there is no substitute for engaging one another on a personal level. In doing so, I have developed friendships from different faith traditions that enrich my life, expand my knowledge, and enhance my sensitivity.

## CATHOLIC-JEWISH RELATIONS

AJC's history in Catholic-Jewish relations goes back to the 1920s, when they filed their first *amicus curiae brief* in the U.S. Supreme Court. The case, *Pierce v Society of Sisters of the Holy Names of Jesus and Mary*, dealt with the right of Catholic parents to send their children to parochial schools in Oregon. It was a landmark case for religious freedom.

In the 1950s, AJC began fifteen years of behind-the-scenes interfaith diplomacy that played a major role leading up to the historic 1965 declarations of Vatican Council II. Catholic and Jewish programs and dialogue groups continued on and off during that time and made up a significant part of Atlanta Chapter's interfaith agenda.

We hosted a number of major events commemorating special anniversaries of Vatican Council II. In each decade we featured distinguished national experts and local clergy, as well as AJC scholars, to discuss the current state of Catholic/Jewish relations. An AJC press release described the first of the community forums.

*Catholic-Jewish Forum Commemorates 20th Anniversary of Vatican Council II*
*Atlanta, Georgia, May 3, 1985*

1985 marks the 20th Anniversary of Vatican Council II. This is a significant event in the history of Catholic-Jewish relations because it marked the end of Catholics teaching that Jews shared the collective guilt for the death of Jesus. Catholic educational materials and liturgy were revised and a new day in Catholic-Jewish dialogue was ushered in.

The American Jewish Committee was the only Jewish organization who participated with Pope John XXIII in these historic Vatican Council II deliberations at the Holy See.

Twenty years later, AJC leaders once again had an audience with the Pope. This time urging the Vatican's recognition of Israel and suggesting the Pope visit Jerusalem.

Three workshops will address these topics:
Education: "What do we teach about each other?"
Liturgy: "How are our roots and traditions shared?"
Joint Social Action: "How do we create a just society?"

In 1993, Rabbi Michael A. Signer, Abrams Professor of Jewish Thought and Culture, Department of Theology, University of Notre Dame, addressed a mixed group of Catholic and Jewish leaders in Atlanta on the topic of the future of Catholic-Jewish relations.

Celebrating each new decade following Vatican Council II provided AJC with an opportunity to expand our work and create new initiatives in this area. On June 19-20, 1995, AJC and the Catholic Archdiocese of Atlanta co-sponsored a two-day symposium titled "Catholics and Jews at the Dawn of the 21st Century." Three workgroups addressed these topics:

- How do we read the New Testament without anti-Jewish bias?
- What does the catechism of the Catholic Church have to say about Jews and Judaism?
- Understanding the relationship between Israel and Palestinians

On December 15, 2005, AJC and the Catholic Archdiocese of Atlanta were joined by the Consul General of Israel to the Southeast in marking the 40th Anniversary of *Nostra Aetate*. The event was titled "Sacred Music Concert of Jewish and Christian Texts." The celebration began with a three-hour scholarly symposium and dinner, following which the community was invited to a free concert.

Michael Jacobs, writing in the *Atlanta Jewish Times* on December 20, 2005, said:

> The occasion was a joint celebration by the American Jewish Committee and the Catholic Archdiocese of Atlanta to mark the 40th Anniversary of Nostra Aetate, Pope Paul VI's declaration on his church's relations with non-Christians. The document came out of the Second Vatican Council, initiated by Pope John XXIII in 1963; the fourth of five sections address the Jews.
>
> In the four decades since, 'Jews have become for us real persons, not simply the Hebrews of old or Christ-killers of Christian polemics,' said Sister Mary Boys, a professor of practical theology at the multi-denominational Union Theological Seminary in New York.

Boys concluded that four decades is far from enough time to undo the damage of two millennia of 'largely tragic relations,' but she looked to Rabbi Tarfon in Pirkei Avot for inspiration in continuing the effort: 'You are not required to complete the work, but neither are you at liberty to forsake it.'

Archbishop Gregory wrote about the event in *The Georgia Bulletin, Archdiocese of Atlanta* of December 22 under the title "What I Have Seen and Heard."

Last week, local Catholics and Jews shared some of our sacred music as an expression of the bonds that we hope will bring us greater understanding and harmony. We celebrated the 40th Anniversary of the issuance of *Nostra Aetate*, the Second Vatican Council document that heralded a new moment of hope for ecumenism and interreligious dialogue and conversation. This special event included an afternoon symposium on the ongoing challenges that we face as Christians and Jews in deepening our understanding of and respect for one another. Then the evening brought a splendid musical program of Christian and Jewish music sung by a mixed choir of Catholics from our Cathedral choirs and the Archbishop Lyke Choir and the choir from The Temple here in Buckhead. The music was spectacular, as the assembly of nearly 500 people attested by their standing ovation at the conclusion of the program. I express my sincere gratitude to all those from the Archdiocese of Atlanta who worked together with our Jewish neighbors and friends to plan and to achieve this event.

When new Archbishops came to serve the Archdiocese of Atlanta, AJC co-hosted events to introduce them to Atlanta's Jewish religious and civic leaders. We welcomed The Most Reverend

Eugene Antonio Marino in May, 1988, The Most Reverend John Francis Donoghue in June, 1993, and The Most Reverend Wilton D. Gregory in March, 2005. As I write this memoir in 2018, I want to express my personal admiration for Archbishop Gregory. Over the years, he has brought extraordinary dedication and leadership to strengthening Catholic-Jewish relations in Atlanta. His unprecedented commitment to interfaith understanding continues to enhance relations between our two communities.

As AJC initiated interfaith coalitions and worked within the community on various interreligious activities, we developed strong ties with and great regard for the Catholic community's tireless and devoted leader, Monsignor Henry Gracz, Catholic Shrine of the Immaculate Conception, a man of deep faith and integrity. Through the decades, Father Gracz continues to participate with AJC in many diverse endeavors. Numerous times he responded to controversial films in the Atlanta Jewish Film Festival which portrayed Catholics during World War II and the Holocaust in problematic ways.

## POPE JOHN PAUL II'S DEATH

The Jewish community responded to Pope John Paul II's April 2, 2005, death with words of admiration and appreciation for his vital role in changing Christian-Jewish relations in this century. It was a tremendous honor for me to receive an invitation from Archbishop Wilton Gregory to join religious leaders at a Memorial Mass on April 7. The service celebrating the Pope's life was an historic time for the Catholic Church, but, for a Jewish professional, being included with such an august group of interfaith leaders to witness this moment was inspirational.

*Dear Ms. Frank,*
*This past Saturday, the Catholic Church lost its beloved shepherd, Pope John Paul II, after twenty-six years as Supreme Pontiff.*

*Over the years, he was a tireless servant of God. In paying tribute to our Holy Father, President Bush said: "Laura and I join people across the Earth in mourning the passing of Pope John Paul II. The Catholic Church has lost its shepherd, the world has lost a champion of human freedom, and a good and faithful servant of God has been called home." As we mourn the loss of Pope John Paul II, we also celebrate his life and legacy, not only to the Catholic Church, but to the whole world. The tributes that have flooded in over the past few days remind us of his tremendous contributions to humanity.*

*I would like to take this opportunity to extend an invitation to join me, the clergy and faithful of the Archdiocese of Atlanta for a special Memorial Mass for Pope John Paul II at the Cathedral of Christ the King, 2699 Peachtree Road, NE, Atlanta on Thursday, April 7 at 6 p.m.*

*I would be honored if you can join me and my flock as we pay tribute to one of the greatest religious and moral leaders of our time. Sincerely in Christ,*
*Wilton D. Gregory*
*Archbishop of Atlanta*

My own words of admiration and condolence and those of AJC's Rabbi David Rosen were reported on April 7 in *The Georgia Bulletin, Archdiocese of Atlanta.*

*Atlanta Jewish Community Remembers Pope*

The American Jewish Committee, an international Jewish organization that has advanced interreligious understanding worldwide for more than half a century, worked with the Pope directly on numerous occasions at the Vatican.

The executive director of the group's Atlanta chapter, Sherry Frank, noted the passing of Pope John Paul II with this statement.

"The American Jewish Committee profoundly mourns the passing of Pope John Paul II. He was the central figure of our times in the remarkable transformation in Catholic-Jewish relations in particular, and Christian-Jewish relations, in general.

"Pope John Paul II will be remembered throughout the world for his unparalleled religious leadership, his historic role in the collapse of communism, and as a universal voice of conscience in troubled times. The Jewish community also will remember him with particular affection—no Pope had ever given the degree of attention to Jewish communities worldwide or received Jewish leadership at the Vatican so readily and so extensively as did John Paul II.

*Jewish Expressions of Condolence Unprecedented*
*Jerry Filteau*

The April 2 death of Pope John Paul II brought an absolutely unprecedented outpouring of condolences, thanks, praise and blessing from religious leaders of the Jewish community.

Their comments indicated how deeply Catholic-Jewish relations have been affected worldwide by the Catholic Church's first Polish pope—who as a youth personally experienced the tragedy of the Nazi Holocaust of the Jewish people in World War II and as pope transformed that experience into an intense Catholic theological reflection on God's eternal covenant with Jews and the sinfulness of Christian anti-Semitism.

"Nobody has done as much to transform Catholic-Jewish relations as John Paul II. He will be forever remembered as a great hero of Catholic-Jewish reconciliation," said Rabbi David Rosen, Jerusalem-based international director of interreligious relations for the American Jewish Committee.

Rabbi Marc Tanenbaum and Ambassador Andrew
Young, Christian Council Prayer Breakfast, 1980

(L-R) Joy Berry, Governor Roy Barnes, Sherry Frank, Georgia Human
Relations Commission Press Conference, Georgia State Capitol, 2000

Interfaith leaders Jan Swanson,
Sherry Frank, Ken Brandt

ITC Seminarian Conference
facilitators Dr. James Costen
and Rabbi James Rudin, 1992

World Pilgrims trip to Morocco, Sherry Frank with
weaver from Hilltop Shepherds' Village, 2015

Muslim leader
and scholar,
Tayyibah Taylor,
and Sherry Frank

World Pilgrims gather in response to death at Tree of Life Synagogue in Pittsburgh.
(L-R) Reverend Angela Rice, Reverend Dr. Gerald Durley, Sherry Frank, Rabbi
Mario Karpuj, Reverend Lanny Peters, and Imam Plemon El-Amin, 2018

# JEWISH COMMUNAL AFFAIRS

THE GIFTS OF JEWISH KNOWLEDGE AND IDENTITY

*If I am not for myself, then who will be for me? And if I am only for myself, then what am I? And if not now, when?*

—Hillel, Ethics of the Fathers 1:14

Although it was unusual for the AJC, a national defense agency, to have a department of Jewish Communal Affairs, it followed national trends in the Jewish world and created one, acknowledging that an external threat to our people also included an internal threat. Along with its hallmark work in interfaith, interethnic, and international relations, the Atlanta Chapter made a unique contribution to its members and the extended Jewish community by adding this new dimension to its scope of work.

Under the exceptional scholarship and leadership of Yehuda Rosenman and then Dr. Steven Bayme, AJC's Department of Jewish Communal Affairs produced landmark studies on Jewish identity, diverse aspects of the Jewish family, communal organizations and professionals, and affiliation and demography.

This work captured my attention and resonated with our Atlanta Chapter's lay leaders as well. From a study on the impact of intermarriage to an analysis of Jewish voting patterns, our Chapter

Annual Reports throughout the 1980s and 1990s described creative and varied programs that actively involved our members, community rabbis and Jewish professionals, local universities, and the media. AJC research and publications in this area were distributed widely, and our members expanded their knowledge of Judaism and Jewish issues.

Atlanta Chapter provided a legacy to Atlanta when it replicated AJC's national work in Oral History. Our outreach to young Jewish adults led to the creation of ACCESS. And an overwhelming response to many years of screening films led to the creation of the Atlanta Jewish Film Festival (AJFF.) I have devoted separate chapters to each of these topics.

This agenda was a central part of AJC's work in Atlanta. Following are descriptions of some of the most successful programs.

## THE JEWISH FAMILY

The Jewish family was experiencing many of the same challenges facing all families in the 1980s, including late marriage, intermarriage, divorce, single parenting, low birth rate, women at work, two-career families, longer life span, mobility, and suburbanization. But the impact on us as a small minority was especially significant. Through AJC's William Petschek National Family Center, we were studying these issues, publishing research reports, and expanding local programs.

The Atlanta Chapter hosted our first city-wide conference on the changing Jewish family in 1981. In 1982, we began focusing on the issue of intermarriage. In 1983 and 1984, AJC co-sponsored a series with Jewish Family Services titled "Interfaith Workshop for Intermarried Couples." In 1983, we brought Paul and Rachel Cowen to Atlanta to speak about their book, *Mixed Blessings: Untangling the Knots in Interfaith Marriage*, and their innovative work in this area.

Also in 1983, AJC co-sponsored a forum with NCJW on Jewish

childcare needs, and, in 1986, we participated in an AJC national research project on Jewish Family Planning. A 1988-1989 national study covered the topic of Jewish lay and professional leadership. Recognizing how important this issue was, Atlanta Jewish leaders and professionals agreed to participate in the study, and its findings and publications were distributed widely.

On March 29, 1992, AJC coordinated a community forum titled "The Battle of the Century: Jewish Survival vs. Intermarriage, Marginality, and Assimilation" co-sponsored with the Atlanta Jewish Federation, the Atlanta Jewish Community Center, Jewish Family Services, and the Atlanta Rabbinical Association.

AJC developed "A Guide for Interfaith Families to Atlanta Area Congregations, Agencies, and Organizations." This 1994 publication provided information on policies and programs in the Jewish community based on data derived from questionnaires completed by congregational rabbis and agency and day school representatives. The Guide was distributed to Jewish agencies, organizations and congregations, as well as to facilities such as pediatric and other doctors' offices.

*Press Release: "A Guide for Interfaith Families..."*
*FOR IMMEDIATE RELEASE... JANUARY 13, 1994...*
*ATLANTA, GA...*

The American Jewish Committee, Atlanta Chapter, is proud to announce the publication of "A Guide for Interfaith Families to Atlanta Area Congregations, Agencies, and Organizations." This new publication details the policies of Atlanta area congregations, agencies and organizations regarding membership and admission policies, participation in religious school and youth programs, life cycle events and ritual observances. This Guide is presented with hopes of encouraging intermarried couples to affiliate with congregations and organizations in metro Atlanta. The American Jewish Committee wants to help strengthen the connections between the organized Jewish community and the growing number of interfaith families in the Atlanta area. We hope it will assist those families who would like to be more Jewishly active and involved in finding a congregation and organizations that suit their needs and interests. And we hope, in turn, that they and their children will contribute to the continued strength and well-being of the Jewish community. Copies are available in our office.

Throughout this period, AJC developed and distributed material on aging and ethnicity, parenting, blended families, divorce, and outreach to intermarried couples. Additional publications included "American Jews: The 1986 Election" and "The Poor Among Us: Jewish Tradition and Social Policy."

## JEWISH IDENTITY AND EDUCATION

Throughout the 1980s and 1990s, AJC facilitated networking and extensive programming for Jewish communal professionals. We annually sent local college professors on AJC's Academicians Seminars in Israel and launched a Jewish Academicians Network in Atlanta.

By engaging with area rabbis and scholars, we enhanced the Jewish knowledge of AJC leaders and members. We developed programs with links to targeted national publications, and others evolved from local initiatives.

AJC created a series of national ads for *The New York Times* featuring a broad range of well-known Jewish luminaries responding personally to "What Being Jewish Means To Me." The Atlanta Chapter developed similar opinion pieces and placed them in the *Atlanta Jewish Times* in the fall of 1993. They included prominent local figures: Stuart Eizenstat, Erwin Zaban, Elise Eplan, Andi Arnovitz, I.J. Rosenberg, and Elie Wiesel (the latter reprinted *from The New York Times*).

# WHAT BEING JEWISH MEANS TO ME

**STUART E. EIZENSTAT**
United States Representative
European Communities

American Jewry is in a quiet state of internal crisis. The threat to Jewish continuity comes not from our external enemies, as was the case for two millennia of Jewish history, but from a growing lack of Jewish identity. This occasions the question "Why Be Jewish."

There are many reasons to remain Jewish and to proudly pass Judaism along to our children and grandchildren. Permit me to share my personal view.

The first reason is that in a rootless and impersonal world, I find Judaism gives me a sense of peoplehood, of belonging to a group with common ideals, values and beliefs. It makes me feel a part of a greater whole, of being one with a historical tradition, the oldest continuous one in recorded history.

Second, by being Jewish today I can participate in one of the greatest episodes of modern history: the rebirth of the Jewish State of Israel after 2000 years.

Israel is the unfolding of modern Jewish history – in taming deserts and swamps, in building a modern infrastructure, in defeating enemies who vastly outnumber them, and, now, in winning the peace Jews have so long sought for their own nation state.

Third, I also find Judaism a total way of life, a guidepost, a reference point, a grounding, a safe harbor. In a materialistic world with multiple pressures and tensions, in which people seek some deeper meaning for their lives, Judaism adds real meaning and richness to the hum-drum of my daily existence. It enormously enriches our entire family.

When I worked at the White House my Jewish background heavily influenced the way in which I looked at issues and their solution. Our sensitivity to the poor and downtrodden, our social activism on behalf of a better society, our strong belief in the importance of education, our views on charity, our whole concept of Tikkun Olam, healing the world, the way in which we relate to our fellow human beings, are powerfully shaped by our Jewish teachings and tradition. These remain invaluable guides to me as they can be to every Jew.

I find that in chanting our time-honored prayers, in following our rituals, in celebrating our holidays, in having a traditional Shabbat dinner at which we discuss the modern relevance of the Torah portion of the week, the spiritual side of life, which is so often pushed to the background in today's world, can be given room to flower.

The totality of my religious observance and participation in Jewish organizational life and Jewish culture, has created a "comfort zone" which strengthens me and my family to deal with the rigors of modern life. By being distinctly Jewish I am also adding to the beautiful Mosaic of diversity which makes the United States such a wonderful country. We do not have to assimilate to be real Americans.

 **The American Jewish Committee**

| Lois Frank | Jane Smith | Sherry Frank |
|---|---|---|
| President, Atlanta Chapter | Chair, ACCESS | Southeast Area Director |

*This message is presented by the American Jewish Committee, Atlanta Chapter, as a service to the Jewish Community. The American Jewish Committee is dedicated to strengthening the Jewish community, enriching the quality of Jewish life, and enhancing the creative vitality of the Jewish people. For information on membership and programs, call 233-5501.*

The American Jewish Committee, Atlanta Chapter
3490 Piedmont Road, N.E., Suite 1310
Atlanta, Georgia 30305

# WHAT BEING JEWISH MEANS TO ME

ERWIN ZABAN
Chairman of the Board
National Service Industries, Inc.

Though I don't follow strict religious practices, being Jewish is more a connection to tradition than religious observance to me. Being Jewish is a great way of life.

I often wonder how much less meaningful my life would be without my being Jewish. There is some sort of kinship between us, a tie that binds one Jew to another.

Recently in a discussion with a non-Jewish friend, we talked about the unique commitment that Jews feel toward meeting the needs of the non-Jewish community as well as those of the Jewish community.

It is amazing how Jews are raised to feel that sense of responsibility to the world around them. I certainly was by the example my family set for me.

My grandfather was charitable and concerned about the community.

My father followed his example and was charitable and very caring.

I have tried to follow in that mold also. It gives me personal satisfaction to be able to give to my community. Now I look with pride at the lives of my children. They are caring and following in the example our family has set for them.

Simply stated, the Judaism that I feel is ingrained in me stems from my sense of tradition. While I identify with my Judaism in this manner, I have strong respect for the Orthodox community. Their adherence to religious observance has strengthened our community and helped assure Jewish continuity.

I'm very happy and proud to be a Jew. Perhaps I've been luckier than some.

*The American Jewish Committee, Atlanta Chapter, is proud to present this message, the fourth in a series, on the meaning of being Jewish today. The Jewish community offers an abundant diversity of intellectual, spiritual and cultural opportunities that can enrich and deepen one's life. Jewish living, we believe, provides rootedness in the present and a link to our history and destiny.*

*We encourage all Jews to explore the many paths to being a Jew in contemporary America, and to experience the joy and beauty of the Jewish heritage.*

## The American Jewish Committee

| Lois Frank | Jane Smith | Sherry Frank |
| President, Atlanta Chapter | Chair, ACCESS | Southeast Area Director |

*The American Jewish Committee is dedicated to strengthening the Jewish community, enriching the quality of Jewish life, and enhancing the creative vitality of the Jewish people. AJC advocates public policy positions rooted in American democratic values and the perspectives of the Jewish heritage. Founded in 1906, it is the pioneer human relations agency in the U.S. For information on membership and programs, call 233-5501.*

The American Jewish Committee, Atlanta Chapter
3490 Piedmont Road, N.E., Suite 1310
Atlanta, Georgia 30305

# WHAT BEING JEWISH MEANS TO ME

ELISE EPLAN
The Atlanta Project

Being Jewish means community, *kehilah*, to me. It means the Jewish community, of which I feel so much a part. It is the feeling of sitting in that big sanctuary at Ahavath Achim on Shabbat morning and having a sense of home. It is knowing that my paternal grandparents and great-grandparents worked to make this sanctuary possible. It is having to think every time I reach up to get a plate, about whether it is milk or meat. It is about the memories of my maternal grandparents who spoke with a Russian accent and built a Jewish life for themselves in the small Southern city of Mobile. It is sharing Shabbat and so many other joyous or sad times with a group of friends that have become like family to me over the last eight years, my *Shabbaton* group.

But there is also a larger community of which I am a part. The words *tikkun olam* resonate for me. Being part of a community is about my desire to leave it better than I found it. I am blessed with a life that has provided me with a nurturing home, educational opportunities and all of my material needs – I need to give something back. My sense of community means that I have the power to do something to chip away at the problems that plague this city. The twelve of us who started Hands On Atlanta have proven that. My grandfather who provided free legal services for poor people knew that. It is for me about reaching out beyond the world in which I exist daily. It is about tutoring and getting to know a child who has not had the privileges that I have had. It is about realizing that I am part of this larger community and its problems – racism, poverty and hopelessness profoundly affect me.

The communities in my life are intertwined. My bloodlines are strong. Being Jewish for me is this sense of family, this feeling of community and this need of mine to leave this world better – all that was passed down to me. It becomes mine to pass on, with my husband, to our children as they become a part of this *kehilah*.

*The American Jewish Committee, Atlanta Chapter, is proud to present this message, the fifth in a series, on the meaning of being Jewish today.*

*We encourage all Jews to explore the many paths to being a Jew in contemporary America, and to experience the joy and beauty of the Jewish heritage.*

## The American Jewish Committee

Lois Frank
*President, Atlanta Chapter*

Jane Smith
*Chair, ACCESS*

Sherry Frank
*Southeast Area Director*

*The American Jewish Committee is dedicated to strengthening the Jewish community, enriching the quality of Jewish life, and enhancing the creative vitality of the Jewish people. AJC advocates public policy positions rooted in American democratic values and the perspectives of the Jewish heritage. Founded in 1906, it is the pioneer human relations agency in the U.S. For information on membership and programs, call 233-5501.*

The American Jewish Committee, Atlanta Chapter
3490 Piedmont Road, N.E., Suite 1310
Atlanta, Georgia 30305

# WHAT BEING JEWISH MEANS TO ME

**ANDI ARNOVITZ**
Artist, Mother, Co-owner Judaic Gallery

When I think about why I am a practicing Jew, it is always with an acknowledgement of where I have come from. I often wonder what my great-great-grandmother would think of me. What might she ask me — were we to have a conversation ...

*"So, after so many years, of so much lost, of so little traditional observance in our family, why be so, so Jewish?"*

What can I say to her – this woman who knew the prayers and holidays by heart – understood them even ... Because I want to remember. I want to be remembered. I want to connect and be connected – to their world – to this world.

*"And keeping kosher? Why that. Today – with so many choices?"*

"Because we have so many choices. To create boundaries. To say you may not take everything you want. You are not exactly like everyone else. You cannot try everything ... Because maybe if my children understand self-restraint with food, they will also understand it with drugs, with sex, with life ..."

*"And Shabbos? You begin to keep this too? And all the holidays – even the little ones ... why now? In this day and age. Why?"*

"No phones. No cars. No errands. No birthday parties. No cooking. No laundry. No work. For twenty-four hours my children have both parents – together – I have my husband and he has me. Oh Bubbe, can you understand how rare this is today? Can you understand what this does for a family? And the holidays give such dimension to our lives. We thrive on rituals. Did you know Bubbe – they've done studies, and families who repeatedly recognize and celebrate events are closer, healthier, more whole. Isn't that incredible! Especially in this day and age. Celebrating nothing gives you nothing and children who believe in nothing. Celebrating Jewish holidays gives you Jewish families."

*"And you paint things – Jewish things – pictures ... Why?"*

Because I need to express this awe – this sense of delight, of gratefulness. To touch others with it. To fill our home with it. To create pictures that say being Jewish is incredible. Being Jewish is a privilege. Being Jewish is a duty, an obligation, an adventure.

*"So you like this being Jewish?"*

"Yes Bubbe. I do. I love being Jewish."

---

*The American Jewish Committee, Atlanta Chapter, is proud to present this message, the third in a series, on the meaning of being Jewish today. The Jewish community offers an abundant diversity of intellectual, spiritual and cultural opportunities that can enrich and deepen one's life. Jewish living, we believe, provides rootedness in the present and a link to our history and destiny.*

*We encourage all Jews to explore the many paths to being a Jew in contemporary America, and to experience the joy and beauty of the Jewish heritage.*

## The American Jewish Committee

Lois Frank
*President, Atlanta Chapter*

Jane Smith
*Chair, ACCESS*

Sherry Frank
*Southeast Area Director*

*The American Jewish Committee is dedicated to strengthening the Jewish community, enriching the quality of Jewish life, and enhancing the creative vitality of the Jewish people. AJC advocates public policy positions rooted in American democratic values and the perspectives of the Jewish heritage. Founded in 1906, it is the pioneer human relations agency in the U.S. For information on membership and programs, call 233-5501.*

In 1992, AJC's publication *Why Be Jewish: In Symbol and In Substance* led to a study group series in Atlanta exploring topics covered in the report.

- *Faith* – A "divine obligation" is what God has decreed for my life.
- *Belonging* – Jewish life provides something profound in contemporary American life, a sense of belonging. Traditional societies emphasized communities, whereas modern culture extols the virtue of individuality. Feeling part of something larger than ourselves is very gratifying.
- *Culture* – Judaism is more than our religion; it's our civilization. It encompasses the Jewish people, its land, language, art, literature, mores, laws and social forms.
- *History* – We are a link in a long chain of the Jewish past to which we owe a debt. We must heed a call to Jewish study to learn its lessons.
- *Personal Meaning* – Judaism provides a repository of personal meaning for contemporary people. It provides intellectual challenge, ethical guidance, and is a binding force for family units.
- *Spiritual Meaning* – It satisfies the hungers of the human soul.
- Political and Social Meaning – It is a source of inspiration for activism and philanthropy.
- *The Meaning of Israel* – This is the most powerful source of Jewish identification in our times. Identification with the Zionist dream has energized Jews and enhanced Jewish self- confidence.

Area rabbis, scholars, and Jewish personalities participated in the series. An allocation from the Atlanta Jewish Federation Endowment Fund enabled this in-depth study program to be edited and recorded by Atlanta Interfaith Broadcasters; it was televised in 1994.

The decades spanning the 1990s and 2000s were filled with activities designed to inform and educate.

- The Chapter held forums with college students and parents to discuss challenges facing students on campus and provided AJC publications to them.
- In 1992, we held the first of five *Shabbatons* to inspire Jewish learning and bonding for participants. Scholars included Rabbis Yitz Greenberg, Daniel Gordis, Brad Hirschfield, and Dr. Neil Gillman.
- "Traveling with the Torah from Sinai to Safed" was the title of a 1993 six-part study series taught by Orthodox Rabbi Binyomin Friedman, Atlanta Scholars Kollel, and Reform Rabbi Philip Kranz, Temple Sinai.
- From 1998 to 2000, the Atlanta Chapter and ACCESS sponsored the study series "One People, One Torah: Interactive, Intimate, Relevant."
- ACCESS members held a study series using the book *The Nine Questions People Ask About Judaism* to broaden their Jewish knowledge. They also created "City-Wide Shabbat," a program where chapter members hosted ACCESS members for Shabbat dinners.
- In 2000, and again in 2005, the Chapter published a five-year calendar listing the dates and brief descriptions of Jewish holidays and distributed it widely throughout the non-Jewish community to address the issue of conflicts as an increasing number of educational, cultural, sports, and civic events were being scheduled on Jewish holidays.
- On April 19, 2004, Judea Pearl spoke about his son, Daniel Pearl, whose life was cut short by terrorists, and whose story he co-edited with his wife, Ruth, titled *I am Jewish: Personal Reflections Inspired by the Last Words of Daniel Pearl*. A record crowd attended this forum, co-sponsored with The Temple, featuring influential Atlanta Jews speaking about what Judaism means to them.
- We commemorated the 350th anniversary of Jews in the

United States in the winter of 2004 with a three-part series co-sponsored with Emory University. On February 7, 2005, Dr. Steven Bayme, AJC's National Director of Jewish Communal Affairs, spoke on this topic at a forum co-sponsored with Atlanta-area synagogues.

## ATLANTA RABBINIC ROUNDTABLE

In the late 1990s, divisive stands taken in Israel on the subject of "Who is a Jew?" polarized the Jewish community. Rabbis around the city of Atlanta addressed this subject during High Holidays, fueling considerable disagreement. Dr. Richard Cohen, AJC's Atlanta Chapter President, met with his rabbi, Temple Sinai's Philip Kranz, to discuss what role AJC might play in responding to these challenges. With the ambitious goal of bringing together rabbis from the different branches of Judaism to foster respect, understanding, and deeper personal relations among Atlanta's growing and diverse rabbinical community, the Atlanta Rabbinic Roundtable was born in December, 1997. The Chatham Valley Foundation and Jonathan Golden provided partial funding; the sessions continued through Spring of 1998.

The group of senior rabbis included two Conservative rabbis, Arnold Goodman of Ahavath Achim Synagogue and Shalom Lewis of Congregation Etz Chaim; three Reform rabbis, Alvin Sugarman of The Temple, Philip Kranz of Temple Sinai, and Stanley Davids of Temple Emanu-el; and three Orthodox rabbis, Ilan Feldman of Congregation Beth Jacob, Binyomin Friedman of Congregation Ariel, and Yossi New of Congregation Beth Tefillah.

From the initial planning, AJC leaders recognized the importance of keeping these discussions confidential; this meant finding a neutral and secure location and identifying an appropriate facilitator. Arrangements were made for the group to meet monthly at the Carter Presidential Library. At the suggestion of AJC's national staff, Rabbi Joseph Rackman traveled from New York to Atlanta monthly to facilitate the dialogue. Rackman is a learned Jew and practicing attorney and is the son of a revered Orthodox rabbi. During one of his visits to Atlanta, he spoke to AJC members at a luncheon addressing the topic "Why Can't Jews Talk To One Another?" True to their commitment, the participants kept the discussions confidential.

In August, 1998, the rabbis met for a one-day Rabbinic Dialogue Retreat at the home of Lois and Larry Frank. In December of that year, the rabbis shared lunch and a discussion with a group of religious and secular Israelis traveling to the United States on a project sponsored by AJC's Institute for American Jewish-Israeli Relations. The goal of this national program was to expose the Israelis to the many dimensions of Jewish identity in the United States. When the rabbis saw how positive this varied Israeli group's experience was, they suggested that they themselves might travel together to Israel. Understanding the special nature of this trip and the significant potential it provided for community building, Erwin Zaban generously donated the funds to underwrite it.

The rabbis began meeting monthly in the fall of 1999 and into 2000 to study and prepare for their July 31–August 8, 2000, itinerary. They planned each day's activities, as well as sites to be visited, and selected speakers to reflect their personal observance, views, and connections to Israel. A decision was made to document the journey, but keep it private. Once again, we deliberated on the appropriate neutral and trustworthy person to record the experience. Tom Teepen, Editorial Page Editor of the *Atlanta Journal-Constitution*, was selected and traveled with the rabbis, five of whose wives accompanied them. Five of the eight rabbis spoke about the trip in High Holiday sermons, but Tom Teepen's report of the deliberations remains secure in the files of the Atlanta Chapter of the AJC and has never been released.

Upon the conclusion of their time in Israel, a statement was released that underscores for me how important communal work is.

*Atlanta Rabbinic Roundtable Mission Statement*

*We continue a process of mutual discovery as we seek to understand one another, both as human beings and as Jews committed to our People's meaningful survival. In this process we have endeavored to become increasingly sensitive to the nuances of each other's ideological, theological and psychological perceptions in serving our Creator and the Jewish Community. The week in Israel is not a culmination of this process, but rather a significant continuation of the odyssey we share with one another.*

Some quotes from letters we received from those involved in this project bear sharing.

From Rabbi Arnold Goodman - July 30, 2000
*Dear Sherry,*

*Many thanks for your good wishes on the eve of our "rabbinic pluralism summit." It promises to be a wonderful learning experience for all of us. The theme of Tisha b'Av and the issue of religious messianism is now being reviewed by Rabbinic voices in Israel. Just today in the Jerusalem Post, Rabbi Lichtenstein argued that true religious messianism is not acquiring or holding onto land, but deepening the moral and ethical infrastructure of Israeli society.*

*I look forward to the session with him and the other scholars with whom we have sessions scheduled.*

*The meeting with other personalities will enable us to get some sense of the post Camp David climate in the country.*

*The Rabbinic Round Table owes you personally, Richard Cohen. Erwin Zaban and the AJC leadership our heartfelt thanks for making this coming week possible.*

*Obviously, I will be delighted to share my reactions and*

*experiences, well aware of our commitment not to go public with-*
*out our joint consent.*
*Rae sends her best.*
*AMG*

*August 9, 2000*
*Dear Friends,*

*I am writing to you on a personal level to thank you for the*
*support of the project involving the eight Atlanta rabbis. Your*
*confidence in our efforts has made these past two years significant*
*for those of us who have been privileged to participate. We feel*
*certain that, at some point in our deliberations, our efforts will*
*bear rich fruit.*

*You must certainly join me in appreciating the vision and*
*dedication of Richard Cohen. His shepherding this project has been*
*exemplary. I am grateful to you and to him for your sponsorship.*
*Sincerely,*
*Philip N. Kranz*
*Rabbi*

At AJC's Annual Meeting in 2000, the Atlanta Chapter won the
Szabad National Program of the Year Award for this project. The rabbis
continued to meet and study together upon their return. In the months
and years that followed, there were tangible signs in statements,
communal programs, and personal relationships that attested to the
significant and lasting impact of this AJC project on its participants.

## COMMENTARY STUDY GROUP

Beginning in 1985, Atlanta attorney David Meltz led a provoc-
ative AJC monthly discussion on the lead article in *Commentary*. I
vigorously argued the opposing liberal view to most articles. The
debates were intellectually challenging, and attendance was strong.

In 1995, we celebrated the 10th anniversary of this popular AJC luncheon series.

Founded in 1945, *Commentary* magazine was published monthly by AJC and read by more non-Jews than any other Jewish magazine. Its articles and perspectives featured some of the most talented emerging scholars, politicians, and recognized experts on subjects of domestic, national, and international Jewish concern. By the 1970s, it had become the key voice for neoconservatism, although a disclaimer appeared in the magazine stating "the opinions and views expressed by *Commentary*'s contributors and editors are their own." AJC published *Commentary* through 2006 and continues to support its role as an independent journal of thought and opinion.

## AMERICAN JEWISH YEARBOOK

AJC's research and publications are highly respected and quoted widely and often by national and international scholars, policy makers, and Jewish lay and professional influentials across a wide variety of fields.

For a hundred years, the agency published *The American Jewish Year Book*. We ordered them each year to give to area rabbis for their offices or their congregation's library. One year, I presented it to a young new rabbi in Atlanta. With delight, he told me he was the son of a rabbi and fondly remembered spending time in his father's office, seeing rows of this Year Book on the shelves. We also presented the book to members of Atlanta's Consular Corps when we visited in their offices.

In my final years at AJC, adult education courses were proliferating across Atlanta. They were provided under the auspices of the Florence Melton Program at the Marcus Jewish Community Center of Atlanta, the Atlanta Scholars Kollel, and new synagogues and Chabad Centers. I am especially proud that AJC played a significant role early in the 1980s to address this yearning for increased Jewish knowledge by our chapter and its leaders. We were blessed with community rabbis and scholars who generously partnered with us on the sacred journey of learning and identity.

(L-R) Bob Evans, Rabbi Donald Tam, Rabbi Ilan Feldman,
Speakers at "Why Be Jewish" program, 1993

# ACCESS

BUILDING FOR THE NEXT GENERATION

---

*It is not your responsibility to finish the work (of perfecting the world), but you are not free to desist from it either.*

—Rabbi Tarfon, Pirkei Avot 2:16

A t a staff retreat in the early 1980s, AJC's Director of Jewish Communal Affairs, Yehuda Rosenman, challenged us to reach out to young Jewish adults. Citing our research, he noted that they were obtaining college and advanced university degrees in numbers disproportionate to their demographics. These well-educated and mobile young adults were likely to identify with AJC's intellectually stimulating and diverse agenda.

This posed a worthy challenge, and I began developing a list of the adult children of our leadership. Our members immediately bought into this outreach. They hosted events in their homes and businesses, spoke at meetings, and generously supported our efforts. The number of interested young leaders from across the community grew quickly, and soon they were attending a variety of programs. AJC's former National Associate Director and head of its Leadership Development Department, Shula Bahat, was especially helpful, encouraging and supporting our pioneering initiative.

Our earliest programming consisted of several three-part series addressing topics reflective of the AJC agenda. One covered *Pro Choice: Where Do You Stand?*; *Israel and the Palestinians*; and *What Makes a Good Jew?* Another tackled *Separation of Church and State: What's It All About?*; *Investments for Young Professionals*; and *Extremism-Terrorist Groups on the Rise or Decline?* While some ideas were generated by the participants, most of the programming was staff-directed. A brochure described these activities.

> *In response to the growing number of young Jewish adults in our city, the Atlanta Chapter is pleased to offer innovative programming, opportunities for networking, and exposure to the dynamics of Atlanta and its movers and shakers. This combination, rooted in excellence, is the hallmark of the American Jewish Committee.*

One of our young volunteers, Mindy Selig Shoulberg, spent countless hours at the AJC office entering information from her address book into our data system. This was long before the availability of current technology, and her address book, along with those of numerous other leaders of the nascent ACCESS, was key to expanding our list of potential members.

During Steve Selig's term as Atlanta Chapter President from 1987 to 1989, the number of participants mushroomed from fifty to three hundred. Initially referred to as View Points and then Young Professionals, the group formed a program committee that evolved into a steering committee. It soon became clear that a more formal structure was needed.

Elaine Alexander, Atlanta Chapter President from 1989 to 1991, along with Chuck Wolf, the board liaison to this emerging young group, gave guidance and leadership to what would soon be called ACCESS. In early 1990, T.J. Bierman and Steve Klorfein volunteered to serve as the first co-chairs of the Steering Committee. Elise Eplan, Joel Arogeti and Beth Paradies were the first program co-chairs.

A defining moment for the group occurred one hot summer evening in July, 1990, when advertising moguls Joel Babbit and Joey Reiman hosted 150 young adults at their rooftop offices. *A View From the Penthouse: The Jewish Entrepreneurial Spirit* featured Chuck Wolf, Buck Goldstein, Steve Selig, Babbit and Reiman. This inspirational event was the first of what would become a highly anticipated annual program focusing on Jewish entrepreneurship. As the fall paid-up membership event, it started the year off with a bang.

In ensuing years, similar gatherings featured every major Jewish entrepreneur. Creative spins on this event focused on young entrepreneurs, family businesses, women, and programs that were industry-specific, such as entertainment and real estate. When the original entrepreneurs entertained once again for the 10th anniversary of ACCESS, membership had grown to 1,000.

At their meeting on November 20, the steering committee was charged to establish Young Professionals' own identity with a new name, logo and stationery. "We want to give young people access to the mainstream of AJC," Steve Klorfein said in an article in the *Atlanta Jewish Times* on February 15, 1991. The word "access" was appropriate because, as a name, it created the special identity of enabling young Jews entrée into the Jewish and general communities through the work of AJC.

AJC's agenda has been central to ACCESS over these more than twenty-five years, spurring on a variety of new initiatives. In recent years, Atlanta's Consular community has grown, and ACCESS members meet with consuls general to advocate for Israel's security as well as issues of anti-Semitism and extremism. Now called *Dinners with Diplomats*, these get-togethers prepare ACCESS members to be articulate spokespeople for the Jewish community. ACCESS leaders have participated in numerous AJC sponsored trips abroad – to Germany, Chile, Switzerland, Mexico, and Croatia -- to continue the agency's important work in global advocacy.

Following the example set by the Atlanta Chapter's achievements in intergroup relations, ACCESS has long been active in the Atlanta Black/Jewish Coalition. They have been leaders in the coalition's Marvin C. Goldstein Project Understanding Black-Jewish Young Leadership Retreat and the biennial Seders. ACCESS has hosted an Asian-Jewish Seder, programs on diversity in the workplace, and has worked with the Hispanic and Asian communities.

Keeping young Jews informed and involved in the community has always been a priority of the Atlanta Chapter and its work with ACCESS. Forums were often held with community rabbis and discussions related to Jewish identity and family issues. Many times in the early years it felt as if we were sponsoring events that could just as well have been found in a synagogue adult education program. They covered how to lead a Seder and how to prepare *Shabbat* and holiday meals. We ran a series entitled *Shabbat Rocks* at many synagogues, offering dinner, services and stimulating discussions with rabbis. Atlanta Chapter members hosted ACCESS members for *Shabbat* dinners and made sure they all had homes to go to for Passover Seders. Hosting the Steering Committee members annually in my *Sukkah* for a *Shabbat* dinner and sing-along is among my sweetest memories.

ACCESS has an exceptional record of achievement in grooming future leaders with skills and commitment for AJC and the Jewish community at large. Three of their chairs, Kent Alexander, Elise Eplan and Beth Paradies, have gone on to serve as Atlanta Chapter presidents.

ACCESS member Leslie Blonder Isenberg was our first young adult to join a major community board when she was elected to serve on the board of the William Breman Jewish Home. When Dina Gerson became co-chair of the Atlanta Jewish Film Festival, it was clear that we had hit our stride. ACCESS members now fill leadership roles in AJC and throughout our Jewish and civic communities.

In an article in the *Atlanta Jewish Times* during ACCESS's 10th year, AJC Executive Director David Harris said "ACCESS is terrific. It's been a pacesetter within the national American Jewish Committee structure for young leadership development and programming."

As a testament to the success and effectiveness of Atlanta's programming, the national organization adopted the name we coined, and all chapter young adult groups are now called ACCESS. AJC's major national meeting, the Global Forum, is currently preceded by a national meeting of ACCESS groups, and our own Atlanta leaders fill top roles at this gathering of over five hundred young adults.

From its inception, ACCESS members participated in AJC fund-raising.They attracted large crowds and new donors with themed events such as an annual Chai Society Party and several silent auctions. For their 10th anniversary party, thanks to the generosity of Doug Hertz and Dave Shoulberg, they held a carnival night at United Distributors. ACCESS members often serve as co-chairs of the Selig Distinguished Service Award Dinner, where their leadership is recognized. Kent Alexander, along with his parents Elaine and Miles, as well as Beth Paradies and her husband Gregg, are recipients of this award.

ACCESS members were integrated into all aspects of the Atlanta Chapter, serving on the AJC Board of Trustees and its various committees. They were active participants in the Atlanta Jewish Film Festival and still host a night at the festival each year. When mentoring programs were initiated, chapter members were both involved in and supportive of ACCESS programming as well as in serving as role models and teachers for ACCESS steering committee members.

In 1993, Richard Cohen, in his president's column in the chapter newsletter, wrote "The record growth of ACCESS has been one of the highlights of these two years. Today over one third of our members are a part of AJC's vibrant young adult division. This will assure us strong leadership for years to come."

When I retired in 2006, I was asked where I would direct funds if donors were to make contributions in my honor. I selected ACCESS, because I am so proud of the dedication and achievement of these young adults and AJC's commitment to invest time, talent and resources into this program.

So many personal stories, including some on uncomfortable moments I've faced, have arisen from meaningful interactions with AJC and ACCESS members. I have often repeated one such story to illustrate an unanticipated situation that had a surprising outcome.

In my early years in AJC, our membership was open to Jews, their spouses, and children. But non-Jews, not related to members, could not join AJC. This was a quiet, internally-known policy that was rarely mentioned and was changed in later years; however, it was debated heatedly by the board and was a highly charged topic for one of our older long-time members.

At one ACCESS program, led by Rabbi Lou Feldstein, I had to face this policy head-on and grapple with it. The subject was how to conduct a seder. For many of our members, this was a hot topic, since they were in Atlanta away from family; they were gathering with friends for Passover, but were novices at leading a Seder. One of our ACCESS members called the office to RSVP for himself and his non-Jewish girlfriend, and I was at a loss as how to respond. Should I say she is not welcome? This was years before the Jewish community put outreach to interfaith couples on our communal agenda. Fortunately, my good sense prevailed, and I took both names and added them to our attendance list.

At the beginning of the evening, Rabbi Feldstein asked participants to introduce themselves and share one Passover memory. I became increasingly nervous about our non-Jewish guest as we went around the room, but I needn't have worried. When it came to her turn to speak, she said "I've come tonight to begin to collect Passover memories." I was moved by her heartfelt words. Today she and her husband are active members of the community, and all their children are Jewish day school alumni.

Over the years a broad variety of programs presented many similar opportunities for us to reach out to and embrace individuals searching for Jewish knowledge and a comfortable place within our Jewish community. This work is a real source of pride for me.

ACCESS continues to thrive. Its steering committee has grown in number. Today their programs are less focused on domestic public policy and Jewish identity issues, and they are doing fewer community service projects. Although there have been changes in direction, its purpose remains the same. Reflective of AJC's national agenda, there is increased focus on international and intergroup relations. The list of highlights, included in the Appendix, demonstrates the diversity and innovation of ACCESS activities.

Programs to provide education, social, and networking opportunities continue to fill the calendars of these activist young adults. New priority outreach initiatives are directed to the ethnic communities – African-Americans, Latinos, and Asians – and in the interfaith community with Muslims.

When I retired in 2006, after a glorious, challenging, and extremely satisfying career at AJC, I was able to look back at some of my most enduring efforts. Among those are the Atlanta Black/Jewish Coalition, ACCESS, and the Atlanta Jewish Film Festival. I am very honored that I was given the opportunity to create an endowment fund that would not only carry my name, but would also ensure the longevity of one of my proudest initiatives. The Sherry Frank ACCESS Endowment Fund was established at my retirement, and funding was increased with the 25th ACCESS Anniversary Celebration in 2016. Pictures from my celebratory retirement event, which coincided with AJC's centennial tribute and concert, are in the Appendix and reflect the wide diversity of people I encountered along my journey.

ACCESS officers:
(L-R) Vice-Chair Jane
Butler, Secretary
David Rubenstein,
Chair Elyse Eplan,
1992-1993

President
Candy Berman
presents Young
Leadership
Award to Leslie
Blonder, 1999

ACCESS 25th Anniversary Celebration (L-R) Jacque Frank
Friedland, Sherry Frank, Ronnie van Gelder, 2015

# ORAL HISTORY PROJECT

## PRESERVING SACRED STORIES

---

*Our lives are shaped as much by those who leave as they are by those who stay. Loss is our legacy. Insight is our gift. Memory is our guide.*

—Hope Edelman

A JC's William E. Wiener Oral History Library was created to record the 20th century American Jewish experience through the recollections of those who have lived it. It was founded in 1969 with a gift from the estate of William E. Wiener and earned additional grants over the years from public agencies such as the National Endowment for the Humanities and a number of private sources. The library has preserved histories revealed through in-depth interviews – on tape and in typescript, indexed and organized – and provides valuable material for authors and researchers.

When I began my career with AJC in September, 1980, our national organization was celebrating its 75th anniversary. Herbert Cohen chaired the Atlanta Chapter's Year of Celebration, during which time three anniversary programs were held: an Oral History panel moderated by ABC news correspondent Herbert Kaplow; a national Inter-religious Affairs Commission meeting in Atlanta that included an award presentation to Dr. Martin Luther King, Sr.;

and a Conference on Human Rights that explored the repression of religion behind the Iron Curtain. William (Bill) Breman received the Chapter's Distinguished Service Award, and Senator Sam Nunn received AJC's Institute of Human Relations Award.

One program at that year's national convention (Annual Meeting) featured an Oral History Panel highlighting famous luminaries. These panels were a long-held tradition at the Annual Meeting, and since the 1970s, Atlanta had been engaged in this area. Past Chapter President Dejongh Franklin headed up a group of lawyers who conducted oral history interviews of influential Atlanta leaders. Miles Alexander, past Chapter President and founder of the local oral history project, sent this letter to then AJC Director Bill Gralnick detailing the continued expansion of the project.

*December 21, 1976*
*Dear Bill,*

*The following is a list of what I understand to be the assignments for interviewing between now and April, 1977.*

*Ruth Gershon and her father will interview Rabbi Epstein; Nancy Saul will interview A.L. Feldman and Josephine Heyman; Richard Flexner will interview David Marx; Mike Ginsberg will interview Bea Haas; you will ask Vida Goldgar to interview Adolph Rosenberg as soon as possible in view of his illness; Joe Haas will interview Edward M. Kahn; I will request John and David Golden to interview their father; I will request Charles Wittenstein to interview Hannah Shulhafer; Larry Bogart will be requested to interview Louis Geffen, Rabbi Tobais Geffen's son who lives in Atlanta; Dennis Meir will be asked to interview Ida Sugarman; Herbert Ringel will interview Mr. and Mrs. Louis Montag; Ted Frankel will be asked to complete the interview of Mendel Romm, Sr.; and I will complete the interviews of Mr. and Mrs. Herbert Taylor and Mr. Neely (through his grandson-in-law, Howard Hoffman)*
*Sincerely,*
*Miles J. Alexander*

The 75th Anniversary Oral History Panel received wide media coverage. It provided information to the community on AJC's Wiener Oral History Collection; it showcased a stellar Atlanta panel; and it reported the formal presentation of the Atlanta Chapter's collection to Emory University's Woodruff Library Special Collections department.

December 29, 1980  *Atlanta Journal-Constitution*
*Racing Against Time: Bill Gralnick Is Trying To Save History Of Atlanta's Jewish Community*
*by Billie Cheney Speed*

When Bill Gralnick of the American Jewish Committee heard that Dr. Joseph Yampolsky had died, he knew a wealth of information about Atlanta's Jewish community had been lost.

"Dr. Yampolsky, a well-known Jewish physician in his 80s, died in October 1978," Gralnick said, "and there was so much he could have shared with us in an oral history."

Since then, Gralnick admitted, he's felt as if he's racing against time, trying to capture and record the careers, lifestyles, ideas and histories of the Jewish experience in Atlanta.

In discussing the importance of oral histories, Gralnick quoted photographer Henri Cartier-Bresson: "Photographers deal in things which are continually vanishing, and when they have vanished, there is no contrivance on earth which can make them come back again. We cannot develop and print a memory."

However, Gralnick said, Milton Krents, chairman of the Wiener Oral History Library in New York, reminds that "(the oral historian) can develop these memoirs in sound and imprint these memories of a passing era permanently in the pages of history."

As a part of the 75th anniversary celebration of the American Jewish Committee, the Atlanta Chapter has chosen to focus attention on oral histories. The resulting event, "The Oral History Program," is scheduled for 8 p.m. Wednesday in the WAGA/TV-5 auditorium, with ABC News correspondent Herbert Kaplow interviewing four prominent members of Atlanta's Jewish community. (Actually, the four participated in earlier interviews, and their responses and memoirs were taped.)

"The people chosen for Wednesday's program have old family ties in the Atlanta area and bring varied backgrounds and much information regarding the growth of the Atlanta Jewish community and Atlanta itself to the interview," said Gralnick, southeastern regional director of the American Jewish Committee. They are Mrs. Sarina Rousso, Gerald Cohen, Cecil Alexander and Elliott Goldstein.

Mrs. Rousso, 81, is an expert on "Romanceros," the old Spanish-Jewish songs which have been passed from generation to generation by word of mouth. She is also knowledgeable of Sephardic customs and rituals and is trying to preserve customs by working with younger generations.

Sephardic Jews, Gralnick explained, come from the Mediterranean countries and the Middle East while Ashkenazic Jews come primarily from Northern Europe.

Gerald Cohen, president of Central Metals Co., is a past president of Ahavath Achim Synagogue and vice president for community relations of the Atlanta Jewish Federation.

Cecil Alexander is chairman of the board of Finch, Alexander, Barnes, Rothschild and Paschal Architects, Inc. Twice he has received the National Council of Christian and Jews Brotherhood Award, and he served as the first chairman of the Citizens' Advisory Committee for Urban Renewal.

Elliott Goldstein is a senior partner in the law firm of Powell, Goldstein, Frazer and Murphy and is past president of The Temple, and former director and vice president of the United Way.

During the same program, Miles J. Alexander, founder of

the Atlanta Chapter's oral history program, will present Emory University with the committee's taped oral history collection, which includes 13 interviews of prominent Atlantans. The tapes will be given to Herbert F. Johnson, director of libraries for Emory's Special Collections Department.

The Atlanta oral history collection will also be sent to the American Jewish Committee's Wiener Oral History Library in New York, which houses a collection of taped interviews with great American writers, entertainers, politicians, scientists. There's also an oral history collection of interviews with survivors of the Holocaust. Wiener is the largest American Jewish oral history library in the nation and serves as an information clearinghouse for American Jewish oral history projects across the country.

The oral histories of five Georgians are already a part of the library: Morris Abram, former president of Brandeis University, now practicing law in New York City; Cantor Isaac Goodfriend and his wife Betty Goodfriend, both survivors of the Holocaust; Elijah Wisebram, a Russian who immigrated to Eastern Europe and then to Rome, Ga. (he founded and still operates the Wisebram Department Store in Barnesville); and Elliott Goldstein, also featured in the Atlanta oral history collection.

*Histories of Influential Jewish Atlanta Families*
*Donated to Emory University*

| | | |
|---|---|---|
| Mrs. Ida Levitas | Mr. Sam Eplan | Mr. Donald Oberdorfer |
| Mr. John Sibley | Rabbi Harry Epstein | Mr. Cecil Alexander |
| Mrs. Ethel Myers | Mr. Sinclair Jacobs | Mr. Gerald Cohen |
| Mr. David Marx | Rabbi Joseph Cohen | Mrs. Josephine Heyman |
| Mr. Albert Mayer | Mrs. Rebecca Gershon | Dr. Nanette K. Wenger |
| Mr. Ed Kahn | Mr. Eldridge Freeborn | Mrs. Sadie Jacobs |
| | Mr. and Mrs. Robert Zimmerman | |

History had largely ignored the work and accomplishments of women, so it was not surprising that in 1980, oral histories of women represented less than 10% of the William E. Wiener Library's total collection of outstanding American Jews. With few exceptions, women's presence throughout the years had been noted as wives and mothers of men who have been the movers and shakers. To correct this omission, the Wiener Library began to focus on documenting the unrecorded past and rapid emergence of the American Jewish woman through her achievements in the Jewish and general communities. The goal of this national project was to study the accelerating role of social change in molding and revising attitudes and lifestyles of American Jewish women. It was the intention that the Library expand by incorporating regional AJC chapter collections.

A national blueprint for action was developed to serve as a guideline for selection of memoirists and the content of memoirs. Definitions were established for terms:

- *Jewish* – any woman who so identifies herself. This runs the spectrum from affiliated, to non-affiliated, to observant, to non-observant, etc. (Within the memoir, we shall ask the interviewee to share her definition of what it means to be "Jewish.")
- *Woman* – It is important to get good representation of the "actuarial imperatives," those now in their 80s and older, since their memories will stretch back to the beginnings of the century and earlier in the memories of their parents... as well as those in their middle years and young women whose careers are still evolving.
- *Achievement* – "Achievement" lends itself to broad definition and should be so viewed for the screening of memoirists. Those who have "achieved" in both the volunteer as well as professional sectors, whose lives, interests and concerns have made a contribution to the society in which they elect

to function – whether the Jewish or general; the business, political, professional or cultural, and/or the family.

Through the active participation of AJC chapters around the country, the national collection would provide a significant contribution toward recognizing the important role of American Jewish women in the 20th century. Fifteen AJC chapters participated in this new oral history project.

In 1982, under the leadership of Dr. Roberta (Bobbie) Golden, the Atlanta Chapter launched its Women of Achievement Oral History Project. The first program was a panel held on May 25, 1983, at WAGA-TV studios. A standing-room only crowd heard fascinating stories from panelists.

- Janice Rothschild Blumberg – Author of the history of *The Temple, "As But a Day: The First 100 Years 1867-1967,"* prominent and beloved leader in Atlanta
- Josephine Heyman – Activist for women's rights and civil rights; Past President of Atlanta Section, NCJW; League of Women Voters; and Women's Division, Atlanta Jewish Federation
- Judge Phyllis Kravitch – United States Circuit Judge, U.S. Court of Appeals, 11th Circuit; first woman Superior Court Judge in Georgia
- Dr. Nanette Wenger – Professor of Medicine (Cardiology), Emory University School of Medicine; Director, Cardiac Clinic, Grady Memorial Hospital; first woman to serve as President of the Georgia Heart Association

In 1985, as enthusiasm for this project grew, the National Council of Jewish Women (NCJW), Atlanta Section, under the leadership of Atlanta Section President, Susan Feinberg, joined AJC as a co-sponsor. Sunny Stern was the staff coordinator, and Phoebe W. Lundeen served as Chairperson of the Advisory Committee.

To assure that the interviews would be consistent and professional, Irma and Milton Krents were recruited to train our volunteers. Milton was a highly regarded broadcast executive and producer of the religious drama and discussion series "The Eternal Light" on NBC radio and television for the Jewish Theological Seminary of America. He later became the director of AJC's Oral History Library Collection, and served as chairman of its advisory board.

After Milton's retirement from this position, his wife, Irma, who had a respected career in public relations and was an award winning script writer, took over as director. When I held office in NCJW's Atlanta Section, Irma was on the national staff of NCJW and headed their public relations department. She conducted a training session concerning the difference between public relations and personal and private relations. Using her own touching and personal story as an illustration, she told us that her son, Harold, was born blind. Facing tough challenges, he became a lawyer and an advocate for the disabled. His story was featured in *Butterflies Are Free*, a first-of-its-kind Broadway play, and later a film starring Goldie Hawn. Her story stayed with me, and I especially loved the connection I had forged with Irma from NCJW to AJC.

By November, thirty volunteer historians had been trained and were beginning the collection of memoirs of Jewish Women of Achievement.

November 15, 1985 *The Southern Israelite*
*'Women of Achievement' selected Asher, Goldgar for oral histories*

Thirty Atlanta volunteer historians have been trained and are beginning the collection of memoirs of Jewish Women of Achievement. This project is co-sponsored by the American Jewish Committee and the National Council of Jewish Women. Co-chairing the project are Dr. Roberta

Golden and Libby Johnson for AJC and Terry Epstein and Beth Isaacson for NCJW.

Barbara Asher, Atlanta City Councilwoman, and Vida Goldgar, Editor and Publisher of *The Southern Israelite*, have been selected to be interviewed by the group of historians. Both group interviews will be conducted at the NCJW offices. Ms. Asher will be interviewed at 9:30 a.m. Wednesday, Nov. 20; Ms. Goldgar will be interviewed at 7:30 p.m. Thursday Nov. 21.

Over the next 12 months, volunteers will be interviewing individual women whose collective histories will paint a vivid picture of the impact that Jewish women have had on every aspect of Atlanta.

On Oct. 21, Ms. Beth Wenger spoke at a monthly meeting of the oral history interviewers. A native Atlantan, she recently completed her undergraduate thesis for Wesleyan University entitled, "The Southern Lady and the Jewish Woman: The Early Organizational Life of Atlanta's Jewish Women." She spoke about the changing roles of women throughout the years. Ms. Wenger emphasized the need for documented women's histories and the lack of information currently available. She applauded AJC and NCJW for meeting this need.

Continuing with their successful model, AJC and NCJW co-hosted an oral history panel on November 13, 1986. The panelists were:

- Spring Asher, Producer WXIA-TV – *Noonday*; author and newspaper columnist; Chair, Advisory Board, Northside School for the Arts; Winner of six Emmys
- Leah Janus, President, Advocacy Network; Past President, Atlanta Chapter, United Nations Association; President,

League of Women Voters, Fulton County and State of Georgia; Past President, Women's Division, Atlanta Jewish Federation

- Dr. Rose Lehman, Graduate University of Toronto Medical School; In practice in Atlanta since June 1948; Specialities: OB/GYN, Endocrinology, and Bariatrics; Past President, Atlanta Branch of American Medical Women's Association.

The oral history panels drew large crowds and provided key opportunities to showcase the project, recruit volunteers, and solicit names of women to be interviewed.

Concurrent with Women of Achievement, the *Zachor* project on Holocaust survivors was being developed. At this time, the Atlanta Jewish Federation recognized that an additional effort to collect oral histories of men was needed. An initial meeting was held on November 20, 1986, to address this issue.

As meetings continued to explore expansion of the Women of Achievement Oral History project, AJC and NCJW members held training sessions and added women's memoirs to its growing collection. In 1987, Esther and Herbert Taylor donated $10,000 to the project to be used for transcribing the tapes. Interviews were transcribed verbatim, and the transcribed copies were kept with the original tapes. In 1988, Karen Piassick, Beth Isaacson, Ray Ann Kremer, and Joel Lowenstein served as co-chairpersons.

On January 5, 1989, Betty Ann Jacobson, the incoming chairperson of the Atlanta Jewish Federation's Heritage Center, invited the Oral History participants for lunch. The meeting's purpose was to officially involve Federation in the expansion of this AJC and NCJW project.

With Federation now co-sponsoring the project, the team of co-chairpersons included AJC, Sara Franco and Ray Ann Kremer; NCJW, Suzi Brozman and Karen Piassick; and Atlanta Jewish Federation Jewish Heritage Center, Betty Ann Jacobson and Jane Lefco. Each organization was responsible for different aspects of the project.

In a memo recapping the February 1 meeting of the Oral History co-chairs, Sunny Stern, AJC Assistant Area Director and project coordinator, included the "Statement of Direction of Purpose for the Project."

*The group agreed that the purpose of the newly aligned and expanded Oral History Project is to document a personal history of the Atlanta Jewish community through the memories, orally taken, of individuals. These Oral Histories are to be used for historical research and will be housed in the William E. Wiener Oral History Library in New York and the Heritage Center of the Atlanta Jewish Federation in Atlanta.*

In March, Irma Krents returned to Atlanta to conduct a volunteer training session for the recently renamed Esther and Herbert Taylor Oral History Library. She also met with the reconstructed Advisory Committee and with the new co-chairpersons. Mimi Alperin, AJC's National Chairperson of Special Projects and Project Coordinator for the Wiener Library, traveled to Atlanta to continue providing national support.

Atlanta area rabbis were asked to suggest names of men and women to interview with the intent to preserve the history of our entire community. We reiterated that it is the "actuarial imperative" to secure the memoirs of older members of our community.

On June 26, 1990, Judith Taylor, presiding over the Advisory Committee, recognized the completion of our first year as the Jewish Oral History Project of Atlanta. We received an additional $5,000 grant from the Esther and Herbert Taylor Foundation to cover the cost of getting the Jewish Women of Achievement Collection ready to send to New York. A list of the tapes was distributed that included the Women of Achievement plus three memoirs done posthumously by those close to the subjects.

| | | |
|---|---|---|
| Hermie Alexander[1] | Edith Elsas | Carolyn Haas Kahn |
| Barbara Asher | Hannah Entell | Helen Kahn |
| Spring Asher | Vivian Frankel | Dr. Rose Lehman |
| Barbara Balser | Miriam Freedman | Miriam Levitas |
| Virginia Barnett | Dr. Regina Gabler | Dr. Mollie Orloff |
| Miriam Belger | Vida Goldgar | Herta Sanders |
| Rose Berkowitz | Rubye Eplan Goldstein | Irene Schwartz |
| Ricky Birnbrey | Irma Goldwasser | Carolyn Selig[3] |
| Ida Sloan Borochoff | Helen Gortatowsky | Leah Janus |
| Sylvia Breman | Be Haas | Beverly Shere |
| Lucinda Bunnen | Betty Haas | Betty Smulian |
| Frances Bunzl | Ruth and Katherine | Esther Taylor |
| Helen Cavalier | Hertzka | Alene Uhry |
| Jean Cohen | Josephine Heyman | Dr. Nanette Wenger |
| Roz Cohen[2] | Carolyn Holland | Ethel Wise |
| Ethel Coplan | Betty Ann Jacobson | Anne Yudelson |
| Marilyn Ehrlich | Fanny Jacobson | Ruth Zuckerman |

1. *Memories shared by Cecil and Helen Alexander, Teresa Lansburgh, Terri Milkey, Hava and Bill Rothschild*
2. *Memories shared by Bruce Cohen, Elliot Penso, Irving Penso, Lena Penso*
3. *Memories shared by Dorothy Joel, Cathy Selig, Steve Selig, Harriet Goldstein*

On May 16, 1990, with a strong sense of "mission accomplished," the William E. Wiener Oral History Library and the entire AJC Oral History Collection was gifted to the Jewish Division of the New York Public Library with the objective of making it more broadly available to students, scholars, and researchers. A letter dated October 24, from Sunny Stern to Sandy Berman, archivist at the Heritage Center, acknowledged that the Women's Collection was being given to the Heritage Center.

> *Dear Sandy,*
>
> *Enclosed you will find the tapes and transcripts of the Atlanta Jewish Women of Achievement Oral History Project. The women in this collection were selected because of their achievements as professionals, volunteers, or homemakers. We are delighted to finally send them to you to be housed at the Heritage Center. Two additional sets now reside in the Wiener Oral History Library in the American Jewish Committee Building in New York City and the Jewish Division of the New York Public Library. This collection is considered to be open-ended in that we intend to add to it as we identify women who should appropriately be included. As these are completed, we will send them to you.*
> *Sincerely,*
> *Sunny Stern*
> *Staff Coordinator*

Training sessions continued to augment the knowledge and skills of our interviewers. Presentations were conducted by area historians and synagogue leaders including Mark Bauman, Doris Goldstein, Ike Habif , and Anna and Louis Geffen. On December 4, 1990, Erwin Zaban provided a unique opportunity as he guided the group on a tour of the National Service Industries' archives and spoke about Atlanta business history. On another occasion, Betty Ann Jacobson led a tour of historic Oakland Cemetery.

By early 1991, plans were underway for three oral history panels and a major year-long exhibit on the Jews of Atlanta to be housed by 1994 at the Atlanta History Center. The exhibit was to be called "Creating Community: The Jews of Atlanta 1845 to the Present." The Jewish Heritage Center of the Atlanta Jewish Federation took the lead in organizing this major exhibit and the year of programming around it.

June 28, 1991  *Atlanta Jewish Times*
*How the Community Preserves Its History*
*by Ellen Bernstein*

The organizers of a recent Atlanta Jewish history program never imagined they would draw such a large crowd for an evening of schmoozing about the old Washington Street neighborhood.

"It pulled people in," said Shirley Brickman, the moderator of the panel discussion. "I think people like to reminisce. These are special memories, family memories."

The venue for the June 10 program changed three times to accommodate the snowballing enthusiasm in the community, Mrs. Brickman said. At the last minute, Ahavath Achim Synagogue agreed to hold the event., which drew well over 600 people. The synagogue was an ideal place for reminiscing since the old AA sanctuary, on Washington Street, was at the heart of the old neighborhood.

The audience was a mix of the 'old crowd,' their children, and grandchildren. But what surprised the coordinators was the large turnout of relative newcomers to the city.

"These people grew up in similar urban neighborhoods. These are shared memories that everyone can relate to," said Mrs. Brickman, a key volunteer in the community's efforts to document its history in recent years. "It's like flipping through a scrapbook. It doesn't have to be your own."

The Washington Street program was funded by the Herbert and Esther Taylor Foundation and sponsored by the American Jewish Committee, the Atlanta Jewish Federation and the National Council of Jewish Women. It is one of several planned for the community culminating in a year-long exhibit on Atlanta Jews in 1993.

The exhibit will be housed at the Atlanta History Center in Buckhead in a $15 million addition to be completed next year.

"Hundreds of volunteers are expected to be involved as researchers and docents for the Jewish exhibit," Mrs. Brickman said.

The exhibit is called "Creating Community: The Jews of Atlanta, 1845-present." Lectures, films and panel discussions will continue throughout 1993 as an adjunct to the exhibit.

"What we plan to do is tell our story. It will provide an understanding of our vibrant community among ourselves and the general public," Mrs. Brickman said.

The Jewish Heritage Center of the Atlanta Jewish Federation has taken the lead in organizing this major exhibit. The Federation employs an archivist, Sandy Berman, who for six years has collected memorabilia from Atlanta's Jewish families.

The Atlanta Chapter of the American Jewish Committee and the National Council of Jewish Women have also taken an active role by building a collection of tape recorded memoirs of Jewish Atlantans.

In five years, Mrs. Brickman said, the community hopes to build a permanent structure to consolidate the exhibit, the archives, the oral history collection and the *Zachor* Holocaust Center, now housed in the Atlanta Jewish Community Center. The Holocaust Center is an educational exhibit, personalized with the stories of survivors now living in Atlanta.

"Heritage means the past, the present and the future," Mrs. Brickman said. "We hope a permanent home for the collections will give us a sense of continuity as a Jewish community."

The three oral history panels drew hundreds and covered a broad cross-section of Atlanta's Jewish community. Topics included:

1.  "Old Washington Street, A Slice of Early Atlanta's Jewish History," held on June 10, 1991, at Ahavath Achim Synagogue. Shirley Brickman moderated. Panelists included Sara Alterman, Dr. Irving Greenberg, Edward Krick, and Dorothy Rosenblum.

2. "Los Muestros: Our People, the Sephardim of Atlanta," held on June 1, 1992, at Congregation Or VeShalom. Joel Arogeti moderated. Panelists included: Emily Amato, Asher Benator, Sol Beton, and Regina Tourial.
3. "Memories: The Temple 1867-1993," held on February 21, 1993, at The Temple. Elmo Ellis moderated. Panelists included: Robert Lipshutz, Sam Massell, Betty Nathan, and Alene Uhry.

At the same time as plans moved forward for the "Creating Community" exhibit, work was progressing on the creation of a new Heritage Center. On April 11, 1994, Sunny Stern wrote thanking Judith and Mark Taylor for the continuing financial support of the Taylor Family Foundation, Inc.

*Dear Judith and Mark,*

*The collection continues to grow. We have nearly 200 memoirs and there are many yet to be interviewed. Excerpts from the transcripts are being used in the upcoming "Creating Community" catalogue and I am told constantly by Sandy Berman, the archivist at the Federation, that writers and other scholars use the tapes and transcripts with great frequency. It is thrilling to be a part of this wonderful and very valuable project.*
*Sincerely,*
*Sunny Stern*
*Staff Coordinator*

A year later, Sunny Stern again wrote to Mark Taylor requesting additional support from the Taylor Family Foundation, Inc.

*Dear Mark,*

*We hope that the new Heritage Center will be ready to house The Esther and Herbert Taylor Oral History Library by the spring of 1996. This, of course, brings with it the need to have the*

*Collection catalogued in a manner which will make it compatible with the newly computerized system scheduled to be in place at the Center.*

*It is very exciting to know that the permanent home for the oral history collection will soon be a reality and access by scholars and historians and the like will be at hand. The generosity and support of The Esther and Herbert Taylor Foundation for this project has made it all possible, and for that, I know that the community is extremely grateful. As I've indicated on many occasions, I feel very proud to be a part of this really wonderful project.*
*Sincerely,*
*Sunny Stern*
*Staff Coordinator*


After speaking at a meeting of the Jewish Oral History Project on May 19, 1998, I received the following letter.

*Dear Sherry,*
*Thank you for sharing your insight and understanding of the Jewish Oral History Project at the meeting on May 19. Your continued support will help to facilitate a smooth transfer of administrative duties to The William Breman Jewish Heritage Museum.*

*The work that has been done by you and others within your respective organizations provides visitors to the Museum with an aspect of local history that differs from that found through the research of historical documents. The transcriptions are used frequently and are a lasting legacy to the memoirists, the interviewers, the staffs at NCJW and AJC, and especially to Sunny Stern.*

*We feel fortunate to take on a more active role in this project and hope that you will continue to participate.*
*Best Regards,*

*Sandra Berman*       *Jane Leavey*
*Archivist*           *Director*

A press release on September 15, 1998, told of the transfer of the Oral History Collection.

*Oral History Tapes Transferred to the William Breman Heritage Museum*

For decades, the AJC nationally was involved in the development of a Jewish Oral History Library Collection. The Atlanta Chapter joined in this project during the 1970s. The Collection first targeted specific groups, such as significant Jews in politics, media, entertainment, business, and Holocaust survivors.

In the early 1980s, when the focus was on women, the Atlanta Section, National Council of Jewish Women joined AJC in this project. Late in the 1980s, the Atlanta Jewish Federation joined and the project was expanded to cover the broad scope of Atlanta's history. Over the years, oral history panels drew large crowds and gave the community new insights and fond memories of the struggles of women in various careers, the development of the Sephardic community, the early days of The Temple and visions of Old Washington Street.

After shepherding the project for more than 25 years, the tapes were officially moved, this summer, from the AJC offices to the William Breman Jewish Heritage Museum. They are valued resources of the people and history of Atlanta's Jewish community and they belong in this beautiful new library and in its archives. AJC, NCJW and Federation will continue to give vision and leadership to this project for years to come.

When I think back on the genesis and development of this project, I am filled with warm memories. As staff coordinators, first Ronnie van Gelder and then Sunny Stern guided the project with great love and professionalism. Committed volunteers became skilled interviewers and even developed personal relationships with the people whose lives they captured. Judith Taylor led the Advisory Committee ably with wisdom, and grace. The Esther and Herbert Taylor Family Foundation, Inc., believed in what we were doing and provided generous financial support at every stage of the project. Three organizations demonstrated over the decades a model of sharing responsibilities and dedication to a single objective – preserving Atlanta's Jewish history.

I treasure the phone calls I received from family members sharing with me the confidential news of a loved one's serious illness and the hopes that we could secure their interview in a timely manner. I checked our list of interviewees whenever the news of a community leader's death occurred and was so relieved to find that most of the time we had recorded their memories. The Oral History collection, initiated by AJC, continues at the Breman Museum.

First Women of Achievement panel (L-R) Dr. Nanette Wenger, Janice
Rothschild Blumberg, Judge Phyllis  Kravitch, Josephine Heyman, 1982

Vida Goldgar being interviewed by Dr. Roberta (Bobbie) Golden, 1985

Erwin Zaban showing National Service Industries' archives with volunteers
(L-R) Erwin, Leon, Elise and Madelyn Eplan, Lois Wender, 1990

Transferring the collection of tapes from AJC to the Breman Museum,
(L-R) Terry Cherniak, Sydney Simons, Virginia Saul, Susan Feinberg, Fayne
Frankel, Sandy Berman, Jane Leavey, Lois Wender and Susan Plasker, 1998

# Black-Jewish Relations

---

*Our struggle is not for a day, a week, or a year, but for a lifetime
if that's what it takes to build the beloved community.*

—John Lewis

I am often asked where my strong interest in Black-Jewish relations
comes from. Upon reflection, I attribute it to events that occurred
after my father's death when I was 11 years old. My dad's brother,
Joe Zimmerman, had a men's store in downtown Atlanta eponymous-
ly named Zimmerman's. On holidays and during the summers when
I was a teenager, Uncle Joe frequently brought me to his store to work,
helping people select shirts and ties and handling the cash register. A
large number of his clients were African-Americans. It was only years
later that I learned Zimmerman's was one of very few places in Atlanta
where African-Americans could try on clothes and get credit. When
my Uncle Joe passed away, Daddy King (Martin Luther King, Sr.)
preached the eulogy at his funeral at Congregation Shearith Israel, an
orthodox synagogue. This was in the early 1960s, and this event was
highly unusual, but it spoke volumes about my uncle and his relation
to the community. I am confident it played an indelible role in shaping
me and my commitment to civil rights and Black-Jewish relations.

When people visit the King National Historic Site, they see not only Dr. Martin Luther King, Jr.'s, Nobel Peace Prize, but also the shirt he wore the day he received it, with the Zimmerman's label on the inside of the collar.

From my teen years in youth groups until young adulthood, I was an active volunteer and expanded my contacts and commitment to Black-Jewish relations. The National Council of Jewish Women (NCJW) had several cultural enrichment projects in the inner-city schools, and I loved working there with black students.

My involvement in Andrew Young's campaign for mayor of Atlanta had another major impact on my work in this area. At the time, I was working closely in NCJW with my good friend, Fran Eizenstat, and her husband, my childhood friend, Stuart Eizenstat. Stuart was deeply involved in the campaign. While I have written details about this in my chapter on Politics and Advocacy, I want to mention here a moment at an NCJW national convention when then U.N. Ambassador Andrew Young spoke. There was a large delegation from Atlanta, and all of the delegates were in awe of his address. I raised my hand for personal privilege to speak and said, "If I knew how far your star would take you, instead of driving a car to bring people to vote for you for congress, I would have driven a bus." This just brought the whole house down at the convention.

Many years later, as I was retiring from AJC, I participated in an Atlanta Chamber of Commerce program titled Principal for a Day. I was assigned to Burgess-Peterson Elementary School and immediately bonded with their principal. The school is in the East Lake area of Atlanta, and the majority of the students are black. That one-day experience led to my reading to first graders and volunteering weekly at the school, an activity I continued for three years.

As I began to do research for my memoirs at the AJC office, I pulled out a multitude of files on Black-Jewish relations and became aware that we were approaching the 30th anniversary of the

Atlanta Black/Jewish Coalition. My attention turned to focusing on this and documenting the Coalition's history. No other city has had a successful Black-Jewish alliance sustained over thirty years with such an extensive amount of programming, interaction, and continued commitment and leadership.

It began with AJC's invitation to Black and Jewish leaders to meet on March 31, 1982, to discuss passage of the renewal of the Voting Rights Act. AJC leader, Cecil Alexander conducted the meeting at which Atlanta City Councilman John Lewis was the guest speaker. The congeniality among participants and enlightened, informative discussion led to an enthusiastic endorsement of our formalizing the group to work together on this specific issue. Cecil and John were asked to serve as co-chairmen, and the Atlanta Black/Jewish Coalition in Support of the Voting Rights Act was born.

In the following months, meetings were held with U.S. Senators Sam Nunn and Mack Mattingly, as well as editorial boards of the *Atlanta Journal and Constitution*, to advocate for the Voting Rights Act. After it was renewed, the group remained together under its new name, the Atlanta Black/Jewish Coalition.

A model was defined for the purpose of the coalition: it employed education, advocacy and action. Over the ensuing three decades, we continued to work together on the important local, national and international issues that faced our two communities. We frequently met at the Martin Luther King, Jr., Center for Nonviolent Social Change and worked together on King Week and Center activities.

The generous funding from AJC's Lois Frank and Terri and Mickey Lubin Atlanta Chapter Endowment Fund, for which I am so grateful, enabled the publication of *Atlanta Black/Jewish Coalition 30th Anniversary 1982-2012*; Diana Silverman was its editor. In the preface I noted how proud I was to have played a role in creating this coalition and providing staff support to it during my twenty five years at AJC.

Specific dates, issues and events recorded in this publication are highlighted in the Appendix. It describes our numerous actions and events, from crossing the Edmund Pettus Bridge in Selma with John Lewis in 1985 to our opposing the Voter I.D. Bill in 2005. However, it cannot convey the depth of the relationships that have continued through the decades, establishing historic bonds of friendship and alliances that have strengthened a wide array of initiatives and programs in our city. We have assembled to celebrate victories and have bonded at sad times in the lives of our members and community. Through differences of opinion, political preferences and challenges in our own community, we have maintained strong ties, mutual respect and shared values.

Stories of my involvement in the Black/Jewish Coalition, and my relationship with special people, programs, activities and advocacy that I have been engaged in permeate nearly every chapter of these memoirs.

## SPECIAL APPOINTMENTS

My work in the general community has given me some special opportunities to go beyond my traditional roles. When Mayor Andrew Young issued a proclamation announcing the dates of July 4, 1987, through June 30, 1988, as the official period of recognition of the City of Atlanta's sesquicentennial, I was asked to serve on the Steering Committee and co-chaired the Celebration Committee with Billye Aaron.

In 2003, after the death of two mayors who made major contributions to the city, Mayor Shirley Franklin asked me to serve on the Atlanta Advisory Commission to Honor the Legacies of Mayors Ivan Allen, Jr., and Maynard Holbrook Jackson, Jr., our first African-American mayor. The committee was co-chaired by A.D. "Pete" Correll and Jesse Hill, Sr. As a result of our deliberations, we renamed the Atlanta airport the Hartsfield-Jackson Atlanta International Airport.

In 2017, the City of Atlanta adopted a resolution that established the Task Force to Determine an Appropriate Manner to Honor Congressman John Lewis. I was proud to serve on this fourteen-member committee with Lois Frank.

## JOHN LEWIS

No chapter on Black-Jewish relations would be complete without additional words about my admiration for and relationship with Congressman John Lewis. My crossing the Edmund Pettus Bridge in Selma in 1985 for the 20th anniversary of the Voting Rights Act, participating in 1988 and 1993 for the reenactment of the March on Washington, and receiving honors from civil rights organizations over the years, all have John's mark on them.

I've described these events in my own words in an acceptance speech at Resurgens Atlanta, and in two articles in the *Atlanta Jewish Times*.

*Resurgens Atlanta Race Relations Award Acceptance Speech* - June 14, 1988

*I remember talking with Mike Gettinger, who for many years was the director of the Atlanta Jewish Federation. I told him I was going to work for the American Jewish Committee and that I felt as though I needed to wake up the following day with a degree in comparative religion and another in Middle East history.*

*Mike wisely advised me to take a deep breath and move into my new career studying my Jewish heritage. What wonderful advice. For I have learned that the more rooted I am in my own faith and community, the more I have to bring to the community at large. I'm thankful for the strength, inspiration and support I have received from the Jewish community and particularly from the American Jewish Committee.*

*I was given good advice from my former boss who advised me to identify a few mentors and listen to their advice and to identify an issue and make my mark in the community. Phoebe Franklin Lundeen was one of my mentors, and I think she would be especially proud of this award I have received today.*

*I started to work for AJC in the fall of 1980 and participated in the interfaith efforts to respond to Atlanta's murdered and missing children. I remember the emotional speeches given by AJC's Rabbi Marc Tanenbaum and Mayor Andy Young at the Christian Council Breakfast that spring. Rabbi Tanenbaum told the crowd that during the Holocaust Jewish babies were thrown into the air and shot like pigeons in rifle practice by the Nazis. He asked the audience, "Is there any doubt that Jews who suffered this pain from the murder of their children now share the pain with our black brothers and sisters who endure the murders of their children?"*

*Perhaps this message of "sharing the pain" is what separates people, cities and institutions. Atlanta has been a city where the pain of segregation and bigotry were to be overcome by courageous leaders and the creation of important organizations like Resurgens Atlanta.*

*Cecil Alexander has been one of Atlanta's courageous leaders and one of my special mentors. Not only did he help create Resurgens Atlanta, but he is a former President of AJC and helped us give birth to the Atlanta Black/Jewish Coalition.*

*Now completing our sixth year, the Coalition initiated by AJC continues to be a force for good in our city. I am indebted to the Coalition members and supporters who have joined with me in creating an organization that has shared the pain and the joy of events in our city and world over these past six years. You have taught me a great deal and my memories are very precious.*

*We marched in Selma, Alabama to celebrate the 20th Anniversary of the Voting Rights Act.*

*We marched in Forsyth County to speak out against racism and anti-Semitism which still flourish in our midst.*

*And when I marched in Washington, D.C., for Soviet Jewry and sang "We Shall Overcome" with 250,000 people assembled prior* to Gorbachev's summit meeting with Reagan, the song's verses had special meaning for me because we had sung it together in celebration of King Week, in rejecting bigotry in our midst and in praying for human rights and religious freedom for all of God's people.

I remember John Cox saying after several years of Coalition lunches, "I can't love those of you in this room any more, let's stop just talking to each other." And so we continue to spread this message and this year the Coalition has begun to bring black and Jewish youth together from NAACP and BBYO chapters. And new people continue to add their names to our rolls.

I have been especially pleased to receive calls from young and talented black leaders who are candidates for political office. They ask to meet with me and question me about the Jewish community, our issues and concerns, our leaders and organizations. Each time, I'm struck with their sincere interest and am confident they will continue to make Atlanta "a city too busy to hate" by their individual efforts to reach out and understand the entire community.

I love when they ask me the state of Black-Jewish relations in Atlanta. I proudly say it's the best in the country. Not because we always agree, but because we have people who care and are willing to share each other's pain and because we have structures in place to meet the challenges that face us individually and collectively.

I'm honored to be the recipient of Resurgens Atlanta's Race Relations Award and am deeply grateful to the AJC and the Black/Jewish Coalition who have made today possible for me.

September 9, 1988 *Atlanta Jewish Times*
*Let Freedom Ring... Reflections on the 25th Anniversary March*

The sun beat down on my shoulders as I marched amongst the crowds to the Lincoln Memorial. We all came to mark the 25th Anniversary of the Great March on Washington. I felt as though I could hear Dr. Martin Luther

King, Jr.'s, words "let freedom ring," as I kept pace with the crowd. Freedom rang all around me in songs and signs. The placards called for support of the ERA, jobs, peace, an end to apartheid, and protested racism in Japan.

Voices from past marches rang out from the podium and new voices with the promise of the future were heard. As an Atlantan, I felt a special pride listening and realizing how much leadership continues to flow from our city to all corners of our world with a message of hope and justice. And as a Jew, I felt a particular calling to be a part of this historic march and to continue to build upon ties between blacks and Jews.

Mayor Andrew Young presided over the program, charging us all to remember that one third of our citizens linger in poverty, not realizing Dr. King's dream.

A strong and passionate Congressman John Lewis called out to the crowd saying the time had come to stop spending money on missiles and bombs and start spending it on education, housing and health care. He noted that in these twenty-five years, we've witnessed a non-violent revolution of ideas and values and urged us not to oppress but to lift up, not to enslave but to set free.

As Congressman Lewis concluded his remarks, Hyman Bookbinder, the American Jewish Committee's former Washington Representative, leaned over to me in the beating sun and whispered, "it was just this hot twenty-five years ago when I sat here." Many like Bookbinder came back to "let freedom ring" with the stirring messages that pricked our nation's conscience and led to major political progress. Today, the message is clearly calling for more economic progress.

One of the most touching moments for me was when James Farmer, founder of CORE (Congress of Racial Equality), described where he was twenty-five years ago. "I was an involuntary guest of the state of Louisiana." He was in their jail and had to be taken out of town in a hearse in order to escape the lynch mob. But he and others in jail with him on August 28, 1963, listened with tear-filled eyes to Dr. King's speech on TV. He said, "our people were of all religions and colors, looking to find ourselves and define ourselves." He ended with a beautiful poem he wrote which asks, "Mirror, mirror, on the wall, what am I when I stand tall?" and concludes with "I won't let race define my soul." His words pierced my soul. Perhaps it was the reason we all came and marched. We want to be defined as more than our race, sex, or religion, but as people with a dream and the courage to act upon it.

Strong voices continued as the hours passed. Dr. Joseph Lowery noted that we had come to the seat of government and the center of this nation's conscience. He said, "new cashiers are needed in the bank of justice."

Coretta Scott King and her four children stood proudly before the crowd as a symbol of the future. Mrs. King steadfastly continues her husband's work and challenges us to awaken the slumbering conscience of this country. She called on us to work for women's rights until women are in decision-making places equal to their numbers in our population. She said, "we must dream of a nation which wages war against sickle-cell, AIDS, cancer and heart disease. This dream is not of utopia but is realistic for the wealthiest nation of this universe.

Governor Michael Dukakis told us we must march on and cited many issues we must work for. He said, "we must march on until racism, anti-Semitism and all forms of discrimination are banished from this land. We must march not only until Mandela is free, but until apartheid is dead and all of South Africa is free."

There was music and singing on this hot afternoon in

Washington. There were people of numerous ethnic and religious backgrounds among the crowd. There was frustration at the progress not yet made, but I felt that there was hope for what we could all do together if we care enough to listen to Dr. King's dream and make it our own. We must care enough to let freedom ring and exercise all the privileges and responsibilities we have living in this democratic nation. The hopes and promises of future generations are in our hands.

It was cold this past December when I went to Washington and marched on Freedom Sunday for Soviet Jews. The precious rights of free speech, religion, assembly, and petition of our government are denied to many people around the world. Congressman John Lewis raised his voice that day also and spoke for universal civil and human rights. Dr. King said it best when he said, "a threat to freedom anywhere is a threat to freedom everywhere."

And so I came back to Washington and marched in the August sun, just one more time, to hear freedom ring for all of God's children.

August 7, 1993 *Atlanta Jewish Times*
*I'll Keep Marching*

I remember feeling a bit self-conscious when we first started marching for Soviet Jewry. It was the early 1970s. There was the Russian circus, the ballet and other performing groups. We went from the Civic Center to the Fox and to the Omni. We wanted the media to see our signs "Let my people go" and we wanted the performers to see our leaflets urging one Soviet leader after another to stop harassing and detaining Soviet Jews.

I remember feeling resolute marching on the steps of the Georgia Capitol on behalf of Georgians for Religious Liberty. Together with a coalition of Christian clergy, civic and political leaders, we were fighting the teaching of creation science in Georgia schools and upholding the wall of separation between church and state.

I remember feeling frightened marching on the cold streets in Forsyth County lined with Ku Klux Klan members wearing hoods and robes. We were marching against fear and intimidation in the week following the violence and attack of civil rights activists who marched the week prior to mark Martin Luther King, Jr.'s, birthday.

I remember being overcome with tears marching in Selma, Ala., with Congressman John Lewis. Members of the Atlanta Black/Jewish Coalition participated in 1985 in the 20th anniversary of the Voting Rights Act. As we reached the crest of the Edmund Pettus Bridge, Congressman Lewis kneeled with Rabbi Alvin Sugarman to kiss the ground. What a sea change had occurred. The police were there to assist marchers. The world's press waited to greet Congressman Lewis rather than police dogs and fire hoses of 20 years earlier.

I remember feeling overcome with emotion, marching with a quarter million American Jews in 1987 on Freedom Sunday for Soviet Jewry. To hear and see Anatoly Shcharansky, and heroes of the refusenik movement was a day I shall never forget. We came to Washington just as U.S.S.R. leader Mikhail Gorbachev was coming to meet President Reagan.

I remember feeling excited marching in the heat in 1988 for the 25th anniversary of the March on Washington. Hearing Dr. King's "I Have a Dream" speech once again in the very spot he first delivered it was a thrill. AJC's Washington Representative, Hyman Bookbinder, and I sat in the VIP area. Bookie, as he is affectionately called, remembered the scene 25 years earlier when he heard Dr. King deliver this historic speech.

Bookie and I made a date to sit together again in 1993 for the 30th anniversary march. I'd never break a date with Bookie.

And so, once again I marched and created new memories.

Bookie brought a worn and faded banner he purchased at the 1963 march. Lois Frank, President of the American Jewish Committee's Atlanta Chapter and Immediate Past Co-chair of the Atlanta Black/Jewish Coalition joined Bookie and me in the VIP section.

The press has criticized this event in terms of numbers and diffuse message. I beg to differ. I think it's remarkable that 30 years after the "I Have a Dream" speech, 75,000-plus citizens traveled to the nation's capital to mark this milestone event in civil rights history. I heard loud and clear that we need more jobs for our citizens, less violence, support for the Brady Gun Control bill and healthcare for all. That message is cogent, relevant and urgent. I was proud that the Black/ Jewish Coalition responded to a quick call for help and underwrote the expenses of 30 Atlanta students at the march. I wonder why the press failed to report how mixed the crowd was racially and religiously. That too is a sign of our progress in civil rights. Bookie noted that no women spoke 30 years ago and half the speakers were women in the 1993 march. That is progress worth noting also.

I seem to feel the heat and the cold more these days, and surely I walk a bit slower. Yet anniversaries speak to me in special ways, and the cause of justice and freedom rouses me out of my complacency, and so I keep my marching, shoes at hand, ready to add new memories to my storehouse of special moments. Freedom needs exercise in words and actions.

We presented AJC's prestigious Atlanta Chapter Selig Distinguished Service Award to Congressman Lewis in May, 1995, on the occasion of the chapter's 50th anniversary.

Through the years, Congressman Lewis continued to demonstrate his support and connection to our Jewish community. This was evident in the invitation I received on January 23, 2004.

*Dear Sherry,*

*I want to invite you to serve on a Jewish Advisory Panel that I am forming through my Atlanta office. The purpose of the panel is to ensure strong communication between my office and Jewish organizations and congregations in my district.*

*As you know, I represent a large Jewish constituency and have always been supportive of the key issues in your community. I will continue to be supportive of Israel and the search for a just and secure peace in the Middle East in this heightened period of international terrorism and the rise of anti-Semitism. I also am concerned about the President's Faith Based Initiative and the need to maintain the wall of separation of church and state.*

*I look forward to working with you.*

*Sincerely,*

*John Lewis*

*Member of Congress*

On March 25, 2017, I had the privilege of presenting John to the NCJW at their national convention where he received their Human Rights Award.

*In 1985, in a smoke-filled room, a group of African-American influentials told City Councilman John Lewis to run for President of Atlanta City Council. They also told Georgia State Senator Julian Bond to run for the U.S. Congress. They didn't want to see, for the first time, two civil rights leaders running against one another. John Lewis' response was, "let the people decide." Throughout his life, John has fearlessly talked truth to power, and the people have decided. Yes, for 30 years and 15 elections, the people have decided that John Lewis is the person we want to represent us in Congress.*

*Through the summer months of his first campaign for Congress, his son, John Miles, spent weekends in my house while John and his late wife, Lillian, campaigned 24/7. John Miles and my son, Drew,* put up yard signs, handed out materials and celebrated their birthday together. We rode in our own special "freedom train," with hundreds of supporters from Atlanta to D.C. for John's swearing into office.

Relentlessly this amazing hero continues to speak truth to power. In 1982, he was the founding co-chairman of our Atlanta Black/Jewish Coalition, which continues to be an effective voice for justice in Atlanta. I fondly remember John joining us at the Black/ Jewish Young Leaders Retreat. Sometimes he walked in casually dressed in shirt and jeans. Other times he was dressed up in a tuxedo, coming from a dinner to benefit the LGBT community or environmental issues or labor relations.

As a freshman Congressman, John was a leader in support of Israel. When he traveled to the Soviet Union with his peers, he was told not to raise the issue of Soviet Jewry. In the Kremlin, John quoted from Martin Luther King's Letter from a Birmingham Jail, telling officials "why we can't wait" to free Soviet Jews. Once again speaking truth to power. Fearlessly facing opposition, he went to jail countless times for civil rights, but also for standing up against apartheid in South Africa and genocide in Darfur. He refused to participate in the Million Man March because of Minister Louis Farrakhan's anti-Semitic statements.

Justice often presents itself in unusual ways. My favorite for Congressman Lewis is his story about being denied a library card as a young boy in Alabama. Today his trilogy, March, has been on the New York Times bestsellers list for months and his most recent one has beat all past records as the top book sold by Amazon.

Can we all recall watching TV coverage of the late night sit-in John led in Congress, demanding a vote be taken on gun violence prevention? Once again daring to speak truth to power.

NCJW taught me, way back in the 60s, that one woman can make a difference. This wonderful organization gave me life skills to live a life of action and purpose.

You, my brother, John Lewis, the beloved conscience of the

*U.S. Congress, are my hero. You live every day proving that one person can truly make a difference. It is with great love and pride that I present you to Debbie Hoffman, President of NCJW, and to Nancy Kaufman, NCJW CEO, and Debbie and Nancy, thank you for the privilege of introducing John Lewis to the National Council of Jewish Women.*

A final personal reflection on my family's relationship to John Lewis: My children, Jacque, Laura and Jake, have all been influenced by my work in this area and our family connection to John, but Drew has been especially connected. In 1988, he introduced the Congressman to his classmates at The Epstein School. Almost thirty years later, as Davis Academy Associate Head of School and Principal, Drew introduced him to students, faculty and friends at a program and book signing. An *Atlanta Jewish Times* article about the event reported that Drew recalled working hard at age ten to get Lewis elected to Congress for the first time. But he was disappointed when Lewis chose to walk to his victory celebration rather then ride in the waiting limousines. Drew was quoted as saying, "John never stops marching."

Over the 2016 spring school break, Drew, his wife, Jana, and their sons, Jordan and Peyton, visited the Congressman in his Washington, D.C., office and attended the congressional screening of his film, *John Lewis: Get In The Way.*

I sincerely believe that if this country is not safe for African-Americans, it will not be safe for Jews either. This guided my work as a young adult involved in NCJW's community service projects in the inner city and continued through my twenty five years at AJC. It is still important to me today and is especially enhanced by my personal bond with Congressman John Lewis and members of our Black/Jewish Sisters Group, whom I have written about in my chapter on Women's Issues.

Congressman
John Lewis
at the Project
Understanding
Young Leaders'
Retreat, 1993

Black/Jewish Coalition's book signing for Congressman
Lewis' *Walking With the Wind*,
(L-R) Ingrid Saunders Jones, Lillian Lewis, Coretta
Scott King, Miles and Elaine Alexander, 1998

Poster at John
Lewis book
signing

Sherry Frank with Cecil Alexander and John Lewis at Edmund
Pettus Bridge March in Selma, Alabama, 1986

# INTERETHNIC RELATIONS

OUR DIVERSITY IS OUR STRENGTH

*Our ability to reach unity in diversity will be the
beauty and the test of our civilization.*

—Mahatma Gandhi

Building bridges of understanding between various communities throughout the United States is a hallmark of the AJC. In the early decades, this work was primarily directed at the religious denominations within Christianity. Major accomplishments were celebrated in Catholic relations, culminating in Vatican Council II and the release of *Nostra Aetate* on October 28, 1965. As America became more religiously diverse, AJC's interfaith work expanded to include new and growing religious communities.

Accompanying these changes, ethnic communities grew as well and expanded across our country. In Atlanta, the number of consular offices increased to serve the needs of their emerging constituencies as well as the significant business and political interests of these groups.

For decades, the Atlanta Chapter had been involved in civil rights and Black-Jewish relations. Then, in 1980, we established an Ethnic Committee to explore coalition efforts with some newer groups. A couple of minor events were held with the Greek community, and limited outreach was initiated to identify the Arab-Christian community.

The focus soon turned to the Hispanic community, where numbers were increasing at a dramatic pace. The Mexican Consulate office in Atlanta was a noteworthy and important participant in intergroup relations. They were an influential voice on social justice and legal issues, and we enjoyed close ties with them. As national Hispanic organizations opened offices in Atlanta, we worked in tandem with them through networking and on legislative issues.

The Latin American Association (LAA) became our partner in a wide array of endeavors over the decades. Meetings were devoted to getting to know one another and learn about issues facing our respective communities. We advocated regularly during the Georgia General Assembly on public policy particularly opposing "English Only" bills. We co-sponsored political forums and held sessions on advocacy skills, public relations, immigration, and acculturation.

The chapter provided outreach to Asian leaders, particularly within the Chinese, Indian, and Korean communities. I have included a chronology of our major activities in the area of interethnic relations in the Appendix to demonstrate AJC's strong, sustained, and informed commitment to the work that we embrace. Three detailed examples of our timely and unique initiatives follow.

## RODNEY KING VERDICT AND KOREAN OUTREACH

Riots broke out in Los Angeles following the April 29, 1992, verdict in the Rodney King case. More than fifty deaths occurred, and the destruction and property damage was staggering. In Atlanta, some African-Americans attacked Korean-owned businesses near the Atlanta University campus. On May 4, at Mayor Maynard Jackson's request, AJC brought the religious and ethnic communities together for a press conference in response to the violence.

Mayor Jackson, we of the American Jewish Committee come here today with the support of many others to offer you our praise for a job well done by you and the Atlanta police and support your decision to contain the unrest in our city and at the Atlanta University campus.

Over the past five days, we have witnessed a tragedy with the loss of lives, injuries, the loss of jobs, as well as up-wards of a billion-dollar loss of property. Even the innocent bystander has been drawn into the conflict. Think of how much good a billion dollars could have done if earmarked for assistance to the disadvantaged.

We stand here today, now, Jew, Christian, Asian, Hispanic, white and black, in solidarity and support for the black com-munity, the students of Atlanta University and the disadvan-taged and disenfranchised of Atlanta. We must find answers.

Out of this chaos and destruction we must create an opportu-nity and go beyond rhetoric and not allow yet again the return to "business as usual" attitude as the embers of the fire grow dim.

We pledge to you as mayor to work as a community to find tangible solutions to the unmet needs and rage that exists in our community.

When I reported to Morton Yarmon, AJC national staff, on June 5, 1992, I elaborated on the press conference as well as additional calls for our help in intergroup relations.

*I hope this is helpful to you in developing the next* Insiders Letter.

*As soon as the Rodney King verdict was announced, we reached out to Mayor Maynard Jackson on behalf of the Atlanta Black/Jewish Coalition, which we initiated in 1982 and continue to staff. On Thursday, April 30th, we asked him to let us know how we could be helpful to him. On Friday, May 1st, the day after the rioting in Atlanta, the Mayor told me that he would welcome some statements of support from the community's religious leaders.*

*We reached out to numerous agencies and religious and ethnic groups. We were overwhelmed with the crowd of 100 leaders who came together to denounce the violence and pledge our support to the city and our commitment to meet the needs in the population which precipitated, in part, the violence.*

*Richard Cohen, Atlanta Chapter President, and Tommy Dortch, the Black/Jewish Coalition Co-chair, ran the press conference. Speakers at the press conference included the Mayor, Eldrin Bell, Chief of Police, and Congressman John Lewis. Most of the members of the Atlanta City Council attended. Other speakers included representatives of the following: Georgia State Human Relations Commission; 100 Black Men; Christian Council of Metropolitan Atlanta; The Korean Association of Greater Atlanta; Atlanta Interfaith Coalition.*

*Acknowledged in the crowd were representatives of the Atlanta Jewish Federation, Atlanta Rabbinical Association, ADL, 100 Black Women, Concerned Black Clergy, Atlanta Presbytery, Atlanta Catholic Archdiocese, National Council of Jewish Women, the Baha'i faith, Martin Luther King, Jr., Center, Georgia Power, the Korean business community, judges, and members of the Georgia Legislature.*

*We had broad pickup on radio, TV, the Jewish press and the Atlanta Journal-Constitution.*

*At the press conference, the Korean community asked us to meet with their leaders. They told us they felt they could learn a great deal from the Jewish community. They invited us to be their guests for dinner on May 18th. This was an exciting evening for all of us and only the first step towards working together.*

Another report I wrote on May 18 recapped our meetings with Korean and Jewish leaders.

*Following a major press conference initiated by AJC at the request of Mayor Maynard Jackson on May 4, 1992, in which nearly all ethnic and religious groups in the city were represented, a member of the Korean Community, Mr. Young Kang, called the AJC office to request a meeting. He invited AJC leaders to meet with leaders from the Korean community over supper on May 18th. Ten representatives from AJC were joined by ten Koreans representing, among others, their Chamber of Commerce, newspapers, the Grocers' Association, the Democratic Party, Community Relations Committee, and Community Service Center.*

*The meeting began with introductions around the table and then the meeting was turned over to Dr. Lee, a physician turned community activist. Dr. Lee stated that they, as a community, were deeply troubled by the conflicts they were experiencing with minorities (Blacks) and were seeking advice from the Jewish community. He then shared some insights about Korean history, citing the German and Japanese goals to control the world. He equated the torment by the Japanese of Koreans with treatment by the Germans of the Jews. The Korean leaders, however, did not publicize their plight as did the Jewish leaders. He told us that during World War II, the Japanese took 30,000-40,000 Korean girls for "recreation." There is the feeling that the Korean immigrants in the United states are following in Jewish footsteps as they buy grocery stores, shoe repair shops, and jewelry stores around the country. Great anger was expressed in describing the fate of many of these shop owners during the riots in Los Angeles and Atlanta, when according to their account, police waited just outside the "square shaped area" in which the rioting occurred. They complained of calling 911 while trapped inside their stores and waiting one hour for a response.*

*The Koreans expressed the sentiment that they sense they have the support of the people in general, but they want to know how to overcome the violence in many of the people they face everyday. When asked if they had done anything in the area of community relations in those neighborhoods, they responded that they came to this country to succeed, and in their businesses the focus is on long hours of hard work with no real thought to community relations. They cited the language and the tall cultural wall which exists between the two communities as real barriers for them. They implored their Jewish guests to tell them what they had done wrong. Incident after incident was described illustrating their vulnerability to crime in the neighborhoods where their shops are.*

*Some of the AJC members spoke of Jewish shop owners understanding the need to become a part of the neighborhood by hiring young people from the neighborhood, contributing to neighborhood causes and generally showing an interest in the folks who live there.*

*The Koreans conceded that, having come to this country after the Civil Rights Era (1969-70s), the problems are more socio-economic than racial. Many in the Black community see the Koreans as taking opportunities away from them.*

*There were questions about the media and some of the distortions which occurred. We suggested that there were more effective approaches than glaring press conferences, including quiet meetings with editorial boards, etc., to express concerns and opinions.*

*There is a Korean community of about 30,000 in Atlanta. The leadership with whom we met expressed a strong desire to have an ongoing dialogue with us. All participants seemed genuinely pleased with the exchanges of the evening and were eager to meet again.*

In 1992, I was already heavily involved in the development of the Atlanta Interfaith Coalition. The riots spurred us past the talking and organizing stage and into action.

The greatest effort in this period took place within the Black/Jewish Coalition. The unrest was a priority topic of discussion at our steering committee meeting on May 12. At the Coalition's 10th anniversary event on May 20, we hosted Gary Rubin, AJC's National Affairs Director, and Milton Morris, Vice President of Research at the Joint Center for Political and Economic Studies, Washington D.C., who both spoke on the topic "Blacks and Jews: Shaping a National Urban Agenda."

On August 26, 1993, Lois Frank hosted and Kent Alexander chaired a program on political issues and advocacy for Korean leaders, featuring three Jewish members of the Georgia General Assembly. It is interesting to note that as a result of the Rodney King verdict and our meetings with Korean leaders, we helped them connect with influential members of the African-American community to develop a dialogue. Relations developed between these groups, and trips to South Korea followed.

As I continued to extend our interethnic outreach, I received a call from a leader in the Indian-American community asking us to meet with them for help on naming a street for Mahatma Mohandas Gandhi. It is a great satisfaction that we have been provided with many opportunities for bridge building, such as this one, because the AJC is held in such high respect.

INSTITUTE OF ETHNIC AWARENESS

We implemented AJC's commitment to learn about and increase our effectiveness working with Atlanta's growing ethnic communities by creating the "Institute of Ethnic Awareness." The following press release, on September 27, 1995, summarizes the project.

The American Jewish Committee, Atlanta Chapter, has, with a grant from Atlanta's Jewish Federation, created a new and exciting program for leaders in Atlanta's Jewish community. "The Institute of Ethnic Awareness" has been designed to enable Jewish leadership to gain knowledge and understanding of the other major ethnic communities which help to make up the ethnic diversity which has expanded so dramatically in Atlanta in recent years.

The Institute will bring participants to sites within each of the five ethnic communities selected, to meet with their leaders, learn about their respective institutions, communal issues and general demographic profiles. The opening session will provide an overview of the multi-ethnic city Atlanta has become and its evolution to this point. The Institute will meet in six sessions, once a month, beginning in October with members of the Latin American, Indian, Korean and Chinese communities.

Participants in the Institute will be selected through an application process. The opportunity to be a part of this very informative program is open to leaders and emerging leaders in all organizations, institutions and agencies in Atlanta's Jewish community.

Project co-chairs, Larry Appel and Ray Ann Kremer, wrote to the AJC Board and ACCESS Steering Committee: "It is our sincere belief that those who become involved in the 'Institute of Ethnic Awareness' will not only bring back to the Jewish community a new and broader insight into the potential for involvement, but will gain tremendous personal enrichment from the opportunity to meet and build relationships with people of different ethnic backgrounds. These individuals, like members of the Jewish community, have a rich heritage and a strong cultural identity which they value and which influences their lives."

The Institute opened with the topic of the demographics of Atlanta's growing ethnically diverse population, presented by Dr. Arthur

Murphy, Chair of the Department of Anthropology at Georgia State University. Each of the six sessions was held at culturally or religiously significant places within the respective communities. Two sessions covered the Hispanic community, one on the Mexican community and one on all of the other Spanish-speaking countries with large populations in Atlanta. The Indian, Korean, and Chinese were the focus of additional sessions. Every session included ethnic food representative of the respective culture. Participants enjoyed a bus tour that included major points of interest to the Asian and Hispanic communities.

Believing that lasting relationships can be built when both communities learn from and find ways to support one another, AJC planned follow-up programs to help expose ethnic leaders to our Jewish community, religious structure, organizations, and issues. We hosted a dinner at the Selig Center (Atlanta Jewish Federation) and included a tour of the William Breman Jewish Heritage Center. In keeping with our tradition of serving ethnic food, our dinner menu included knishes, kugel, roast chicken, tzimmes, and strudel. (Perhaps newer to our visitors than their food was to us.)

As a result of information obtained from a questionnaire distributed at this dinner, another meeting was held with specific agency leaders and staff. It was interesting to learn what they wanted to know about the services we provided that would be helpful in their efforts to respond to the needs of their respective communities. Most were curious to know how we used volunteers and how we accessed state and federal funds for direct services. The Indian community wanted to know more about programs for the elderly, not direct services. They had brought their parents to Atlanta and felt responsible for keeping them occupied and stimulated while they, the community leaders, were at work. A workshop featuring staff from Jewish Family and Career Services addressed many of these issues. Useful materials were distributed and networking opportunities continued after the session.

January 26, 1996  *Atlanta Jewish Times*
*Strength in Numbers: Atlanta's Jewish organizations forge relationships with other ethnic community leaders*
*by Melanie A. Lasoff*

When the Georgia legislature introduced a bill two years ago that required all children to have social security numbers to be in school, Maritza Keen of the Latin American Association was upset. The bill would have discriminated against immigrants, Ms. Keen believed, because social security numbers are only issued to U.S. citizens.

Ms. Keen, whose agency provides assistance to Atlanta's Hispanics, wanted to challenge the bill. But she needed some support. So she called her friend, Sunny Stern, assistant Southeast director of the American Jewish Committee, to generate a group that would testify against the legislation. "There's strength in numbers," says Ms. Keen.

Larry Appel, an AJC board member, joined Ms. Keen before the State Senate Education Committee to speak against the proposal. It was defeated. Ms. Keen says the presence of another Community at the committee meeting showed officials that the issue concerned more than a single ethnic group.

"The only way we are going to be strong and build public policy in our interests is to form coalitions and bring people together," she says.

When members of ethnic groups forge relationships, they strengthen the entire Atlanta community, organization leaders say. And many turn to the Jewish community because it is well-organized and established.

"If this is an international city, we can only all benefit from really getting to know each other and not confining our activities to our own quadrant of the city," Ms. Keen says.

In another example of such teamwork, the AJC, a national

organization to protect the right of Jews, joined hands with members of Atlanta's Korean community after Los Angeles police officers were found innocent of beating Black motorist Rodney King in 1993. Some Korean Atlantans worried that their small businesses would be looted by outraged Blacks.

Korean leaders and representatives from the AJC, and other groups, held a press conference stressing ethnic unity, says Ms. Stern. The event helped allay the Koreans' fears, she says.

Sometimes professional relationships between ethnic representatives become friendships. That's what happened between Ms. Keen of the Latin American Association and Ms. Stern, who met during a Leadership Atlanta conference in 1991. Since then, Ms. Keen says she often solicits the AJC for advice on immigrant issues, such as overcoming language barriers and finding access to services.

The Indian community looks to emulate Atlanta Jews, says Subash Razdan, of the National Federation of Indian-American Associations. When ethnic groups interact, members discover similarities, he says. "Our problems are very similar," Mr. Razdan says, citing discrimination, prejudice, and mixed-marriage.

The Indian community in Atlanta hopes to continue building a relationship with area Jews, he says. "The Jewish group has outstanding connections, and we would like to draw on their strengths."

Ms. Keen, Mr. Razdan and others hope to expand their relationships with local Jews by participating in the AJC's Institute of Ethnic Awareness. During six monthly programs, which end in March, up to 25 Atlanta Jews share a meal native to an ethnic community and listen to speakers discuss their national culture, politics, and Atlanta involvement. Participants have met with members of the Latin

American and Indian communities, and planned events with Chinese and Korean representatives.

"It's important for the Jewish community, as a minority community, to recognize we're not alone," says Mr. Appel of the AJC. "The greater community benefits if the parts understand each other and work together."

Mr. Razdan says he looks forward to more opportunities to work with the Jewish community.

"There is strength in diversity," he says. "The different cultures each have different treats, different things to offer. We can learn from each other."

## GEORGIA INTERETHNIC COALITION

On January 22, 2003, AJC gathered leaders of a large number of ethnic groups to a luncheon meeting to form the Georgia Interethnic Coalition and develop its mission statement and goals. The impetus for this was sparked in the fall of 2002 with a hugely successful screening of the film "What's Cooking?" The film tells the story of four families, living in the same neighborhood, preparing for Thanksgiving dinner. The audience enjoyed film, food, and discussion, and left with a desire for more formalized and continuing interaction.

The Coalition's first formal gathering received generous media coverage.

April 9, 2003 *Atlanta Journal-Constitution*
*Curious About Cultures: New Interethnic Coalition picks Indians as starter*
*by Rick Badie*

A coalition seeking to link metro Atlanta's diverse cultures has chosen Indian-Americans as its inaugural community to study.

The Georgia Interethnic Coalition, a months-old group, is hosting its first event Thursday night, and metro Atlanta's 50,000 or so Indian-Americans will be the topic of discussion. The event is set for 6:30 p.m. at the Palace Restaurant in Norcross.

A panel discussion will be led by Jagdish Sheth, a marketing professor at Emory University; Beheruz Sethna, president of the State University of West Georgia; and Samar Mira, a retired Emory professor.

The coalition grew out of a holiday feast hosted by the Southeastern office of the Atlanta-based American Jewish Committee.

The event, held Nov. 13 at the Woodruff Arts Center, drew 300 African-Americans, Jewish and non-Jewish whites, Asians, and others who dined together, then saw "What's Cooking?" a comedy-drama about four diverse middle-class Los Angeles families who gather to celebrate Thanksgiving.

Sherry Frank, who oversees the American Jewish Committee, used the event to launch the coalition. Its mission: to build relations among ethnic communities, resolve issues and learn about one another. The group, with a 200-person mailing list, hopes to expose members to a different immigrant group every other month.

"We're at an embryo stage," Frank said, "but it's exciting. We want to go out in the community and experience the Indian-American community, the Chinese community, the Hispanic community, and the Black community."

There's territory aplenty to cover. The 2000 census says Georgia's Latino population shot up 300 percent in the 1990s. About 435,000 Latinos live in the state. Asians, meanwhile, saw their numbers increase 135 percent statewide during the same period; about 173,000 live in Georgia. A majority of the newcomers settled in metro Atlanta.

But little, generally, is known about immigrants such as south Asians, said Amitabh Sharma, a Stone Mountain resident who runs a software company. He called the coalition a "step in the right direction for people to learn about a rich heritage and culture that needs to be understood and comprehended."

"We have very much in common with America," said Sharma, who devotes time to "propagate the right tenets of the culture."

"We believe the world is one common village," he continued, "and that there should be a lot of brotherhood, love and compassion."

Narender G. Reddy, a Duluth commercial Realtor and Republican activist, called the coalition one avenue to end the "self-imposed segregation" often practiced by ethnic groups as they "preserve their own cultures."

Besides learning about the life of immigrants, Frank wants the coalition to foster change, "a great example being the way Blacks and Jews are working on the Georgia flag issue."

The April 10, 2003, inaugural dinner was the prelude to a host of activities. In ensuing years, varied programs were presented, dialogue groups were formed, and political forums and voter registration drives were held. Significant relationships were created and existing ones were strengthened. AJC continued to provide staff while lay leaders guided the work of this Coalition.

Along with Atlanta's dramatic population growth, diverse ethnic communities were increasing in numbers, and additional consulate offices were opening. When I retired in 2006, the Consul General of India serving the entire Southeast was stationed in Houston. Today there is an additional consulate in Atlanta. Following a tradition of the Indian Embassy in Washington, D.C., that co-hosts a *Hanukkah* celebration with AJC, this event is now an annual AJC-India Consulate reception in Atlanta, bringing leaders of our two communities together in a pleasant social evening.

Jews are accustomed to reading the *Haggadah* at our Passover Seders. Through these pages, we retell the story of the Jews' exodus from slavery in Egypt to freedom. Interspersed with text and prayers, this narrative uplifts us spiritually.

*America's Table®: A Thanksgiving Reader* was created by AJC recognizing a need for spirituality and togetherness following the terrorist attacks of September 11, 2001. Over the years it has been incorporated by many as a holiday ritual that helps all Americans find common ground in a world where divisiveness too often takes center stage.

An annual Atlanta tradition began in 2003, when AJC first hosted a pre-Thanksgiving luncheon at which *America's Table®* was read. Congressman John Lewis was our co-sponsor in the first few years. Ethnic and religious leaders and a large representation of Atlanta's Consular Corps attended this luncheon.

The reader was published by AJC until 2011, in cooperation with numerous national civic, religious, and ethnic organizations. It highlighted the struggles and journey of diverse populations trying to obtain the safety and freedom of America. In 2005, *The New York Times* printed the America's Table Reader® in its entirety.

I brought the reader to an elementary school classroom and had students discuss it. One particular edition included Reverend Dr. Gerald Durley's story. He read it with great enthusiasm at our crowded pre-Thanksgiving luncheon. AJC continued bringing together interfaith and interethnic leaders and members of the Consular Corps at Thanksgiving events for several years after this publication was discontinued.

## PROJECT INTERCHANGE

Through the decades, the Atlanta Chapter has strengthened its ties with a wide range of ethnic leaders, inviting them to participate in AJC's Project Interchange. This institute provides valuable educational seminars in Israel encouraging influential leaders to build understanding of and support for Israel. In addition, this AJC Institute extends the same experience to national and international movers and shakers from a wide variety of disciplines including, religion, civic, political, academic, media and the diplomatic corps.

Black/Jewish Coalition Co-chairs Lois Frank and Tommy Dortch speak at press conference after Rodney King verdict, Atlanta City Hall, 1992

# ATLANTA JEWISH FILM FESTIVAL

## BUILDING BRIDGES OF IDENTITY AND
## UNDERSTANDING THROUGH FILM

*Film as dream, film as music. No art passes our conscience
in the way film does, and goes directly to our feelings,
deep down into the dark rooms of our souls.*

—Ingmar Bergman

In 1994, the Atlanta Chapter marked its 50th anniversary. We began a year-long celebration with the *50th Anniversary Film Series* by screening one film from each of the Chapter's five decades. For several years leading up to this anniversary, AJC had hosted successful Jewish film screenings and discussions, and there was a lot of enthusiasm and support as celebration plans developed.

*Press Release: American Jewish Committee 50th Anniversary Film Series*

The American Jewish Committee is proud to present, in honor of its 50th Anniversary year in Atlanta, an innovative Jewish Film Series which will explore the Jewish image in American film through each of the agency's five decades. A discussion will follow each film session.

The series begins on October 13th with "Gentleman's

Agreement," starring Gregory Peck in the classic exploration of anti-Semitism in America. The discussion facilitator will be Janice P. Alper, Executive Director, Jewish Educational Services. On November 2nd, the feature will be "Marjorie Morningstar," the first film to focus on a young Jewish woman and an upper middle-class milieu. The discussion facilitator will be Deborah Goldstein, Director of Judaic Studies, Atlanta Jewish Community Center. On December 14th, "The Fixer" will explore the unjust imprisonment of a Jewish handyman in turn-of-the-century Russia. Facilitating the discussion will be Rabbi Shalom Lewis of Congregation Etz Chaim. "Hester Street" will be the January 3rd film, which looks at the experience of Russian Jewish immigrants on the Lower East Side. Steve Chervin, Director of Jewish Continuity for the Atlanta Jewish Federation, will lead the discussion. The final program on January 31st, "Crimes and Misdemeanors," deals with American Jews grappling with their own identity and the concepts of guilt and atonement. Rabbi Ilan Feldman of Congregation Beth Jacob will be the discussion leader.

This Film Series and the Jewish Communal Affairs Committee are chaired by Cathy Selig and Robbie Kremer. The 50th Anniversary Committee chairs are Linda Selig and Dr. Arnold Rubenstein.

The film series was so well received that it became an annual AJC event. In 1997, 1998, and 1999, The Temple joined AJC as a co-sponsor and series host. With each ensuing year, the audience continued to grow, and space quickly became an issue.

At the same time as Atlanta was experiencing success with its series, Jewish film festivals were becoming popular across North America, and other cities began sponsoring similar community-wide events. Chapter board member Cookie Shapiro, a film enthusiast, had attended the *San Francisco Jewish Film Festival* and was convinced this was a project Atlanta would embrace.

Atlanta Chapter's membership had reached 2,000, the largest in the country, and new ideas for programming in all areas were being sought to serve our expanding numbers. I remember telling Cookie that if she wanted to develop a Jewish film festival, she should go out and raise the money to hire additional staff to support it. Cookie did just that. With a supportive lay leadership and a healthy dose of determination, she set about raising funds and serving as chairperson of the festival. Thanks to initial support from corporations, foundations, and individual donors, the Atlanta Chapter hired Candy Berman's firm, A New Angle, to staff our first festival. Judy Marx, AJC's Assistant Area Director, became its coordinator.

Over the next two years, committees met to screen films, develop materials, and recruit volunteers. Many other related activities followed at a hectic pace as excitement grew throughout the community for this ambitious undertaking.

Joey Reiman offered the creative genius of his firm, BrightHouse, to help imagine the breadth of the festival and envision the logo and tagline for it. The iconic director's chair became the graphic image of the soon-to-be-launched 2000 Atlanta Jewish Film Festival (AJFF). *Not Just Another Night at the Movies* was the selected tagline. AJC's 1999 executive summary describes the film festival's scope and its initial goals.

> *The American Jewish Committee, Atlanta Chapter, is initiating a major community program for the year 2000. AJC will join the circuit of over 35 communities that now host city-wide Jewish film festivals. The ATLANTA JEWISH FILM FESTIVAL (AJFF) will showcase films that impart Jewish values, contemplate Jewish issues, and explore Jewish themes. Through viewing and discussing these films, we will explore universal themes that impact the total community, such as immigration, identity, prejudice, and ritual.*

*AJFF will strive to strengthen our community's consciousness of Jewish culture, identity, history, and values. The organizers hope to provide a dynamic forum for the community to engage in dialogue with the filmmakers, actors, directors, and other artisans who create and influence films with Jewish content. This event will strive to promote awareness, appreciation, and pride in the diversity of the Jewish people. The goals of AJFF are to:*

- *Create an awareness and appreciation of Jewish film*
- *Reach out to unaffiliated Jews in metropolitan Atlanta*
- *Collaborate with Jewish and arts organizations for sponsorship and promotion*
- *Educate audiences on Jewish issues*
- *Attract demographically diverse communities outside the Jewish community*
- *Enhance Jewish life in Atlanta*

*The ATLANTA JEWISH FILM FESTIVAL will be a community-wide celebration, lasting eight days, showcasing 20 films that highlight diverse cultural, ethnic, and religious experiences. It will reflect the broader human relations mission of the AJC, supporting its goal of nurturing pluralism and building bridges of understanding. In order to attract audiences from the entire Atlanta metropolitan area, AJFF films will be shown at theaters throughout Fulton, DeKalb, Gwinnett, and Cobb counties as well as in the City of Atlanta.*

*The Atlanta Chapter of the American Jewish Committee, the Southeast's premier human relations organization, is extremely proud to be producing Atlanta's first-ever Jewish film extravaganza. With support from local philanthropic foundations and corporations, the ATLANTA JEWISH FILM FESTIVAL will be a major success and an annual cultural event in our community.*

Strobe lights and a red carpet imbued an atmosphere of

glamour and importance to the Opening Night Gala of the AJFF at the Woodruff Arts Center's Rich Auditorium on October 29, 2000. Jason Alexander's comedy film, *Just Looking*, made its southeastern premiere. After the showing, screenwriter Marshall Karp and actor Rick Licata responded to the film's premise and held a discussion with audience members. The program for the evening listed Jane Fonda as Honorary Festival Chairperson, Jason Alexander as Honorary Gala Chairperson and Director of *Just Looking*, Cookie Shapiro as AJFF Chairperson, and Cathy Selig and Michael Coles as Gala Chairpersons. Producers were BrightHouse, Delta, Salomon Smith Barney, Robinson Humphrey, The Coca-Cola Company, Arthur M. Blank Family Foundation, Harry Norman Realtors, Ketchum, and the Rich Foundation.

AJC Chapter President, Buck Goldstein, and AJFF Chairperson, Cookie Shapiro, provided the welcome in the Program Guide.

> *Welcome to the premiere of the Atlanta Jewish Film Festival. Comedies, dramas, documentaries, animation, and shorts… our inaugural year has it all. "Not just another night at the movies" is our tag-line and our pledge to every festival movie-goer.*
>
> *For more than two years, members of the American Jewish Committee's (AJC) Atlanta Chapter have been engaged in raising funds, screening films, recruiting volunteers, and developing public relations materials in an effort to bring the best ever film festival to Metro Atlanta. The Atlanta Jewish Film Festival (AJFF) takes the broad human relations mission of the AJC, nurturing pluralism and building bridges of understanding, and brings it to the big screen for your exploration and enjoyment. The films selected for the AJFF offer universal appeal in a thought-provoking manner while representing a diverse cinematic experience through a variety of Jewish themes.*
>
> *Film has an unparalleled immediacy and vibrancy and captures a wonderful range of languages and stories. Each of the twenty-three films from nine countries are creative and dynamic in themselves.*

*Together, the AJFF films of 2000 are guaranteed to inform, entertain, encourage lively discussion, and allow for personal reflection.*

*Films such as the powerful* Chronicle of Love, *the hilarious* Just Looking, *the innovative* Genesis, *the stunning* Soleil *with Sophia Loren, and the Academy-Award-winning* The Personals *offer unique opportunities to consider our past and contemplate our future in the dawn of the 21st century. Many of the artists, producers, directors, and writers will share personal stories expressing their works of art from the inside.*

*We appreciate the support we received from our generous sponsors who put their faith in the AJC's ability to produce this top-quality festival. We look forward to greeting you personally throughout the Atlanta Jewish Film Festival.*

The reception for that initial festival was a harbinger of the success that was to come. In addition to the Rich Auditorium, films were screened at AMC Mansell Crossing, AMC Phipps Plaza, and the Selig Center. The audience was asked to judge films, and the feature, documentary, and short receiving the highest marks were brought back for an awards event at a post-festival screening. From the beginning, an ACCESS night for young adults was an integral part of the festival.

Early on, Kenny Blank transitioned from being a member of the film screening committee to a member of the staff and ultimately became the festival's Executive Director. Staff size increased in response to the development, program, communications, and technology needs of the festival. A greater number of venues was required as the AJFF strived to reach a broader audience representing Atlanta's growing Jewish community and, because of repeated requests, to show films multiple times.

The size of the audience became larger every year, as did the number of films. Dynamic and thought-provoking speakers and panelists, including actors, directors, and community celebrities and specialists, added greatly to the film experience. In the early years, there were special screenings during school hours, and black and Jewish middle school and high school students were brought together for film and discussion. Russian and Yiddish films were scheduled for Soviet Jewish seniors who were bussed from their housing units to share lunch, film, and camaraderie.

The Opening Night Gala attendance quickly outgrew the Woodruff Arts Center, and we relocated it first to the Fox Theatre, and ultimately to the Cobb Energy Center. Closing night also expanded beyond theater capacity and soon required two screenings at the Rich Auditorium. By 2016, closing night was so well subscribed that it was held at Symphony Hall at the Woodruff Arts Center. In 2018, both opening and closing nights were held at the Cobb Energy Center to accommodate the large audiences.

In recent years, movie theaters began renovating and seating capacity was reduced. At the same time, the complex City Springs was being built and included the Sandy Springs Performing Arts Center with seating capacity of over 1,000 in its Byers Theatre. The 2019 AJFF held a large number of screenings in this new, impressive, state-of-the art facility. Additional screenings were held around Metro Atlanta.

The Atlanta Chapter continued to provide a significant amount of lay and staff leadership, time, financial support, and office space to the AJFF. As the festival concluded in 2014, talks were underway regarding the future of the AJC's involvement in the AJFF. The Marcus Foundation provided funds to hire a consultant to evaluate the festival's future needs. Numerous focus groups met, and individual interviews were conducted with various community stakeholders. As a result of this comprehensive evaluation, in 2014, AJC and AJFF drafted an agreement that enabled AJFF to establish operational, financial, and artistic independence.

*Atlanta Jewish Film Festival Becomes Independent as New Arts Non-Profit*
*AJFF Will Continue Partnership With Founder, American Jewish Committee*

*Atlanta – September 18, 2014 – The Atlanta Jewish Film Festival (AJFF), and its founder American Jewish Committee Atlanta (AJC), announced the festival's independence as a new non-profit arts organization. The new entity officially became operational effective August 1, 2014, after AJC Atlanta's board unanimously voted to ratify a mutual agreement to establish AJFF as a separate 501(c)(3) organization. This milestone decision will allow AJFF to operate as an autonomous arts and cultural institution, while continuing an active partnership with American Jewish Committee Atlanta, which founded the film festival as an advocacy project some 14 years ago. AJFF Executive Director Kenny Blank will remain at the helm of the new organization, after leading AJFF through ten years of extraordinary growth.*

*"Every year, AJFF sets the highest standards for showcasing outstanding world cinema and a first-class audience experience," said Blank. "Our newfound independence puts AJFF squarely in the marketplace of other great Atlanta arts institutions and international film festivals, and best positions us to explore future programming opportunities."*

*AJC and AJFF will continue to collaborate around areas of joint interest, including utilizing the festival as a platform for dialogue among ethnic, religious, and national communities. "AJC is proud of how the film festival has evolved," said AJC Atlanta's Regional Director Dov Wilker. "With its day-to-day operations supported by a new entity, AJFF will continue to be a gift to our community. Meanwhile, AJC will continue to focus on its core advocacy mission, enhancing the well-being of the Jewish people and Israel and advancing human rights and democratic values in the United States and around the world."*

*"We are excited that an independent AJFF will give us new opportunities for collaboration. Our local bridge building has always been enhanced by the film festival, and we look forward to continuing to see the fruits of this partnership," says AJC Atlanta President Lauren Grien.*

*Blank also sees the new relationship as a windfall, saying: "The film festival could never have achieved the success it has today without the foundational support of AJC. Going forward as distinctive partner organizations allows both AJC and AJFF to focus on what we do best and together take full advantage of our strengths." In the coming months, AJFF will embark on a strategic plan to chart a path forward to ensure organizational, programmatic, and fiscal vitality and stability.*

*Steve Labovitz, an AJC Atlanta Vice President, former Chief of Staff for the City of Atlanta and partner at McKenna Long & Aldridge, will lead AJFF's inaugural Board of Directors. His many years of experience in private-public partnerships and economic development are seen as crucial as AJFF navigates independence. "We have two jobs," Labovitz said. "First, we're going to secure the programming of the film festival, so audiences can continue to enjoy it for years to come. Second, we're going to take the incredible talent and expertise we have developed, and we're going to do even bigger and better things."*

*For more information on the Atlanta Jewish Film Festival, please visit AJFF.org.*

*The Atlanta Jewish Film Festival (AJFF) was founded in the year 2000 by the Atlanta Regional Office of the American Jewish Committee (AJC), a global advocacy organization that enhances the wellbeing of the Jewish people and Israel through education, outreach, and diplomacy. Through the power and shared experience of cinematic storytelling, AJC and AJFF foster stronger bonds within the Jewish community, and intergroup relations with Atlanta's diverse cultural, ethnic, and religious communities. Today, AJFF is an independent non-profit arts organization that continues an active partnership with its founding agency, American Jewish Committee.*

A comprehensive five-year strategic plan was implemented, and the AJFF has flourished as an independent agency. Additional arts grants and corporate and individual funding have been secured, and the staff has been enlarged. Activities now include year-round programming, education, and outreach. AJC has continued to be involved in the festival, and its role as partner and founder is always publicly acknowledged.

In its 15th year, with over 38,000 tickets sold, Kenny Blank proudly reported that "thanks to our enthusiastic and loyal audience, our supremely dedicated volunteers, and our tremendously generous supporters, the AJFF became the world's largest Jewish film festival."

On January 26, at the Opening Night of the 2016 AJFF, Kenny announced the creation of the annual ICON Award for contributions to the cinematic arts. It was presented by the AJFF, in partnership with ArtsATL, to its first recipient, Lawrence Kasdan, on Sunday May 22, at the Woodruff Arts Center. A press release for the award noted Kasdan's significant accomplishments as a writer, director and producer.

When asked how I fill my days since retiring in 2006, I need no encouragement to brag about the time I spend with the AJFF. In the Development Committee, I make countless phone calls to secure sponsors. I attend Program Committee meetings to recommend speakers and panelists for specific films. I have co-chaired the Engagement and Outreach Committee to inform about and attract individuals, agencies, and organizations to films with universal themes which include interfaith, human rights, immigration, and more. And it continues to be a joy for me.

I can't wait to receive the AJFF program guide each year. I clear my calendar as best I can, labor over the wonderful and diverse offerings, and fill my twenty-three days of the festival with more than two dozen movies. I am still asked to introduce some films and facilitate the question and answer sessions following others.

It is hard to quantify the impact of the AJFF, but I am confident that the level of our community's Jewish identity, knowledge, and pride is dramatically and positively affected by the films seen by thousands of people over the nearly month-long festival and the endless conversations they stimulate. Synagogues and organizations utilize the festival for programming with their members. Families bring children for a shared and creative Jewish learning experience. It seems significant that over 20% of the audience are non-Jews whose understanding of Jews, Judaism, and our history is enhanced by the films and the discussions that follow. Unaffiliated Jews are brought closer to our community through these films and the audience experience of community that it fosters.

The AJC gave a magnificent gift to Atlanta in 2000. How lucky I am that I was the Executive Director of the chapter at that time and was able to play a role in bringing the festival to Atlanta. In addition, I served as Secretary of the AJFF during the period of transition from AJC to the Atlanta Jewish Film Society, Inc.

Of course, a project of this magnitude involves the contributions of hundreds of committed and involved people. Steve Labovitz provided outstanding leadership as president in the independent festival's three formative years. I want to single out two other individuals without whom the AJFF would likely be in a very different place. First is Judy Marx, who tirelessly devoted her time and talent in the festival's early years when the demands of a project in its infancy were daunting. And second is Kenny Blank, whose skill and professionalism is unmatched, and whose continuing efforts, along with those of the lay and staff team, have brought us to today's level of excellence.

(L-R) Dov Wilker and Kenny Blank, planning AJFF, 2018

Sherry Frank and Sandy Abrams, opening night

# LEGAL CHALLENGES

*Justice, justice shall you pursue.*

—Deuteronomy 16:20

F rom its earliest days, the AJC dedicated itself to protecting the civil, political and human rights of all people, frequently working on legal issues and through the court system. We often brought Sam Rabinove, AJC's National Legal Director, to Atlanta to brief our members, particularly the lawyers, on cases the organization was addressing. These included those of church-state separation, civil rights, religious liberty and discrimination. Since specific legal challenges emerged in different ways, we were required to tailor our response to each case. Our work advocating for a posthumous pardon for Leo Frank, monitoring a court case on potential claims of anti-Semitism and discrimination at Kennesaw State College, and exposing and combating Holocaust denial in Emory Professor Deborah Lipstadt's trial are examples that demonstrate the approaches we used.

William (Bill) Gralnick was AJC's Southeast Regional Director when I joined the staff as Assistant Director in the fall of 1980. Bill had experience in law enforcement, was active in combating anti-Semitism, and had a keen interest in the media. One of his media connections was with John Seigenthaler, a legendary Nashville journalist and fierce advocate for racial equality. John was editor and publisher of *The Tennessean* and later added to his distinguished career in journalism by becoming the founding editor of the *USA Today* editorial pages. In several exchanges with John, Bill discussed his growing concern with extremism and paramilitary camps in Tennessee. As a result of these conversations, staff writer Jerry Thompson spent an amazing eighteen months undercover inside the Ku Klux Klan. Bill and John helped prepare Jerry for his infiltration of the group, concealing all of his ties to the staff of *The Tennessean* and fabricating a false personal history and identity. They were both secretly in touch with Jerry throughout the entire experience. This was a totally fascinating story.

I had followed this series of events from my early days at AJC, and when Bill left Atlanta to direct AJC's Florida office in June, 1981, my knowledge of the situation was up to date. I met Jerry for the first time on August 13, when he and Bill spoke at an Atlanta Chapter program. Later that year, Jerry received a national award from AJC in Houston, Texas, as well as a nomination for a Pulitzer Prize for his series on his experience in the KKK. Jerry's award-winning book, *My Life in the Klan*, was published in 1982. The book's jacket cover distilled the magnitude of Jerry's work and pointed out the difference between what other journalists learned about the Klan from the outside versus the extended time and personal experiences he gleaned from his eighteen months inside this dangerous paramilitary organization. Jerry gave me a copy of his book for my birthday and inscribed it:

*To Sherry Frank — I can never thank you enough for all the help and support you've provided. You're without a doubt my "Atlanta" girlfriend. Love, Jerry Thompson 11-11-82 (Happy Birthday)*

It would be difficult to overstate the danger Jerry faced after leaving the Klan; *The Tennessean* had to provide him with round-the-clock protection. However, the information he uncovered while on this daring mission was valuable beyond measure. It was during this time that one of Jerry's security guards told him about a relative, Alonzo Mann, who related a story he wanted to tell before he "met his Jesus." This information provided an unexpected link to what would become Jerry's next explosive story – one that had a deeply personal Atlanta connection.

The guard related that his relative had, as a teenager, witnessed a crime in Atlanta many years earlier for which the wrong person had been convicted. Although John Seigenthaler questioned why this story was important – *The Tennessean* didn't sell many newspapers in Atlanta – he nevertheless gave approval to Nashville reporter Bob Sherborne to join Jerry in uncovering Alonzo Mann's story about the death of Mary Phagan. This led to the ultimate and historic pardoning of Leo Frank.

Because he had close and trusted ties to AJC, Jerry was comfortable calling me to say, off the record, what his next assignment entailed. Jerry and Bob made several visits to Atlanta investigating the history of the Leo Frank case. I connected them with lawyers who were able to secure helpful documents, and they continued to gather information about this story. We were advised in advance when their blockbuster report was to be released in a special Sunday edition of *The Tennessean*.

Having this inside information, we decided to change the board meeting date from its usual Thursday to a Monday when Jerry and Bob were scheduled to be in Atlanta and could attend. On the Friday afternoon prior to our Monday meeting, I made several calls inviting

Stuart Lewengrub, Anti-Defamation League (ADL) Director, Vida Goldgar, *The Southern Israelite* editor, and other influential people to attend as well. I told them to read up on the Leo Frank case over the weekend, because some new and significant information would soon be released. Miles Alexander gave me a rare, out-of-print, book about the Leo Frank trial, *Night Fell on Georgia*, by Charles and Louise Samuels, which I shared with Vida.

On Sunday, March 7, 1982, *The Tennessean* printed a special ten-page news section titled "An Innocent Man Was Lynched" that included the statement Alonzo Mann had given to the paper and the Georgia Board of Pardons and Paroles. Mann recounted that when he was called as a witness in the trial, his mother advised him not to say a word about what he had seen and to only answer questions directed to him. He said that Jim Conley, the chief witness against Leo Frank, fabricated a bizarre and detailed report of the incident regarding where Leo Frank was in the building and who was holding Mary Phagan's body. Anguishing over this for many years, he wondered if he could have saved the lives of Mary Phagan or Leo Frank if he had responded differently. He had shared his secret with several people, including his wife, other relatives, friends, a soldier in the army in World War I and a reporter, but was repeatedly advised not to make his story public for various reasons, including that it would not bring back Leo Frank or Mary Phagan. Mann also testified that others had lied in the trial when they said Leo Frank had women and liquor in his office.

In Vida Goldgar's March 12, story in *The Southern Israelite*, she wrote:

After talking with Mann "for many hours over a three day period and many hours since," Thompson and Sherborne asked for and received a sworn affidavit. The Tennessean also arranged for Mann to submit to two lie detector tests: a polygraph and a psychological stress evaluator. "He passed them both with flying colors," Thompson said.

> In his sworn affidavit, Mann said, "Leo Frank was con-
> victed by lies heaped on lies. It wasn't just Conley who lied..."
>
> "Leo Frank was a good office manager. He always was
> proper with people who worked for him. There were wit-
> nesses who told lies, and I remained silent."

Needless to say, this news story was followed by a flurry of activity. AJC, ADL, and the Atlanta Jewish Federation co-sponsored a program on April 1, at which Jerry spoke about his investigation and *The Tennessean* story. A legal committee comprised of representatives of these three agencies met for months and submitted a request to the members of the State Board of Pardons and Paroles for a full and complete pardon exonerating Leo Frank of any guilt for which he was convicted by the Superior Court of Fulton County in 1913. Co-signers for the agencies included Charles Wittenstein and Dale Schwartz for ADL, David Meltz for AJC, and David Minkin for the Atlanta Jewish Federation.

On August 31, 1983, Bill Shipp wrote an op-ed in the *Atlanta Constitution* titled "Time to Lay the Burden Down" in response to a blatant show of anti-Semitism – a planned Klan march in Marietta, to the grave of Mary Phagan.

> It is time we all laid that burden down. Leo Frank ought
> to be pardoned. Gov. Joe Frank Harris should publicly recom-
> mend that the State Board of Pardons and Paroles give Frank
> a full posthumous pardon, and the Board should adopt his
> recommendation.
>
> But the most important aspect of the Frank case is not
> whether he received a fair trial – but that we countenanced
> lynching and mob-rule. If the state lets the Klan demon-
> stration at Mary Phagan's grave pass without comment or
> reaction, it will stand as evidence that official attitudes have
> not changed much since that dark day in 1915.

> The state should answer Klan bigotry with a clear rebuke. It should let the world know that Georgia does not condone terroristic rule by robed riffraff; it should let all know that we recognize injustice and are willing to undo it, even at so late a date. The state should pardon Leo Frank immediately.

Alonzo Mann was deeply disappointed when, in December, 1983, the State Board of Pardons and Paroles denied a posthumous pardon to Leo Frank. He advocated for Leo Frank's innocence until his death in March, 1985. Finally, on March 11, 1986, an article in the *Atlanta Constitution* was able to report "Georgia Pardons Victim 70 Years after Lynching."

> But the board reversed itself and granted the pardon today after the Anti-Defamation League, the American Jewish Committee and the Atlanta Jewish Federation submitted a new petition arguing that they should not have to prove Mr. Frank's innocence, only that he was denied justice.
>
> The board said Mr. Frank was pardoned because the state failed to protect him and because officials failed to bring his killers to justice.

In addition to the press releases of the local agencies involved, AJC's national office released a statement.

> New York, March 11... The following statement was issued today by Howard I. Friedman, President of the American Jewish Committee, and David M. Gordis, its Executive Vice President:
>
> "The American Jewish Committee hails the news of Leo M. Frank's pardon by the Georgia State Board of Pardons and Paroles as justice long overdue. As has many times been proved,, an innocent man was convicted by perjury, misconduct of prosecutors, and religious prejudice. The innocence of Leo Frank has

now been upheld forever, and his soul can finally rest in peace. Our Atlanta Chapter – indeed, the entire Jewish community of Atlanta – is in our debt for the tenacity and dedication with which it pursued justice in this case over close to three-quarters of a century. For the nation, the Leo Frank case stands as a reminder that mob rule and anti-Semitism, racism and bigotry, have no place in our society.

(For your information: Leo M. Frank, a young Jewish businessman, was lynched by a mob in Marietta, Georgia, in 1915, two years after he was unjustly convicted of the murder of Mary Phagan. Several years ago, a witness broke a 70-year silence with a sworn statement to the effect that Frank was innocent of the murder, and Atlanta's Jewish community has since been urging the State Board of Pardons and Paroles to take today's action.)

It continues to amaze me that this sensitive piece of Georgia history still remains controversial. Descendants on all sides stick firmly to their views of Frank's guilt or innocence, in many cases despite the clear evidence that exonerated him.

Our Jewish community will forever be indebted to John Seigenthaler and Jerry Thompson for their commitment to justice and the truth. Their work exposing the Klan and its ultimate connection to the Leo Frank pardon provided a long awaited opportunity to write about Leo Frank's innocence for posterity. My warm relationship with Jerry and my inspiring meeting with Alonzo Mann -- on one of their visits to Atlanta they brought Mann to my office – are among my cherished AJC memories. A picture of me with him hangs on my wall at home.

KENNESAW STATE UNIVERSITY

In July, 1994, I became aware of some anti-Semitic incidents targeted at faculty at Kennesaw State College (KSC), renamed Kennesaw

State University (KSU) in 1996. By November, several AJC lay leaders and I had received briefings from Jewish faculty members who had lost their positions at the college. This was the beginning of a four-year process closely monitoring the legal cases brought by Candace Kaspers Ph.D., who was not Jewish, and Jewish faculty members Alan Howard Schwartz, Ph.D., Bari R. Levingston, Nadine Sue Koch, Ph.D., and Judy R. Palmer, Ph.D. The lawsuit was described in an article on May 19-25, 1995, in the *Atlanta Business Chronicle* © **1995 Atlanta Business Chronicle. All rights reserved. Reprinted with permission.**

*Kennesaw State suit says anti-Semitism cost professors jobs*
*by Adam Feuerstein*

A former department head at Kennesaw State College (KSC) has filed a federal lawsuit claiming that she and two Jewish professors lost their jobs due to rising anti-Semitism among campus administrators.

Candace B. Kaspers, the former chair of the Communications Department at KSC's School of Arts, Humanities and Social Sciences, alleges that she was asked to resign on Nov. 1, 1994, after raising concerns that an announced reorganization of the Communications Department eliminated its only two Jewish professors, Alan Schwartz and Bari Levingston.

The reorganization and Kaspers' resignation were ordered by Lois Muir, Dean of KSC's School of Arts, Humanities and Social Sciences, according to the lawsuit filed April 12 in U.S. District Court in Atlanta.

Kaspers' fear of rising anti-Semitism on campus stems in part from anti-Jewish Neo-Nazi tracts that were slipped under the office doors of at least two Jewish professors at state-funded KSC during the past year, including Schwartz.

The disagreement between Kaspers and Kennesaw State College might have been dismissed as a personality conflict

From the earliest time that the charges were made, President Betty Seigel denounced anti-Semitism in writing and gave assurances that KSU was not a college that discriminates on the basis of religion in its employment practice. Timothy (Tim) Mescon, Ph.D., Dean of the Michael C. Coles School of Business, met with us and wrote frequent letters and newspaper articles in defense of all actions taken by the college. He led a KSU Task Force commissioned to make recommendations and work on these varied issues of concern. Over the two years since news of the pending lawsuit had been released, we met several times with faculty members and interested community leaders, as well as Betty Siegel.

On February 14, 1997, Atlanta Chapter President, Arnold (Arnie) Sidman assembled journalists at a special luncheon to raise awareness of the case. Candace Kaspers and other professors involved in the suits were available to answer questions. In July, we alerted the media to the upcoming trial.

The American Jewish Committee is a human rights organization that monitors questions of discrimination, particularly allegations of anti-Semitism and organizational insensitivity to Jewish issues.

The first of five lawsuits charging Kennesaw State University with religious discrimination will be heard, beginning August 11th, before Judge William S. O'Kelley, Senior Judge of the United States District Court for the Northern District of Georgia, at the Richard Russell Courthouse. The plaintiff in this lawsuit is Dr. Candace Kaspers, a former Kennesaw State University administrator. Dr. Kaspers held this position for more than three years before being asked to resign less than 24 hours after she questioned the termination of the only two full-time Jewish faculty members in her department. Dr. Kaspers, who is not Jewish, was highly regarded at Kennesaw State as the Chair of the Communications Department.

In addition to Dr. Kaspers' lawsuit, four other individuals, all former professors at Kennesaw, have filed suit against the University, alleging religious discrimination.

The American Jewish Committee is watching these cases closely and believes that it is incumbent upon the media to provide sufficient coverage of these cases to enable the public to understand what has transpired at this public university.

We urge full press coverage of this trial and exploration of the allegations of Dr. Candace Kaspers.

AJC staff and lay leaders observed the court proceedings, *Candace B. Kaspers v Board of Regents of the University System of Georgia*, from the beginning of the trial on August 11, 1997, until the verdict was given on August 21. Candace Kaspers was formidable when questioned in the trial; she was poised, articulate, knowledgeable and had an impressive career history at the college. It was surprising, however, to watch Betty Siegel on cross-examination, as she seemed, to me, to lack full grasp of the situation.

We were elated when we heard the verdict in U.S. District Court. Candace Kaspers was awarded a $275,000 judgment for retaliatory discrimination, falling just short of the maximum of $300,000 allowed in such cases. The day after the verdict was announced, we hosted a crowded press conference in our AJC office. Candace spoke along with her attorney, Richard Gerakitis, and Bari Levingston and Alan Schwartz, the two Jewish faculty members in the Department of Communications whose jobs were eliminated. Extensive press coverage followed, including an article the next day in the *Atlanta Journal-Constitution* titled "Kennesaw University Loses Suit." The

*New York Times* published an article on August 24 titled "Teacher Demoted Over Dismissal of Others is Awarded $275,000."

Dr. Kaspers was understandably relieved and pleased with the verdict and the legal decisions. She received an additional award at a later hearing regarding compensation and faculty opportunities. On September 19, a Settlement and Full Trial Release of All Claims was signed by all parties involved in this lawsuit, granting Dr. Kaspers a sum of $750,000.

Dean Muir was subsequently dismissed by the university. President Betty Siegel said in a statement that she was disappointed in the verdict, but her spokeswoman, Annette Hannon Lee, said the university did not plan to appeal. Candace Kaspers and Alan Schwartz were quoted in an article in the *Atlanta Jewish Times* on August 29 titled "Former Kennesaw Chair Wins Lawsuit."

"I would have been derelict in my duties if I did not speak up," Kaspers said. She was thankful the jury agreed with her, clearing her name and restoring her reputation.

"This gives the Board of Regents an opportunity to focus on issues of concern at the college," she also said Friday. "I hope they take this seriously and investigate the issues raised by me and four other Jewish faculty members."

"The jury's verdict proved that she was right," said Alan Schwartz, one of the Jewish professors who lost his job during the department reorganization Kaspers opposed.

"I would see this trial as a sort of vindication," he said during the press conference at the American Jewish Committee offices. "I feel vindicated."

On September 4, 1997, AJC hosted a program titled "Justice Prevails" and invited its members and the community to "please join us to hear about this riveting case and to pay tribute to the courageous actions of this righteous Christian, Dr. Candace Kaspers."

On October 15, Candy Berman, Chapter President, and I wrote to Betty Siegel thanking her for coming to the AJC office to meet with us. As she had requested, we gave her a list of recommendations to improve the community relations climate at KSU after the *Kaspers v Board of Regents* trial.

*Dear Betty,*

*In response to your request, we brought this issue to our Executive Committee and share this list with you of constructive steps we recommend to you.*

- *Host and participate in AJC's Campus Bigotry workshop. Ken Stern, AJC's Program Specialist on Anti-Semitism and Extremism, has conducted these workshops with major universities throughout the U.S.*
- *Amend the KSU student activity form as soon as possible so that it includes the voluntary lines for religious affiliation.*
- *When and if anti-Semitic incidents occur in the future at KSU, respond in a public way, i.e. press conference, press release, etc. A quick and strong public response, rather than internal campus memos, will send a much clearer statement to the campus community, as well as the general public, that these evil acts of hatred and bigotry will not be tolerated at KSU.*
- *Call on AJC as a resource, when needed, to assist in either developing your response to incidents or in helping publicize your response to these despicable acts.*
- *Establish an Interfaith Council at KSU which would include representatives of the various religious groups on campus.*
- *Co-sponsor events at KSU with AJC or other Jewish organizations on topics of interest to your Jewish students and faculty and inclusive of your total campus community.*

*We wish you good luck and want to stay in touch with you*

*so that we can report on your progress to the community. We all*
*know that actions speak louder than words.*
*Cordially,*

*Candy Berman*                           *Sherry Frank*
*President, Atlanta Chapter*             *Southeast Area Director*

We continued to follow the legal cases of the four Jewish faculty members alleging religious discrimination: Schwartz, Levingston, Koch, and Palmer. On August 28, 1997, AJC received a generous donation from Bari and Keith Levingston. Bari finally had reason to celebrate in late February, 1998. After the suit was settled, we received an additional generous donation and heartfelt thanks from them. An article in the *Atlanta Jewish Times* on March 13, titled "Board of Regents to Show Her the Money," captures the story.

> "I don't know how long the administration can treat religious discrimination as a non-issue," said Bari Levingston, who announced last week she received a $150,000 settlement from the Board of Regents.
>
> Levingston claimed she lost her job as a communications professor in 1995, because she is Jewish.
>
> "While the Board of Regents legally doesn't admit guilt, the six-figure settlement sends a strong message that Levingston's claims of religious discrimination are serious," her lawyers said during a press conference at the American Jewish Committee's office last week.

AJC's press release on March 4, invited members and the press to hear Bari Levingston discuss the facts and terms of her settlement.

> "This is a significant settlement regardless of disclaimers by Kennesaw State University and the Board of Regents that religious discrimination was not or is not a problem at the University," said

Elaine B. Alexander, National Board member and past Atlanta Chapter President of the American Jewish Committee.

According to one of Ms. Levingston's lawyers, Craig M. Frankel, "The jury in Dr. Kaspers' case sent a clear message to the Board of Regents that religious discrimination will not be tolerated at Georgia's state universities. By agreeing to pay Ms. Levingston a six-figure amount to settle her discrimination claim, the Board of Regents has taken a much-needed step to condemn discrimination on our state's campuses."

While we monitored these legal cases and statements of faculty in leadership positions at KSU, we asked Governor Roy Barnes for guidance regarding the role of the Board of Regents and to help us secure a meeting with Chancellor Stephen R. Portch. We had a productive meeting with Governor Barnes in April, and on August 17, 1999, a small group of AJC leaders met with Chancellor Portch. I summarized this meeting in my August 20 letter.

*Dear Governor Barnes,*

*Betty Smulian, Clyde Rodbell, Arnie Sidman, and I had a very satisfying meeting with Dr. Stephen Portch on Tuesday, August 17. We had an open and thorough review of our concerns about the management of Kennesaw State University. Dr. Portch was very candid with us, and we assured him that we would respect the private nature of our conversation.*

*We were impressed with Dr. Portch's sincerity and his knowledge. We learned a good deal about the role of the Board of Regents and the grievance process for concerned students and faculty.*

*Thank you so much for helping us secure the meeting.*
*Warm regards,*
*Sherry Frank*
*Southeast Area Director*

Unfortunately, the outcomes of the remaining cases were not successful. Dr. Alan Schwartz's lawsuit was dismissed by a federal judge. Drs. Palmer's and Koch's cases were tried in federal court where the juries found KSU not guilty in both instances.

Times change, and, hopefully, people with good intentions learn from past mistakes. In ensuing years, with new people in top leadership positions and proactive steps for inclusion, KSU has become a welcoming university for Jewish students and faculty. Numerous programs and exhibits on issues of concern to Jews, including Israel and the Holocaust, are being promoted as a matter of course. As Atlanta's Jewish community continues to grow, KSU attracts its increased support and participation.

## DEBORAH LIPSTADT TRIAL

The issue of Holocaust denial continued to surface periodically throughout my tenure at AJC. Sometimes it was written about in newspapers on college campuses. Other times we had to respond to statements made by extremists or anti-Israel speakers in our own community.

Ken Stern, AJC's Program Specialist on Anti-Semitism and Extremism, spoke numerous times at programs we sponsored, and we widely distributed his publications on Holocaust denial. In the fall of 1993, Ken, along with Deborah Lipstadt, spoke and signed their respective books on this topic at the MJCCA (Marcus Jewish Community Center of Atlanta) Jewish Book Festival.

The issue came to a head with the trial of *David Irving v Penguin Books, Ltd., and Deborah Lipstadt.* In 1994, Emory University Professor, Deborah Lipstadt, published the book, *Denying the Holocaust: The Growing Assault on Truth and Memory,* in which she described the British historian, David Irving, as a Holocaust denier. In response, Irving filed a libel suit against her and her publisher, Penguin Books, Ltd. The trial, which attracted broad international coverage, presented a particular challenge, because in England, unlike in America, one is presumed guilty until proven innocent.

A staggering $3 million was needed for Deborah's defense. David Harris, AJC's Executive Director, was asked on behalf of the organization to chair a quiet, behind-the-scenes fundraising campaign. For three years, AJC worked tirelessly to help raise the required money, but never uttered a public word about its role. The professor's lawyers feared that Irving might use this information to depict himself as a victim of a "worldwide Jewish campaign" and thereby gain sympathy and support. AJC was the first to donate, contributing $50,000. The staff was asked to donate as well, and I am so proud to have made a personal gift. While other organizations and leaders participated, AJC took the lead. Ken Stern devoted several years to this work and became an unofficial member of the legal team.

I viewed this as the most important Jewish trial of this century and was determined to sit in on it. From the early days of its preparation, chapter leaders were updated at board meetings. I was invited to a dinner hosted by Felicia and Joe Weber the evening before Deborah left for London, and I was flattered to be included in the celebratory reception hosted by Glenda and David Minkin upon her return to Atlanta. In one of Deborah's remarks that afternoon, she spoke about the gratitude expressed by countless survivors, which led to someone giving her the special title of "Deborah, High Priestess of Memory."

When it came time to observe the trial, many Atlanta Chapter members traveled to London. In preparing for the day in court, Deborah had advised visitors to arrive hours ahead of time to get in line, as the crowds attending the daily courtroom proceedings were so big that they had to move to a larger courtroom. Several hours into the trial, she passed by the visitors' area en route to the restroom. She looked at us and said, "Welcome to the theater of the absurd." (I used that statement as the title of several speeches I gave upon my return home.) I closely followed the court proceedings through media reports, especially those by Douglas Davis in the *Jewish Telegraphic Agency* (JTA), and included highlights in my speeches.

*I traveled to London last week (on February 20, 2000) to walk down the beautiful lobby of the Royal Courts of Justice. The arched ceilings stretched several stories as I followed the winding hallways and stairways until I reached Courtroom 73.*

*I was told "Get there at 9:00 a.m. if you want to get into the courtroom at 10:30. The halls will be packed with press waiting in line also; they fill the courtroom in the morning in order to file their stories after lunch."*

*As the door opened, and I prayed there would be one more seat left for me, Deborah Lipstadt came through the crowd and ushered me in with her. "Sit here in the front row," she said. "Look down two seats; Abe Foxman is here today." Among the seven or eight people seated in my row were the ADL's national director and national president, an attorney and former Wexner Fellow from Boston who studied with Deborah, and two non-Jewish colleagues of hers from Emory University, one a professor of Christian Thought; another who team-taught a course with Deborah.*

*As the people continued in, a man with a yarmulke walked in – no other than Israel Singer, President, World Jewish Congress. When we broke at 1:30 for an hour for lunch and cleared the courtroom, I realized that Sally Levine, a teacher at the Hebrew Academy, was seated in the gallery. When we reassembled after lunch, Deborah pointed out that Martin Gilbert, the great historian of world Jewish history and author of countless books, was in the gallery.*

*I mention these people just to emphasize the importance and magnitude of this case in our own Jewish world. I mention it also because everyone asks me "How's Deborah Lipstadt holding up?" and "How's the case going?" Deborah seems strong and energized by the support that is a constant in the courtroom. They've moved* to bigger chambers, just to accommodate the crowds who want to witness this trial. She seems confident as well by the proceedings and breadth of evidence being presented in her defense.

Still, one wonders how the judge will rule. Will it be a mixed decision leaving some new questions about some aspects of the Holocaust?

Just a word about the actual setting of the courtroom. The contrast between the architectural splendor of this landmark building and the stark courtroom is tremendous. You feel as though you are in a college classroom or storage room of a local library. The room is small and plain. Microphones hang from the ceiling, and shelves, stacked high with notebooks filled with discovery transcripts line both sides of the courtroom. The visitors' seats are plain and stacked close together in rows. The press sits to the right, and a small aisle divides the visitors on the left. Sitting on the first row, I could look into the laptop computers of the nearly a dozen law clerks working throughout the proceedings, rising to retrieve one notebook of testimony after another. I wondered where they might be in 20-30 years from now. The presiding judge, referred to repeatedly as "My Lord," wore the high collared shirt, tails and silly wig. Defense Counsel Richard Rampton and two others in the courtroom also wore wigs, which didn't cover their hair, and included rows of curls and two long braids in the back.

On the one hand, you felt as if you were in a storage room and not a courtroom. On the other hand, you saw, in close view, the defendant, Deborah Lipstadt, her lead attorneys, Julius Lester and Richard Rampton, and the leading Holocaust denier in the world, David Irving.

I had to keep reminding myself that this was real and not a mirage. Was it possible that a respectable court of law could be considering:

- Were there death camps in Europe?

- *Did Hitler know about the Final Solution?*
- *Is it possible that nearly one-half million Hungarian Jews were killed and buried in the summer of 1944?*
- *Did Hitler organize mass emigration of East European Jews and not mass murder?*
- *Were there only one million Jews who died in this period?*
- *What is it about Jews that make them picked on for pogroms, etc?*

*On January 11, 2000, the trial began, with Irving suing Lipstadt and her British publisher, Penguin Books. Charles Gray, one of Britain's most experienced libel lawyers, was the presiding judge in the case. The case stemmed from Lipstadt's book, Denying the Holocaust, where she says that Irving is "one of the most dangerous spokespersons for Holocaust denial." She further states that "he bends historical evidence until it conforms with his ideological leanings."*

*He claims that by calling him a denier rather than a revisionist with a different view of history, she has robbed him of his livelihood.*

*David Irving is a tall, broad man. His determination, at times impatience, comes through in the courtroom. His fingers twitch, reflecting the strain he's under, yet his calm voice prevails. No one can deny his encyclopedic grasp of the Third Reich and his knowledge of the German side of the Second World War.*

*When I was in the courtroom, Professor Richard Evans, a Cambridge scholar, whose discovery transcripts exceeded 700 pages, was questioned by Irving about such things as:*

- *Wasn't it possible that Jews died of carbon monoxide and factory fumes in Treblinka and Belzech?*
- *Where are the archeological proofs from mass graves that prove so many Jews were killed there?*
- *Isn't the issue about scale, not fact, regarding these numbers?*

- *"Don't you acknowledge that I've worked for 30 years on Hitler's words and actions and 15 years on Goebbels? Wouldn't I know what they knew and what they ordered to be done?" Irving asked. Professor Evans answered "it's how you work and the conclusion you want to draw."*
- *The questions back and forth continued for hours between Irving and Evans. Irving: "Hitler ordered mass emigration" – Evans: "That's a euphemism for mass murder." – Irving: "Hitler ordered the Jews to be sent to Siberia and Madagascar" – Evans: "That's a camouflage for sending them to Auschwitz." Then there were the long debates over translation of German words "total destruction vs. war of extermination," "Jews are dying like flies" vs. "Jews are being killed like flies." Then there was a clarification of Hitler's reference to Jews as racial pests, similar to agricultural varmints or public pests, similar to rapists, train robbers or other criminals.*

*Throughout the six hours, Professor Evans turned toward the judge, refusing to face Irving. Refuting every conclusion Irving reached, Evans challenged his ability to objectively draw facts from anywhere or anyone.*

*JTA, February 7*
*At one point, the court was shown a video of Irving addressing a right-wing American organization, the National Alliance, in Tampa, Florida, in October, 1995, when he discussed the "legend of the Holocaust." Irving denied any association with the National Alliance, but Rampton pointed out that he had spoken at their events eight times between 1990 and 1998.*

*JTA, February 14*
*After producing a 740-page critique of Irving's historical method, Evans said he had been unprepared for the "sheer depth duplicity"*

*he had found in Irving's treatment of Holocaust-related historical sources.*

*The court proceedings reinforced the view he had expressed in his report that Irving had fallen so far short of accepted standards of scholarship that "he doesn't deserve to be called a historian at all."*

*Earlier, military historian Sir John Keegan, compelled by subpoena to testify for Irving, said he found Irving's ideas to be "perverse," while his claim that Hitler did not know about the fate of the Jews until late 1943 "was so extraordinary it would defy reason."*

*JTA, March 5*

*Rampton quoted from a 1991 speech in Canada in which Irving told his audience that he saw no reason to be "tasteful" about Auschwitz.*

*"It's baloney, it's a legend," he told his audience. "Once we admit the fact that it was a brutal slave labor camp and large numbers of people did die -- as large numbers of innocent people died elsewhere in the war -- why believe the rest of the baloney?"*

*"I say quite tastelessly, in fact, that more women died on the back seat o f Edward Kennedy's car at Chappaquiddick than ever died in a gas chamber in Auschwitz."*

*At an earlier hearing, Hajo Funke, a professor at the Free University of Berlin, told the court he considered that Irving, 62, had "committed himself wholeheartedly" to neo-Nazism in Germany. He said Irving had used Germany as a "playground" for his right-wing extremism until he was expelled in 1993.*

*JTA, March 7*

*Rela Geffen Monson (Gratz College and a friend of Deborah's) said*

*"How can we be listening to someone argue in a serious court of law that Jews tattooed numbers on their arms to get money from the German government for Israel?"*

*In the last few days of the trial, Irving was on the stand and truly interrogated – one might say destroyed – by experts on extremism in Germany and the U.S. about his close and undeniable ties to radical, extremist, right-wing groups – all the way back to his toast at the anniversary of Hitler's birthday. This case closed on Monday, March 6, and recessed for a week. Closing arguments were presented on Tuesday and Wednesday, March 13 and 14.*

*JTA, March 15*

*David Irving told the High Court in London this week that some of the world's largest Jewish organizations are involved in an international conspiracy against him.*

*The trial, which has attracted international attention, has been described as the most important trial involving the Holocaust since Adolf Eichmann, the chief engineer of the Holocaust, was convicted in Israel in 1961.*

*The plaintiff and defendant have shown sharply contrasting styles. Irving – who served as his own attorney and appeared to relish the spotlight – wasted no opportunity in and out of court in making statements supporting his claims that Auschwitz was not a death camp, or that there was no systemic, mass destruction of Jews; Lipstadt, a professor at Emory University in Atlanta, has sat silently throughout the proceedings.*

*Irving has described Auschwitz as a "fable" and insisted there was no evidence to suggest that Hitler ordered the systematic mass destruction of the Jews.*

*In his 24-page closing address, defense lawyer Richard Rampton declared that the trial had exposed Irving's views as a "fraud."*

*The reasons, he continued, were not hard to find. "As the evidence in this court has shown," Rampton said, "Irving is a right-wing extremist, a racist, and, in particular, a rabid anti-Semite."*

The weight of this trial was enormous, and its implications will resonate around the world for the foreseeable future. It informed my speeches in the months that followed as I described the apprehension we felt as we prayed and awaited the verdict.

After a month's recess, on April 11, Judge Gray considered the evidence and ruled in Deborah's favor. He didn't mince words when he declared that Irving was a Holocaust denier, anti-Semite, and racist. He went on to say, "Irving was motivated by a desire to present events in a manner consistent with his own ideological beliefs, even if that involved distortion and manipulation of historical evidence." AJC responded to the verdict in a press release.

*American Jewish Committee Applauds Court Condemnation of Holocaust Denier*
*Atlantans who attended the trial in London express satisfaction with verdict*

Atlanta, GA, April 11, 2000.... The American Jewish Committee today called the verdict in *David Irving v Penguin Books, Ltd., and Deborah Lipstadt* a landmark victory for historical truth.

American Jewish Committee, Atlanta Chapter, members were in the courtroom in London during every week of the historic trial. "We were witnesses to the truth, lending our emotional support to Dr. Deborah Lipstadt, a revered member of our Atlanta community," said Sherry Frank, Southeast Area Director of the American Jewish Committee, who sat in Courtroom 73 in February. "David Irving's distortion of facts and despicable hatred of Jews received full light of inspection in this courtroom. Justice, truth, and free speech prevail. We applaud this judgment."

"Truth prevailed, and anti-Semitism and the historical fraud of Holocaust deniers were exposed for all to see," said David A. Harris, Executive Director of the American Jewish Committee. "The court has shown that the insidious efforts of David Irving and other Holocaust deniers to manipulate historical facts do have limits."

Mr. Harris and Ms. Frank both commended Dr. Lipstadt for her "courageous defense" and Penguin Books for standing by her. "Many publishing houses would have looked at the cost of libel litigation and settled. Not Penguin, to its credit," Mr. Harris said, "Penguin's steadfast support of Dr. Lipstadt has been a profile in courage."

Judge Charles Gray held that Dr. Lipstadt was justified in calling Mr. Irving a Holocaust denier in her book "Denying the Holocaust: The Growing Assault on Truth and Memory," published in England by Penguin Books, Ltd.

I was moved by Deborah's speaking in her own words about this trial. She wrote an Op Ed piece in JTA, April 25, 2000, titled "My ordeal with Irving showed I was wrong to laugh 20 years ago."

In 1995, when I opened a letter informing me that David Irving was suing me for libel for calling him a Holocaust denier, I had precisely the same reaction that I had 20 years earlier when I first heard that there were people who denied the Holocaust. I laughed.

Why, I wondered, take this seriously? Holocaust deniers reminded me of flat-earth theorists. The idea was preposterous.

I never anticipated the havoc this fight would wreak with my professional and personal life. At the post-verdict news conference, I was asked: "Given all that has happened, would you write the same things about Irving?"

The answer was "No." Were I writing my book now, I would write even more harshly about him. This legal action, which he instigated, allowed my lawyers to demand the release of reams of his personal papers documenting his activities. We know far more about him than we ever did before. We hoisted him on his own petard.

I fought him because I could not run from evil, even when

the evil is rooted in nonsense, for nonsense can cause significant damage. *The Protocols of the Elders of Zion* are proven forgeries that are based on a ludicrous premise. Nonetheless, they continue to circulate. The Holocaust teaches that evildoers must be stopped early, before they can inflict much damage. Hitler was far less of a foe in the early 1930s than in the 1940s. So too, deniers must be stopped now.

I have not yet fully unpacked what it meant to be a defendant in a libel suit that brought together the Holocaust, free speech and historiography. I shall never forget as I entered court on the first day being told by survivors: "We are counting on you."

Nor shall I forget being enveloped after the trial by a man outside the courtroom who said: "My parents died in Auschwitz. In their name, thank you."

I was wrong to laugh 20 years ago when I first heard about the deniers. I was wrong to laugh when I opened the letter informing me that Irving was considering a suit. And I was entirely wrong to assume it was just a nuisance. It was far more than that.

But David Irving was far more wrong than I if he thought that I would "crack up and cop out." I did neither. I fought this charge with all my strength. It was a demanding battle. Yet, on some level, it has also been a surprisingly rewarding endeavor. It taught me much about evil, but it also taught me about goodness, friendship, and about doing the right thing. That too is part of this story.

This trial and the issue of Holocaust denial continues to be a topic of study and discussion. Emory University houses major documentation on the subject as well as the trial. AJC and ACCESS hosted a conversation and book signing with Deborah on June 22, 2005, after the release of *My Day in Court with David Irving: History on Trial*. Co-sponsors included The Davis Academy and Temple Emanu-El.

Deborah is an effective and valuable guest speaker and panelist for Holocaust-related films at the Atlanta Jewish Film Festival (AJFF). I was especially thrilled to be in the audience when the AJFF co-sponsored a screening of the film *Denial*, which depicts the trial, before its public release. At this event, Deborah responded to the film and shared personal reflections on those challenging years. The audience was filled with friends, colleagues, and supporters who embraced Deborah before and after the screening. While she thanked everyone who had been there for her, she expressed special gratitude to her Emory University colleagues for their unflagging support throughout the entire ordeal.

After the release of the film, I was again asked to speak about the trial. I found it so personally rewarding to know Deborah and to have worked with her. Because the trial was so contentious and dramatic, it was satisfying to witness a piece of history and bring the story back to Atlanta audiences. I will always be especially pleased to talk about the major behind-the-scenes role – financially, legally, and morally – that was played by the Jewish community around the world and the unique and significant part played by the AJC.

Sherry Frank meets with
Alonzo Mann at AJC office

*Nashville Tennessean* reporters,
(L-R) Robert Sherborne and
Jerry Thompson, review AJC
files on Leo Frank case

Press conference at AJC office celebrating the verdict in the Dr. Candace Kaspers case, (L-R) Alan Schwartz, Bari Levingston, Richard Gerakitis, Candace Kaspers (at the mic), Sherry Frank, and Arnie Sidman, 1997

(L-R) Brooke Blasberg, Cookie Shapiro, Deborah Lipstadt, Ken Stern (AJC national staff,) Barbara Babbitt (Fleming) at book signing, MJCCA Book Festival, 1993

# ANTI-SEMITISM, DISCRIMINATION AND EXTREMISM

## SAFEGUARDING DEMOCRACY AND PLURALISM

*I have decided to stick with love. Hate is too heavy a burden to bear.*

—Martin Luther King Jr.

nti-Semitism -- prejudice about or discrimination against Jews -- can have different bases. The oldest one is religious-based, blaming Jews for the death of Jesus. In 1965, Vatican Council II repudiated the deicide charge and identified anti-Semitism as a sin. Additional declarations over the decades by other Protestant denominations has led to the decline of religious-based anti-Semitism.

Although Judaism is a religion, Jews are a people as well and at times are erroneously considered a distinct race. It was race-based anti-Semitism that fueled Nazi Germany's demonizing of Jews and ultimately led to the Holocaust. It is the basis for the ideology of white supremacist groups, Neo-Nazis, the Ku Klux Klan, and a wide array of other extremist hate groups. Race-based anti-Semitism has its own literature. *The Protocols of the Elders of Zion* argues that Jews secretly meet to control the world; *The Secret Relationship Between Blacks and Jews* distorts the history of slavery to paint it as a Jewish attack on black people.

The newest form of prejudice against the Jews is political anti-Semitism. The late Abba Eban, Israeli diplomat and scholar, once said in explaining this phenomenon: "classical anti-Semitism denies the rights of Jews as citizens within society. Anti-Zionism denies the equal rights of the Jewish people to its lawful sovereignty within the community of nations… all that has happened is that the discriminatory principle has been transferred from the realm of individual rights to the domain of collective identity."

We continue to see the rise of political anti-Semitism expressing itself as anti-Zionism, with declarations by the United Nations (UN) and its affiliate organizations, by some Christian denominations, at international forums, and on college campuses. There continues to be a growing Boycott, Divestment, and Sanctions (BDS) movement worldwide.

Rabbi Jim Rudin describes the expression and growth of anti-Semitism well. He states in an article in *Kiwanis*, May, 1992, "The lesson is clear. If respectable people use toxic language, it provides a license for the violent people in our midst. If, by our language, we devalue the worth of a person or group, such a person or group becomes an 'acceptable' target for rhetorical and ultimately physical assault."

Rabbi Rudin's words were prophetic. On Shabbat morning, October 27, 2018, the worst attack in history on the American Jewish community took place with the murder of eleven Jews at Tree of Life Synagogue in Pittsburgh, Pennsylvania. Anti-Semitism and white supremacy remain on the rise, fueled in part by the polarizing and combative rhetoric of the Trump Administration.

During my years at AJC, there were times when I received hate mail and malicious phone calls. It was upsetting, of course; but instead of being a deterrence, it had the effect of emboldening me. With support and the knowledge that AJC has always been a leading voice in responding to all kinds of bigotry, I was able to respond effectively when its various forms presented themselves.

I took great pride in the quiet diplomacy we demonstrated. We were faced with issues that required patience and steadfast determination, working with our members and like-minded community leaders, to witness and effect change.

## Ku Klux Klan

It is one thing to write about the Klan. It is completely different to see them up close. This frightening experience played out for me on the streets of Cumming, Georgia, in Forsyth County.

Forsyth County had a long history of violence on the part of segregationists. At noon on January 17, 1987, Hosea Williams led a racially mixed group of fewer than ninety civil rights leaders into Forsyth County for a "March Against Fear and Intimidation." They were violently attacked by the Ku Klux Klan and their allies. A week later, 20,000 marchers, including many AJC members, returned to Forsyth County to complete the earlier march. It turned out to be the largest civil rights march since the 1960s.

I was at the center of the weeklong planning for this march, and worked side by side with major civil rights leaders and key members of the Black/Jewish Coalition. I was asked to identify a Jewish participant who had marched in the 1960s to speak in Forsyth County, and I turned to AJC's Rabbi Jim Rudin who, I knew, had taken part. With only three days notice, he flew to Atlanta to march with us and retell the experiences he had in Hattiesburg, Mississippi, in 1964.

I will never be able to erase the sounds and visions of the more than one thousand demonstrators — young men, women, teenagers and children — shouting racial epithets, wearing KKK robes, waving Confederate flags and making Nazi salutes. The memory of the screaming of the "N" word and the hateful hand-written signs, including "James Earl Ray (assassin of Martin Luther King, Jr.), American Hero" and others, still haunts me.

We were terrified and felt surrounded by danger, even with 2,300 heavily armed officers from the Highway Patrol, Cumming Police, National Guard, Georgia Bureau of Investigation, and sheriff's office, providing a corridor for us to march through or perched on roof tops while low flying security helicopters flew above us. In total, fifty-five agitators were arrested, including David Duke, Klan leader.

In 1912, white residents terrorized and drove out the black population of Forsyth County. The 1987 march was a step along the way to repair this injustice. Today, demographic changes, an influx of newcomers moving to the area, and a Georgia highway linking it to the larger city have made Cumming part of the suburban sprawl of Atlanta. But a history of turbulent race relations will always require diligent monitoring.

As time went by, I was involved in less significant, yet still notable, efforts to confront Klan-related issues. In June, 1987, we learned that David Duke was planning an event at the Waverly Hotel to announce his candidacy for President of the United States. We alerted the hotel about Duke's background on June 2.

*Dear Mr. Guilbault,*

*On behalf of the Atlanta Chapter of the American Jewish Committee, I want to thank you for the bold action you took in canceling the meeting of David Duke on June 8th or 9th at the Waverly Hotel, at which time he was to announce his candidacy for President of the United States.*

*Duke, a former head of the Knights of the Ku Klux Klan and present leader of the National Association for the Advancement of White People, is an affront to the fair and decent people of this country. His inflammatory remarks only serve to incite hatred and violence.*

*The American Jewish Committee for 81 years has worked to combat bigotry and extremism and enhance intergroup relations for all people.*

*We thank you for your action and hope that David Duke and others like him who poison the political process will be exposed for the evil they espouse.*

*Sincerely,*

*S. Stephen Selig*

*President, Atlanta Chapter*

In 1990, AJC joined other area organizations in filing an *amicus* brief, *The State of Georgia v Shade Miller, Jr.*, supporting the constitutionality of the 1950's anti-mask laws. Thankfully, in Georgia, Klansmen can no longer legally hide behind their masks when on public property.

It is sad to note, that as I write this memoir in the summer of 2018, the KKK and other hate groups, fueled in part by the Alt-Right, have marched in the streets of Charlottesville, Virginia, and other cities spreading their insidious message of hate. This is an unfortunate reminder that the battle against anti-Semitism, discrimination and extremism is never over.

## RADIO TALK SHOW

In July, 1987, AJC conducted a nation-wide survey of call-in radio programs to determine their levels of bigotry – anti-Jewish mainly, but also anti-Black, anti-Catholic, and other types of intolerance. This was especially timely, as we were involved with this issue on the local level. On Friday, July 8, WGST Radio show host Ed Tyll said extremely offensive things about Congressman John Lewis. Two days later, during a phone interview, he was so rude to Senator Wyche Fowler that the Senator hung up on him. Community response was instantaneous; calls for Tyll to be fired and protest marches in front of the radio station garnered wide media, print, and TV coverage. John Lauer, Vice President and General Manager, and Eric Seidel, Station Manager, expressed the station's regret for the inappropriate remarks and, on July 11, apologized to Congressman Lewis. Noting that Ed Tyll's remarks were uncalled for, unprovoked and unconscionable, they assured him that they would not tolerate this kind of insult and expressed their sorrow that it took place.

On July 13, I was the single white member of a delegation of black community leaders who met with WGST's John Lauer and Eric Seidel to respond to Tyll's comments. There were representatives of the NAACP, SCLC, Concerned Black Clergy, president of the Black Bar Association of Atlanta, a member of the Atlanta City Council, and one member of the College Park City Council. The meeting began politely, but quickly became hostile. The delegation called for the station to fire Tyll, or at the very least to do more than give him their proposed one week suspension. It was agreed that another meeting would be scheduled on July 20 for the group to meet with Tyll.

After a short suspension without pay, Ed Tyll issued a statement regarding the unwarranted and insensitive comments he made on his program regarding Congressman John Lewis. In it he expressed his sincere apology to Congressman Lewis and the listening audience and acknowledged that his characterization of the Congressman was both contemptible and insensitive. He also admitted that he had abused the privilege of expression with his comments on the public airwaves in his talk-show.

On behalf of the Atlanta Black/Jewish Coalition, Elaine Alexander and Ozell Sutton wrote to the editor of the *Atlanta Journal* on July 16 expressing outrage at the offensive statements made by talk-show host, Ed Tyll. They questioned the wisdom of allowing divisive and inflammatory comments on air. "This kind of programming ... doesn't enhance intergroup relations, but rather incites racism, anti-Semitism and bigotry. Ed Tyll's personal attack on Congressman John Lewis on the air was entirely inappropriate."

At the July 20 meeting, Ed Tyll made a long and passionate apology for his offensive remarks against Congressman John Lewis and his rudeness to Senator Wyche Fowler. He claimed that he wasn't a racist and had learned a great deal from this experience.

To our surprise and dismay, on Wednesday morning, July 22, at 9:00 a.m., John Lauer made a statement saying that Tyll's suspension would be lifted and his show would resume at 1:00 p.m. Ed Tyll was back on the air only two days after our meeting. Lauer said that radio talk-shows all over the country were watching this case and "he was not going to yield to black pressure." We began to receive shocked and angry calls in the AJC office. We were indignant over attempts to portray this as a black issue, when clearly it was not.

To offer an opposing view, the CBS affiliate (TV-5) asked Elaine Alexander, Atlanta Chapter Vice President and Co-chair of the Black/Jewish Coalition, to come to the station for an interview. Tyll repeated his apology on air and continued to denounce his previous actions. Meetings followed with individuals and organizations that had participated in our two meetings at WGST. We decided to continue and expand our involvement in this area. As a result of our strategy session, we formed the "Coalition for Fairness in Media."

Unfortunately, this was not to be the end of controversies involving Ed Tyll. On October 29, during the AJC's National Executive Council meeting in Atlanta, a forum was held on "Countering Bigotry on the Air." Panelists included media professionals and Elaine Alexander, and a reporter from WGST radio covered this meeting. The next afternoon Tyll made inflammatory remarks on the air about the meeting and the panelists, the American Jewish Committee and the Black/Jewish Coalition. The Atlanta office and Steve Selig, Atlanta Chapter President, received numerous calls from people who were offended when they listened to the program.

On Thursday, November 19, at the request of Steve Selig, Eric Seidel set up a meeting for us to listen to tapes from Tyll's Friday, October 30 show. I participated along with Steve, Tom Asher, Atlanta Chapter Past President and National Board of Governors member, and Ronnie van Gelder, Assistant Area Director. After listening to the tapes, Steve wrote to John Lauer.

*Dear John,*

*Thank you for allowing us to listen to the tapes from Ed Tyll's show on Friday, October 30, 1987. If you haven't already done so, I strongly urge you to listen to this tape.*

*Ed used character assassination and irresponsible mudsling-ing. He knows nothing about the organizations that he is malign-ing as evidenced by his statements that the Black/Jewish Coalition is a very dangerous organization; perhaps more dangerous than the fascists in Italy in the 1930s and calling the American Jewish Committee an enemy of the people that is out to regulate speech just the way the Nazis burned books. The American Jewish Committee is this country's premier human relations organization with an 81-year history of enhancing intergroup relations and protecting human rights.*

*His reckless and unfounded rhetoric repeats the pattern that led him to his intemperate remarks about Congressman John Lewis that led us to your office initially. It underscores our concern about "shock radio" and its potential for inciting intergroup tensions and community unrest.*

*The undisciplined venom of Ed Tyll erodes the standards of public service that we believe should guide a station committed to serving the community.*

*Sincerely,*

*S. Stephen Selig, III*

*President, Atlanta Chapter*

In the following years, talk-show hosts on WGST continued making offensive statements, and we quickly responded when they crossed the line from civility to bigotry and incitement. After the April 29, 1992, Rodney King verdict in Los Angeles and the violence that followed there and in Atlanta, the evening program host Ralph from Ben Hill urged his listeners to "take it to the streets" while he played the song "Burn, Baby, Burn." His comments encouraged violence and were a serious threat to safety in our city. He included anti-Semitic and anti-Korean charges as well. In May and June of that year, we were openly critical of the program and its frequent statements attacking Jews.

On May 24, journalist Colin Campbell wrote an article in the *Atlanta Journal-Constitution* titled "Hate Radio – in Context." He began by pointing out the false statements WGST talk-show host Neal Boortz claimed Colin had made regarding Israel. After correcting the errors attributed to him, Colin went on to make these points:

> WGST kicks off its mornings with Neal Boortz, then passes its afternoons with Rush Limbaugh, then greets the evening by broadcasting local black Muslim talker, Ralph from Ben Hill. (I suppose this is "balance.")
>
> When racial violence broke out in Atlanta after the Rodney King beating verdict, I wasn't the only listener to hear Ralph spouting anti-Semitic nonsense. He called Los Angeles Mayor Tom Bradley, an "Uncle Tom" controlled by "the Jews." He said, "Burn, baby, burn." He sounded as if he wanted to incite a riot.
>
> Is this how WGST and its corporate parents, Jacor, make money?
>
> Under cover of entertainment, opinion and information, it has been broadcasting angry and socially divisive words that do entertain some listeners, including me at times, but that are also abusive, inflammatory, inaccurate, racist, anti-Semitic, insulting to women and obsessed with violence.

Once again, I arranged for a delegation to meet with Eric Seidel. On June 17, a group including Reverend Perky Daniels, Atlanta Interfaith Coalition; Tommy Dortch and Lois Frank, Co-chairs, Atlanta Black/Jewish Coalition; and Paula Bevington, Chair, Georgia Human Relations Commission, all went to the station. The next day I received a letter from Eric emphasizing how important it is to hear from community organizations and how dedicated the station is to being responsible broadcasters. He expressed his desire to continue the communication and said he hoped we would get together for an informal lunch later in the summer.

Even though we were diligent in meeting with the station after incidents and did what we could to mitigate the conversations, the problem wouldn't go away. On February 5, 1999, Candy Berman wrote to Randy Michaels, CEO of Jacor Corporation, about anti-Semitism on the radio.

*Dear Mr. Michaels,*

*We would like to bring to your attention recent anti-Semitic and racist comments made on Jacor's Atlanta radio station, WKLS (96Rock). Several weeks ago, the morning show began running a segment called "Ask the Jew" (a call-in show when listeners can call the station and ask Larry Wachs, one of the hosts, questions about Jews and Judaism). While the title itself is somewhat problematic, in that it proclaims a certain expertise about Jews and Judaism, of greater concern is the content of the on-air discussion. Not only is the station broadcasting incorrect information, but racist and anti-Semitic attitudes are deemed acceptable. It is, in fact, unacceptable to use vulgar references to any ethnic or religious group, to perpetuate stereotypes, or to denigrate in any way individuals or beliefs in the name of "parody" or "satire."*

*Since early January, this office and other Jewish organizations and synagogues in the Atlanta area have received calls from constituents expressing outrage. Many of our members have indicated that they will no longer listen to 96Rock until they hear from us that the tasteless and inflammatory discussions have ceased.*

*The American Jewish Committee has always been at the forefront of fighting prejudice in whatever form that it takes. We will continue to monitor the 96Rock morning show and will alert our members and affiliated organizations when this disrespectful and offensive attitude is changed.*

*Sincerely,*

*Candy Berman, President*

Show hosts had claimed the term "Jewing someone down" was not a pejorative, knocked the act of circumcision as barbaric, joked about facial characteristics of Jews, and questioned security in Israel. The program was ultimately taken off the air. Radio talk shows continue to be a source of information, entertainment, and sadly, at times, divisive and offensive rhetoric.

## AGNES SCOTT COLLEGE

The case for Agnes Scott College and its policy of not hiring Jewish faculty was an issue that took decades to make right. It was the subject of *The Southern Israelite*'s February 24, 1967, article titled "Faculty Restrictions Stun Friends of Agnes Scott." Exactly fifty years later, on February 24, 2017, the *Atlanta Jewish Times* referred back to that column in "Remember When, February 24, 1967."

The Atlanta Jewish Community Council's community relations committee plans to meet to consider a response to a statement from the board of trustees of Agnes Scott College. The board of the 78-year-old, Presbyterian-aligned women's institution reaffirmed a longstanding policy against the hiring of non-Christian faculty. Charles Wittenstein, the Southeast director of the American Jewish Committee, said it was hard to understand the importance of religion for faculty teaching subjects such as French and mathematics.

The article caught my eye. Even though I had been involved in this issue for some time, I didn't realize how long this had been the college's policy. When chapter President Joel Goldberg asked David Baker, an attorney with Powell Goldstein, to chair a new legal committee, I seized on the opportunity to thank David for accepting this invitation and to propose several issues we might want to address. In my letter of August 16, 1983, I noted that a Jewish professor was denied tenure at Agnes Scott. Indeed, the school has *never* granted tenure to a Jewish professor. "We have reason to feel that discrimination was involved in this case."

Our staff met with attorney David Meltz, to hear him present the background of this case. Mr. Meltz was planning to represent a professor at Agnes Scott College who had completed five years on the faculty and had consistently received positive evaluations but was denied tenure. He learned that it had never been granted to a Jewish faculty member.

Lawrence (Larry) Gellerstedt, Jr., was serving as chairman of the Board of Agnes Scott College at the time. When we brought this issue to his attention, he was both surprised and embarrassed. He urged us to keep the story out of the public news and vowed to stay on top of it until the situation was corrected.

On March 21, 1984, David Meltz , now an Atlanta Chapter board member, wrote to G. Conley Ingram, an attorney and board member of Agnes Scott College, inquiring about progress in addressing the problem. He assured Mr. Ingram that this was a private matter, and that he had no desire to pressure or embarrass the College, but he looked forward to the day when this problem had been rectified.

Six years later, on September 24, 1990, I was surprised, yet delighted, to receive a letter from Agnes Scott's Professor Alberto Sadun.

*Dear Sherry,*

*I am writing to bring you up to date on some news that may be of interest to you. A few years ago you asked me to keep you informed as to my status at Agnes Scott College. I am pleased to tell you that I have recently been granted tenure, and have been promoted as well to the position of Associate Professor of Astronomy (a rare if not unprecedented decision at Agnes Scott, coming together as it does with the tenure decision). In addition, I have been appointed as Chairman of the Department of Physics and Astronomy. I guess for the time being the administration is pleased with my work.*

*I am well aware of the checkered history Agnes Scott College has had in terms of human relations (including religious prejudice). As far as my own personal experience is concerned, I have not felt any discrimination or other kinds of prejudice expressed during the years I have spent at Agnes Scott.*

*I am motivated to write this letter because of my tremendous respect for the work of American Jewish Committee as an information agency, and so I simply want to provide as much information as I can on this subject.*

*Sincerely yours,*

*Alberto C. Sadun*

This issue had a successful ending, illustrating the patience required to reach it as well as the quiet behind-the-scenes work of the AJC. It is also a fine example of the friendship and support we have in the non-Jewish community as exemplified by the efforts of Larry Gellerstedt, Jr., an outstanding and admired business and civic leader. Today, in 2019, Agnes Scott College boasts increased Jewish activity and is a welcoming place for Jewish faculty as well.

WESTMINSTER SCHOOL

In April of 1991, a heated debate was going on at the Westminster School regarding their long-standing policy of hiring Christian-only faculty.

April 11, 1991 *Atlanta Journal*
*Westminster's tug with the past*

Westminster, a private institution, has every right to the practice, once common to schools that grew out of religious institutions. It should be proud of the Christian mission that has led it to rank as one of the South's top high schools. In the eyes of many educators and college admissions officials, it is the pre-eminent college preparatory school in the region. Precisely because of that standing, Westminster's long-term interests and those of its students and alumni argue for change.

The internal controversy at Westminster is maddening, not because it is bigoted, but because it is… stubbornly old-fashioned. It is also a disservice to its many alumni and friends, who though they may profess a different faith or none at all, have shared in the institution's values and respected its heritage. That respect should cut both ways.

April 12, 1991  *Atlanta Constitution*
*Westminster in need of an enlightenment*

Forty years ago, when officials of what later became The Westminster School adopted the policy of excluding non-Christians from the faculty and governing board, they did wrong. When Westminster board members voted recently, presumably in more open-minded times, to re-affirm those prohibitions, they compounded the error.

Westminster, one of the nation's finest prep schools, is a private, Christian institution, and it can draw up its rules and make its choices accordingly. Yet the board members who defeated a motion made by Cox Enterprises Chief Executive Officer James Cox Kennedy that would have rescinded the exclusionary policy must recognize its inherent contradictions.

Would changing the policy undermine Westminster's basic Christian foundations? It's hard to see how. There is no special Hindu interpretation of geography or Jewish spin to teaching phonics. And no one questions the school's right to provide Bible instruction and offer devotionals as it sees fit.

On behalf of the 1,200 members of AJC, Elaine Alexander, Atlanta Chapter President, wrote to James (Jim) Kennedy, Chairman and CEO of Cox Enterprises, Inc., and Larry Gellerstedt, III, President and CEO of Beers Incorporated, thanking them for their courageous stand on this issue. Jim Kennedy's response acknowledged the difficulty of challenging Westminster's stand as well as disagreeing with his friends on the board who support this archaic policy. He expressed his belief that the goal of deliberations was to make a good school even better.

All throughout the next year there were meetings with faculty and families of Westminster students. In August, 1992, John (Jack) Harrison, President of *The New York Times* Regional Newspaper Group, wrote a statement to the Westminster board in anticipation of their upcoming vote on this issue. He questioned whether Westminster was practicing discrimination in hiring only Christian faculty and pointed out the inclusive nature of Christianity and the need for its trustees and its school to practice this openness to all people. Noting the resilience of the Christian faith, he said he believed it would not be diluted by including Jewish faculty in the school.

Word of Westminster's hiring policy reached the most prestigious universities in the country. Questioning this practice, some decided to boycott Westminster functions to which they would usually send recruiters, as was reported in an op-ed in the *Atlanta Journal* on November 26, 1992, titled "Westminster's clear call for change."

November 24, 1992 *Atlanta Journal*
*Westminster's very stature demands openness*
*by Dick Williams*

The problem at the Westminster Schools is that they have succeeded. College admissions directors know well that the northeast Atlanta prep schools are the best in the South. That status places a special burden on the institution. And it's why

Westminster is catching the flack it is from Georgetown, Duke, Tufts, MIT, Harvard and Yale.

When the debate over the rights of private institutions and their heritage is over, Westminster finds itself facing one human question.

How can it say to its Jewish students, you are brilliant, but you may not teach here?

That's not a legal question. It's chillingly personal.

The shame of it is that is it unnecessary and un-Christian. A school that discriminates openly violates Christian teaching.

Jack Harrison put it more bluntly when he resigned from Westminster's board. "Immorality," he said.

In December, 1992, Steve Selig wrote to Cody Laird, Jr., Chairman of the Board of Westminster Schools.

*Dear Cody,*

*As a long time member of the Westminster family, I am heartened by the recent developments of your board. I sincerely appreciate the leadership you are bringing to this issue and the extensive amount of meetings and input you have invited on this subject. In my opinion, it is time for Westminster Schools to change its hiring policy for faculty.*

*I wish you good luck as you guide the Westminster board forward. I hope you will share this letter with your board. I look forward to the day when this issue is resolved and Westminster's hiring policy is open to the most qualified individuals regardless of their religion.*

*Sincerely,*

*S. Stephen Selig, III*

As the issue gained increased attention, ACCESS added their support.

*Dear ACCESS member,*

*As you know, the American Jewish Committee is an organization that speaks out when it sees injustice or prejudice in our society. The Atlanta Chapter has expressed our concern with the discriminatory hiring practices that exist at The Westminster Schools. I am asking for your help in providing a voice from ACCESS to do the same.*

*Many of you graduated from, or know someone who graduated from, Westminster. The issue of not hiring non-Christian faculty has been revisited recently, and it offers us a chance to express our opposition to the policy. Hearing from graduates of the school can make a tremendous impact, and I urge you to write a letter to the Headmaster and the Chairman of the Board of Trustees. Indicate in your letter that you hope they will share your letter with their board.*

*Scott Smith, a 1980 Westminster graduate and member of ACCESS, has provided a few key "talking points" for you to include in your letter, if you care to use them. They are only there to offer ideas – we encourage you to express your opposition in any way you wish. The most important thing is that you write.*
*Sincerely,*
*Elise Eplan*
*Chair, ACCESS*


On December 10, we wrote to Cody Laird.


*Dear Cody,*

*We appreciate the depth of feeling on this issue and are gratified to learn of the increasing efforts to explore and hopefully change the current policy.*

*While we respect your commitment to maintaining the Christian philosophy of your school, we can assure you that hiring non-Jewish faculty has in no way diminished the Jewish nature of the Epstein School, Hebrew Academy or Yeshiva High School. All of these private Jewish schools in Atlanta have strong religious, cultural and Hebrew language programs and yet benefit from outstanding non-Jewish faculty who teach diverse subjects including math, sciences and the arts.*

*It is time for letters to the editors, cartoons and the like to cease linking Westminster Schools with charges of anti-Semitism, discrimination, etc. This will happen, we believe, when the hiring policies for your faculty are changed.*
*Sincerely,*
*Richard W. Cohen, M.D.*          *Sherry Frank*
*President, Atlanta Chapter*       *Southeast Area Director*

In a dramatic move, on December 10, 1992, Jack Harrison resigned from the Westminster board in protest of its hiring policy. That same day, he wrote a compelling article in the *Atlanta Journal-Constitution* titled "Conscience of Atlanta Can Change Westminster" decrying anti-Semitic actions. "You will change the policy because the people of Atlanta, the city with a conscience, demand it," he wrote. "In the mid '80s, a board subcommittee recommended the policy change and the chairman never presented the findings to the board. Shame. Shame on your secretive ways that affect 1,600 families, the parents and children of Westminster."

That December, staff writer Laura Wisniewski at the *Atlanta Journal-Constitution* reported on surveys taken at the school and suggested that the trustees reconsider this policy.

*Students, Faculty Favor Making Change*

While Westminster's leaders continue to grapple in private over the school's Christians-only hiring policy, students, parents, alumni and faculty are coming out strong against the practice. Separate faculty and student surveys, conducted by the school's newspaper, *The Bi-Line*, showed 65 percent of the high school students said they wanted the policy changed. Of Christian students surveyed, 55 percent wanted it changed.

The survey results came out Thursday in a special issue of *The Bi-Line* that also carried several articles about the controversy. The faculty survey, taken by a teacher, is expected to be presented to the school's board of trustees soon.

Many people associated with the school speculate that the trustees may reconsider the policy in February – sooner than the original October date – after the board hears from all concerned.

This issue drew national attention when it received coverage in *The New York Times* on December 23, 1992, in an article titled "Atlanta School's Ban on Hiring Non-Christians Opens a Debate." It raised the points that Westminster's policy of hiring only Christian faculty has attracted criticism from some of the best colleges, and that parents are concerned about whether it could affect their children's applications to these schools. The controversy generated questions for Christians about the meaning of a Christian school in a secular world and for Jews what it means to be a minority in a majority Christian world.

After so many years of debate, Cody Laird was able to notify the Westminster family about the document adopted by the board at its meeting on February 25, 1993. A press release, titled "Westminster Trustees Adopt a Long-Range Plan," included a statement recognizing the school's desire to "develop the whole person for college and for life" and therefore to appoint faculty who both excel in their fields and who support the Christian values of Westminster, thus acknowledging that skilled faculty of all faiths could be eligible to teach at the school.

The Westminster story illustrates how slow change can be and how frequently it meets with resistance. Fortunately, as the City of Atlanta grew, diversity became more valued, and brave leaders rose to face new challenges. This was evidenced by the decision of the Westminster board. One of the strongest voices for that change was Jim Kennedy of Cox Enterprises, who had received  AJC's prestigious Human Relations Award in 1991 for his years of outstanding leadership throughout the civic and business communities. Today Jewish students, faculty and lay leaders are valued and active in the school.

## MINISTER LOUIS FARRAKHAN

In the 1990s, Minister Louis Farrakhan and Nation of Islam leaders were among the most outspoken proponents of anti-Semitism and were distributors of offensive and historically incorrect materials. Many times we had to respond to challenges they presented for Atlanta. One of these was in October, 1992, when they were in our city to celebrate Saviour's Day, the Nation of Islam's annual commemoration of the life of its founder, the Reverend Elijah Muhammad.  Their advance staff was in town weeks ahead of time and tried repeatedly to secure meetings between Jewish leaders and Minister Farrakhan, provoking tense discussions with Jewish leaders and rabbis and black leaders and clergy. When the Jews refused to meet, it drew media attention. An *Atlanta Journal* article by Paul Kaplan on February 7, 1993, was titled "Farrakhan's visit left no lasting black-Jewish rift."

Blacks and Jews have a history of cooperation in Atlanta, but the friendship was strained last October when Nation of Islam leader Louis Farrakhan, who has called the Jewish faith a "gutter religion," came to town for a rally.

Gov. Zell Miller appeased some Jews by rescinding a letter of welcome his office had sent to Minister Farrakhan, but Mayor

Maynard H. Jackson refused to rescind his office's letter. Instead, he urged Minister Farrakhan to apologize to Jews and urged both groups to discuss and resolve their differences.

Jewish leaders refused, saying there was nothing to talk about until Minister Farrakhan apologized for, or retracted, his anti-Semitic remarks.

"I have no apologies to make; I have no words to retract," Minister Farrakhan told 40,000 followers at the Georgia Dome.

Ms. (Sherry) Frank thinks "there was some damage that was done that, over the years, will be fixed." She still recalls "anguishing over the Farrakhan visit" one night and deciding to call John Lewis, the black congressman from Atlanta who is adept at building black-white coalitions.

"He urged me to put it in perspective: Farrakhan's visit will be short-lived in Atlanta, and the divisiveness will quickly become eclipsed by other things, and years of work in black-Jewish relations will stand for much more than one visit by Farrakhan in the Dome. I think the congressman was right."

In January, 1994, the Black Students Association and the Black Law Students Association extended an invitation to Farrakhan's assistant, the activist Khalid Abdul Muhammad, for a February 8 speaking engagement at Emory University. After a few tense days, the invitation was rescinded.

AJC joined several community agencies, Emory students and faculty, and the director of Hillel, in developing a plan of action for both alternatives – if he spoke, or if the talk was cancelled. In an effort to continue to educate our community about anti-Semitism and strengthen relations in the Black/Jewish Coalition, we took several actions.

1. We invited the Chair of Emory University's African-American Studies Program to meet with the Steering Committee of the Black/Jewish Coalition. We wanted to

learn about campus activity and offer help in bringing black and Jewish students together. On January 27, 1994, we wrote to Dr. Billy Frye, Interim President of Emory University.

*Dear Dr. Frye,*

*On behalf of the American Jewish Committee, Atlanta Chapter, we want you to know how pleased we were to learn that the scheduled speech by Khalid Abdul Muhammad for February 8th at Emory University has been cancelled.*

*We are deeply offended at the hate-filled message he delivers and are pleased that our community will not have to respond to this raw bigotry.*

*We would be happy to work with you, your faculty and/or students in building a more tolerant environment.*

*Sincerely,*

| | |
|---|---|
| *Lois Frank* | *Sherry Frank* |
| *President, Atlanta Chapter* | *Southeast Area Director* |

2. The Atlanta Black/Jewish Coalition commended the Reverend Jesse Jackson for his condemnation of the statements of Khalid Abdul Muhammad, spokesman for the Nation of Islam. In a January 29 letter to the editor of the Atlanta Constitution, Dianne Harnell Cohen and Thomas (Tommy) Dortch, Jr., quoted Jackson as saying the speech was "racist, anti-Semitic, divisive, untrue and chilling." He conveyed similar concern expressed by other prominent black leaders, including Reverend Al Sharpton, William Gray, III, Kweisi Mfume, and the Reverend Benjamin Chavis, whom we applauded for speaking out in the face of demagoguery, hate mongering and blatant anti-Semitism.

3. Lois Frank, Atlanta Chapter President, and I sent a February 10 letter to the editor of the *Atlanta Journal*.

*More of the Same Old Hate.*

The American Jewish Committee is appalled by Louis Farrakhan's comments. It is the same old bone-chilling hate.

Farrakhan reaffirmed the Nation of Islam's ongoing program to spread hate against whites, Jews, gays, Catholics, and others. He stood by the substance of the bigoted and racist remarks of his associate Khalid Abdul Muhammad at Kean College, while rebuking only his associate's "manner."

He demonstrated the Nation of Islam's agenda through his wholehearted endorsement of its virulently anti-Semitic book, *The Secret Relationship Between Blacks and Jews.* This book has been roundly criticized by scholars, black and white, as a distortion of history designed to promote anti-Semitism within the African-American community.

It is past time for people of good will of all religions and races to denounce the hate mongers in our midst.

Standing up against the frightening statements and actions by Farrakhan and his followers emboldened us. The Saviours' Day event could have caused another anti-Semitic incident in Atlanta. Fortunately, we have long-standing and strong relations with many of Atlanta's most admired leaders. This is especially true of my personal relationship with Dr. Johnnetta Cole, President of Spelman College. A February 24 press release from AJC acknowledged and praised her actions.

The American Jewish Committee, Atlanta Chapter, commends Spelman College and its President, Dr. Johnnetta Cole, for their unequivocal stand against bigotry by cancelling the "Saviours' Day Celebration 1994," sponsored by the Lost-Found Nation of Islam scheduled in Sisters Chapel on Sunday February 27th. This forthright action was taken as a result of the circulation of a vile anti-Semitic flyer promoting this event.

On March 4, the *Atlanta Jewish Times* reported on the praise Dr. Cole received from the Jewish community and concerns raised in some parts of the black community regarding distancing them from Farrakhan and the Nation of Islam.

Farrakhan's frequent television appearances and speeches at large community events were receiving increased attention. On February 24, AJC placed an ad in *The New York Times* in response to this heightened anti-Semitism. Dr. Cole joined with 250 other leading Americans in signing this ad. It affirmed the diversity of faith, ethnicity and race that has brought us to this country in different ways and unites us in a common campaign for civil rights and justice for all. Atlantans joining with Dr. Cole included Mayor Bill Campbell, Dr. James Costen, Senator Paul Coverdell, Archbishop John F. Donaghue, James Kennedy, Coretta Scott King, Congressman John Lewis, Bernard Marcus, Governor Zell Miller, Dr. Louis Sullivan, and the Honorable Andrew Young.

Farrakhan's 1995 Million Man March sparked numerous discussions and responses. On November 10, we reprinted an ad in the *Atlanta Jewish Times* that AJC had placed in *The New York Times* the week before. It was titled "Count Us Out" and made it clear that racism and anti-Semitism are not debatable issues.

> *As long as the Minister and his aides continue to engage in broad scale attacks against Jews and other groups, both in speeches and publications, there's simply nothing for us to discuss.*
>
> *Minister Farrakhan and his movement cannot have it both ways – one voice that today purports to speak of dialogue and ecumenism and another that obsessively demonizes Jews and others.*

At the same time as he was calling for African-American men to take more responsibility for their families and community, Farrakhan continued to spout his relentless anti-Semitic statements.

At a December 6, 1996, conference on "Hate in America" sponsored by the Center for Democratic Renewal, I spoke about the series of burned churches, the rise of the militia movement, the white supremacist's espousal of conspiracy theories and Holocaust denial, the increase in hate crimes, and concern with bigoted lyrics in some of Michael Jackson's songs. I also addressed the hateful message delivered by Farrakhan.

> *The Jewish community watches the rise of Minister Farrakhan with great concern. The Black separatist Nation of Islam contin- ues to distribute messages of hate, from the sale of the book* The Protocols of the Elders of Zion, *sold at their forums, the Million Man March and in their bookstores, to the speeches of Minister Farrakhan. In the weeks preceding the Million Man March, he reiterated to the media his opinion that Jews were the "blood suck- ers" of the Black community. This poisonous rhetoric continues to flow from him and his deputies including the reinstated Minister Khalid Abdul Muhammad.*

During my tenure on staff and on occasions when people spoke about AJC and ADL,  I heard it said that both organizations were involved in work in a "growth industry" of persistent anti-Semitism, racism, sexism, homophobia, and all forms of bigotry. I will forever be grateful that AJC provided me with a powerful platform to speak out on these issues.

Tom Asher and Steve Selig listening to tape of radio talk-show, 1987

# SOVIET AND ETHIOPIAN JEWRY

## LIBERATION MOVEMENTS OF OUR TIMES

---

*They tried their best to find a place where I was isolated. But all the resources of a superpower cannot isolate the man who hears the voice of freedom, a voice I heard from the very chambers of my soul.*

—Anatoly Shcharansky (Natan Sharansky)

The exoduses of Soviet Jews and Ethiopian Jews will long be celebrated as heroic stories of world Jewry that took place during my lifetime.

## SOVIET JEWRY

Early in my involvement in NCJW, I became aware of the struggle to free Soviet Jews, and I wanted to help those who reached America adjust to our country as much as I possibly could. NCJW had always had an active Service to New Americans Committee, resettling immigrants from all over the world. In Atlanta, Hannah Entell was chair of this committee from 1964 to 1973, primarily assisting Jews from Western Europe. She paved the way for meeting future resettlement challenges. In 1974, NCJW presented its highest honor, the Hannah G. Solomon award, to her for her tireless work over the decade.

With the emerging Soviet Jewry movement, a new chapter in resettlement was opening up, requiring different initiatives. In June, 1974, working closely with the Jewish Family and Children's Bureau (later named Jewish Family and Career Services – JF&CS,) NCJW restructured their Service to New Americans Committee. NCJW Vice President Fran Eizenstat guided the effort. Jody Franco, Anne Birnbaum, Laura Dinerman and Nancy Pollard provided additional leadership to the new team of fifty volunteers. In September Atlanta welcomed the first twenty-five Soviet Jews to our community. An article on different facets of the Soviet immigration situation was included in the *NCJW Bulletin*.

HIAS (Hebrew Immigrant Aid Society) has predicted that 4,800 Soviet Jews will arrive in the United States due to the loosening of immigration laws in Russia. And we feel that we have the rare opportunity to help these people in adapting to our country and to our community.

As Eli Wiesel has said,

> *Alone, the individual Jew would have been lost many times and long ago, but a Jew is never alone... Jews have never before been so organically linked to one another. If we shout here, we are being heard in Kiev. If Jews cry in Kiev, they are heard and worried over in Jerusalem, and if Jews are sad in Jerusalem, we are moved to tears here.*

And so, it is for us in our own way to lift the shackles of oppression experienced by these people and to expose them with patience, pride, and faith to a new way of life in America. Council's role is significant, because we are completely furnishing an apartment for all families who arrive. Relatively simple things to us, such as learning how to use public transportation, paying one's bills, going to the grocery store and buying nutritional food, learning a new set of cultural values, or speaking English, are taught to the newcomer by a team of volunteers assigned to each family.

"The Soviet Union – It's a Tough Place to Live, It's a Tougher Place to Leave" had been  the theme of the third annual Women's Plea for Soviet Jewry on Human Rights Day, December 10, 1973. This event was a major forum for education and advocacy, and it provided a springboard for future action.

The April, 1974, *NCJW* Bulletin printed the "Matzah of Hope."

That the Jews of the Soviet Union may know that they have not been forgotten and that we are one in brotherhood.  The National Conference on Soviet Jewry, an association of 34 national Jewish organizations and hundreds of Jewish community councils and federations in support of the struggle of Soviet Jews to attain freedom and equality, urges that the following statement be read at the Seder of every American Jewish household.

The leader of the service takes up the matzah, sets it aside, and says:

*This Matzah, which we set aside as a symbol of hope for the Jews of the Soviet Union, reminds us of the indestructible links that exist between us.*

*As we observe this festival of freedom, we know that Soviet Jews are not free to leave without harassment; to learn of their past; to pass on their religious traditions; to learn the languages of their fathers; to train teachers and the rabbis of future generations.*

*We remember with bitterness the scores of Jewish prisoners of conscience who sought to live as Jews and*

I loved including this new liturgy at my Seder. It reflected contemporary struggles and launched a large number of new readings and *Haggadot* produced over the decades since the Soviet Jewry movement of the 1970s. At community Seders I attended, we added new words to the Negro spiritual "Go Down, Moses,"calling it "Freedom Land." It was particularly powerful when sung jointly with the Atlanta Black/Jewish Coalition. *Tell the Kremlin to let our people go!* Ending with the words *"Am Yisroel Chai."*

Towards the end of the 1970s, I spoke about Soviet Jewry, presenting a comprehensive review of the history and current status of the movement, traveling to Charleston, South Carolina; Sarasota, Florida; Memphis, Tennessee; Tulsa, Oklahoma; and Atlanta, Georgia.

On November 7, 1975, I joined a demonstration with hundreds of Atlanta Jews at the Fox Theatre where the Moscow State Symphony was performing. One of the protestors carried a sign saying, "Without freedom, life is not a symphony." My poster read, "Let my people go," and I was quoted in an *Atlanta Constitution* story saying, "We applaud cultural exchange, but oppose cultural repression. We are in no way trying to undermine the performance." This was the first of many rallies we held over the decades when Russian groups performed in our city.

NCJW's November/December 1978 *Bulletin* carried an article titled "Mayor Maynard Jackson Returns from the Soviet Union."

Mayor Maynard Jackson returned from the Soviet Union recently after leading a delegation of mayors in a State Department-sponsored two-week visit.

Before and after his visit, he invited several community leaders, including a representative from NCJW, and professionals to meet with him to hear their concerns regarding Soviet Jewry.

Following the suggestions of the Jewish leaders, the Mayor made some meaningful contacts with Soviet Jews which he reported to the heads of all Jewish organizations at a special meeting held on October 4.

In addition to meeting with the Rabbis of Kiev and Moscow and sending New Year's Greetings from them, Mayor Jackson visited refusenik Dr. Benjamin Levich in his Moscow apartment. He described a very moving experience when he met Dr. Levich, his wife, and several friends.

We thank the Mayor for his participation in the trip and relating his experiences to us.

During NCJW's annual installation meeting on May 21, 1979, we phoned Yakov Ariev in Riga. His cousin, Bella, who was in the room with us, spoke to him in Russian and translated into English. We learned that his family and neighbors had recently been refused exit visas and were fearful for their future. Sending greetings of friendship, we committed to continue to advocate for their release.

As the years passed, I added to my button collection supporting the release of Soviet Jews. I joined the thousands of Jewish activists wearing bracelets and necklaces bearing the names of leading refuseniks.

From 1972-1987, Sister Ann Gillen served as the Executive Director of the National Interreligious Task Force for Soviet Jewry. She worked closely with AJC's Rabbi Jim Rudin, and I enjoyed collaborating with her and hosting her in Atlanta. We created the Atlanta Interreligious Task Force on Soviet Jewry and Human Rights and through the years advocated with an impressive list of clergy, civic leaders, and elected officials in an official and public capacity.

Speaking about Soviet Jewry resettlement at NCJW's Southern District Convention in 1978, I ended with this story.

*I still have chills when I remember visiting a family on their first day in their new apartment and at the end of their long journey for freedom when, in broken English, a young teenager said "It's like 'once upon a time,' and the story is about me." For these people, reality is two women talking to each other. One is a Russian immigrant, the other is an American. A favor is needed, and a favor is done. The Russian lady, her face filled with emotion, says "If only I had the English words to tell you my thoughts. I have so many Russian words I know to say." "Say them," said the American lady. "I'll understand with my heart." "I wish the Soviet government would listen with their heart," replied the Russian lady. But we in Council will reply with our hearts and heads in advocacy and in action. We will make sure the quiet diplomacy works, because we will initiate public awareness and agitation, and we believe that human rights are self-evident and transcend political boundaries, and we know that our children will look on the chapter in history in which we lived and they will know that we were not silent. And the physical annihilation of our people in the 1940s will not bear witness to the spiritual annihilation of our people in the 1970s.*

I was serving a four-year term on NCJW's National Board when an August 22, 1981, press release reported on my continuing involvement in Soviet Jewry. It announced "New NCJW Manual Aids Professionals and Volunteers Working With Russian Jewish Immigrants."

Since 1972, more that 80,000 Russian Jews have resettled in the U.S. For many, the flight from Soviet oppression has come only after long years of waiting for exit visas. Many of these immigrants arrive in America bewildered, confused by the unfamiliar environment, and often with unrealistic expectations. They need help in adjusting to a new life in a strange land; many speak no English and need interpreters; their immediate requirements include everything from clothing, to a roof over their heads, to finding work.

To aid in this resettlement process, the National Council of Jewish Women has recently published a manual entitled, *Community Partners: the Staff-Volunteer Team in Soviet Jewish Resettlement.* The publication, underwritten by a $50,000 grant from the Council of Jewish Federations, is the product of a year of intensive study, field interviews, pilot training and in-depth contributions from Jewish communities throughout the country.

*Community Partners* was developed under the auspices of NCJW's Soviet Jewry Grant Committee, co-chaired by Elaine Sterling and Sherry Frank. Ms. Sterling, an NCJW National Vice President from South Orange, N.J., has expertise in developing training modules and materials. Ms. Frank, a National Board Member from Atlanta, GA, has had extensive involvement in the resettlement of Soviet Jews.

By the spring of 1981, NCJW Atlanta Section volunteers had assisted in furnishing 450 apartments. In my professional role at AJC, I was working on new ways to advocate for Soviet Jewry.

I went to the Soviet Union from April 15-26, 1987, to meet with Jews struggling to leave that country. It was a transformative event for me. In preparation for our visit, David Harris, AJC's Executive Director, visited Atlanta to brief the five of us making this trip – Beatrice Gruss, Rabbi Robert Ichay, Cookie Shapiro, Larry Thorpe and me. He gave us detailed instructions on whom to meet with in Moscow, Leningrad (now St. Petersburg), and Riga, how to contact them on the phone and how to connect with them at the train station.

We were told what clothing items we should bring that could be sold on the black market to help pay rent and other necessities of the activists, and we were asked to bring medicines that had been requested of previous visitors. We were to bring back information on the health of specific individuals and new needs of others. David advised us to contact and meet with the U.S. Embassy and gave us suggestions for dealing with expected KGB surveillance.

Our mission was all at once exciting, scary and sacred. We traveled during Passover at a time when many Russian Hebrew teachers were in prison. Rabbi Ichay had a recorder and filled blank tapes with recordings of Torah that we left for the activists in each city.

On the plane home, I recounted my experience in the Soviet Union in a report for Atlanta Chapter members.

*Dear AJC Member,*

*I'm writing this letter in flight returning home from an emotional 10 days in the Soviet Union. From its inception, the American Jewish Committee has been devoted to protecting the rights of Jews throughout the world. We began 81 years ago by responding to pogroms in Kishinev. As part of our 80th Anniversary, chapters were encouraged to travel back to where we began, to give hope to our brave sisters and brothers locked in a cruel and inhumane society.*

*From the moment the plane touched down in Moscow, on to Riga and throughout Leningrad, everything was grey. It's cold, snowy and rainy three-quarters of the year. The streets are cracked, sidewalks are combinations of pavement and mud puddles, water is undrinkable, cabs are scarce, information is censored, propaganda flourishes, no one smiles, few speak English, and the military presence is everywhere. The only bright spots in this enormous stretch of land are the Jews of hope. Strong, courageous people who make us cry with their stories of horror and renew our faith with their sense of destiny and unbroken spirit.*

*Five of us from AJC's Atlanta Chapter, Cookie Shapiro, Larry Thorpe, Rabbi Robert Ichay, Beatrice Gruss, and I, spent a memorable Passover in Moscow. We brought Kosher food, items of Judaica, medications, magazines, books, and assorted clothes and gifts. We met with well-known refuseniks, women who were fighting to get their husbands out of prison, parents who longed to be with their sons and daughters in Israel and the United States who had never seen their grandchildren, people who had spouses abroad and were denied visas to join them, families praying to leave before their sons went into the army and sick people needing medical help abroad.*

*We met Nadazhda Fradkova, the only woman sentenced to a forced labor camp, drugged with narcotics in mental hospitals and given sulfur injections which induced near fatal temperatures and days of excruciating pain. We heard Marina Furman tell about the KGB threats that her baby would not be born alive if she continued her activist role. When she went into labor, the KGB kept the doctor from her and she nearly died. Rabbi Ichay held her precious five-week-old daughter and blessed her in Hebrew, and that picture still lingers in my mind. Tanya works tirelessly for her husband, Uli Edelshtein's, release from a prison camp where he was critically ill with a broken leg, hip, and urethra. For a month he was given no medical treatment and was close to death. Still weak, but recovering, he now is assigned to hard labor working on a conveyer belt, and if he doesn't do his work fast enough, he'll be punished further.*

*We mixed with refuseniks in front of the Moscow Synagogue at dusk on* Shabbat. *I stood and hummed, captivated by two young singers and a man playing guitar, as dozens of refuseniks gathered around to sing Hebrew and Yiddish songs for nearly two hours. We visited one family who received a letter to come to the authorities to discuss their visa application. They asked us to come back two days later after they went to the authorities. Refused for* the seventh time, the Uspensky's were told not to re-apply until 1992. Their 16-year-old son, a member of the religious community, was teary eyed when Cookie gave him a Chai she bought in Israel. We saw David Laikhtman one evening, and while we returned to our hotel, their family received a call from authorities telling them they had permission to leave the Soviet Union. We received a call from David later that evening, and we felt their joy and drank toasts at dinner, at last some good news.

Everywhere we went, other refuseniks came to see us. Each thanked us for coming and told us their only hope of survival is in our hands and the hands of our American government. They told us of the Seder in the American embassy in Moscow attended by 100 refuseniks. Secretary of State George Shultz made a moving speech, which touched them deeply. He went around the room saying something personal to everyone and giving them gifts. He gave Iosif Begun an ancient Haggadah. This experience had a rippling effect, and all of the Moscow refuseniks were reinforced by this American support in such a public manner.

We asked refuseniks what they thought of Gorbachev and Glasnost and how it would affect them. Most felt Gorbachev was better than past leaders and wanted to improve the system. The weight of history was against him, and unless he's in office for 15-20 years, only limited improvements are possible, in their view. They feel the new emigration laws are terrible and are concerned with the increased number of refusals given for reasons of "state secrets," when the refuseniks have had access to no secrets in their work in the last 15 years. State secrets are even being used to deny visas when a distant relative might have worked in sensitive areas.

Some refuseniks are cautiously optimistic that more permissions to leave will be given, but not to long-term active refuseniks and not to those who most want to go to Israel. In several visits we learned about the anti-Semitic posters, books and pamphlets recently published, and we brought back samples with us.

We had a fascinating meeting with Shaun Byrnes, Director of Political Affairs, in the U.S. Embassy in Moscow. We talked in rather guarded terms, because he told us they are operating with the attitude that the entire U.S. Embassy is bugged. He and the other staff members are closely in touch with the refuseniks and very sensitive to their plight. He felt, as the refuseniks did, that there is some reason for hope and increased emigration, but it is far too limited, and the doors could shut tight at any moment. He was concerned about the 10,000 being discussed to leave when 400,000 have applied. He told us the United States is committed to the Helsinki guarantees of free emigration. The sight of the American flag warmed our hearts as we approached our embassy, and after meeting with Burns, we were even prouder of the posture of our government and its unyielding support of human rights.

We asked every person we met with what we could do for them. We told them other Atlantans would be in Russia in June and asked what material items they needed. We took careful notes and will fill each request.

Larry Thorpe took a chance on getting film out of the Soviet Union and brought a camcorder. We have incredible stories on film. We have personal interviews and stories of horror and bravery. We have messages in Russian to send to families abroad. I presented three brave women, who continue their husbands' struggle for them while they are in jail, books autographed by Coretta Scott King about her life with Martin Luther King, Jr.

Throughout the trip, I kept humming the music to the song "We Are One," and through the tears Beatrice said, "We Jews come from strong stock." Our people survive, they reach out to one another and give each other strength. In a small way, we added our support to that 2,000 year chain of Jewish survival. More Jews need to travel to Russia. I'm deeply grateful for this memorable opportunity. The faces and stories will be with me forever. I urge you to consider making this journey also.

Safely home, I could share with friends, family and community some of the "off the record" intrigue that had surrounded us. When talking in our rooms, we had played music so we could not be overheard by the KGB's bugging devices. We arranged our personal articles in drawers in such a way that we could tell if our rooms were checked when we were out, and found, when we returned, that things had been slightly moved. We spent hours touring famous places and filming them before recording our meetings with activists in the hopes that if we were being followed, we would be seen as ordinary tourists, and, if our film was checked, only the beginning minutes would be watched. At the U.S. Embassy, we wrote the name of an activist urgently needing help on a kids' "magic drawing slate," — one of those old fashioned toys that can be erased when the top plastic sheet is lifted and there is no record left behind. Weeks later, we were excited to hear that her release had been secured.

Freedom Sunday, the most significant event in the history of the Soviet Jewry movement, took place on December 6, 1987, just before the Gorbachev-Reagan summit. A quarter of a million people demonstrated in Washington, D.C. David Harris took a leave of absence from AJC to serve as the national coordinator of this event. In the weeks prior to it, Chapter leaders and staff worked encouraging participation around the country. AJC members and staff were invited to stay over for a private dinner honoring Natan Sharansky, providing a truly special experience for us all. The *Atlanta Constitution* published an editorial I wrote on December 5, 1987.

*Freedom Sunday is chance to affect history*

We don't get to choose moments in history; they are chosen for us. Such is the case with the upcoming Gorbachev-Reagan summit.

But we do have the power to affect those moments in

history, and that is the driving force behind the Washington Mobilization tomorrow called Freedom Sunday.

Twenty-four years ago, thousands of people from across the United States stood in our nation's capital and heard the piercing words of Martin Luther King, Jr., as he described his dream for his people. That march, that dream, that movement, in 1963 changed the course of history for black citizens of our country and for other minorities, women and the handicapped.

Tomorrow, thousands of Jews from across the United States will march together with concerned citizens of all races and religions in support of Soviet Jewry.

We will hear from Natan Sharansky, Ida Nudel and other heroes of the struggle for religious freedom in the Soviet Union. Vice President George Bush and congressional leadership will reinforce the strong commitment this country has to human rights and religious liberty, a message at the top of the agenda when President Reagan meets with Mikhail Gorbachev. As former President Carter said, "America didn't invent human rights, human rights invented America."

Leaders of the National Council of Churches and the National Conference of Catholic Bishops also will participate.

As we march together, we will speak of our dream for our brothers and sisters in the Soviet Union. We have a dream that the Soviet Union will honor the international documents it has signed and allow Soviet Jews to practice their religion, study Hebrew, observe holidays, train rabbis and teachers, and establish Jewish cultural activities. We have a dream that Jews in the Soviet Union will no longer face discrimination in jobs and higher education. We have a dream that the Soviet Union will allow those Jews who wish to leave, their basic rights guaranteed by international law, to emigrate. We have a dream that the Soviet Union will cease to be the world's leading publisher of anti-Semitic and anti-Israel propaganda.

Numbers speak loud and clear. Six million Jews (one-third of world Jewry) were murdered in the Holocaust. Today, one-fifth of the Jews in the world are trapped in the Soviet Union. The future of those 2.5 million Jews rests on the hearts and minds of Jews in the free world. We will not stand idly by.

From 1968 to December 1986, nearly 650,000 Soviet Jews were sent the necessary personal affidavits of invitation submitted by Israeli citizens and registered in the Israeli Foreign Office. (This is the first step for Jews in the emigration process.) During the same period, more than 266,000 Jews left the Soviet Union with Israeli visas. Therefore, nearly 385,000 who remain, at great personal risk, have taken the initial step to leave.

The new Soviet law that allows only for those with parents and children abroad to emigrate would cut eligibility for Soviet Jews wishing to leave by 90 percent.

In 1979, more than 51,000 Jews left the Soviet Union. The number was down to 914 in 1986. In 1987, about 800 a month are being granted permission to leave, a dramatic decrease from the 4,000 a month in 1979.

The summit meeting next week between Reagan and Gorbachev has the promise of moving our world a little closer towards peace.

There should be no misunderstanding. Support for human rights in the Soviet Union need not in any way suggest opposition to an arms reduction accord. An intermediate-range nuclear forces agreement that serves America's security interests and contributes to a more peaceful world would benefit Americans and Russians alike.

But there remains the lingering question of whether the Soviets can be trusted to keep their word on this or any other agreement. Through their action in upholding human rights agreements, Soviets can build trust in our country.

> Three thousand news people will be in Washington for
> the summit. The eyes of the world will be watching. Perhaps
> the course of history for Soviet Jews will be dramatically
> affected by our presence.
>
> We hope Freedom Sunday will live on in our history as a
> proud moment and turning point in the eternal struggle for
> international human rights and freedom for Soviet Jewry.

Mayor Andrew Young issued a proclamation declaring December 8, 1987, "Freedom for Soviet Jewry Day." At our invitation, Congressman John Lewis spoke at the demonstration saying "Twenty-five years ago, I marched here in Washington to focus the nation's attention on the injustices and the oppression of segregation. Many of my Jewish friends were with me then, and today I am proud to take part in your march for freedom for your people who are oppressed in the Soviet Union."

Although Coretta Scott King was unable to accept our invitation to speak, she sent a message that was read by Congressman Lewis in which she wholeheartedly endorsed the rally, noting that her husband, Dr. Martin Luther King Jr., had been concerned about what he called "spiritual and cultural genocide" being forced on Soviet Jewry by the Soviet government.

Throughout the 1980s, Jewish community organizations cooperated on resettlement. There were demonstrations when Russian groups performed in Atlanta, and we intensified our personal connections with specific activists in Russia. We secured tickets to cultural events for the Russian Jews in Atlanta, including the International Ballet Rotaru and violinist, Itzhak Perlman. When Soviet Jewish activist Lev Shapiro came to Atlanta on September 1, 1988, I arranged an editorial board meeting at the *Atlanta Journal-Constitution* for him and scheduled several additional press interviews.

Many dedicated Atlanta leaders were involved in this effort, and among the most committed were Kathy and Howard Sachs and Judith and Elliott Cohen. Howard was deeply engaged politically with members of Congress and went on to serve as President of the National Conference on Soviet Jewry. The Cohens were among Atlantans who traveled multiple times to the Soviet Union and met with refuseniks around the world. In 1989, Judith spent several months in Ladispoli, Italy, teaching English to Soviet émigrés who were hoping to come to the U.S.

We received outstanding and significant support from our political and civic leaders throughout the 1980s. The Jewish community should feel a special sense of pride and gratitude for this advocacy on behalf of our Jewish brothers and sisters in the Soviet Union.

- July 2, 1981 – A letter was sent to President Leonid Brezhnev, written on Georgia Institute of Technology stationery and signed by a dozen chemistry professors, urging the release from exile of Dr. Viktor Brailovsky. He, his wife Irina, and son Leonid were denied exit visas. The letter closed with:

  *We as scholars and educators are sensitive to the importance of a free and nurturing atmosphere in which to develop and communicate and we submit that this issue transcends the scientific and educational community and reaches fully to the human community worldwide. Until everyone everywhere is free of oppression, we shall all suffer.*

- July 20, 1981 – Mayor Maynard Jackson wrote to Alexander Lerner.

  *Word has reached the United States of the death of your wife, Judith, on July 7. I send you my deepest heartfelt condolences and sympathy in what is undoubtedly a trying and tragic time for you and your family.*

  *I recall our meeting during my visit to the Soviet Union in the Fall of 1978, and will never forget you and your friends, Benjamin Levich and Yakov Alpert.*

  *The passing of your wife, Judith, is all the more tragic since she was unable to fulfill her great wish to reunite with her family in Israel. It is my hope that the Soviet authorities, in the name of humanity, will permit you and your son to accompany your wife's remains to Israel.*

*Your struggle for human rights for Soviet Jews is a struggle for humankind to share.*

- February 14, 1985 - Congressman Wyche Fowler sent a letter on behalf of the Congressional Coalition for Soviet Jewry.

  *As you may know, the formation of the Congressional Coalition for Soviet Jewry was announced on January 30 in Washington. I, along with Rep. Jack Kemp (R-NY) and Senators Lugar (R-IN) and Sarbanes (D-MD), will serve as co-chairs of the Coalition. This bipartisan coalition will serve as a focal point for congressional activity on behalf of Soviet Jews. Our ultimate goal is to encourage all governments throughout the world to support private and public advocacy efforts on behalf of Soviet Jewry.*

  *The situation for Jews in the USSR has worsened in the last five years. During both my visits to the Soviet Union (1973 and 1983), I was struck by the inhumane treatment and total lack of respect for human dignity and freedom on the part of the Soviet authorities. At present, the immigration numbers are lower than ever – only 896 Jews were allowed to leave in 1984. In addition, anti-Semitic attacks and harassment have risen to frightening proportions.*

  *The time to take action is now. We must bring attention to the plight of our brethren in the USSR. It is my sincere hope that the Congressional Coalition will be a moving force in the effort to grant freedom and justice to Soviet Jews.*

- December 11, 1986 – Konstantine Kharchev, Chairman, Council of Religious Affairs, USSR, was in Atlanta. Mayor Andrew Young met with him and raised our concern about Soviet Jews. Coretta Scott King hosted a luncheon with him and invited me to join in the discussion. These were important opportunities for our advocacy.

- April 24, 1987 – *Atlanta Jewish Times* published a piece titled "Getting Involved." An accompanying photo showed Sherry Frank giving John Lewis and his wife, Lillian, AJC publications on Soviet Jewry.

  *Mrs. Lewis will be part of a five-member delegation representing the Congressional Wives for Soviet Jewry in Vienna this spring at the Helsinki Review Committee.*

- July 16, 1987 – Congressman John Lewis wrote to me expressing his support and apprising me that Congresswoman Constance Morella was joining him as a co-chair of the Congressional Coalition for Soviet Jewry Freshman Class. In his letter he said, "Ms. Morella and I are looking forward to our trip to Israel later this year."

- November, 1988 – Congressman John Lewis attended a Human Rights Conference in Moscow. As a freshman legislator on this trip, he was advised not to raise the issue of Soviet Jewry. On December 1, he spoke at a program sponsored by AJC and the Ahavath Achim Synagogue repeating the address he had made to the Body of the Supreme Soviet.

*Mr. Chairman,*

*I want to thank you and the members of the Supreme Soviet for hosting this meeting. Chairman Hoyer and Co-Chair DeConcini, I am pleased, grateful, and delighted that you invited this very freshman member of the Congress to be a participant in this very important and historic dialogue during this week. We have had some open and frank discussions; for the issue of human rights is a serious and urgent matter for the people of our two countries.*

*I will be brief, however, Mr. Chairman. I want to convey a sense of urgency, a sense that we must move with speed to affirm the Helsinki Accords, and to affirm and respect the human rights of all humankind.*

*I want to say to my Soviet colleagues that what affects the people of the Soviet Union affects the people of the United States of*

America including my city of Atlanta, Georgia. As nations we may be independent, but as a people and as members of the community of nations, we are interdependent. We are all in the same boat.

As one who has tasted the bitter fruit of racism and discrimination in my own country, I can tell you that the issue of human rights will not go away and that time is neutral. We must all play an active role in enhancing the human rights of our fellow human beings.

In my country, under the rule of law, in the areas of civil and human rights, we have witnessed a nonviolent revolution. We had that nonviolent revolution because under the First Amendment of our Constitution, we are committed to the freedom of assembly, the freedom of speech, the freedom of the press, and the freedom to protest for right.

We must remember this is 1988, and we are moving toward the 21st Century. To tell a refusenik to wait and be patient until 1991 or 1995, when we will again consider your application, is to prolong the psychological pain, the hurt, and the suffering. It is to further compound the denial of basic human rights. Brothers separated from brothers, husbands separated from wives, sons and daughters separated from mothers and fathers.

I appeal to you, the members of the Supreme Soviet, to use your power and influence to open the doors and let those out that have a desire to leave, and affirm the rights of those that desire to remain in this country.

So, I say that this member of Congress will not be satisfied, will not be patient, as long as one person is denied the right to leave and return to his country. I will not be satisfied, will not be patient, as long as one person is not allowed to carry out his religious beliefs. I will not be satisfied, will not be patient, as long as a Jew cannot be Jewish in his own country. I cannot be satisfied or patient as long as one person of conscience is held in prison.

We must use the power of our two great nations not to destroy, but to build; not to divide, but to bring people together; not to oppress, but to uplift; not to enslave, but to set free. True peace is not *the absence of tension; it is the presence of justice. So there cannot be real, true and lasting peace on this planet without a commitment to human rights. As one American, Martin Luther King, Jr., stated on one occasion, "We all must learn to live together on this planet as brothers, or we will perish as fools."*

*It is my hope that these discussions will continue in a fruitful manner.*

*Thank you Mr. Chairman and my colleagues of the Supreme Soviet.*

- July 5, 1989 – Senator Wyche Fowler sent a letter to me on funding for refugee assistance.

*Dear Sherry,*

*I am pleased to report that an important initial step has now been taken toward reducing the Soviet refugee backlog. My colleagues and I on the Appropriations Committee have approved an $85 million supplemental appropriation for refugee assistance. This legislation was passed by the full House and Senate and, on June 30, was signed into law by the President.*

*It is estimated that as many as 200,000 Soviets may apply for admission to the United States in the coming fiscal year. Thus, if we are to avoid another crisis, we must move now to formulate a comprehensive, long-term plan that ensures a refugee policy that is both efficient and humane.*

*I want to assure you that, through my positions on both the Appropriations Committee and the Helsinki Commission, I will continue to work diligently toward this goal.*

*Sincerely,*

*Wyche Fowler, Jr.*

*U.S. Senator*

Natan Sharansky was the guest speaker at the Ahavath Achim Synagogue's June, 1988, Eizenstat Family Lecture. My friend,

Ambassador Stuart Eizenstat, told me that Sharansky wanted to hear the words spoken by Dr. Martin Luther King, Jr., and asked if I could make arrangements for him to go to the King Center. I contacted Martin Luther King, III, who rearranged his schedule so he could join us. It was an extraordinarily moving experience sitting in the executive conference room with Sharansky watching a video of Dr. King speaking. At one point, Sharansky began to talk to the monitor, as if speaking directly to Dr. King, acknowledging that he felt the same way – physically locked up in prison, yet spiritually free in conscience and soul. When I reflect on this experience, I have a sense of awe and wonderment for the spirit, faith, and strength that emboldens our heroes.

Greeting Jews that we had met in Russia and being with them again once they were living free in Israel was an indescribable thrill. Nothing could have been more fulfilling for a Soviet Jewry advocate than standing on the tarmac at Ben Gurion airport to witness a plane's landing and the arrival of new *olim*. As the airplane doors opened, hundreds of new immigrants looked out to see an equal number of us waving Israeli flags, singing songs, and wiping tears as Jews from one part of the world to another, strangers -- now family -- joined hands and danced joyfully in the cool night air. There was simply no better thanks for the years of waiting and working than sharing that moment of exodus and freedom.

In March, 1990, as our advocacy efforts for the release of Soviet Jews continued, a large number of those immigrants arrived in Atlanta. An urgent call for help went out from JF&CS with a special request for families to host the newcomers for Passover. My family had been invited to have Seder at the home of Lois and Larry Frank, and, as usual, Lois volunteered and opened her home to new arrivals. The Khodorkovsky family (name later changed to Kodor) – Sasha, Dmitri, and their son Alex – joined us for dinner. They were deeply moved by the hospitality, bounty of food, and free expression of ritual and Jewish tradition. There were tears, hugs, thanks, and simply, without language, hearts communicated with hearts. I will never forget that evening, and later that week, when I called JF&CS to sign up as a volunteer to "adopt a family," I asked if I could be assigned to the Khodorkovskys.

That match began a friendship with people who today are now part of my extended family. Sasha became an editor of the Russian monthly newspaper, *Russia House*. In December, 1995, she wrote an article in the *Atlanta Journal-Constitution* which I have excerpted here.

I didn't know what a menorah was until Hanukkah came along. Every *Hanukkah* evening, my grandmother would take out a bunch of candles from a cabinet and place them in a glass jar.

As she lit them, one by one, she would say, "Tonight, all my people light up a candle. There are no rich or poor, fortunate or unfortunate Jewish people – before the candles, everyone is equal and all are united."

"Why can't it always be like that?" I would ask. "One must pray to God," she would answer, without answering.

Many years have passed; now I live in the United States. But some things don't change. I remember celebrating my first *Hanukkah* in Atlanta among my new American friends at the home of Sherry Frank (the Southeastern director of the American Jewish Committee). It was like being back in my childhood – candles, latkes, sweets, children receiving money and adults exchanging gifts. Sherry gave me mine and said, "This present for your family I have brought from Israel. Happy *Hanukkah.*"

I unwrapped my present and saw an elegant, shining menorah. Small candle holders curved up, like strings pointed to the sky. I touched them, and as if by magic, I heard sounds of music.

Those strains of Jewish melodies uplifted everybody.

> Old men straightened up and joined the circle of children and grandchildren. Shoulder to shoulder, we danced, holding each other tightly. No one could break our circle or stop our *Hora*.

In 1991, Senator Sam Nunn wrote letters on behalf of Dmitri's extended family and supported our efforts to secure their freedom. Unfortunately, Dmitri's father passed away before receiving permission to leave, but in 1993, his mother, Zina, and his brother, Leonid, arrived in Atlanta along with Leonid's wife Ludmila and their daughter Maria. It was wonderful being a small part of this family reunion.

Replicating a timely national program, our Atlanta Chapter invited participants from the large Atlanta Russian community to apply for AJC's 1999 Leadership Institute for Jews from the Former Soviet Union. Funding was provided with a grant from the Atlanta Jewish Federation. Jeanney Kutner, longtime activist and chairperson of this program, said, "the Leadership Institute will help strengthen our Jewish organizations and congregations as well as provide a stronger voice for the Jews from the Former Soviet Union."

When I see my own children inspired to become involved, I realize how powerful and effective a tool leading by example is. My daughter Jacque, a young professional in San Francisco, reached out to Soviet Jews in that community and volunteered to assist two young families. After marrying and moving to Toronto, she and her husband, Tom, continued that outreach and "adopted" a Soviet Jewish family new to Canada. These families continue to play important roles in our lives, participate in our holidays and *simchas*, and remind us of the phrase describing Jewish peoplehood, "we are one."

On July 25, 2017, we were once again together with the Kodors having dinner at Lois and Larry Frank's home. Jeanney Kutner, also a close friend of the family, was with us. I had brought along a copy of a moving article titled "Happy New Year" that Sasha had written in 1994 that I had unearthed while researching these memoirs. I read it aloud. In it, she described the family's life in Russia. It was emotional, troubling, warm and fascinating at the same time. Dmitri and Alex commented on how superb the translation was from Russian to English, and Jeanney noted that her son, Rob, who spoke Russian, must have translated it. Sasha's article appears in the Appendix.

## ETHIOPIAN JEWRY

It is really a wonder that Ethiopian Jews have continued to exist. These remote, third-world Jews kept their religion alive for centuries against all odds, separated and isolated from mainstream Judaism. The stories about their secretive escape and rescue are equally miraculous. The role of American Jewry, Israel, and the U.S. in this saga is a part of modern history and is ongoing. I feel very proud to have been involved, both professionally and personally, in the part played by AJC and our Atlanta Chapter.

Uriel Heilman's article, "The Falash Mura's Fate," for the *Jewish Telegraphic Agency* on February 16, 2006, provided a brief historical background.

Until the late 1970s, very few Ethiopian Jews had ever wandered beyond the borders of their country and made it to Israel.

But in 1979, an insurgency in northern Ethiopia opened an exit route to Sudan, and thousands of Ethiopian Jews – who called themselves Beta Israel, but were known to outsiders as Falasha – began fleeing the famine and war of northern Ethiopia on a journey they hoped would end in Jerusalem.

Along with thousands of other Ethiopians fleeing their country, which at the time was ruled by Communist dictator Mengistu Haile Mariam, the Jews settled in refugee camps in Sudan and waited for Mossad operatives to take them out.

For the first few years, those who were taken to Israel left in one of three ways. Some were given forged documents and put onto planes in Khartoum bound for Athens. Once in Europe, they then were quietly put onto planes to Israel. Others were moved from their Sudanese refugee camps at night to Port Sudan, where Israeli naval commandos put them onto clandestine naval vessels and then transferred them onto ships headed for Israel. A few were airlifted directly to Israel from the Sudanese desert on illicit flights.

A famine in Ethiopia in 1984 lent great urgency to the effort to rescue Ethiopia's Jews, many of whom were dying of starvation and disease in refugee camps in Sudan while they waited to be taken to Israel.

In the covert maneuver Operation Moses, Israel began airlifting large numbers of Ethiopian Jews from Sudan's desert beginning in November, 1984. Leaks about the operation and growing risks forced its early end in January, 1985, after more than 8,000 Jews had been brought to Israel in the space of just six weeks.

Thousands more remained stranded in Communist Ethiopia.

Barbara Ribakove Gordon, a Senior Editor of *Health Magazine*, traveled to Ethiopia in 1981 and witnessed firsthand the plight of these Jews. In 1982, she founded the North American Conference on Ethiopian Jewry (NACOEJ) with a small group of friends. AJC offered support for this new organization by providing office space in our national headquarters, collaborative work with our international affairs professionals, and connections to our chapters. When David Harris suggested we bring Barbara to our communities to tell about and secure help for Ethiopian Jews, I jumped at the opportunity and immediately confirmed program dates.

I met Barbara for the first time in March, 1987. In an evening meeting held at The Temple, she related the astounding story of

Ethiopian Jews, their struggles, their spirit and their needs. She showed a slide of a beautiful, young, wide-eyed Ethiopian boy born with a spinal deformity who walked  bent over on his arms and legs, just like a small dog. I couldn't get that picture out of my mind for months. Years later, I would learn that this precious child had made it safely to Israel, and caring doctors had him standing erect, walking like a normal, healthy child.

I had scheduled a breakfast meeting for the next morning at the AJC office for those unable to attend the previous evening's presentation. As soon as I got home that night, I called Dr. Steve Kutner, an ophthalmologist and close personal friend, and told him he simply had to come to my breakfast meeting, insisting he cancel any early appointment he had, and he agreed. After one hour with Barbara, Steve was ready to help in every way possible and volunteered to travel with her to Ethiopia in June.

Richard Bono's March 13, 1987, article in the *Atlanta Jewish Times* titled "Atlantans Reminded of Jews in Ethiopia," reported on Barbara's work.

> As she travels around the country talking about the plight of the Jews of Ethiopia, Ribakove Gordon reminds Americans, whose attention span is often limited, that Operation Moses did not do the whole job. In the Gondar Province of Ethiopia, where most of the Jews live, the ravages of oppression, famine and civil war are beginning to take their toll.
>
> "And the point is, they can be saved," she said. "It's not like the Holocaust; they are not in concentration camps. They are not beyond our reach."

Steve wasted no time preparing for his mission, educating himself about third world diseases and pulling together medicines and resources. Upon his return from Ethiopia, he began speaking about his experiences, amassing supplies and recruiting supporters and volunteers to travel with him on future trips. He wrote a moving article in the *Atlanta Jewish Times* on July 24, 1987, titled "Atlanta doctor makes emotional trip."

Last spring I had the opportunity to meet the director of an organization dedicated to the survival of this remnant community and to their ultimate exodus to Israel. The North American Conference on Ethiopian Jewry's (NACOEJ) Barbara Ribakove Gordon visited Atlanta under the auspices of the American Jewish Committee. I was so moved by her message and plea for assistance that I committed to help.

Just returned from a mission to Ethiopia, where I had the most meaningful experience of my personal and professional life, I want to share some part of the incredible emotion generated.

During the four days, we were able to visit and treat about 2,000 Ethiopian Jews scattered across the province. The country was magnificent, but the remaining Jewish communities were in horrible condition. The standard of living and medical health was appalling and catastrophic. The range of medical problems was mind-boggling.

Although there was little malnutrition, we treated hundreds of cases of neglected wounds, infections, and diseases related to poor hygiene, inadequate water supply and lack of sanitation. I treated eye diseases I had seen only in textbooks. The people were desperate for care and were so grateful for so little.

As our mission touched down in Israel for debriefing on our return, we felt we had come home. All of us knew that our lives would never be the same again, and when we visited HaKotel (Western Wall), we looked up with a tear, a prayer and a promise to always REMEMBER.

Barbara expressed her gratitude for our work in Atlanta in a heartfelt letter to Joel Goldberg, Chairman of the Chapter Task Force on Ethiopian Jewry.

*Dear Joel,*

*A few days ago, I received copies of the letters you sent to Melvin Tillem, Cantor Isaac Goodfriend, and Allen Soden. I want to tell you how grateful I am to you, to Sherry Frank, and to all the wonderful people at the Atlanta AJC Chapter for what you have done on behalf of Ethiopian Jews. Your warmth, your empathy, the energy that you have put into helping us make our June mission a success, are extraordinary – and extraordinarily effective, too.*

*Above all, I want to thank you for Steve Kutner, not on behalf of NACOEJ, but on behalf of the community of Ethiopian Jews to whom he was simply a miracle that appeared in their midst. From the Kes of Aba Entonius, who will now be able to read the Torah again, to the child in Etege out of whose ear he pulled parasites, to the Ministry of Culture staff person in Addis Ababa whom he examined and supplied with medicine unobtainable in Ethiopia, Steve is a never-to-be-forgotten wonder-worker. For those of us in the group that had the privilege of traveling with him and assisting him, he is simply the best of the best – modest, kind, tireless, able to do splendid work under the most difficult circumstances, and to become a friend to his co-workers as well.*

*I am looking forward so much to being in Atlanta again in September, to say thank you in person to all of you. We couldn't have done it without you.*

*Sincerely,*

*Barbara Ribakove Gordon*

I sent my national colleagues and Barbara the media coverage we had secured. On August 14, she wrote a warmly personal letter to the *Atlanta Jewish Times.*

I am writing to tell you how very moved I was by the coverage the *Atlanta Jewish Times* gave to our June mission to Ethiopia.

The pictures brought back so vividly the days we spent in Jewish villages in Gondar, among people we have come to know and love. The beautiful article by Dr. Steve Kutner made me weep. As we left one village, Steve told me he would never forget the sight of people holding out their cupped hands for the little tubes of eye ointment that could keep them from going blind.

Well, the people whose lives we touched in June will never forget Steve either. He worked tirelessly, patiently and cheerfully, even when the rain was pouring down his neck or the sun glaring into his eyes. Under the most primitive conditions, he gave careful examinations, prescribed medicines and treatments, waiting patiently while the words were translated into Amharic for mothers in ragged shawls who held out babies with illnesses never seen in more fortunate parts of the world.

Along with the other two members of our volunteer medical team, the extraordinary "ordinary" people who joined us from all over the United States, Steve was a miracle that came to pass in Gondar.

Thanks to the wonderful people at the Atlanta Chapter of the American Jewish Committee, I'll have a chance to come back to Atlanta after Labor Day to say thank you in person. Have you got any more at home like Steve Kutner? It doesn't seem possible, but if you do, I hope they read the editorial that accompanied Steve's story, and come out to join us. We can't have enough of such a good thing.

Thank you for caring so much.

On September 8-9, 1987, we brought Barbara back to Atlanta. Steve

Selig, Atlanta Chapter President, and Joel Goldberg encouraged the attendance of Atlanta area doctors at gatherings where she spoke.

Quiet meetings, as well, were held with business owners, and connections were made with private schools and institutes in the area for under-the-radar work involved with specific rescue efforts for Ethiopian Jews.

Passover is my favorite Jewish holiday, and for decades I have been leading Seders and collecting new and contemporary readings to add to my *Haggadah*. I began an annual tradition of sharing a small collection of these with my friends and members of AJC's Board of Trustees. In March, 1990, Barbara sent me a beautifully designed and moving reading to be told at the Seder about Elana's story and the experiences of separated families and those still trapped in Ethiopia. I included it in my readings that year.

Dr. Kutner's work continued for many years with additional trips to Ethiopia, serving on the NACOEJ Board and doing exceptional work in Israel training doctors to help Ethiopians arriving in Israel with specific medical issues. Through Project Vision, which he founded, he restored eyesight to thousands. Steve continued his work with the Ethiopian *olim* (immigrants) through Jewish Healthcare International, also created by him, and with the Jewish Agency for Israel.

No phone call I ever received in my twenty five years at the AJC was more significant than the one I answered midday on Friday, May 24, 1991. In a conference call to all of our chapter offices, David Harris told us, "the airlift is underway." What would soon be known as Operation Solomon was being carried out, with forty jets coming and going in thirty-six hours, bringing 14,000 Ethiopian Jews safely home to Israel. We were told to share the news with area rabbis right away, as *Shabbat* would keep them from learning about it on television. We asked them to join with their congregations in prayer for the safety of this secret and dangerous rescue. All these years later, I still choke up thinking about this mission and the enormity of its accomplishment.

Barbara traveled again to Atlanta for a July 10 program that AJC co-sponsored with The Temple. The title was "Last Flight Out of Ethiopia," and the flyer's text promised an exciting meeting.

*Summoned to Addis Ababa in secrecy weeks ago, Barbara Ribakove Gordon helped prepare for the miracle rescue of 14,000 Jews from Ethiopia. She has amazing stories and pictures about this rescue and the four flights she participated in including the last plane of Operation Solomon.*

The next week, the *Atlanta Jewish Times* covered Barbara's presentation in an article titled "Ethiopians Went to Israel 'In Pure, Perfect Faith'."

On the eve of Operation Solomon, Barbara Ribakove Gordon was given the painful task of separating the 14,000 Ethiopian Jews about to be airlifted to Israel from their few remaining possessions.

"Every bundle would take the space on the airplane that might have been taken by a baby," said Ms. Gordon, an American who was a member of the team at Israel's embassy in Addis Ababa, Ethiopia, that processed the Jews for their hurried departure. "There was no time to check those bundles for security."

"Half of Addis turned out at the Israeli embassy," Ms. Gordon said. The civil war was in its death throes and the capital was poised to fall to the rebels. Everyone wanted to leave.

The Israelis established a circular course around the embassy compound to process the Ethiopian Jews. The Jews could be distinguished by a plastic card which identified each family and included a photograph of the head of the household. After 36 hours, the airlift was over.

This story had a unique black-Jewish aspect to it. Over the years, when Ethiopian Jews, now Israelis, came to Atlanta, we arranged programs for them to meet with our members, the press and, on occasion, black leaders. Two actions taken by Atlanta black political leaders drew national attention. The first was after Operation Moses in 1984. Marvin Arrington, Atlanta City Council President, wrote an op-ed in the *Atlanta Journal-Constitution* on January 20, 1985, responding to the Ethiopian airlift. "Israelis have demonstrated to the world that there is a brotherhood of man, and that it is not bound to race." ... "That a nation of white men should care enough about the survival of starving blacks, to literally 'take them home with them,' took several moments for me to grasp." Citing Martin Luther King, Jr.'s, contribution, he movingly said "Martin, look how well your dream works."

The second action was on September 15, 1991, after the historic rescue of Ethiopian Jews in Operation Solomon, when AJC published a full page ad in *The New York Times* titled "We have a stake in Israel – America's Black Mayors." Thirty-six black mayors, including Atlanta's Mayor Maynard Jackson, signed the ad.

Facets of my work often overlapped, and so it was with the black doll project, which I described in my chapter on South Africa. Black dolls, initially made in the U.S. and sent to South Africa and later made in South Africa and sent to the U.S., were now going to Ethiopian Jews in Israel. What a global world we live in!

The struggle of Ethiopian Jews continues today; the small group remaining in Ethiopia is still trying to get to Israel, and the complicated challenge of resettlement in Israel is ongoing. A few of my precious artifacts remind me of this distant community. The villagers in the Gondar Province set out handmade artwork on the ground for purchase. Participants in the missions bought them all in order to provide financial support to the community and to assure that they would be able to return in their life-saving missions. I have a small clay animal, rather primitive in design, that was one of these items. In addition, I treasure my Ethiopian-designed throw pillow that we use every year at Passover while following the tradition of reclining when telling the Exodus story; it seems particularly appropriate. Whenever I see other Ethiopian handcrafts around my synagogue and in friends' homes, including *tallitot* and matching bags, challah covers, and decorative throw pillows, I am reminded of that extraordinary journey to freedom.

The ancient biblical story of the Exodus is a defining chapter in the history of the Jewish people. For Jews living in the 20th century, we were blessed to witness and take part in historic exodus stories in our own generation. The phrase "Let my people go" has a new relevance and will forever be etched in our hearts and in our memories.

Dr. Steve Kutner in Ethiopia, 1987

Ronnie van Gelder and Congressman John Lewis at Washington
March for Soviet Jewry, "Freedom Sunday," 1987

Martin Luther King, III, presenting book on Dr. Martin
Luther King, Jr., to Natan Sharansky, 1988

Standing on the tarmac in Israel waiting to greet arriving Soviet Jews,
(L-R) Sherry Frank, David Harris, Larry Thorpe, Cedric Suzman, Hyman
(Bookie) Bookbinder, 1990

Reunion with Soviet Jews in Israel (L-R) Larry Thorpe, Cookie Shapiro, Beatrice
Gruss, Soviet Jewish activists Tanya and Yuli Edelstein, Sherry Frank, 1991

# GERMANY AND THE HOLOCAUST

## FACING EVIL AND RESCUING TREASURED ARTIFACTS

*We must always take sides. Neutrality helps the oppressor, never the victim. Silence encourages the tormentor, never the tormented.*

—Elie Wiesel

W hen I began my career at AJC in 1980, the agency launched a groundbreaking German-Jewish exchange program in partnership with the Konrad Adenauer Foundation. Chapter members participated in these exchanges for many years. AJC created additional partnerships with Germany, and our Atlanta Chapter hosted several groups of visiting German leaders. We participated in numerous events co-sponsored with the German Consuls General serving the Southeast, dealing with issues relating to the Holocaust, including restitution, textbook study reviews, and US and Israel relations with Germany. I prize the two pieces of the Berlin Wall that I received as gifts from our leaders who traveled with AJC to Germany. One bears the dates of the wall, August 13, 1961-November 9,1989. Another is inscribed "Berlin Wall June 10, 1990."

On March 25, 1988, I received a letter from Alexander von Schmeling, Consul General of the Federal Republic of Germany, informing me that "the German Academic Exchange Service has selected you to be invited to their Special Information Program *Germany Today* from June 26- July 13, 1988, in Berlin and Bonn." This was an opportunity too good to pass up, and it became a cherished learning experience.

Most of the time was spent in Bonn, a quaint and beautiful city that was the seat of the government when I first visited in 1988. Our days included study at the university and some tourist activities. A boat ride down the Rhine river had us marveling at the amazing medieval castles high above on the hillside. Our charming boutique hotel was one of many small hotels, cafés and shops that surrounded a large and lively plaza. Before the sun came out in the morning, we heard the streets being washed and the carts bearing fresh fruit and pastries enter the area.

From Bonn we traveled to Munich and toured Dachau; it was my first experience at a concentration camp. Dachau opened in 1933 and was a brutal forced labor camp for political prisoners. It was embedded in a neighborhood, and it seems impossible that the people living close to it were unaware of the horrors taking place in the camp.

I was involved in numerous other community and specific AJC activities related to Germany and the Holocaust, but four are particularly memorable.

## 50TH ANNIVERSARY OF KRISTALLNACHT

In 1988, AJC created a multi-faceted project to commemorate the 50th anniversary of Kristallnacht. It was detailed in a letter to religious leaders signed by Atlanta Chapter President Steve Selig and Interreligious Affairs Vice President Cookie Shapiro.

*The National Conference of Catholic Bishops, the National Council of Churches, and the American Jewish Committee joined together to prepare the enclosed research materials for use in churches, synagogues, educational institutions and community centers. People of faith throughout the United States will commemorate this anniversary. We invite you to join us in Atlanta by participating in any or all of the following:*

- *Keep lights on in synagogues and churches on the night of November 9 "to dispel the night of darkness" of 1938.*
- *Use the enclosed materials in sermons and educational classes during the week of November 6.*
- *Attend the community-wide observance commemorating the 50th anniversary of Kristallnacht on November 9, 1988, 8:00 P.M., at Ahavath Achim Synagogue. A specially commissioned oratorio, "Stars in the Dust," will be performed by members of the Atlanta Symphony and a 16-voice choir directed by Fletcher Wolfe.*
- *Join Mayor Andrew Young and other religious and political leaders to light a memorial candle and sign a proclamation on Wednesday, November 9, 12:00 noon, at Atlanta City Hall.*

*We offer this material in loving memory of the victims of Kristallnacht, indeed, in memory of all the victims of the Holocaust. WE SHALL REMEMBER!*

Religious leaders representing the Catholic, Baptist, Episcopal, Methodist, Presbyterian, and Jewish communities all participated in the November 9 observance. The Christian Council of Metro Atlanta, Concerned Black Clergy, and the Atlanta Rabbinical Association also took part.

Mayor Andrew Young and Fulton County Commissioner Michael Lomax provided the opening remarks. Cantor Isaac Goodfriend, Ahavath Achim Synagogue, spoke, and Steve Selig called on political and religious leaders to light a memorial candle and sign the City of Atlanta proclamation.

*WHEREAS November 9-10, 1988, marks the fiftieth anniversary of Kristallnacht – The Night of Broken Glass, a night of terror sanctioned by the Nazi state and its offices;*

*WHEREAS during Kristallnacht the criminal government of the Nazis roused the German and Austrian peoples to the frenzy of violence that shocked the civilized world;*

*WHEREAS during Kristallnacht hundreds of synagogues in Germany and Austria were destroyed, hundreds of businesses and homes were ransacked, scores of innocent people were killed because they were Jews, and thousands of others were arrested, humiliated and sent to concentration camps;*

*WHEREAS the lack of an active response by civilized nations encouraged in the perpetrators an arrogance that led directly to the carnage of the Second World War;*

*WHEREAS Kristallnacht paved the way for future atrocities culminating in government sponsored mass murder on a scale unparalleled in history;*

*WHEREAS Kristallnacht marked the prelude of the outbreak of war and the murders of millions of innocent people;*

*WHEREAS the rule of the Nazis represents one of the darkest periods ever to have befallen mankind, when barbarity was praised and learning and culture scorned;*

*WHEREAS an essential lesson of Kristallnacht is that evil must be recognized, confronted, and opposed, and ignorance fought;*

*THEREFORE, be it proclaimed that the week of November 4-10, 1988, be declared a Week of Remembrance for Kristallnacht, in memory of all those who suffered and perished in its wake and marking our determination that acts of wanton violence never again be perpetrated, and that the great cause of truth and justice be forever served.*

*Michael Lomax, Chairman, Fulton County Commission*
*Andrew Young, Mayor, City of Atlanta*
*Martin Luther King III, Fulton County Commissioner*

*Father Alan Dillman, Atlanta Catholic Archdiocese and the Church of the Immaculate Conception*

*Reverend Joseph Roberts, Ebenezer Baptist Church*

*Rabbi Harvey Winokur, Temple Kehillat Chaim and Atlanta Rabbinical Association*

*Father Stacy Sauls, St. George's Episcopal Church*

*Dr. Bill Hinson, Christian Council of Metro Atlanta*

*Reverend McKinley Young, Big Bethel AME Church and Concerned Black Clergy*

*Rabbi Arnold Goodman, Ahavath Achim Synagogue*

*Samuel Lean Wilson, Sr., Hillside Chapel and Truth Center*

*Reverend Randall Williamson, Methodist Center*

*Reverend Marion M. Pierson, District Superintendent – Atlanta, College Park United Methodist Church*

*Barbara Asher, Atlanta City Council*

*Jim Maddox, Atlanta City Council*

*Reverend P. C. Ennis, Central Presbyterian Church*

*S. Stephen Selig, III, President Atlanta Chapter, American Jewish Committee*

*Sherry Frank, Southeast Area Director, American Jewish Committee*

AJC delivered special materials for religious services to 600 congregations in Metro Atlanta. A story in the *Atlanta Daily World*, November 13, 1988, included a picture of Steve Selig, Cantor Isaac Goodfriend, Fulton County Commissioner Martin Luther King, III, and Mayor Andrew Young.

## Traveling to Berlin and Bonn

For nearly two decades, my boss and the director of AJC's Community Services Department was Eugene (Gene) Dubow. Gene made frequent trips to Atlanta and developed close ties with our leadership. On his final visit, he told us about his plans to open AJC's office in Berlin on July 1, 1997. This would be American Jewry's first Berlin-based office.

Gene said he hoped to address the lack of knowledge Germans have about Jews, Judaism, and the American Jewish community. He planned to lecture to German students, reach out to German Jews, evaluate the country's Holocaust curriculum, and expand adult exchange trips between Germany and the United States. He noted Germany's strength within Europe and its important economic ties to Israel.

Some Chapter leaders suggested that we plan a visit to Germany to meet with Gene in the new office. We soon finalized plans, and from October 22-29, 1998, we traveled to Berlin and Bonn. During that time – on Wednesday, October 27 – the new government took over. (The Capitol would move from Bonn to Berlin in early 1999.) At our orientation session, Gene told us the AJC office is seen as an "Embassy of the American Jews" that has contact with the government. The points they stress include the following:

- 6,000,000 Jews in America care about Israel's security.
- We're very interested in the Jews in Germany.
- There are still many Jews in Eastern Europe.
- Anti-Semitism is an ongoing concern of ours.
- We're watching how democracy works (is safeguarded) here.
- We should advocate for pensions for Holocaust survivors.
- Slave labor during the Holocaust is under discussion. Chancellor Kohl said this is a corporate issue. Chancellor Schroeder said this is a government issue as well.
- Germans know so little about American Jewry. AJC is a bridge in this area.

While we were traveling, an October 26 AJC press release described the visit.

Representatives of Atlanta's Jewish Community will be in Bonn to witness the changing hands of the German government. Nineteen members of the Atlanta Chapter of the American Jewish Committee will meet with government officials and representatives of Israel and the United States who are stationed in Germany.

Among the eight Chapter board members in the group are two past Chapter presidents, Tom Asher and Joel Goldberg, as well as Rabbi Alvin Sugarman of The Temple. On Tuesday the group will be traveling from AJC's office in Berlin to Bonn. The schedule will include:

Reinard Weiner, Counselor with Political Section of the North American desk

Ari Primor, Israeli Ambassador to Germany

Lunch with Konrad Adenauer Foundation members at the Foundation

Peter Wichert, State Secretary of Defense

Reception hosted by the American Embassy at the U.S. Embassy American Club

Our itinerary contained stimulating briefings and informative tours and was filled with emotional moments. We visited the Berlin site of a book burning where a transparent sidewalk reveals an underground display of pieces of glass and empty bookshelves. At the House of the Wannsee Conference, where the "final solution" was sealed, we viewed the exhibition "The Wannsee Conference and the Genocide of European Jews." A poignant visit was paid to the memorial site and museum of the Sachsenhausen Concentration Camp. It was a blessing to go there with Rabbi Sugarman. He led us in prayer as we toured Sachsenhausen, pausing in a bunker for reflection. I put my emotions to pen and paper and wrote a prayer for our Memorial Service. Upon our return, I shared it with my AJC leaders and colleagues, and the *Atlanta Jewish Times* printed it on November 13, 1998.

*Prayer for Memorial Service Sachsenhausen Concentration Camp*

God of wonder and majesty, we stand in this sacred place made holy by the suffering of our people.

We thank you for giving us courage and wisdom to make this journey and the heart to ache for what we see.

Bless us as we wrestle with the inability to understand the evil in mankind that made the Holocaust possible.

Be with us as we pray for the Jewish souls who were innocent victims and help us not to make victims out of the innocent young men and women in Germany today.

Help us comprehend the great accomplishments taking place in this country, stained with Jewish blood in the past, yet moving with speed into the millennium.

Make sense out of all the dichotomies that abound all around us.

We see... the high speed trains being built to bring closer together the peoples of Europe. And we remember... the train tracks all around us that sped our people to their deaths.

We see... the industry and building, the cranes and signs of progress. And we remember... the enormous effort to mobilize this country for war and destruction.

We see... the lights illuminating the beautiful boulevards. And we remember... Kristallnacht and the light of fires that burned Jewish books and synagogues.

We see... immigration laws being enacted and a multi-ethnic society being embraced. And we remember... the words of Judenrein and Aryan Nation.

We are fortunate to witness the pendulum swing from a Jewish community being decimated to one proud of its rapid growth.

We thank you God for the wonder that helps to soothe

the pain, for the hope that defines our people that will never die.

Give us the courage to continue to face our past and strength to keep our world safe from madness.

We Jewish community professionals do what we do out of commitment and love of the work. Still, it means so much when we are recognized by our peers, and I was touched to receive a very complimentary memo from David Harris, AJC's Executive Director, on December 19, 1998.

*Dear Sherry,*

*Yesterday evening I had a chance to read the prayer you composed for the Chapter visit to Sachsenhausen. I was profoundly moved by your words, as I'm sure everyone present was. In all, it sounds as if it was a very successful trip to Germany, and I couldn't be more delighted that the Chapter organized the journey.*

*As you know, I count myself one of your biggest fans. The prayer is just one of the many reasons why. You've led the Atlanta Chapter from strength to strength through your devotion, passion, dynamism, creativity, and indefatigability.*

*I look forward to my visit in April.*

*David*

Rabbi Sugarman captured many of our thoughts in his November 13 *Atlanta Jewish Times* article, "A Sea Change in Germany."

There are precious few experiences that sear themselves into the very fabric of our being, but for me, one of them surely was the visit to Germany late last month of 19 Atlantans under the auspices of the American Jewish Committee.

Encounters with officials in the German government on all levels made clear that a very large portion of the German people are confronting the harsh realities of their Nazi past and seem absolutely determined to guard the future of their democracy so that never again will Nazism gain dominance over them.

But we saw something else happening in Germany as well, and it began on our first night in Germany. It happened to be a Friday evening in Berlin, and we all went to Shabbat evening services at the Synagogue Pestalozzisstrasse. The rabbi was a young man trained at the Leo Baeck College in London, which is an institution belonging to the World Union of Progressive Judaism, the world-wide arm of Reform Judaism. The cantor was a survivor of Auschwitz now in his 80s, and on that Friday evening, our eyes filled with tears to hear the incredibly beautiful liturgical music and to worship with the different generations present, including a group of Israeli youth. Perhaps the most poignant moment of all came when a *bar mitzvah* was called to the pulpit, held up his *kiddush* cup and led all of us in the chanting of the *kiddush*. Here we were, a group of Atlanta Jewry, worshipping in the heart of Berlin, not far away from the Reichstag, which is being rebuilt, hearing the beautiful strains of the *kiddush* coming from the throat of a young German Jewish boy. His presence symbolized for us how powerful, strong and resilient is our Jewish faith. Even on the ashes of the Holocaust, in the cradle of Nazism, there yet arises new Jewish life and hope. And that is the way it should be, for we are Jews who go on living…

This was only one of many unforgettable trips I took abroad during my years with AJC. The other participants who shared this experience were Tom and Spring Asher, Burton and Barbara Gold, Joel and Carole Goldberg, Charles and Barbara Golsen, Barbara Klineman, Jarvin Levison, Henry and Joyce Schwob, Sidney Simons, Alvin and Barbara Sugarman and Mark and Judith Taylor.

After we returned from our Berlin visit in November, 1998, my brother-in-law, Charles Golsen, told me about a discussion he had with his good friend Jack Bolton. Jack is married to Iris Bolton, a nationally acclaimed expert on suicide who runs a non-profit counseling center in Atlanta called The Link. Iris' father, Curtis Mitchell, was a Colonel in the U.S. Army and was stationed near Bergen-Belsen when it was liberated in 1945. He secured a photographer to document what he found at the camp and later wrote a powerful article entitled *Belsen Revisited*. He later gave the photographs to Jack and Iris.

Jack asked Charles to share the photos and article with me. The pictures had since been declassified, but they still bore their "classified" stamps; they were dated April, 1945. Colonel Mitchell's article was extremely moving, and I have excerpted a small part of it, omitting much of his writing about the horrors of the camp.

Each Spring of every year, I hold a small private ceremony. In April, when the leaves on my trees grow fat again with sap, and men's minds, released from winter's torpor, begin to ferment with fresh contrivances and inventions, I take a photograph from my desk and look at it. It shows a man – myself – staring into a huge open grave in which lay sprawling corpses of several thousand political prisoners of the Bergen-Belsen Camp in the Nazi Germany of 1945.

It is a matter of record that more bodies were broken and more minds unhinged in Belsen in a shorter time than at any prison in modern history. Within a fortnight, at the peak of the Nazi campaign of extermination, almost 20,000 humans died of hunger, typhus, and such other diseases as came in the wake of planned starvation. Their bodies were carted away in trucks to huge dumps that were common graves, where at last, man's ultimate indignity was hidden in the innocent earth.

Belsen is not a place to forget, neither by those who saw it nor by the world which read of it. Belsen is a symbol of dismal, human failure and its appalling significance may help erect some useful defense against our current world's sweet complacence....

....That about finishes it, I guess, except that my photographer did take the pictures we came to get. Some of them were pretty grim but they were useful at the Nuremberg trials and elsewhere. One picture showed me standing on the edge of that open grave. It was shot on purpose, because I suddenly thought of all the people I knew with short memories who someday would be doing business in the same old way, conniving for special privileges and using prejudice and bigotry and hatred to achieve their ends. They would be the ones who would say, "Nonsense, Mitchell. Belsen couldn't have been that bad. You've dreamed the whole thing up."

Here are my final thoughts. When enough people tell you a thing, you begin to believe it. That's why I look so hard at that picture each anniversary of the surrender of Bergen-Belsen and its dead. I didn't dream up any part of this story. But I wish I had.

*Charles Curtis Mitchell, Colonel, Author, Writer, died March 15, 1998.* **Copyright 1998 Bolton Press Atlanta**

I was unsure of the best way to handle such a rare find, so I brought the book of graphic and powerful photographs to Sandra Berman, the archivist at the William Breman Jewish Heritage Museum in Atlanta. Although some of the pictures were used in the Nuremberg trials, most had never been seen. She was anxious that they stay in Atlanta.

I sought additional advice from David Harris who suggested that I bring the pictures to Washington, D.C., when I attended AJC's Annual Meeting. He arranged for me to meet with staff at the U.S. Holocaust Memorial Museum where we were taken to a room filled from floor to ceiling with scrapbooks labeled with the names of various concentration camps. The staff pulled out the material labeled Bergen-Belsen. We turned page after page until, to my great surprise, we came across blurry low-quality copies of the thirty-eight photographs I had brought with me. As it turned out, I was holding the original set. Charles had learned through an internet search that because the British liberated Bergen- Belsen, rather than the Americans, there are precious few pictures available, making the ones we had especially valuable.

A series of meetings followed to decide what to do with our important find. After much deliberation, we agreed that this was an Atlanta story and that the artifacts should remain in our community. Iris Bolton and her family offered to participate in any way we desired and generously donated the photographs, along with the article, to AJC. We targeted Spring of 2000, the 55th anniversary of Bergen-Belsen's liberation, to share this story. A statement was released on February 7 to the press by Joel Goldberg, AJC Past President and project co-chair.

> The journal, written by Curtis Mitchell (father of Iris Bolton), and the 38 photographs are an important documentary to the horrors of the Holocaust. The American Jewish Committee is sincerely grateful to Iris and Jack Bolton for giving this collection to our organization. We are especially appreciative of the relationship that Charles Golsen has with the Boltons and AJC. It was Charles who was first shown the collection after returning from an AJC trip to Germany. He realized how valuable this collection was and brought the Boltons and AJC together.

After several AJC meetings, which included discussions at the U.S. Holocaust Memorial Museum in Washington, D.C., and the Breman Museum in Atlanta, the Atlanta Chapter Board of Trustees recommended that the original script and photographs be given to the William Breman Jewish Heritage Museum. AJC will send digitized copies of this collection to:

Yad Vashem in Israel

Bergen-Belsen in Germany

Fred Crawford, Witness to the Holocaust Collection at Emory University

The U.S. Holocaust Memorial Museum in Washington, D.C.

Plans are underway for a program on May 1st when the community will be able to view the photographs and hear the Boltons' story.

The Breman Museum mounted a beautiful exhibit displaying the framed photographs and incorporating the moving words of Colonel Mitchell. A community forum on May 3, co-sponsored by AJC and the Breman Museum, drew a large crowd to open the exhibit. Both Jack and Iris Bolton spoke and were thanked for their generous and significant donation to our community.

The long and meaningful journey that began with our desire to travel to Germany to see AJC's Berlin office in 1998 culminated with the addition of a very special collection for the Breman Museum in 2000.

## LITHUANIAN TORAHS

My ties to AJC and Congregation Or Hadash often merged seren-dipitously in co-sponsored events and through shared materials. One of the most significant happenings that bound us together was AJC's discovery of Judaic items hidden in Lithuania at a time my synagogue was hoping to acquire a Holocaust Torah.

AJC's part of the story began in 1997 when Rabbi Andrew Baker, Director of International Jewish Affairs for the organization, first heard about a trove of Lithuanian scrolls. He was in Vilnius to discuss the dispensation of thousands of Jewish books and Yiddish newspapers that had been hidden first from the Nazis and later the Soviets. While he was touring the collection at the National Library, the library's Director, Antanas Ulpis, showed him a collection of old scrolls stored in the basement. Years of difficult work followed trying to persuade Lithuanian officials to return them to active use. They ultimately agreed that a number of the Torahs were to remain in the country at the state library and with the Jewish community's few active synagogues and that the remainder would be distributed to synagogues, schools and organizations throughout the world.

Rabbi Baker returned to Vilnius in January, 2002, along with Israeli Deputy Foreign Minister Michael Melchior. There they received more than three hundred Torahs and other religious scrolls from the Lithuanian government that they brought to Israel for examination, repair and international distribution.

On February 8, 2003, *The Washington Post* reported on this story and the important role the U.S. government had played in securing the release of the sacred texts. At a ceremony sponsored by AJC on February 2, Lithuanian Prime Minister Algirdas Brazauskas presented the first recipients of these historic artifacts to three Washington D.C. synagogues representing the major streams of Judaism.

At the time the public coverage of this story occurred, we were actively engaged in creating Congregation Or Hadash. Synagogue leader Elliott Cohen was interested in our having a Holocaust Torah for our synagogue, and he and his wife, Judith, offered to donate the funds to cover costs if we could locate one.

I spoke with my AJC colleagues, Rabbi Baker in Washington and Rabbi Ed Rettig in Israel, and we began the process of requesting a Lithuanian Torah. Elliott Cohen wrote persuasively to Mr. Moshe Moskovic at Israel's Hechal Schlomo Jewish Heritage Center on August 25, 2003.

Dear Mr. Moskovic,

I write this letter to you as a Vice-President of Congregation Or Hadash in Atlanta, Georgia; as the previous donor of a Westminster scroll to the Holocaust Museum at the Bremen Heritage Center of the Jewish Federation of Atlanta; as a founding Co-Chairman of the State of Georgia Commission on the Holocaust; and as a 17-year Board member of the American Jewish Joint Distribution Committee.

I have dedicated much of my adult life to ensuring that the tragedy of, and the lessons from, the Holocaust do not fade with the passage of time. There is no better reminder than a scroll salvaged from that time. It is a continuing, vivid reminder that the Jewish people continue to vibrantly survive and a continuing memorial to those who are no longer themselves able to read from it the beauty of its words.

As with so many Jews in America, many of us in the Atlanta area trace our roots back to Lithuania — for example, my step-father's parents came from Lithuania, and he lived with deep memories of the Old World traditions taught to him by his parents.

Were Or Hadash fortunate enough to be awarded one of your scrolls, it would take a place of honor in our Congregation. It would be used to the maximum extent possible. Having imagined the horrors of the sterile concentration camps I have visited over the years, I believe with every fiber of my body that only education of the young will ensure that the memories never fade. I have spent much of my life so far in this cause. A Lithuanian scroll would be a physical testament to the lessons to be learned.

I realize that your supply of Torahs is limited and their placement is of great importance to you and the other members of the International Committee. I can only hope that Or Hadash will be one of the fortunate congregations to have the privilege of owning a living reminder of the past to use for the protection of the future. Very truly yours,

Elliott Cohen

By December, 2004, I was corresponding with Rabbi Rettig to ask where to send the check for the Torah and how quickly it would be repaired. Our hope was to have it in Atlanta in advance of March, 2005, so Judith and Elliott's grandson, Jordan, could be the first to read from this sacred scroll when he celebrated his becoming a *bar mitzvah*.

Carefully packed in bubble wrap, securely taped, placed in a plastic bag and finally inserted into a plain black duffel, Congregation Or Hadash's Lithuanian Torah flew on February 16, 2005, from Israel to New York in its own first class seat accompanied by Rabbi Rettig. When they landed in New York on the next day, they were met by Emory University professor Ken Stein, a congregation leader, who had volunteered to bring the Torah to Atlanta. Once again, the scroll traveled in a seat of its own to its new home.

In moving words, Ken described the night he spent guarding the Torah until the flight home the next morning. When he was thanked, he responded "I feel great for doing it; thanks are not necessary....Just to know that thousands of times this scroll was read by so many... that this Torah represents exactly who we are... we take it from place to place, it survives and we come back if necessary to claim it, and when we do not have it in front of us, we adhere to its ethics and its contents as best we can."

Ken told me that after he returned from New York, he called his mother, Tillie, and asked her to come to his house to see something he thought she'd be interested in. When she got there, she saw the wrapped package on the dining room table and asked what it was. He opened it for her, and, for the very first time in her ninety-one years, this Orthodox woman from Germany touched a Torah. Ken's wife, Lynn, and Gita Berman, both synagogue officers, witnessed this emotional moment with great joy.

On March 10, at AJC's open Board of Trustees meeting, I cited Ken's role in the scroll's journey home to Atlanta and related the history of our Torah.

Prewar Lithuania had a Jewish population of over a quarter million. Its capital, Vilna, often referred to as "the Jerusalem of Lithuania," was home to one of the eighteenth century's leading Jewish scholars, the Vilna Gaon. The Gaon was the foremost advocate of the rigorous, scholarly study of rabbinic Judaism. Vilna remained a center of Jewish rabbinical studies well into the twentieth century, at which time it was also the hub of a thriving Yiddish culture.

When German troops entered Lithuania in 1941, all this quickly came to an end. The Nazis set about systematically killing the country's Jewish population and looting their properties. By 1944, over 200,000 Jews were dead. Many of the Jewish books, Torah scrolls and religious articles that had been stolen by the Nazis had already been taken out of the country. But some articles still remained in Lithuania.

After the war, a few librarians at the Lithuanian State Book Chamber traveled the country collecting Jewish books and religious scrolls. (They also collected Christian religious articles, which were equally endangered in the new Lithuanian Soviet Socialist Republic.) The Library's director defied Soviet orders to send the religious items to Moscow, and instead set about hiding them in Vilnius. Many of the books were intentionally misfiled among the state collections, while the scrolls were dispersed in buildings throughout Vilnius. When independence came to Lithuania forty-five years later, the National Library had in its collection over 130,000 Jewish books and several hundred Torah scrolls and megillot.

After the Holocaust, most of the Jews still living in Lithuania left for Palestine or America. Today there are perhaps no more than 3,000-4,000 Jews in Lithuania.

After prolonged discussions with Lithuanian government officials, spearheaded by Rabbi Andrew Baker of the American Jewish Committee and others, the Lithuanian Prime Minister agreed

*that most of these scrolls should be returned to synagogue use –
in Lithuania, in Israel and elsewhere in the Diaspora. In 2002,
over three hundred scrolls and fragments were taken to Israel on
a specially chartered El Al flight, where they have been examined
and maintained.*

The Nazis confiscated countless numbers of scrolls and religious
materials in hopes of creating a "museum to an extinct race" in
Germany. Rabbi Baker believed these items were the true Holocaust
survivors.

After welcoming the Torah to Congregation Or Hadash, Judith and
Elliott Cohen were thanked for their generous gift, and their grandson
Jordan Cohen read from it on March 19, 2005, at his *bar mitzvah.*

Kristallnacht observance at Atlanta City Hall, (L-R) Cantor Isaac
Goodfriend, City Councilwoman Barbara Asher, Steve Selig,
community ministers (unidentified,) Mayor Andrew Young, 1988

# SOUTH AFRICA

## TRAVEL AND INSIGHT

---

*What counts is not the mere fact that we have lived. It is
what difference we have made to the lives of others that
will determine the significance of the life we lead.*

—Nelson Mandela

M y in-laws connected with our family from South Africa
in the mid 1950s. I first met cousins Saide and Izzy Frank
in the early 1960s when they came to Atlanta for a family
wedding. In the years that followed, they traveled to Atlanta well
over a dozen times. Their visits usually coincided with Passover,
and we spent time together, shopping, cooking, and just enjoying
each other's company. They told me about South Africa, their home
in Cape Town, and about our Frank family tree. Saide was born
in Rhodesia, now Zimbabwe, and Izzy, a CPA, was born in South
Africa. Whenever she visited, Saide brought us beautiful tablecloths
and spent hours watching American television, which she adored.
That family connection kindled an interest in South Africa that
would later inform much of my work in this area.

Beginning in the 1970s, South Africa and Soviet Jewry were becoming hot issues for both the AJC and the Black/Jewish Coalition.
American Jewry was advocating for freedom for Soviet Jews, and

we supported the Jackson-Vanik Amendment to the Trade Act of 1974. Named for its two major sponsors, Senator Henry (Scoop) Jackson of Washington and Congressman Charles Vanik of Ohio, this provision in U.S. federal law intended to affect U.S. trade relations with countries with non-market economies (originally countries of the communist bloc) that restricted freedom of emigration and human rights. The Trade Act of 1974 passed both houses of Congress unanimously, and President Gerald Ford signed it into law with the adopted amendment on January 3, 1975.

Shortly after that law's adoption, the Sullivan Principles were developed to apply economic pressure on South Africa in protest of its system of apartheid. Developed by the African-American preacher Reverend Leon Sullivan, the principles promoted corporate social responsibility, integration and equality and supported sanctions against South Africa until change occurred. They gained wide support for adoption among U.S.-based corporations and became an important advocacy issue for African-Americans.

In 1984, legendary University of Georgia football coach Vince Dooley was scheduled to lead an alumni trip to South Africa. Members of the Atlanta Black/Jewish Coalition met with the coach and urged him to refrain from traveling there as a protest to apartheid. Still, Coach Dooley insisted on taking the trip, challenging the country to accommodate his alumni, both black and white. The following year, the Coalition held a press conference at Atlanta City Hall to oppose the ongoing system of apartheid and South Africa's recently imposed state of emergency.

On February 11, 1986, the President of the Soviet Union, Mikhail Gorbachev, released refusenik and human rights activist Natan Sharansky from prison after a nine-year term. Four years later to the day, anti-apartheid activist Nelson Mandela was released from prison by Frederik Willem de Klerk, President of South Africa. He had served twenty-seven years in various prisons. I make note of these two internationally recognized activists and their releases, because there was a moment in history when they were supposed to be set free on the same date; however, it was not to be, since Mandela suffered four more years in prison.

FACT-FINDING TRIP

Throughout AJC's history, we have been dedicated to the safety and security of Jews around the world. To this end, I was asked to staff a 1990 fact-finding mission to South Africa, but having urged Coach Dooley not to go to South Africa in 1984, I was conflicted about going myself. I sought advice from Coretta Scott King and Andrew Young. Both suggested that with Mandela's release and the promise of reform taking place, this was the optimal time to go. Along with Dr. Cedric Suzman, a native of South Africa and Atlanta Chapter leader, they helped prepare me for what turned out to be an eye-opening visit.

We were in South Africa during Nelson Mandela's historic trip to the U.S. Led by AJC national board member Martin Kellner, our group included thirteen members of the Los Angeles Chapter and two from the St. Louis Chapter. We traveled from June 22 to July 4 to Cape Town, Durban, Ulundi, Johannesburg, and Pretoria meeting with distinguished people from across the length and breadth of the country. These included influential members of the Jewish community, as well as leaders in business, government, political and labor parties, education, media, research, advocacy, and social service agencies.

In each of our meetings, we told the speakers about the AJC and that our purpose in coming to South Africa was to listen to numerous points of view to learn about the current situation. Our visit came at an important moment in their country's history. Strong winds of change were being described as irreversible.

Fran Rothbard's *Atlanta Jewish Times* article on September 21, 1990, captures the essence of what we learned on this trip.

*Out of Africa: American Jewish Committee representative Sherry Frank found the South African Jewish community standing strong in the midst of sweeping changes*

South Africa is a study in contrasts. There is the striking difference between the third world poverty and first world bustling cities; the contrast between the breathtaking beauty of the plains and the squalor of Soweto shanty towns.

It was that diversity that Sherry Frank found so unexpected during her July tour of South Africa as part of an American Jewish Committee study mission.

"You touch down in Cape Town, and it's on the water; either you're looking at the water or you're looking at these table-top mountains. It's so beautiful that it also defies the evil that's around it," she said.

The dismantling of 50 years of apartheid is marked by continued strife, not only between the white government and the black majority, but also between black tribal factions. Rapid urbanization and economic instability have added to the tensions.

Ms. Frank said the group wanted to know: "Did they feel that a peaceful change was possible, or did they feel there was no future for the Jews of South Africa? Were they panicked or hopeful?"

The travelers found a vibrant and cohesive Jewish community, due largely to the polarized society in which they lived. "It's not only the whites and the blacks," Ms. Frank said. "In a segregated society that's that polarized, it almost forced the Jewish community to be closely knit. Consequently, you have this community that's very structured and organized."

Meeting with the chief rabbi of South Africa, Rabbi Cyril Harris, and Jewish leaders in Cape Town, the group discovered:

- The Jewish population in Cape Town is 25,000; about 70,000 Jews reside in Johannesburg.
- In Cape Town, 80 percent of Jewish children are in day schools.
- The intermarriage rate is only 10 to 15 percent.
- Almost every Jewish family has close relatives living in Israel. Consequently, most South African Jews are strong Zionists.
- Eighty-five percent of Jewish people there are Orthodox.
- The Jewish community has enjoyed tremendous religious freedom.

Ms. Frank said most of the people she met expressed hope about the changes in the country. President F.W. de Klerk, in February "unbanned" the African National Congress and promised a new constitution.

"On the other hand, they are positive toward Nelson Mandela, even in light of what he says about Israel," she said. "Most South African Jews are able to separate their support for Mr. Mandela from their support for Israel," she added.

Ms. Frank also indicated that Mr. Mandela and President de Klerk are viewed as the "moderate middle." Mr. de Klerk's National Party has extremists on the right, while Mr. Mandela faces radical left-wing movements.

The travelers were favorably impressed when they met with Chief Buthelezi, the leader of the Zulu nation, according to Ms. Frank. His Inkatha movement encourages education and espouses non-violence.

Still, it was another study in contrasts seeing the different approaches of the Zulus and ANC. "It was clear that the

ANC and the Zulus have a lot of friction between them," said Ms. Frank.

She explained how many blacks stopped going to school in the 1970s when the government declared that the language in schools had to be Afrikaans. Consequently, many blacks dropped out of school because they did not speak Afrikaans. "There is an enormous illiterate society – a lost generation – because of the lack of education," Ms. Frank said.

"But among the Zulus, there is a push for education. So most blacks see the Zulus with disdain as people who really coopted for the government," she said.

"The future needs both parties," she observed.

The group met with leaders of other political parties as well. "Our most frightening meeting," she said, "was when we met with the head of the Conservative party, and it was like sitting and having a meeting with a Neo-Nazi." The Conservative party holds 20-25 percent of the seats in parliament and is based on white supremacy and segregation. "Hearing them espouse it as though it were legitimate is pretty frightening," she said.

The role of economic sanctions was another disturbing factor for Ms. Frank. "I went there believing that sanctions were an important thing to use as leverage," she said. "And I personally feel that sanctions played a role in bringing the government to the point where it began to dismantle apartheid."

But even the best intentions for political reform could be undone unless there's a strong financial base, she said. "There is such an enormous illiteracy and morbidity and rapid urbanization, with not enough medical care," she said. Without a strong economy to educate and train workers and provide housing all the progress so far could be undone.

> Ms. Frank said she understood that sanctions were one of the only negotiating tools left to Mr. Mandela. "But I do see the time coming when that sanction movement will have to be lifted."

At a meeting of the South African Zionist Federation in Cape Town, we learned that the Jewish community was not only the first to condemn apartheid, but they were also actively opposed to it. We met with Jewish Parliament members Harry Schwartz, Tony Leon, Lester Fuchs, and Zack DeBeers. Helen Suzman, white opposition party leader and world-renowned human rights activist, was not in the country during our trip, but I met with her several times when, as a frequent guest of her nephew, Cedric Suzman, she spoke in Atlanta. We also spoke with black leaders Walter Sisulu and Alfred Nzo (ANC), Joe Slovo (Communist Party), and Zulu Chief Mangosuthu Buthelezi (Inkatha Freedom Party) to gain their unique perspective on societal concerns.

I experienced a remarkable day in Soweto with Lydia D. Ramagaga learning about the numerous projects at the Funda Centre. The women working with mothers and young children told us about the first time they left home and traveled to Israel. They brought a program, known as HIPPY, back from Israel to the township. I couldn't believe what I was hearing. In 1974, on my first trip to Israel, I went with NCJW to dedicate their Research Institute for Innovation in Education at Hebrew University on Mount Scopus. One of their early, and most successful, projects was the Home Instruction Program for Preschool Youngsters (HIPPY), also sometimes called Home Instruction for Parents of Preschoolers. It was developed in 1969 by Dr. Avima Lombard to address the problem of immigrant children falling behind their peers, even when attending the same preschools. Dr. Lombard created home-based services to address the educational enrichment of the child and to strengthen the mother's self-esteem through her activities as an educator. This program was widely adopted throughout Israel.

NCJW's South African counterpart, Union of Jewish Women, sent black teachers and social workers to Israel for training and brought HIPPY to the townships. The Israeli project director comes to South Africa twice a year to train people in the program. This program has had an amazingly broad reach. In the 1980s, First Lady of Arkansas, Hillary Clinton, brought HIPPY to her state as a way to help parents with limited resources prepare their children for school. It has since expanded in the U.S. to more than twenty states. Twenty years after its inception in Israel, it was extraordinary to see HIPPY being used in Johannesburg.

Before returning home, our group spent two totally glorious days on a safari in Kruger National Park at Sabi Sabi Game Reserve. I never imagined how exciting it would be to see so many animals in their natural habitat.

The trip had given us volumes of information and understanding of issues, and after we returned home, I was able to write an informed and lengthy report. I also spoke at numerous forums on South Africa, highlighting its history and current promises for a bright future.

## PROGRAMS AND ACTION

South Africa provided a significant agenda item for AJC and the Black/Jewish Coalition. Both before and after Nelson Mandela's release from jail and subsequent election as President of the Republic of South Africa, we hosted several informational programs, often co-sponsored with the Southern Center for International Studies (SCIS). Chapter leader, Dr. Cedric Suzman, Vice President of the SCIS, assisted with these events. A broad spectrum of interfaith co-sponsors participated as well.

- May 24, 1993, at the King Center – "Personal Views on South Africa" with speakers Jean Young, wife of Mayor Andrew

Young, and Helen Lieberman, social activist, philanthropist, and founder of Ikamva Labantu ("the future of our nation")

- September 2, 1993, at SCIS – Reception and Briefing with Les Dishy, Mayor of Johannesburg, South Africa
- June 21, 1994, at The Temple – "South Africa Elections: First Hand Reports of History in the Making"
- September 22, 1994, at SCIS – "Building on Democracy in the New South Africa," co-sponsored with The Institute for Democracy in South Africa (IDASA)
- November 1, 1994, at The Temple – "Reconciliation in Post-Apartheid South Africa," a dinner and discussion with 28 clergy from the Dutch Reformed Church in South Africa

After winning the April 26-29 elections, Nelson Mandela was inaugurated on May 10, 1994, as South Africa's first black president. AJC's Executive Director, David Harris, and National President, Alfred Moses, sent a congratulatory letter to the new South African president and released a statement titled "The Triumph of Democracy in South Africa."

*The embrace of democracy and the flowering of pluralism in South Africa, a land stained by a long history of racial oppression, are triumphs of politics and the human spirit. The American Jewish Committee commends the vision and perseverance of the leaders of South Africa's past and present Governments for crafting a new political order for their nation out of the principles of equal rights, tolerance, and justice, and applauds the particular and remarkable good will of South Africans across the racial spectrum.*

*We recall the President's assertion to American Jewish Committee leaders in 1991 and 1993 of the importance of close cooperation with the Jewish community in his country and ours, and his pledge that religious freedom would be an entrenched right in the new South African constitution.*

*As we praise President Mandela, we likewise pay tribute to the leader of the National Party and immediate past President, F.W. de Klerk, whose visionary, courageous and moral leadership throughout the difficult process of political transition has set a new standard of statesmanship.*

*We cannot conclude a statement on the South African transition to democracy without recording the admiration and fondness of the American Jewish Committee for His Excellency Harry Heinz Schwarz, the Ambassador of South Africa to the United States, who continues to represent with extraordinary grace and effectiveness the Government, the people, and the hopeful future of South Africa.*

During my years at AJC I had countless opportunities to expand my knowledge on a wide array of subjects. When Atlanta Mayor Andrew Young asked me to speak about the 25th anniversary of Sharpeville on March 21, 1985, I knew next to nothing about this topic, but I accepted the invitation because of my long term and trusted relationship with the Mayor. This was years before you could easily google information, and I called my national AJC colleagues to understand why the event was significant. I learned that in 1960, police fired into a crowd of peacefully protesting men, women, and children in the South African township of Sharpeville, killing 69 and wounding 176. Currently, March 21 is a public holiday in South Africa in honor of human rights and to commemorate the massacre.

In the fall of 1995, AJC and Leadership Atlanta co-sponsored a trip to South Africa for their members and alumni. This was an opportunity to gain first-hand knowledge of changes taking place in the country as well as to tour and connect with people involved in affecting the new face of South Africa. AJC leaders and native South Africans, Lana Imerman and Cedric Suzman, played key roles in planning the itinerary and briefing participants who came away from the experience with new insight.

In the mid-1990s I was introduced to the work of Linda Tarry, an African-American woman living in New York who was studying to be ordained as a minister. She had created a project producing black dolls for the townships of South Africa where self-esteem was in short supply. She was bringing it to Georgia. Black/Jewish Coalition members Lois Frank, Leslie Breland, and I traveled to Soperton, Georgia, to get a firsthand view of this little cottage industry that had such far-reaching effects.

To support the program, AJC co-hosted a holiday party with the Atlanta Black/Jewish Coalition, Jack and Jill of America, Inc., the William Breman Jewish Heritage Museum, the *Atlanta Journal-Constitution*, and Publix Supermarkets. We invited friends and families to the December 13, 1998, "A Celebration of Chanukah, Christmas, and Kwanzaa" held at The Selig Center. The invitation described the project, the details of our program, and our goal to sell dolls.

> *Project People is a U.S.-based, non-profit organization founded by two dynamic leaders, Linda Tarry, an activist and African-American seminary student, and Helen Lieberman, a Jewish leader and community activist in South Africa.*
>
> *The Project began in 1995, sending 15,000 black dolls to provide children in townships in South Africa with lovable sources of self-esteem. It evolved into a factory in Cape Town that manufactures and distributes black dolls throughout South Africa, Israel, and the United States, providing adults with jobs, skills, and the hope of economic independence.*
>
> *A new project, "Crafting Social Change," replicates the program in the United States and will allow poor women in rural Soperton, Georgia to move from welfare to work in a doll manufacturing business and job readiness center.*
>
> *At this multicultural celebration, you will see beautiful dolls*

*on display and have the opportunity to purchase them for donation to children at Atlanta homeless shelters.*

*Also featured, along with music, dancing, crafts, and doll making activities, will be a reading on the children's book* King Solomon and the King of Sheba *by Linda Tarry. Linda co-authored the book with Blu Greenberg, a prominent Jewish writer and speaker. Bring your whole family to this special celebration!*

A press release following the program reported on the success of the event.

> More than $1,600 was raised at the holiday event through the sale of 80 hand-crafted black dolls that were distributed to homeless children in local shelters after the celebration.
>
> "The dolls represent so much more than the materials they're made from," remarked Linda Tarry, the President and co-founder of Project People Foundation. "They signify the empowerment of the women who make them and they provide a positive, cultural, ethnic image for the children who will receive them."
>
> "Project People Foundation has demonstrated a strong commitment to our community," stated Sharon Campbell, co-chair of the Atlanta Black/Jewish Coalition, which co-hosted the evening. "Not only do they bring culture, pride, joy, and hope to underprivileged women, but they provide a framework for the future."

The dolls were delivered to the Council on Battered Women and Children, Genesis Shelter, and CHRIS homes. As I had seen HIPPY, developed in Israel, expand to strengthen families in South Africa and the United States, I now saw that these three countries were connected again. The black doll project demonstrated how, in our global society, issues impacting one country can impact another.

At this time, Ethiopian Jews were arriving safely in Israel, and Atlanta Jews traveled there to meet them with these dolls in hand. Ronnie van Gelder reported that on a Temple trip, the first stop her group made after landing was at an absorption center where Ethiopian children were thrilled to receive these beautiful black dolls clad in bright African-themed clothing.

Three years later, the black doll project brought Helen Lieberman back into my life. I first met her in 1993 when she spoke at a Black/Jewish Coalition meeting, I will always feel a special connection to Helen because of her personal relationship with my daughter Jacqueline (Jacque) and her husband Tom Friedland. Before Jacque and Tom married, they both left their jobs, Jacque's in San Francisco and Tom's in Toronto, and traveled around the world for a year. Tom had a deep interest in South Africa, and they spent six months in the country; this was when the Constitution of the Republic of South Africa was enacted. During their time in South Africa, they celebrated Passover with Helen and her family. They volunteered with Helen's *Ikamva Labantu* project. Jacque worked with the black doll project, and Tom introduced Ultimate Frisbee in the townships.

In October, 2002, Congregation Beth Tefillah, whose membership is thirty percent South African, hosted the exhibit "Looking Back: Jews in the Struggle for Democracy and Human Rights in South Africa." The brochure is excerpted here.

*Looking Back is a photographic exhibit that highlights a time in South Africa, which the world would like to forget. To some extent it represents to South Africans what the Civil Rights in the South of the USA represents to Americans.*

*This particular exhibit highlights the Jews of South Africa who dared to challenge the government of South Africa for its inhuman practices and face threats, brutality, and even death. It is a celebration of the fact that people cannot sit by and watch other people suffer without becoming enraged and outraged and taking risks to make a difference.*

This exhibit, created in Cape Town's Jewish Studies Center, was showcased at an AJC national meeting and traveled to many chapters. Under the leadership of Congregation Beth Tefillah president Kevin King and exhibit chairman Leslie Rubin, a South African Emory professor, daily tours were held from October 7-30, 2002, at their synagogue. A number of community forums featured noted human rights speakers, expanding the experience of the exhibit.

Christina Campbell attends holiday party highlighting donation of South African-made black dolls to Atlanta homeless shelters, 1998

# Israel and
# the United Nations

*It isn't enough to talk about peace.  One must believe in it.
And it isn't enough to believe in it.  One must work at it.*

—Eleanor Roosevelt

As early as I can remember, we put coins in the iconic blue JNF box, and I brought money to my synagogue religious school for the Jewish National Fund (JNF) to buy trees in Israel.  Israel was deeply imbedded in my identity as a Jew, and it remained a central part of my concern, study and advocacy in my adult life. I went to Israel over a dozen times with different groups, Jewish and non-Jewish. I first traveled there with NCJW; I went on several trips with the Atlanta Jewish Federation; and once, after I retired, I went with my rabbis Analia Bortz and Mario Karpuj and Congregation Or Hadash members and families. Most of my travel to Israel was with AJC, and it included staff study trips, Project Interchange Women Leaders Seminar, my Black/Jewish Sisters Group, African-American leaders, and special AJC missions.

On one AJC trip, in August, 2002, I stayed over a couple of days after the planned program because I was given the exceptionally rare opportunity to travel to Jordan with a small delegation of staff and lay leaders. The whole experience was surreal. On the short flight to Jordan, we flew in planes that each held only three passengers and the pilot. We could easily see the land beneath us, and I noticed a stark difference between the two countries' landscapes. Israel was green and lush, but as we flew over the border with Jordan, all we saw was brown. I thought to myself, Jordan needs a JNF, a national movement to make their desert bloom.

We landed at a small airport and traveled by car through the capital, Amman, to one of the residences of King Abdullah bin Hussein and Queen Rania Al-Abdullah. There were numerous signs along the way. AJC's Israel and Middle East Director, Dr. Eran Lerman, who spoke Arabic, was with us and said they were political, tied to the upcoming election. The queen had advocated for more women to be elected to government positions, and the signs supported female candidates.

When we arrived, we were greeted warmly by the king and queen, a handsome and gracious couple. The conversation was easy, and their knowledge of and support for stronger U.S. and Israeli relations was evident. I could not help being taken by the lavish decor in the room. Jeweled swords on the tables and miniature silver soldiers on the shelves reminded me we were in the presence of a proud military leader. As we left this memorable meeting, we took a group photograph that I treasure to this day.

My remarkable experience in Jordan gave me firsthand appreciation for the singular access AJC has with heads of government, the effective way we advocate for Israel and the Jewish people worldwide, and the cooperation and admiration AJC has with American and foreign government officials.

Israel was a high priority in all of the organizations in which I was involved, and as a Jewish professional, I felt my connection to Israel grow even stronger. My work took on several dimensions. First was knowledge-based. AJC produced analysis and reports, engaged top-level experts and provided background material and program support for chapters throughout the country. Emory University's Dr. Kenneth (Ken) Stein, Professor of Contemporary Middle Eastern History, Political Science and Israeli Studies, lent his expertise freely and gave us numerous briefings over the decades. We worked together co-sponsoring countless programs on Israel and the Middle East and benefitted from the scholars and Israeli leaders Ken brought to Atlanta.

Unique among our programs on Israel was a January forum we co-sponsored for a decade with the Ahavath Achim Synagogue titled, "Israel: A Look Back at the Past Year and Forward to the Year Ahead." Rabbi Arnold Goodman, Ken Stein and key political, media and international relations professionals were our speakers. Large crowds attended our annual scholarly Flagship Series, later named the Sol Golden Memorial Flagship Series. Ken brought outstanding Israeli authors, politicians and experts to Emory University as visiting teachers for a semester. Michael Bar-Zohar, author and former Knesset member, was a visiting professor over several years and was frequently featured in our AJC programs.

Outreach to the non-Jewish community to foster understanding about and support for Israel comprised another aspect of my work. The bottom line for all of this was AJC's priority of advocating for Israel's safety and security at home and abroad in the world of nations.

As I worked to defend Israel, I often found that the United Nations (UN) and its affiliate organizations were a major source of anti-Israel and anti-Semitic statements, reports, and resolutions. For nearly fifty years, I have had a keen and personal interest in this area. It permeated my work with NCJW and AJC, my advocacy on women's issues, and my commitment to support Israel and combat anti-Semitism. Responding to the challenges presented by the UN required AJC to work in many arenas, including national analysis and publications, outreach to diplomats, media, and influentials, coalition building and general education within and outside the Jewish community.

Some background on AJC's historic ties to the UN is important in understanding our initial and continuing concern about and response to its actions. AJC was in the forefront of non-governmental organizations that welcomed and supported the adoption of the United Nations Charter in 1945 and contributed to the drafting of its human rights provisions. AJC also played a particularly active role in the drafting of the Universal Declaration of Human Rights and in the creation of the United Nations Commission on Human Rights.

## THE UN DECADE FOR WOMEN: MEXICO, COPENHAGEN, NAIROBI, AND BEIJING

As a feminist and active NCJW member, I was particularly interested in the UN Decade for Women. Our national leaders were involved in official capacities, and I followed the deliberations prior to the forum and policies adopted at its conclusion. The UN Decade for Women held its first international conference in Mexico City from June 19 to July 2, 1975.

In a climate of hostility to Israel, the delegates passed the Declaration on the Equality of Women and their Contribution to Development and Peace. Resolution 32, which equated Zionism with racism, was included in the declaration with other extraneous and unacceptable political statements. It singled out "Palestinian and Arab women" for special attention, appealing to women around the world "to proclaim their solidarity with Palestinian women" and to give "moral and material support in their struggle against Zionism." The U.S. drew the line and voted "no." From 1975 forward, the issue of equating Zionism with racism fueled many of my actions in both NCJW and AJC.

Speaking about the deliberations in Mexico City, Karen DeCrow, President of the National Organization for Women (NOW), told AJC leaders at their National Executive Council Meeting on October 31, 1975:

> *"It was disgraceful," she said, "but it was also unfortunately part of a pattern. Even though the delegates to the conference were women, they couldn't endorse a statement condemning sexism because most of the nations of the world, which they represented, approve of sexism and practice it. On the other hand, they could endorse a statement condemning Zionism because, tragically, the same nations are anti-Semitic and practice anti-Semitism."*
>
> *Ms. DeCrow recalled the scene at the Mexico City conference when the Arab and Third World delegates (led by Jihan Sadat) walked out of the meeting as Leah Rabin went to the podium to speak. Mrs. Rabin, the wife of Israel's Prime Minister, headed the Israeli delegation to the International Women's Year Conference.*
>
> *"It was a humiliating experience, not only for Ms. Rabin, but for all of us there who believe in sisterhood and justice."*

The UN Mid-Decade Conference for Women took place in Copenhagen, Denmark, July 14-30, 1980. In September, I joined the AJC staff, right in the middle of my 1978-1982 term on the National Board of NCJW. Esther Landa, NCJW Immediate Past National President, had been an official U.S. delegate, appointed by President Jimmy Carter, and Ruth Winston-Fox, Vice-President of the International Council of Jewish Women, had represented the United Kingdom. They wrote about their experiences at the Mid-Decade Conference and excerpts were printed in the October, 1980, *NCJW Bulletin.*

Esther Landa: "I went to Copenhagen expecting three of the most miserable weeks of my life, and my expectations were fulfilled."

"The U.S. Delegation to Copenhagen was struggling

with three issues: Zionism, Racism, and Feminism. It was clear, to me at least, that United States foreign policy could not be changed by the delegation to the Mid-Decade Conference. The U.S. would oppose any document which contained a listing of Zionism among the other isms the automatic majority in the UN castigates. The U.S. would support Israel and would support the peacemaking process outlined in the Camp David Accords."

"The PLO hijacked the Conference and kept it hostage to the political question of a Palestinian state. Many times when the U.S. tried to take the initiative with a global statement, the Arab-Soviet-G77, et al, bloc amended it so perversely that we could not even vote for our own resolution."

Ruth Winston-Fox: "Except for the two sessions which I have attended, the PLO and the Arabs have used every opportunity possible to disrupt and avoid explanation of issues concerning Palestinian refugees equating the situation with Apartheid and comparing it even with the Nazi holocaust."

The 1980 Programme for Action contained anti-Israel and anti-Semitic statements reaffirming the Mexico City Declaration equating Zionism with racism, which the U.S. once again opposed. It also repudiated the Camp David Accords and supported assistance to Palestinian women in cooperation with the PLO.

In the fall of 1980, Judith Taylor hosted, and I moderated, an NCJW and AJC co-sponsored women's program on the forum in Copenhagen. One of the speakers was Leah Janus, an Atlanta leader in women's and Zionist organizations and an early advocate in support of the UN. A highly regarded activist and intellectual, Leah had this to say about the Copenhagen conference:

*The dramatic moments of the Conference came unfortunately not from the women's agenda; not from a splendid breakthrough towards achieving the goals of the Decade; and not from a great leap forward in realizing their aspirations for a better life through adequate health care and expanding educational and employment opportunities. The scenes we cannot erase from our minds are those generated by the propaganda demonstrations directly related to the foreign policy agenda, which was superimposed on the Women's Conference by the United Nations General Assembly. Is it any wonder that serious-minded and solution-oriented women at the Conference came away agonized and abandoned?*

*The Copenhagen Conference served as another opportunity for the G77 to play out their now familiar scenario of hostility to the United States and hatred of Israel. The subversion of the Women's Conference to their political aims is the latest and perhaps most cynical example of a carefully planned strategy to impose their will whenever it suits their aims.*

Researching this chapter, thirty-seven years after the event, I found a copy of Leah Janus' paper "Personal Perspective on Copenhagen." Planning to quote from it, I wondered if she had actually attended the conference or simply written about it from news reports. I couldn't remember if Leah had been one of our speakers at the program at Judith Taylor's home, and I called Judith to ask. She wasn't sure but told me that she had been in touch with Leah a while back and knew her daughter, Raizi's, phone number and married name. I went to elementary school and Hebrew school with Raizi, and getting in touch with her was reconnecting with an old classmate. So I called her and I identified myself and the reason I was calling to the man who answered. He suggested I call Raizi's mobile number as she was currently with her mother! I never expected to be making this connection as I dialed and spoke to Raizi Janus Sloop. When I asked if she knew if her mother actually went to the UN Decade for Women Conference in Copenhagen in 1980, she replied, "here, you can ask her yourself," and passed the phone to her.

It seemed unreal when I heard Leah's voice. She had moved from Atlanta many years before to be closer to her family. I told her I was writing my memoirs and asked her if she had attended the Forum in Copenhagen, and she replied, "yes, I did!" And did she remember speaking about it at a program sponsored by NCJW and AJC that I moderated at the home of Judith Taylor? This amazing 102-year-old woman responded, "Absolutely, I did."

Raizi asked me to send her a copy of my book when it was completed and said she would read it to her mother. I told her I would send this chapter as soon as I had it typed and edited. It still amazes me to think about this phone call, and I love telling the story, especially to the many people in Atlanta who knew and admired Leah Janus.

Bias against Israel was still evident as preparations were made for the final conference for the UN Decade for Women to be held July 15-26, 1985, in Nairobi, Kenya.

Inge Lederer Gibel, AJC's Program Associate in Interreligious Affairs, spoke on "Anti-Semitism, Its Role in International Politics and the Women's Movement," at a convention of the Federation of Jewish Women's Organizations of Maryland on March 21, 1985. In a lengthy review of anti-Semitism around the world and the persistence of anti-Jewish propaganda, publications, and actions, she noted using academic freedom and anti-Zionism as excuses for teaching material dangerous to the Jewish people. Inge wrote a beautiful defense of Zionism.

> *Zionism is the national liberation movement of the Jewish people. It has its roots in our Scripture, as we wept for Jerusalem, in our Babylonian captivity, and swore to return, a pledge we made yearly for nearly two thousand years, a faith that kept us whole through persecution and pogrom, through our golden age in Spain and through the longer periods when there seemed to be no light at all. Though political Zionism was most often expressed in secular*

*terms, particularly by mainstream Zionism, to despise Zionism is to despise Judaism and the Jewish people.*

In discussing the UN Decade for Women, Inge pointed out that men were the ones pulling the strings. Male government officials, not women, ran most of the meetings and delegations; however, the Palestinian delegation in Copenhagen was led by female airline hijacker and terrorist Leila Khaled. Inge noted that it was well understood by most of the women present, even if their governments made them speak the right line, that the "International Zionist Conspiracy" was not the root of their problem. She concluded her remarks saying:

> *Jewish feminists must not let themselves be pushed out of the women's movement or turned against the goal of equality for their sisters and daughters all over the world. We must make that clear, at home and in Nairobi, while never forgetting that the destruction of the Jewish people or the Jewish State — and for me they are inextricably linked — would make the pursuit of other goals impossible.*

I had followed the UN Decade for Women from the beginning, and the concluding Conference in Nairobi had a particular impact on my job at AJC. From the early 1970s, I worked closely with Susie Elson, a past president of NCJW's Atlanta Section; we later served together on its National Board. In 1984, Susie was Chair of AJC's National Committee on Women's Issues and was appointed to co-chair a delegation to the July, 1985, meetings in Nairobi along with Mimi Alperin, Chair of AJC's Interreligious Affairs Commission, and Inge Lederer Gibel, who served as the senior staff consultant. Other AJC women leaders from around the country were invited to participate in the Forum for Non-Governmental delegations and individuals.

The convener of Forum '85 was Dame Nita Barrow, President of the World Council of Churches and former President of the World YWCA. Inge Gibel began a fruitful relationship with her, facilitated by her many years of experience working with American and world Christian communities. Preparatory meetings and interaction with other American delegations armed a strong twenty-two woman AJC delegation to Nairobi with two important documents written by staff, one on Palestinian women and another on Israel and South Africa. They went committed to advancing the broad range of women's issues, while prepared to combat anti-Zionism statements.

The AJC women hosted two events, a *Shabbat* service and a workshop on Women of Faith. Dame Nita Barrow, at a demonstration against apartheid, Israel, and U.S. intervention in Nicaragua, ordered the placards that would divide the women to be discarded. "Those who called for 'No to Zionism' should be withdrawn," she said. "I am with you so long as we are calling for peace. When one speaks against another, we are divided. I am not going to be part of anything that will hurt another woman here." An AJC press release on August 2, 1985, described the more subdued nature of the meetings.

Nairobi was very different in both spirit and substance from the earlier U.N. meetings in Mexico City (1975) and Copenhagen (1980). Those were dominated by extremist rhetoric that was destructive of the U.N. Decade's goals," Ms. Elson and Ms. Alperin asserted. Forum '85, the non-governmental meeting in Nairobi, was a huge plus for the women of the world despite the efforts of a small minority of the participants to blame all the problems of the world on the United States and Israel. The overwhelming majority of the 12,000 women present, representing over 150 countries, and all the religions of the world, simply refused to be diverted from the three goals of the Decade: equality, development, and peace," the AJC leaders declared.

Ms. Elson and Ms. Alperin added: "we believe the

positive momentum of the Forum carried over to the governmental meeting, and helped produce a final document that was free of any explicit anti-Zionist or anti-Israel language."

Ms. Gibel paid special tribute to the "magnificent efforts" of Dame Nita Barrow of Barbados, the Forum's Convener: "Dame Nita made a difference in preventing another 'Copenhagen.' She was aided in this effort by many Third World women, especially those from Africa."

These international forums provided substance for important discussions and programs. On September 19, 1985, AJC sponsored a program titled "Nairobi: A Global View of Women's Issues." It was held at Georgia State University and featured speakers who attended the Forum in Nairobi.

Ten years later I was still personally and professionally involved in the UN deliberations about women. After a year of planning for the 1995 Beijing World Conference on Women, AJC sent a nine-member delegation to attend the NGO Forum, held October 13-15, 1995. The governmental conference, from October 17-21, was where Hillary Rodham Clinton gained notoriety over her historic statement, "women's rights are human rights, and human rights are women's rights." The conference agenda included "actions that can be taken to counteract the problems facing women worldwide, such as violence against women, restrictions on employment and education, and repression inspired by religious fundamentalism."

Felice Gaer, Director of the Jacob Blaustein Institute (JBI) for the Advancement of Human Rights of the AJC was the only non-governmental human rights advocate appointed to the U.S. delegation and the only representative of a Jewish organization. Veronica Biggins, former assistant to President Bill Clinton, Director of Presidential Personnel, Atlanta businesswoman, and community leader, was Vice Chairman of the U.S. delegation. Veronica is also one of the women in my Black/Jewish Sisters Group.

The Beijing conference inspired several AJC programs. Assistant Area Director, Jean Saul, moderated a forum titled "Back from Beijing" on November 6, 1995, at Peachtree Christian Church, co-sponsored with NCJW and six major Christian organizations. On November 8, AJC sponsored "Beijing: An Inside Perspective" at Spelman College featuring Veronica Biggins and Felice Gaer.

Finally, unlike previous conferences, the 1995 Beijing World Conference on Women was not highjacked by non-democratic countries nor derailed by the anti-Israel and anti-Semitism of earlier UN-sponsored women's forums.

## UNITED NATIONS RESOLUTION 3379: ZIONISM EQUALS RACISM

Shortly after the Mexico Conference, on November 10, 1975, the UN General Assembly adopted its infamous Resolution 3379 designating Zionism a form of racism, and our work was cut out for us. Atlanta prides itself on being an international city and is home to an ever-expanding diplomatic corps. Throughout the 1980s, regular meetings were scheduled at consulates, and we developed close ties with consuls general and their colleagues. AJC's national staff provided background material for meetings with specific foreign officials, and issues related to the UN and Israel were at the top of our agenda. Anti-Zionism and anti-Israel rhetoric at the UN was discussed, and we consistently urged countries to vote to repeal Resolution 3379.

We distributed publications produced by AJC's Jacob Blaustein Institute for the Advancement of Human Rights (JBI) regarded as the definitive analysis of the resolution. On several occasions, we hosted receptions for the Consular Corps and featured David Harris as our guest speaker. An article in the *Atlanta Jewish Times* on October 12, 1990, quoted him as telling the diplomats, "This resolution has been a factor contributing to anti-Semitism. Sooner or later, the resolution must be repealed so the credibility and integrity of the UN will be restored."

Chuck Taylor, Atlanta Chapter board member, wrote an article in the *Atlanta Jewish Times* on November 9, 1990, titled "Zionism Is Not Racism; Repeal the Big Lie."

November 10 marks a sad day in the history of modern civilization, the 15th anniversary of the United Nations Resolution 3379 equating Zionism with Racism.

This resolution, while devastating and hurtful to Jews around the world, should also disturb non-Jews, for when a law embodies bigotry, everyone suffers. The United Nations was created to govern conduct among civilized nations, and the official promulgation of such a pernicious lie, one which sanctions hatred and anti-Semitism throughout the world, strikes at the very integrity of that institution, and thus the societies it was designed to serve.

Dr. Martin Luther King, Jr., once observed that "when people criticize Zionists, they mean Jews," and the syllogism that "Zionists are racists, Jews are Zionists, and therefore Jews are racists" has been used to justify anti-Semitic activities worldwide.

The lie of "Zionism equals racism" has been taught to students of international law; the State University of New York offered a course in which students were asked to write a paper on the topic "Zionism is as much racism as Nazism"; and on and on.

On July 2, President Bush signed a resolution of Congress denouncing 3379 and calling for its repeal.

Sen. Daniel Patrick Moynihan called 3379 "one of the most pernicious lies of our time; one which licensed anti-Semitism and granted it a new international respectability."

Over Memorial Day weekend in May, 1991, when 14,000 Ethiopian Jews were airlifted to Israel in a dramatic and dangerous rescue, I wrote a letter to the editor and sent it to *The Atlanta Inquirer* and *The Atlanta Voice* about this rescue. Dr. Richard Cohen, Atlanta Chapter President, and Chuck Taylor had a similar article printed in the *Atlanta Jewish Times* on June 7 titled "Zionism isn't racism for Ethiopian Jews."

> On November 10, 1975, the United Nations passed Resolution 3379, which classified Zionism, the belief in a homeland for the Jewish people and the philosophical underpinning of modern Israel, as a form of "racism and racial discrimination." Recent events again demonstrate how ludicrous and evil that lie is.
>
> To the Ethiopian Jews, Zionism is their lifeline to rescue. Unlike European Jews trying to escape pogroms, inquisition and holocaust, these people of color have a place to go, a place created on a philosophy the United Nations deems racist.
>
> This historic airlift clearly demonstrates what Zionism is, and what it is not. Zionism is not, as codified by the United Nations, racism. Zionism is a belief that Jews, regardless of color, should have a homeland, a place of refuge in which to escape whatever form of discrimination, persecution or genocide is in fashion from time to time.
>
> But for the Jews from Ethiopia, people of color, Zionism exists not as a theory, but as a savior, Israel.

By the fall of 1991, AJC chapters, particularly those in cities with consulates, were actively engaged in a full-court press to urge repeal of Resolution 3379.

On November 18, letters were sent to every consul general in Atlanta over the signature of Dr. Richard Cohen, Chapter President, and Scott Dayan, Chair, Consular Program. The letter reminded each diplomat of our prior conversations about Resolution 3379.

*We were heartened by President Bush's strong condemnation*

*of UN Resolution 3379 and his call for its repeal when he addressed the UN General Assembly this fall. We understand that momentum is growing among the nations of the world to repeal it as well.*

*We are writing to you to ask you to contact your embassy and express our strong plea for your country to sign on as a co-sponsor of this initiative and to help assure its repeal.*

*We thank you for conveying this message for us. We would welcome hearing from you about your government's position on this initiative.*

We had maps and flags in our AJC office tallying the responses that we received, one on November 25, from Canadian Consul General James A. Elliott confirming Canada's co-sponsorship of the declaration to repeal the resolution. Another, dated December 13, from British Consul General Barry T. Holmes reaffirmed the British government's long-held and strong opposition to the resolution.

Over the two-year period of 1990 and 1991, Chapter members and staff were involved in twenty-eight official meetings working toward this historic victory and repeal of UN Resolution 3379. It was heartening that on December 17, 1991, after years of advocacy, the UN General Assembly voted overwhelmingly to revoke this notorious resolution.

Marcia Kuntsel, of the Washington Bureau, reported on the UN General Assembly vote to repeal the 1975 resolution equating Zionism with racism. Her article, titled "UN drops racism tag on Zionism," in the December 17, 1991, *Atlanta Journal-Constitution* quoted me. "Atlanta's Jewish community was thrilled to learn of the repeal," said Sherry Frank, Southeastern Director of the American Jewish Committee (AJC). In Ms. Frank's view, the "Zionism-is-racism" resolution legitimized anti-Semitism as well as anti-Zionism. "Today's vote says something to us in the Jewish community about the growing acceptance in the world that discrimination against Israel should not be tolerated and should not be promoted through a world body," Ms. Frank said.

Our involvement in UN-related issues never waned. The U.S. Commission on Improving the Effectiveness of the United Nations, established by Congress in late 1987, held a hearing in Atlanta on March 12, 1993. We were invited to present our views on the UN system and its role in post-cold-war U.S. foreign policy. Steve Cooper, Chapter board member and co-chair of our Israel Committee, presented testimony on our behalf. He called on the United Nations to demonstrate change in the broader area of human rights policy.

Steve also addressed the next major UN-related issue in which AJC would launch a vigorous public-action campaign across the country and around the world.

> *Israel holds the unique status of being the only long standing member of the United Nations that is not a member of any regional group, and thus has been denied the possibility of assuming key positions, such as non-permanent membership on the Security Council, the presidency of the General Assembly, chairmanships of various committees, membership in specialized U.N. bodies that are selected based on these groupings. Israel's natural membership would be the Asian Group, but the Arab and Muslim nations, and their allies in this group, prevent it.*

We advocated for Israel's inclusion in a regional group. My October 7, 1997, memo to Atlanta area rabbis was "A Call to Action."

> *The American Jewish Committee is calling on members of the Jewish community across the country to make their voices heard on a most urgent matter.*
>
> *Astonishingly, forty-seven years after becoming a UN member, Israel is still not eligible to sit on the Security Council and other key*

*UN bodies. As you can see from the enclosed advertisement, 184 member countries, including sponsors of terrorism like Iran, Cuba, Libya, North Korea, Sudan, and Syria, are eligible. Yet Israel, a democratic nation and member of the UN since 1950, is not.*

AJC's Atlanta Chapter placed a full-page ad in the *Atlanta Jewish Times* on October 1 asking readers to take part in a write-in/mail-in campaign urging Israel's acceptance as an equal member of the UN system. Similar ads, submitted by the national organization, ran in the *International Herald Tribune* on September 20-21, 1997, and *The New York Times* on September 23.

Careful briefing on the topic was required before we could enlist community support and promote action. In order to fully participate in the UN, a member state must belong to one of the five existing regional groups – Asian, African, Latin American, East European, or WEOG. By geography, Israel belongs to the Asian group, but Iran, Iraq, Saudi Arabia and others have long blocked its admission. That leaves only WEOG, whose members include Australia, Canada, and the U.S., all of which, like Israel, are non-European countries.

Community leaders stepped up when we solicited their involvement. Coretta Scott King graciously lent her name to the list of endorsers of the appeal to admit Israel as a temporary member of the Western European and Others Group (WEOG). In addition, she sent letters to UN Secretary-General, Kofi Annan; EU Delegation Chairman, Ambassador Jean-Louis Wolzfeld; and US Ambassador Bill Richardson requesting their support and expressing her strong feeling about this glaring injustice.

On April 7, 1998, Candy Berman, Chapter President, wrote to Neil Rubin, Editor of the *Atlanta Jewish Times*.

The American Jewish Committee commends the Secretary-General of the United Nations for his call to end the UN bias against Israel. Kofi Annan's recognition of frequent and historical UN bias against Israel and his plea for the normalization of Israel's status within the world body are welcome changes from the one-sided condemnations of Israel that are all-too-commonplace in the international community.

The UN Secretary-General publicly acknowledged the perception of an anti-Israel bias at the UN, called for Israel to be permitted to join a regional group, condemned terrorism and criticized anti-Semitism – including anti-Semitic remarks and resolutions at the United Nations itself.

AJC stays with issues until they are resolved, and we went all out on this one. We were gratified to see it end well. In May, 2000, Israel finally became a full WEOG member on a temporary basis, subject to renewal, and in 2004, obtained a permanent renewal to its membership.

## UN WATCH AND UNESCO

The 60th anniversary of the UN was marked in 2005. As world leaders gathered in New York to observe this milestone event, we continued speaking out and defending Israel, guided by AJC's statement on UN reform.

- Reiterating our commitment to the founding goals of the UN as written in its charter
- Acknowledging the current global challenges facing the UN
- Urging an end to its decades of bias and discrimination against Israel

Since my 2006 retirement, I continue to follow these issues and read with special interest the newsletter, reports and emails from

UN Watch, a non-governmental organization that, among other things, champions human rights, combats anti-semitism, and defends Israel's treatment at the UN. This important agency, based in Geneva, Switzerland, was established in 1993 and has historic ties to AJC. Its mandate is to monitor the performance of the United Nations "by the yardstick of its own Charter."

The organization's founder and first president, Morris Abram, was a past national president of AJC. Following Abram's death in 2000, David Harris was elected Chairman of UN Watch. Another former national president of AJC, Ambassador Alfred Moses, currently serves as chairman. While an independent organization today, it continues to be loosely affiliated with AJC. Executive Director of UN Watch, Hillel Neuer, international lawyer, diplomat and human rights activist, is highly regarded throughout the world for his intellect and principled leadership.

In the six years (1978-1983) I served as NCJW's Non-Governmental Organization (NGO) representative on the U.S. Commission on UNESCO (United Nations Educational, Scientific and Cultural Organization), I was often exposed to the bias at the UN and its affiliate organizations. The anti-Israel "Zionism equals racism" resolution was ever-present in our meetings. I served on the Commission with Dr. Thomas Buergenthal, one of the foremost scholars on international human rights, and heard him discuss the harmful impact of this resolution and its inclusion in textbooks on human rights.

My final reflections on the UN and its antipathy towards Israel are in response to the outrageous resolution passed by UNESCO in May, 2017. It claimed that Israel had no legal or historical rights anywhere in Jerusalem. On October 12, the State Department announced the U.S. withdrawal from UNESCO. An opinion piece titled "Adieu, UNESCO" was in the *Atlanta Jewish Times* on October 20.

> • UNESCO is supposed to be a stalwart in the fight
> to preserve cultural heritage and spread education,

science and free expression. But it has an ugly history of promoting an agenda opposing American values.

- Under President Barack Obama, the United States stopped paying its UNESCO assessment (more than $70 million in 2016) because of a law passed under President Bill Clinton that bars funding to any U.N. agency that admits "Palestine" as a nation, something UNESCO did in 2011.
- From 2009 to 2014, UNESCO passed 46 anti-Israel resolutions, one critical of Syria and none against any other nation. Those resolutions don't include the measures enacted last year that seek to sever any link between Jewish history and the land of Israel.

After decades of personal and professional connections to the UN, I continue to hope for the day when it will live up to its noble purpose and principles and be a place for protecting women's rights, Israel's security and human rights for everyone throughout the world. Until that time, I will make my voice heard when those fundamental rights are violated.

Participants in AJC and Ahavath Achim Synagogue annual program on
Israel, looking at the past and towards the year ahead (L-R) Steve Cooper,
Sherry Frank, Rabbi Arnold Goodman, Professor Ken Stein, 1994

Mission to Israel, (L-R) Steve Selig, Candy Berman, Isabel Gulden,
Sherry Frank, Jerry Horowitz and Jane Fischbach, 1991

Members of Black/Jewish Coalition traveling to
Israel with AJC's Project Interchange
(L-R) Sherry Frank; Myrtle Davis; Richard Sinkfield;  Ozell
Sutton; Israel's Minister of Foreign Affairs, Moshe Arens; Tommy
Dortch; Gordon Joyner; Reverend Dr. Joseph Roberts, 1989

Reverend Dr. Joseph Roberts, Gordon Joyner, Ozell Sutton, Tommy
Dortch, Myrtle Davis, with Project Interchange, 1989

AJC diplomatic visit to Jordan (L-R) Jason Isaacson, AJC Associate Executive Director for Policy; Samuel Fishman, lay leader; Eran Lerman, Director AJC Israel and Middle East office; King Abdullah II of Jordan; Queen Rania of Jordan; Robert Goodkind, AJC National President; Shula Bahat, AJC National Associate Director; Valerie Hoffenberg, AJC Paris Director; Sherry Frank, 2002

# REMEMBERING WOMEN OF DISTINCTION

THEIR GOOD DEEDS ENDURE

---

*Count your garden by the flowers,*
*Never by the leaves that fall.*
*Count your days by golden hours,*
*Don't remember clouds at all . . .*
*Count your nights by stars, not shadows,*
*Count your life with smiles, not tears.*
*And all throughout your lifetime,*
*Count your age by friends, not years.*

—Anonymous

S everal wonderfully special women in my life, with whom I worked both as a volunteer and as a Jewish professional, have passed away leaving a great void. Each woman had a unique connection to my work in the National Council of Jewish Women (NCJW), Black-Jewish relations, and the American Jewish Committee (AJC). It gave me a deep sense of pride to know them, write about them, and share tributes to them at their funerals and at AJC meetings. I want their good deeds and my fond memories of them to live on in the history of our Atlanta community.

I found my first "organizational home" in the National Council of Jewish Women. Those were the days when most women stayed at home with their young children, rather than seeking paid employment, yet still found time to volunteer endless hours in the community and leave a mark upon it.

Roz Cohen was one such bright and shining star, an inspiring and enthusiastic young leader. Full of energy and passion for Atlanta, she juggled her job with three small children, a home and husband, and volunteer work that included presidency of the Atlanta Section of NCJW from 1979-1981, with lively grace and humor. She died tragically of cancer in 1984 at the far-too-young age of thirty-nine. Throughout her illness, her devoted husband, Bruce, kept in touch with Roz's network of close friends, and we were all at her side in the hospital when she took her last breath. It was devastating.

The next 48 hours before her funeral are still vivid in my memory. After I left the hospital, I went to a bookstore to buy the book *Leaves of Gold* and searched for a special poem, "The Scent of the Roses," written by Thomas Moore. It had brought me comfort when I was a pre-teen, decades earlier, after my father's passing.

That evening was AJC's large donor event, the Grand Affair. I attended with a heavy heart, barely holding back tears as word spread around the room of Roz's death. Late that night I spoke to Bruce and shared the words of the poem, hoping it would offer some consolation. It was the same poem I quoted several times over the years that followed when dear friends passed away. The next day I was scheduled to fly to Virginia Beach with my family for my niece's *bat mitzvah*. When Bruce called to ask me to speak at Roz's funeral, I accepted but couldn't imagine how I could actually attend the mid-morning funeral and still make my plane on time. My NCJW connections saved the day. City Councilwoman Barbara Asher, a past NCJW president, contacted Atlanta City Police Chief

Eldrin Bell for help. While my family left for the airport with my baggage, I had a police escort that drove me to the funeral and afterward sped me to the airport.

Touching and memorable tributes were shared at Roz's funeral on April 27, 1984. Among them was the eulogy given by Rabbi S. Robert Ichay of Congregation Or Veshalom.

*The tears which one sheds at the loss of a righteous person are as dear in the sight of God as the costliest treasures.*

*She achieved in a short time what many of us cannot even dream to achieve in a normal lifetime. But in truth, her many achievements give us only a glimpse of what Rosalind truly was. She graduated from Vanderbilt University Magna Cum Laude, and ever since consecrated her life to every worthwhile endeavor.*

*Roz served as President of the Atlanta Section of the National Council of Jewish Women from 1979 to 1981; she was an honoree of the Barbara Lipshutz Young Leadership award; she participated in the first young leadership mission to Israel, and in the Irving Goldstein Young leadership enrichment program. She was very active as a community volunteer. She served on the board of the Louis Kahn group home for senior citizens and the Epstein School P.T.A. She is an alumni of Leadership Atlanta in 1982 and TOYPA in 1980.*

*She loved her city and her country and found time to be involved in the political scene, as a coordinator of the Wyche Fowler Campaign for President of the City Council and Volunteer coordinator for the McGovern Presidential Campaign.*

*Rosalind was very interested in Italian Renaissance Art History and was able to spend three years in Florence giving walking tours of the city and working at the restoration of the city's art works after the damage caused by a flood.*

*In all these endeavors she excelled, for she gave herself unreservedly, unselfishly and totally with love, enthusiasm and devotion.*

On May 4, the words I spoke at the funeral were printed in *The Southern Israelite.*

### The Scent of the Roses

*Let Fate do her worst; there are relics of joy,*
*Bright dreams of the past, which she cannot destroy;*
*Which come in the night-time of sorrow and care,*
*And bring back the features that joy used to wear.*
*Long, long be my heart with such memories filled,*
*Like the vase in which roses have once been distilled.*
*You may break, you may shatter the vase if you will,*
*But the scent of the roses will hang round it still.*

*There is beauty in the light of the Shabbat candles that pierces the heart and reaches deep within one's being. The flicker of the flames moves freely, shedding light and warmth around the room.*

*The serenity and beauty of the Shabbat candles touched my dear friend, Roz Cohen. On her last Shabbat, Roz was in the hospital. Bruce, Brandon, Seth, and Ross brought Passover sweets and wine and candles to the hospital so they could welcome in the Shabbat together as a family. Roz called me later that evening as she watched the candles glow. It meant so much to her to be with her family and to continue to be a strong link in the chain of 4,000 years of Jewish survival.*

*In typical Roz tradition, she told me about her nurse that evening who saw the candles and identified herself as a Jew. Roz immediately told her that she should call Shalom Atlanta and get connected within Atlanta's Jewish community.*

*I laughed with Roz about the fact that even sick in the hospital, she was still an extraordinary volunteer.*

*Roz knew who she was: a proud Jew, a devoted mother, a loving wife, a caring daughter and sister, and a compassionate friend. She was a non-traditional woman deeply rooted in traditional values of loyalty to family and commitment to community.*

*She was a free spirit and a champion of many causes. She crossed religious and racial barriers, and was dedicated to citizen advocacy and protecting the democratic process. She was bright and well read, sensitive and deeply motivated.*

*For those of us who had the privilege of working with Roz in the community, we remember her boundless energy and the dedication she brought to every task.*

*She reached out to others as few people have the capacity to do. She touched our lives in ways that will linger on in our fondest memories.*

*Her legacy is the example she set in her brief and yet meaningful days spent in our midst.*

*In remembering Roz, may we be touched by the flicker of the* Shabbat *candles and may we feel the peace and contentment she found in the warmth of their glow each* Shabbat.

Congressman Wyche Fowler sent a letter of sympathy to Bruce that was included with additional readings and information in a special NCJW newsletter titled "In Memoriam Rosalind Penso Cohen 1944-1984.".

*Dear Bruce,*

*As I am in Central America, I have asked that this letter be sent to you in the event that our worst fears are realized.*

*I am overwhelmed with sadness and share, in a deeply personal way, the intensity of your grief.*

*I loved Roz, as did all who were privileged to know her. Her exuberance for life – and her ability to communicate that exuberance – is a human legacy that will never be forgotten.*

*I do not know why Roz died, Bruce. But I do know why she was chosen to live. She lived to bring joy and love and friendship – and in the end courage – to her friends, her family, her children, and her husband. In this she succeeded so grandly as to be an eternal example of how one person's life can shine radiantly. She was a beacon for us all.*

*Please accept my deepest sympathy.*
*Sincerely,*
*Wyche*


The day after Roz's funeral, her friend Ben Johnson authored a beautiful article for the editorial page of the *Atlanta Constitution*. It was titled "Roz Cohen was one special citizen, the best of Atlanta." I didn't know Ben at the time, but later learned that he was Roz's neighbor. Their families had close and warm personal relations. Over the years I grew to admire him and the many extraordinary leadership contributions he made to our city.

He captured Roz's true spirit when he said "For the past year, Roz Cohen looked death in the eye – joyously and courageously. She did not seek to be consoled but to console. She laughed and conquered, while we hesitated and trembled. Now she's gone, and many of us are caught up in some expressible combination of grief, guilt, and anger. But it must be said – for the mother who raised her, for the husband who cherished her, for three young sons who may not read it for years, for friends who need the reassurance of having it said -- she was our best."

NCJW, together with Roz's family, established the Roz P. Cohen Memorial Fund and appointed Susan Feinberg, one of her closest friends, to chair its advisory committee. Its goal was to perpetuate Roz's memory and the good work she did in the community. On April 16, 1986, the first Roz P. Cohen Community Forum and awards program was held with longtime friend Ann Wilson Cramer as the featured speaker. The new forum included the presentation of the Community Action Award and a Community Action Grant to an agency meeting an unmet community need. Roz's close friend Wyche Fowler received the award, and the $1,000 grant was given to one of her favorite non-profits, the Louis Kahn Group Home for the Elderly (now called the Cohen Home – no relation to Roz). It was my honor to present the award to Congressman Fowler, whom the *Atlanta Constitution* called "the most effective Congressman in our history."

In 1990, I once again presented this award to a friend of Roz's, admired religious leader, the Reverend Dr. Joanna Adams. Over the years, the Roz Cohen Fund evolved and helped to fund NCJW's interfaith luncheons and other worthy activities.

## BARBARA ASHER

As I became increasingly involved in NCJW, I began accepting leadership positions for Atlanta Section. I participated in our long executive committee meetings and enjoyed the gracious home hospitality and elegant luncheons NCJW President Susie Elson provided for her meetings.

Susie's style and that of our next president, Barbara Asher, provided a stark contrast that we can laugh about today. When the cerebral Barbara hosted, the meetings were long and the food sparse. It seemed that she was never hungry, or perhaps she was too busy strategizing and planning to spend time with kitchen details. Things changed when I followed Barbara and began serving bountiful lunches during our executive committee meetings. This continued for years until more women went back to work and meetings became shorter and moved to office settings.

My relationship with Barbara was redefined as she entered politics and I joined the AJC staff. We both continued to serve NCJW on the regional and national levels, but we also developed new ties working on Black-Jewish relations. On September 19, 1988, I was the one to present Barbara with NCJW's most prestigious Hannah G. Solomon Award and noted some of her many accomplishments.

*There are three kinds of women, I learned early in my NCJW days. Those that watch things happen, those that wonder what* happened, those that make things happen. City Councilwoman Barbara Miller Asher is truly one woman who makes things happen.

When she was President of our Atlanta Section NCJW, our National Convention theme was "One Woman Can Make a Difference." Barbara certainly has made a difference in this community.

She's willing to start small, and begin with a pilot program or initial analysis, but she's always thinking big. She doesn't give up, but plugs away until the task is complete.

I saw this pattern when I watched Barbara work with the establishment of an NCJW center for emotionally disturbed pre-school youngsters. The project's success was only a beginning for Barbara. She didn't rest until the State took responsibility for providing these services for all Georgia's children with special needs.

In Atlanta, we participated in a national NCJW study on day care. Barbara didn't stop when the report was typed and mailed. She persevered until Grady Hospital, with NCJW's assistance, opened a daycare center for patients and staff who desperately needed this service.

A passionate supporter of the needs of our elderly citizens, she was a guiding force behind a succession of NCJW projects, the Golden Age Information and Referral Service and the Nursing Home Referral and Ombudsman program.

She climbed the NCJW ladder and became District President and a member of our national board. Barbara's record is legend in the non-profit community: United Way, Society of International Business Fellows, Metropolitan Atlanta Community Foundation, Leadership Atlanta, Leadership Georgia, Atlanta Women's Network, Atlanta City Club, Resurgens, Friends of Piedmont Park, Georgia Women's Political Caucus, Council for Children, Atlanta Ballet, Northwest Georgia Girl Scout Council, Atlanta Regional Commission Task Force on Aging, Georgia State University Allied Health Advisory Committee, and on and on.

Hannah Solomon, NCJW's founder, "went into the community

*to do what her conviction demanded." She entered arenas women had not yet entered before and championed unpopular causes.*

*Our founder would have been proud to see Barbara serve as chairperson of the Zoning Review Board for the City. In 1977, she was elected as an at-large member of the Atlanta City Council. She's completing her third four-year term and has served on all nine standing committees. In 1987, she was President Pro Tem of the Council and presently chairs their Public Safety Committee.*

*Barbara Asher is more than her impressive resumé suggests. She's a loyal friend, a loving mother and wife, and a caring member of our community. Fame and power never went to her head, and she's still available and accessible to all of us.*

In 1992, a special dinner, co-hosted by Dr. Johnnetta Cole, President of Spelman College, and Dr. Richard Cohen, AJC's Atlanta Chapter President, marked the 10th anniversary of the Atlanta Black/Jewish Coalition. I was unable to attend the dinner due to my mother-in-law's passing away, but I received a phone call the next day saying the evening was a great success, and the women attending were committed to meeting regularly. This was the origin of our Black/Jewish Sisters Group, comprised of six African-American women and six Jewish women. Barbara was a valued member of our group as we shared frequent dinners and discussions and attended cultural events together. I was sure she would one day serve as our mayor, as her influence on Atlanta City Council and throughout the community increased.

Tragically, after a series of complicated medical issues, Barbara died at the age of fifty-nine. Our Sisters were asked to serve as pallbearers at her funeral two days later on December 8, 1995. I was chosen to speak on behalf of the Group. Once again I used the poem "The Scent of the Roses" to begin my speech.

*Long, long will the memories and deeds of Barbara Asher*

*endure. Each of us knew her, admired her, and loved her in a different and personal way.*

*I followed her as President of the Atlanta Section of National Council of Jewish Women. What large footsteps she left behind in the NCJW. During Barbara's presidency, our national theme was "One Woman Can Make a Difference." This was the creed of Barbara's life. She believed it, she lived it, and this city bears witness to it.*

*Barbara taught us so much.*

- *She taught us that programs were needed for emotionally disturbed preschool children.*
- *She taught us that we could and must open a childcare center for the children of Grady Hospital outpatients.*
- *She taught us that you could discuss the most daunting challenges of the world while tagging and pricing clothes for Bargainata.*
- *She taught us that the elderly in our city needed both information and nursing home referral services.*
- *She taught us that there was a need to create Volunteer Atlanta, and housed it in NCJW's offices.*
- *She taught us that public officials could be brought closer to the issues of anti-Semitism, Soviet Jewry and Israel.*
- *She taught us that you could balance family, work and civic responsibility.*
- *She taught us that a Jewish woman in northwest Atlanta could run for and win a citywide seat on City Council.*
- *She taught us that sweet 16 wasn't only an age to be celebrated, but a milestone in City government to be marked.*
- *She taught us that all segments of our city needed a voice and a seat at the table – regardless of race, religion, economics or sexual orientation.*

- *She taught us that power and influence could be an enabler and not a corrupter.*

*Barbara was always available, to speak, to guide, to open doors, to inspire.*

*In recent years, we've been part of a special dialogue group made up of six Black and six Jewish women. We call each other "sisters." One of the sisters expressed her sadness last night that we had not been able to wrap our arms around Barbara during these last difficult weeks. Another sister responded: "Barbara's arms are wrapped all around us – pulling us closer to one another."*

*That is Barbara Asher's legacy. She wrapped her arms around her entire community and pulled us closer to one another.*

*One woman has made a difference. Long, long will the scent of roses and memories of Barbara endure.*

Legislation, conceived and introduced by Councilman Doug Alexander and co-sponsored by all members of the City Council, established a memorial for Barbara in the heart of downtown Atlanta. On the birthday of our beloved Barbara Asher, May 29, 1998, accompanied by our Black/Jewish Sisters, I spoke at the dedication of this monument – a statue in her likeness in a square named for her.

*It's hard to believe that 30 years have passed since Barbara Asher and I began to work together as volunteers in the National Council of Jewish Women. I followed Barbara as President of the Atlanta Section and continued to walk in the giant footsteps she made as she climbed up the rungs of national leadership in the National Council of Jewish Women.*

*Barbara was a visionary and an inspiration. She was a woman who made a difference in everything she undertook. She thought beyond her own neighborhood and her own personal needs. Barbara was on the one hand task oriented, organized, articulate* and driven to succeed. She was a natural for the challenge of political campaigns. On the other hand, Barbara was a people person who cared about her family, the disadvantaged, the handicapped, the vulnerable young and the fragile elderly. Barbara reached out to friends and colleagues in quiet, tangible behind-the-scenes ways offering support in difficult times. I know this first hand, because she helped me through personal troubles in my life.

I was blessed, as many of us are here today, to have worked with Barbara in so many ways. We were partners in volunteer efforts and on numerous civic and organizational boards, activists in political campaigns and on public policy issues, advocates against forces of intolerance and bigotry that continue to polarize and pollute our city, and respected colleagues in the appointed and elected positions of responsibility in which we serve.

Barbara was a professional in every way and a mentor and role model for countless people. She was the ultimate trainer in leadership development, management, communications and political action. She was a feminist and a proud member of the Jewish community.

During Barbara's last three years, I knew her in still another up close and personal way. We were sisters in a group of six Jewish and six African-American women. Together, we would share personal family stories and bring our unique perspectives to dinner discussions of some of the most daunting challenges facing our city. Barbara would glow as she spoke of her grandchildren and her pride in her children, Lee and Helen. Barbara and her husband, Norman, had much to be grateful for and she found strength in this. When Barbara spoke, we all listened. Her insights were fair, clear and reasoned.

Johnnetta Cole is one of our Sisters in our group. Last night I glanced through her recent book, "Dream the Boldest Dreams and Other Lessons of Life" to find a few words of wisdom for this very special occasion. No one says it better than Johnnetta and no one deserves it to be said of them more than our dear friend Barbara Miller Asher. Here are a few of these quotes:

*"The ultimate expression of generosity is not in giving of what you have, but in giving of who you are."*

*"How much better our world would be if each of us respected difference until difference doesn't make any more difference."*

*"Is it not the courage of conviction that moves mountains and parts oceans?"*

*"We had nothing to do with who our ancestors were. But we can have so much to do with who our children become."*

*"The best leaders follow their hearts as well as their heads, and they never ever leave their principles behind."*

*"It is those with the boldest of dreams who awaken the best in all of us."*

*These are the images we bring to this wonderful living memorial to former City Councilwoman Barbara Asher. She now stands forever in the midst of the city she loved with a visionary blueprint for action in her hands. God bless our sister who dreamed the boldest of dreams.*

I learned so much from Barbara, especially in the days before technology changed the way we do things... when you could help change the world with passion, determination, boundless energy, and simple pen and paper. I think of her often when am I doing my best planning and writing on a legal pad.

## CORETTA SCOTT KING

For many years the Atlanta Black/Jewish Coalition held meetings and programs at the Dr. Martin Luther King, Jr., Center for Nonviolent Social Change. Coretta Scott King often participated in these events and generously lent her support whenever asked. She joined us to host a large reception at the King Center welcoming Israel's first Arab Consul General, Mohammed Massarwa, to Atlanta. We worked together on commemorative events reenacting the March on Washington, supporting efforts to create a national holiday honoring Dr. King, and planning the Annual Celebration once the King Holiday was passed by Congress and signed into law by President Ronald Reagan in 1983.

Mrs. King was with us in more challenging times as well, speaking against the anti-Semitic statements of Minister Louis Farrakhan and signing ads organized by AJC for *The New York Times*, condemning anti-Semitism and supporting Israel when it was under attack.

My most intimate meetings with Mrs. King took place when we were working on the details of King Week activities, particularly the annual interfaith service. I introduced her when she gave her "State of the King Center" speech on the Sunday prior to the 1991 holiday's Monday observance. I likened her to the biblical Miriam who led her people, timbrel in hand, through the parted sea. She, too, was a musician who led her people to follow the unfinished work of Dr. King.

The many letters I received from Mrs. King are personal treasures. Following are two that demonstrate her warm gratitude.

*February 22, 1991, (excerpted)*
*Dear Ms. Frank,*

*Please accept my personal thanks, that of the Board of Directors and the King Week Steering Committee for serving as a Co-Chairperson of The Fifteenth Annual Interfaith Service which contributed greatly to the success of the Sixty-Second Birthday Celebration and Sixth National Holiday honoring Dr. Martin Luther King, Jr.*

*Your continued support of the King Center was never more important. Your personal involvement never more needed. Faith has brought us this far and faith will enable us to achieve Dr. King's Beloved Community and World House.*
*Sincerely,*
*Coretta Scott King*
**Reprinted by arrangement with CSK Legacy, LLC**
**(as Manager for the Estate of Coretta Scott King)**

*September 22, 1993*

*Dear Sherry,*

*On behalf of my Co-convener Reverend Joseph E. Lowry, I would like to say how very grateful we are to you for taking the time out of your busy schedule to serve as Co-chair of the Southeast Coalition for the mobilization of the March on Washington 30th Anniversary. Your wonderful team-work as a Co-chair is to be commended.*

*I especially want to thank you for your leadership in making sure buses were secured to get our youth to Washington. Your commitment to making the Southeast mobilization efforts a success is greatly appreciated.*

*Sherry, I also want to express my gratitude to you for your efforts toward mobilizing the Jewish Community for the celebration.*

*Again, thanks for your continued support and commitment.*

*Sincerely,*

*Coretta Scott King*

**Reprinted by arrangement with CSK Legacy, LLC**
**(as Manager for the Estate of Coretta Scott King)**

Aside from the formal activist persona Mrs. King projected, she was a proud and warmly devoted mother. I was privileged to know this side of her as well. On election night 1987, she invited me to campaign headquarters to hear the results of her son, Martin Luther King, III's, campaign for Fulton County Commissioner, a post he served in from 1987-1993.

Breaking news on January 30, 2006, of Mrs. King's death, shocked and saddened me. I called David Harris at once and asked him to give me an hour to gather my thoughts about her. I wrote a memo listing significant times when Mrs. King had stood with the Jewish community, in addition to all the well-known public actions she had taken since her husband's death.

I also wrote a quick letter to the editor that was printed in the *Atlanta Journal-Constitution* on February 1.

*Friend to the Jewish Community*

Coretta Scott King is gone. The King family lost a beloved mother and relative. The civil rights movement lost a devoted activist. The country lost a champion for justice and the Jewish community lost a loyal friend.

Countless people, touched by Mrs. King's kindness and inspired by her determination to continue the struggle for a better America, feel a deep sense of pain and loss.

I share that sense of pain and loss, yet also feel so blessed to have been able to work with Mrs. King and witness firsthand her concern for people and her unwavering commitment to Black-Jewish relations.

Goodbye, Coretta Scott King. Thanks for casting such a giant shadow and allowing me to walk among the thousands in your path.

On January 31, AJC released a statement repeating some of the content of my letter to the editor.

*The American Jewish Committee mourns the passing of Coretta Scott King*

Her commitment and passion in carrying on, after the assassination of Dr. Martin Luther King, Jr., a life dedicated to human rights and justice is her everlasting legacy.

Among the many AJC leaders who worked closely with Mrs. King over the years was Sherry Frank, longtime director of AJC's Atlanta Chapter. "I feel so blessed to have been able to work with Mrs. King and witness first-hand her concern for people and her unwavering commitment to

Black-Jewish relations," said Frank, who participated in the annual King Week events, the periodic reenactments of the historic March on Washington, and in other programs that brought together blacks, Jews, and other Americans.

AJC will long remember Mrs. King's selfless solidarity with the Jewish community, especially in joining the fight for the freedom of Soviet Jews, and in supporting the state of Israel in her quest for peace and security.

I was immeasurably touched to receive a call from the King Center the next day, inviting me to speak at Mrs. King's funeral on February 7, and notified the AJC national staff.

*I just received a call on behalf of the King family asking me to speak on behalf of the Jewish community on Tuesday at Mrs. King's Memorial Service. They asked me to use the words printed in the* Atlanta Journal-Constitution *letter that I submitted.*

*I am deeply honored by this invitation. I will be given 2-3 minutes to speak and thus can use the entire text of my original piece, which recalls so many times that Coretta Scott King stood by our Jewish community.*

*While I am personally honored, this is a wonderful tribute to the importance of the American Jewish Committee's decades of work in intergroup relations, and Black-Jewish relations in particular.*

I received a humbling response from David Harris.

*Dear Sherry,*

*I was profoundly moved by the news you conveyed to me this morning. That you were selected to speak on behalf of the entire Jewish community at Coretta Scott King's funeral on Tuesday is a remarkable testament to your own relationship with her, to your lifelong commitment to the civil rights struggle, and to your leadership through AJC in advancing the relationship between Blacks and Jews. What a well-deserved honor!*

*All of your "kvelling" friends and colleagues will be with you in spirit as you stand up before as many as 14,000 people in the hall, and probably a global television audience, to deliver your eulogy.*

*We will, of course, feature your words on our website homepage and distribute the text to AJC leaders, and encourage the media to include references in their reporting.*

Shabbat shalom,

*David (Harris)*

There were public events for several days prior to the service celebrating her life while her body lay in state at the Georgia State Capitol. In the days that followed, there were announcements that one dignitary after another would be participating in what was to be called "Celebrating Her Spirit: Celebration of the Life of Coretta Scott King, April 27, 1927- January 30, 2006."

The service was to be held at New Birth Missionary Baptist Church, a megachurch in Lithonia, Georgia, several miles away from downtown Atlanta. Late at night on February 6, I received a call from a King Center staff member advising me to come to Mrs. King's condominium the next morning; I would be driving to the service with dignitaries in a limousine.

February 7 was a day I will never forget. I arrived at Mrs. King's condo around 9:00 a.m. I was greeted by her daughter, Yolanda King, and ushered into a room filled with elderly friends of Mrs. King, devoted staff members and Yolanda's minister who had traveled with her from California. Older ladies wearing hats and gloves wandered around the condo, glancing at family pictures, framed photos with legendary heroes, and mementos from the civil rights movement. We gathered in a circle for prayer, led by Yolanda's minister, before leaving the condo and filing into several long limos.

The police escorted our caravan through downtown Atlanta

to the home where family members, including Dexter, Martin III, and Bernice King, were waiting to be picked up and brought to the service. I was in the car with staff members, and we shared stories and discussed plans for the remainder of the day. Everywhere we went, thousands of people were lining the streets, paying tribute to this remarkable woman.

It was a good thing that I didn't drive myself, because even with a police escort, we had difficulty getting through the parking lot. It was only when we told police that I was one of the speakers that we were waved through the innumerable buses and limos and allowed to enter the church.

The day's program included a four-page Order of Service, and it was surreal to see my name listed among the participants. I would speak in front of three U.S. Presidents. The program listed "Official Tributes" and included President George W. Bush, Governor Sonny Perdue, Mayor Shirley Franklin, and Zanele Mbeki, First Lady, Republic of South Africa.

After one of several musical tributes, the program listed "Civil and Human Rights Tributes" that included Dr. Dorothy Height, Chairman of the Board, National Council of Negro Women; Reverend Dr. Joseph Lowery, President Emeritus, Southern Christian Leadership Conference; and me, Executive Director, American Jewish Committee, Atlanta Chapter. Once again, there was music and a list of "Special Tributes" that included Presidents James Earl Carter, Jr., George H.W. Bush, William Jefferson Clinton, and Senator Hillary Clinton.

Hours passed, and speeches were given by family members and friends, nationally prominent clergy, Senator Edward Kennedy, and Representative John Conyers. Stevie Wonder sang "His Eye Is On the Sparrow," Dr. Maya Angelou recited a poem, and the Honorable Andrew Young gave a personal tribute. And then it was my turn.

I worked closely with Judy Marx, AJC's Assistant Area Director, for nearly a decade and often read her my speeches. After hours of crafting my remarks, I showed her my statement about Mrs. King signing onto an AJC ad in *The New York Times* supporting Israel. Judy suggested I add the phrase, "once again supporting Israel's quest for peace." I was actually startled that when I said those words, the large crowd broke out in thunderous applause. It took my breath away, and I have a picture from that moment when my hand is clasped over my heart. Even now I replay the emotions I felt as I delivered this reflection.

*Coretta Scott King Cast a Long Shadow*

*Coretta Scott King is gone. The King family lost a beloved mother and relative. The civil rights movement lost a devoted activist. The country lost a champion for justice, and the Jewish community lost a loyal friend.*

*Countless people, touched by Coretta Scott King's kindness and inspired by her determination to continue the struggle for a better America, feel a deep sense of pain and loss.*

*I share that sense of pain and loss, yet feel so blessed to have been able to work with Mrs. King and witness first hand her concern for people and her unwavering commitment to Black-Jewish relations.*

*As I think about my work with the American Jewish Committee over these past 25 years, I remember fondly her participation in the meetings of the Atlanta Black/Jewish Coalition, Co-Chaired by Congressman John Lewis, and held often at the King Center.*

*I remember the gratitude we felt when Mrs. King joined members of the Coalition in denouncing anti-Semitism and honoring Holocaust memory.*

*I remember Mrs. King hosting a reception with us to welcome Israeli Consul General Mohammed Massarwa, Israel's first Arab member of their diplomatic corps.*

*I remember telling her that I was going to the Soviet Union to meet with Soviet Jews, including the wives of refuseniks whose* husbands were in prison for their activism. She autographed three of her books and asked me to bring these to them in solidarity with their struggle to be free.

I remember the reenactments of the historic March on Washington. One year most Jewish organizations chose not to participate due to concern with the extremist positions of some co-sponsors. Mrs. King refused to let that cause a rift in the long history of strong Black-Jewish relations. The Jewish community held a rally at the King Center before she left for Washington and the first speech she made after returning to Atlanta was Shabbat morning at Congregation Shearith Israel.

I remember calling her to ask if we could list her name in an ad the American Jewish Committee placed in The New York Times calling on Iraq to stop firing SCUD missiles into Israel. She signed the ad, once again rejecting violence and supporting Israel's right to live in peace.

I remember marching in Selma, Forsyth County and Washington with her. Her strength gave us all strength. Her tireless dedication to the cause of equality inspired generations.

I remember our hard work and the enormous thrill of success in achieving a National Holiday to celebrate the life and work of Dr. King. My favorite thing in my office is the flag from the first holiday observance.

I remember the countless meetings planning King Week activities and her sensitivity to including Jewish participation. Each November I anticipated the call from Dora McDonald, in Mrs. King's office at the King Center, asking for the name of a rabbi to read from the Scriptures at the Ecumenical Service on the King Holiday.

I remember the pride I felt when Mrs. King asked me to introduce her before she gave her State of the King Center Address during King Week. I likened her journey to that of biblical Miriam who led her people through the parted seas with music and timbrel in hand. Mrs. King, a gifted musician, also led her people through the troubled waters of our times.

I feel a tremendous loss today. Goodbye Coretta Scott King. Thanks for casting such a giant shadow and allowing me to walk among the thousands in your path.

May her memory forever be a blessing.

The service that had begun at noon lasted until the sun had set. Back in the limo, we headed to the King Center, where Mrs. King would be laid to rest next to her beloved husband, Dr. King. The evening sky was bright and clear. A brief service followed her internment, and white doves were released into the evening sky to spiritually represent love, peace and the soul. With a sense of calm, grief, and fatigue, we headed to a downtown hotel to gather for nourishment and comfort with family, friends, and dignitaries who had traveled from near and far for this historic occasion. Xernona Clayton, a close friend of Coretta's, orchestrated this final gathering, and the hotel management joked with her about an intimate reception that turned out to be quite the opposite.

In the days that followed, I was touched to receive calls from close and distant friends across the country who heard me speak, and it meant the world to me to receive accolades from my AJC staff and lay leaders.

From Shula Bahat, AJC's Associate Director:
You were inspiring, eloquent, forceful, serious, earnest, and as you spoke about Coretta one could really understand how important she was in her own right. The legacy she is leaving behind is hers, and hers alone. You managed to weave into your remarks so many important themes and to remind the audience of important historic events and forgotten values and aspirations. You were, in short, absolutely terrific.

Institutionally, you made us all so proud of AJC and your

*presence on the podium. AJC was highlighted amply in your remarks.*

*Your Jewishness was so evident, every Jew watching you must have identified with you. Especially gratifying was to hear the audience reaction to your mention of Israel.*

*Thank you for being who you are, for achieving such stature. I am so proud to be your friend and colleague.*

From Bob Goodkind, AJC National President:

*Extraordinarily well done! Congratulations again. May the memory of the day and your success therein stay with you for a lifetime.*

*Have now read your eulogy which was poetic -- and as I knew it would be -- moving, eloquent and from the heart. Again, congratulations and thanks. Best regards, Bob*

Since Mrs. King's death Dr. Bernice King has frequently invited me to speak about her mother at forums where students are brought to the King Center to learn about Dr. King, Coretta, and the civil rights movement. I am included annually in events that commemorate her birthday. I will always treasure my relationship with this extraordinary woman, the amazing honor of speaking at her funeral and the continuing relationship I have with the King Center and King family.

In reviewing my AJC files, I reread my words commemorating the first observance of the American federal holiday, Martin Luther King, Jr., Day. They were printed in *The Southern Israelite* on January 10, 1986, and expressed my esteem for both Dr. King and Mrs. King and my personal commitment to continue their work.

On January 20, 1986, we will celebrate the historic first national Martin Luther King, Jr., Day. We are fortunate to be a participant in what hopefully will be an American tradition of genuine significance. Martin Luther King, Jr., was a remarkable human being. His impact on our society left an indelible mark for future generations. When he spoke, he gave people hope; when he acted, he gave people strength to continue the struggle; and when he reached out, he acknowledged the diversity of the people of the world.

In the period since he spoke about his dream for America, his vision of freedom has inspired others in our society to speak out forthrightly for their freedom, America's women, ethnics, handicapped, and elderly.

His own words bear remembering at this important moment in history.

About community, he said: "Through our scientific genius, we have made of our nation – and even the world – a neighborhood, but we have failed to employ our moral and spiritual genius to make it a brotherhood."

About social justice, he said: "We must affirm that every human life is a reflection of divinity, and every act of injustice mars and defaces the image of God in man."

In support of non-violence he said: "Violence as a way of achieving racial justice is both impractical and immoral. It is impractical because it ends up creating many more social problems than it solves. It is immoral because it seeks to annihilate the opponent rather than convert him. It destroys community and makes brotherhood impossible."

Martin Luther King, Jr., left a moral legacy. He was true to his own people, and spoke eloquently about the need for nonviolent change in this country. But he was true to the broader community of the human family. He spoke out against all injustice.

In Martin Luther King, Jr., American Jews always had a friend and ally who understood Jewish agony even as we tried to understand the agony of his people.

Again, let us pause to remember his own words remembering that he said these things prior to 1968.

Of anti-Semitism he said: "We cannot substitute one tyranny for another, and for the black man to be struggling for justice and then turn around and be anti-Semitic is not only a very irrational course but it is a very immoral course, and wherever we have seen anti-Semitism we have condemned it with all our might."

Of Israel, he said: "I see Israel, and never mind saying it, as one of the great outposts of democracy in the world, and marvelous example of what can be done, how desert land almost can be transformed into an oasis of brotherhood and democracy. Peace for Israel means security, and that security must be a reality."

Of Soviet Jewry, he said: "While Jews in Russia may not be physically murdered as they were in Nazi Germany, they are facing every day a kind of spiritual and cultural genocide... the absence of opportunity to associate as Jews in the enjoyment of Jewish culture and religious experience becomes a severe limitation upon the individual."

Coretta Scott King has continued to keep Dr. King's dream alive. But she has done much more than treasure memories of past struggles and victories. Throughout the year, and particularly during King Week, she works to focus public attention and foster creative solutions for the pressing problems facing humanity.

She has continued, as did Dr. King, to reach out to the Jewish community, and to be sensitive to our struggles. She has spoken out in support of Israel and Soviet Jewry. She signed an ad in the *New York Times* criticizing President Reagan's Bitburg visit, and spoke out against Minister Farrakhan's anti-Semitic statements. She continues to offer her support in all programs designed to strengthen relations between the black and Jewish community.

How often we rally together when there is a crisis and

our issues are threatened. Unfortunately, with the rise in world terrorism, we feel even more vulnerable.

Let us gather together during King Week '86 to celebrate what is good in our nation. Let's rally our support around the King family and the numerous events taking place in Atlanta to mark this historic national observance.

Let us celebrate the first national Martin Luther King, Jr., Day by recognizing that Dr. King's dream was a dream we all shared and his life was a moral legacy that touched us deeply. His non-violent strategy offers a sensible alternative to the madness of war and nuclear threats. His dream is still yet unfulfilled. We have the capacity to bring the world closer to that dream if we roll up our sleeves and join the struggle.

## LILLIAN LEWIS

One of the special benefits I received creating the Atlanta Black/Jewish Coalition in 1982 was my warm and personal relationship with John Lewis. As we began to work together, I got to know his wife, Lillian, as well and learned that their son, John Miles, and my son, Andrew (Drew), were the exact same age, both born on May 24, 1976.

Lillian and I became close friends, spending long hours on the phone late in the evening. Politics, family, community and recipes all were familiar topics of our conversations. Lillian became an active member of the Black/Jewish Coalition, helping with contacts for programs with her colleagues at Atlanta University.

When John decided to vacate his seat on the Atlanta City Council to run for Congress in 1986, our conversations transitioned to lengthy meetings reviewing lists and discussing donors and campaign events. Working for a non-profit organization and mindful of protecting our tax exempt status, I was careful that all of this political activity was behind the scenes and off the record.

Through the summer months of John's first campaign their son, John Miles, spent almost every weekend at my house. He and my son, Drew, put up yard signs, wore campaign shirts, and often attended campaign events. We celebrated the election night victory in Atlanta and rode the train to D.C. together for John's swearing into office. Lillian and I looked down from the balcony onto the floor of Congress, where John Miles and Drew sat on either side of the Congressman for that historic moment.

Over the years, Lillian and I shared long phone calls and increased involvement in each of John's campaigns for reelection. I got to know her family when they visited from California, and Lillian and John attended my family's life cycle events, including weddings and *bar* and *bat mitzvahs*. It was an honor to be included in a small dinner party marking their special anniversary. My thank you letter sent December 30, 1993, expressed my heartfelt appreciation.

*Dear Lillian and John,*

*I'm still enjoying the warm memories of the elegant and intimate celebration of your 25th anniversary.*

*John, how lucky you are that "Mrs. Miles" kept calling your office that fateful summer 26 years ago. No one could ask for a more ardent supporter and advocate for all the good that you do than your wife, Lillian.*

*And Lillian, how lucky you are to have such a romantic husband and extraordinary social planner. That dinner was stupendous and the gifts John gave you were really sentimental and lovely. John's attention to every detail should make you feel so good.*

*You are both special to me, and I was honored to be included in your milestone anniversary. Please be sure I am on the list for your 50th!*

*Happy New Year.*

*Love, Sherry Frank*

In later years, when Lillian became ill and incapacitated, I often spoke to her on the phone and went to see her in the hospital and later in a nursing home. I visited with her for the last time just before Christmas in December, 2012. John was with her, and they had just celebrated their 44th wedding anniversary.

Just a week later, when I was out of town, I heard the news that Lillian had passed away. I called John and spoke to Michael Collins, his longtime chief of staff and devoted friend. Michael told me that John wanted me to speak at Lillian's funeral. I went over to their home the next day after returning to Atlanta. The house was already filled with John's and Lillian's friends, community and political leaders, family and devoted caregivers. When I asked John about some of Lillian's credentials, biographical information that I was unfamiliar with, he said, "just talk about your friendship, the personal things that matter in life."

On Monday, January 7, 2013, I arrived at Ebenezer Baptist Church an hour before the scheduled service. My daughter, Laura, came with me, and was in awe of the entire experience. We had a reserved parking space at the church and were ushered into a private room with the other speakers. We visited with Ambassador Andrew Young and reminisced for nearly an hour about John, Lillian, and Black-Jewish relations over the decades.

I sat next to Anita Hill, attorney and Professor of Social Policy, Law and Women's Studies at Brandeis University (yes, the one from the notorious Clarence Thomas hearing.) Until then, I had been unaware of her friendship with Lillian. As each person spoke, I grew prouder that I had been blessed to have Lillian in my life. She touched so many individuals in such a special and enduring way. The church was filled to capacity with members of Congress, civil rights legends, civic and religious leaders, relatives and friends. The program for the service was titled "Celebrating the Life, Legacy, and Spirit of Lillian Miles Lewis, March 3, 1939 – December 31, 2012."

Contributing to the service's beautiful music were Jennifer Holliday, singing "The Last Mile of the Way," and Mary Gurley, singing "If I Can Help Somebody." The Reverend Dr. Joseph Roberts, Senior Pastor Emeritus, spoke and the Reverend Dr. Raphael Warnock, Senior Pastor, gave the Eulogy. Reflections were presented by Christine King Farris, Ambassador Andrew Young, Reverend Jesse Jackson and Xernona Clayton, civil rights leader and broadcasting executive. I was included in the second set of reflections along with Warren Hayes and Anita Hill.

As I spoke, I kept looking out at the front row where John sat next to his son, John Miles. When I talked about our young boys, I was warmed by John Miles' big smile. These were my words, spoken with a heavy heart.

*In 1982, at a staff retreat with my colleagues at the American Jewish Committee, our Washington Representative, Hyman Bookbinder, affectionately called, "Bookie," told me this was the year the Voting Rights Act was up for renewal. He suggested I bring Black and Jewish leaders together to work for its passage, noting the long history of our shared work on this issue.*

*I followed his suggestion, and that was the beginning of the Atlanta Black/Jewish Coalition, which John Lewis co-chaired until he was elected to Congress. This past August we celebrated the 30th Anniversary of the Coalition. Among the many blessings of my work with the Coalition was the gift of thirty years of friendship with Lillian and John Lewis.*

*Lillian and I quickly discovered that her son, John Miles, and my son, Drew, were the same age and born on the same day. We planned their joint birthday parties together when the boys were seven and eight years old.*

*By the time John ran for Congress in 1986, we were like family. Throughout the summer, Lillian would bring John Miles to my house on Friday afternoon after I returned home from work. Lillian* and John would come pick John Miles up on Sunday evening after a full weekend of round the clock campaigning. They were often famished, and I loved having noodle kugel and other Jewish dishes waiting for my hungry and exhausted friends.

Lillian grew up in Los Angeles and attended schools with such large Jewish populations that they were closed on Jewish holidays. Chicken soup and other traditional foods were some of her favorite things to eat.

I brought Drew to many campaign events so John Miles would have someone to play with. I remember them running up and down escalators at many hotels while John was speaking and Lillian was greeting supporters and collecting checks, names and addresses.

We spent many long nights on the phone and productive days creating fundraising lists in those early campaigns when computers and staff were not as efficient as they are now. I always marveled at Lillian's dedication to her husband's work, her interest in his issues and her tireless energy devoted to his campaigns.

The Bible teaches us when God created Adam, he created Eve to be his helpmate. Lillian was truly a helpmate and partner to John. She was a loving wife and mother, devoted to her family.

While we can all speak volumes about Lillian Lewis' wonderful attributes, those who knew her well know how totally unforgiving she was towards anyone who had an unkind word or disagreement with John. We loved her loyalty and support for our esteemed Congressman.

Congressman Lewis, I bring you heartfelt condolences from the American Jewish Committee and the entire Jewish community.

Lillian was a great storyteller and conversationalist. She was a talented leader, a gifted educator and a voracious reader. She was a true intellect with a keen interest in world affairs, developed from her early years with the Peace Corps in Nigeria.

She told the truth and was genuine to the core. Rudyard Kipling's poem speaks to Lillian's virtue: "If you can talk with crowds and keep your virtue, or walk with Kings - nor lose the common touch." Lillian never lost the common touch.

Memories are a gift that death can never take away from us. I will always cherish memories of my friend Lillian.

I will remember how she didn't want the spotlight and was thrilled with John's accomplishments. In later years she didn't want her illness to distract John from his life's work.

I will remember the early years in the Black/Jewish Coalition. After the Martin Luther King, Jr., Holiday was passed, Lillian was on one of our first teams going into Atlanta public schools and Jewish Day Schools conducting "teach-ins" about Dr. King.

I remember how hard she worked on our Coalition programs on Jewish ties to Israel and Black ties to Africa. She was so knowledgeable about the world and proud to bring her Atlanta University scholars from Africa to these programs to educate us and build bridges of understanding.

I remember how Lillian didn't fly and what fun we had on that long train ride to Washington for John's first swearing in. Lillian and I looked down from the Congressional balcony where our young sons sat side by side on the seat with Congressman Lewis during the ceremony.

I remember what a sweet tooth Lillian had and how she loved chocolate. I brought some of my homemade cookies to her at the nursing home and she ate so many chocolate cookies that she had trouble falling asleep that night.

I remember sadder times visiting with Lillian in the hospital and nursing home. Johnny, her aide for over five years, was caring for her so lovingly. They were like sisters, sharing deep personal ties and an unbreakable bond.

I remember how Lillian looked at you with her beautiful brown eyes. In a way, she spoke with her eyes and touched your soul. She never complained, but rather wanted to know about you, your family and your life.

*I visited with Lillian the Sunday before Christmas, December 23. When I walked in the room there was a beautiful vase of red roses from John. Lillian told me their 44th wedding anniversary was the day before.*

*As soon as I learned of her death, I thought of those roses and the poem "The Scent of the Roses." (I read the poem aloud as I had done at Roz Cohen's funeral.)*

*Roses are a thing of beauty. Lillian was a beautiful person. John you shared a beautiful relationship. May Lillian Lewis' memory always be a blessing to those whose lives she touched and enriched.*

For several years after her death, John hosted a December gathering of Lillian's friends and family. It was a bittersweet time to share memories and reflect on how special Lillian was to so many of us. I treasure my special relationship with Congressman Lewis, and I know my friendship with Lillian is a tie that will always bind us.

## SUNNY STERN

My relationship with our fantastic staff is at the top of my list of the many things I am thankful for in my years with AJC. Over the years, we worked together seamlessly in the office and became family as we shared joy and sadness in our personal lives. We gave one another strength and support individually and professionally.

Sunny Stern and I had worked together in NCJW and the Ahavath Achim Synagogue before she joined our staff as AJC's Assistant Area Director. Sunny was a lawyer, and her keen insight enhanced our public policy work. She was a dedicated and knowledgeable Jew and brought this talent to our Oral History Project as well as our young adults in ACCESS. Most of all, she conveyed her kindness, steadiness and dedication to AJC and the numerous community partners with whom we worked. Sunny was admired by and a confidante of AJC staff members around the country.

We worked together many nights, and, on occasion, my young son Drew spent the evening with Sunny's loving husband, Marty, filling vending machines for his business. Marty wasn't a babysitter, but a kind friend and extended family member. Tragically, he passed away unexpectedly in August, 1996. Then, in May of the next year, Sunny discovered a mass and began her year-long battle with cancer, always positive, always strong.

Her death on May 8, 1998, was heartbreaking for all of us in the AJC world – staff and lay leaders – and friends throughout the community. At the request of my AJC colleagues, I spoke at our staff retreat on May 16.

*Thank you for joining with me in this time of reflection as we remember our beloved colleague, Sunny Stern.*

*Sunny Stern's life was a blessing to all who knew her. We were doubly blessed in AJC that she spent over nine productive years in our midst. Her death leaves a huge void and a profound sense of loss. As I have done over the years, when someone I treasure has passed away, I turned to a short poem titled, "The Scent of the Roses." It concludes with these words:*

*You may break, you may shatter the vase if you will,*
*But the scent of the roses will hang round it still.*

*Sunny's memory will linger like the scent of the roses in the vase. Her life had so much meaning because she made time count.*

*I knew that Sunny was slipping away from us during these past three weeks, particularly the last ten days when she was in the hospital. By Wednesday, two days before her death, I stayed late in the office to begin collecting lists of who we would need to call with details of her funeral – Board members, ACCESS Steering*

Committee, Black/Jewish Coalition, ethnic, religious, political leaders, media, Jewish professionals – Sunny's quiet reach was deep and wide. Her nine years with AJC were filled with accomplishments and trusted relationships.

One of the rabbis on our board offered me support, and I took him up on it. I called him at home Friday morning when I received the call that Sunny had passed away. I knew it was imminent. Sunny slipped into a coma Thursday evening. Rabbi Stanley Davids was at our office within hours. Jean Saul Jackson was at Sunny's house bringing some fresh Kosher food for the family. She stayed for a couple of hours, visiting with Sunny's 92-year-old mother, who had traveled in and out of Norfolk, Virginia, this past year to take care of Sunny. We turned off the answering machine at Rabbi David's direction. Lillian Troop and Dale Shields, our two secretaries, and I prayed, and we cried, and we thanked God for the blessing of knowing, loving and working with Sunny. She was deeply religious, and we knew she would have been pleased that we turned to faith and tradition for support.

I knew I couldn't do anything productive, so I asked Dale to help me clean a small stack of 1996 files that needed to be put in archive boxes. I picked up a stack, and there was a file marked Sunny Stern. Just a few thank you notes were in Sunny's file in addition to this memo from Geri Rozanski (AJC's national staff.)

"Despite the rain and wind, it is always Sunny in Atlanta, due in large measure to your remarkable disposition. To watch you on the phone managing the teen retreat (which by now is over – I hope it was the success you have come to expect) or the way in which you manage the very many administrative tasks required of you, to the genuine collegiality you showed Joan Silverman, is to be reminded that there are indeed people who can be thoroughly professional without once losing any of their humanity. How fortunate for Sherry, how fortunate for AJC, and how lucky for me, having a colleague like you. You are a rare and special treasure."

I called Geri Rozanski and Shula Bahat with the news of Sunny's death, and shortly after my call, Geri sent her beautiful memo marked – re:"Sad News."

Phone messages have poured in from groups as diverse as Planned Parenthood, ACLU, Rainbow Coalition, and ethnic and religious leaders. Two messages I picked up on my answering machine were particularly moving.

Reverend Joanna Adams called to express her sympathies. She said, "Sunny was such a great ambassador of warmth and graciousness to me. She was a terrific person. I give thanks to God for her life. She touched a lot of people's lives in a very positive way. Blessings on you, Sherry, my friend."

Congressman John Lewis called and said, "I'm truly and deeply sorry and sad to hear about the passing of Sunny. It's a great loss to you, AJC, the Black/Jewish Coalition and Project Understanding. Be strong and I will keep you in my prayers."

A special obituary printed in the Atlanta Journal-Constitution on the morning of her funeral on May 10 read:

"Sunny Stern, 60, worked to decrease hatred and prejudice in Atlanta by bringing people of different races and religions face to face. Mrs. Stern coordinated seven retreats for African-American and Jewish teens. She created seminars to bring people from different religious backgrounds together and worked to foster relationships among Jews and Asian and Hispanic leaders. 'When you're not looking for credit, you can accomplish so much, and that was Sunny,' said AJC Southeast Area Director, Sherry Frank. 'She impacted everything we did.'"

The Atlanta Jewish Times wrote of Sunny's death, "Sunny Stern, 60, whose humble qualities made as great an impact on others as her professional successes, died Friday, May 8. 'How fitting that today is Mother's Day, because family was Mom's prized possession,' her son, Dr. Mark Stern, told the several hundred people who gathered at the graveside funeral services Sunday, May 10, at

Arlington Memorial Park. 'In raising children, many people think about the mistakes their parents made, and I just think of how I want to raise my children exactly the same way she raised me.' Rabbi Arnold Goodman said, 'She believed in creating a society where people loved one another, or at least respected one another.'"

Sunny worked until her last three weeks. She was always cheerful, positive and optimistic. She reached out to others with cancer and did research on the internet. She found it difficult to lose her hair and got a wig. No More Bad Hair Days was a book that brought her laughter and the author became a new friend who was also struggling with cancer. Sunny's hair grew back grey, and looked great, a bit artsy. When she had more treatment and lost her hair again, she decided to buy a second wig. This one was grey and short cropped, and she looked so good to us. She laughed when people complimented her on her "new look." I've brought pictures with me to pass around. I want you to see Sunny's big smile and how good she looked just weeks before she passed away. I also want you to see her precious granddaughters, Ariel and Julia, and her family: son and daughter-in-law, Mark and Tamar; son, David; and mother, Bubbie "B."

The first time in this year of struggle that Sunny broke down was in my office after Passover. She was weak and beginning to feel her body failing her. She wept and said she couldn't believe how loving everyone was to her. Sunny gave love so easily, and at the end she knew how much love was returned to her by her devoted family and amazing cadre of dear friends.

In my last phone conversation with her, she told me about all the time she was spending during her week of chemotherapy watching TV. She said, "What we do in AJC is so important." It amazed her how much trivia was on the TV, in contrast to how much of significance was on our AJC agenda.

Sunny's work gave her life great purpose and satisfaction. She was an attorney and brought her keen intellect to everything she *did at AJC. But most of all she was gentle and kind and patient and fair and understanding and interested in everyone she touched. She represented AJC so well throughout the Jewish and general communities.*

*Our ACCESS members were especially close to Sunny as she modeled leadership and responsibility for them.*

*It's hard to move forward, to think of programs without her, board trainings, campaigns, dialogues, ordinary routine work. I'm not ready to hire anyone. Sunny was one of a kind – bright, selfless, righteous, truly a blessing to all who knew and loved her.*

*She taught me many things:*

- *Resolve to be cheerful and helpful. People will repay you in kind.*
- *Resolve to listen more and to talk less. No one ever learns anything by talking.*
- *Be chary of giving advice. Wise men don't need it, and fools won't heed it.*
- *Resolve to be tender with the young, compassionate with the aged, sympathetic with the striving and tolerant of the weak and the wrong. Sometime in life you will have been all of these.*

*One of my favorite quotes best describes my relationship with Sunny.*

> *Do not walk in front of me – I may not follow.*
> *Do not walk behind me – I may not lead.*
> *Just walk beside me – and be my friend.*

*Sunny was a great gift, a dear friend. Together we walked side by side for nine productive years. I miss her so.*

When I spoke about Sunny at our Board of Trustees meeting on May 19, I repeated some of the things I shared at the staff retreat and added these statements.

> *Sunny Stern's life was a blessing to all who knew her. We were doubly blessed in AJC that she spent over nine productive years in our midst. Her death leaves a huge void and a profound sense of loss. As I have done over the years, when someone I treasure has passed away, I turned to a short poem titled, "The Scent of the Roses," by Thomas Moore.*
>
> *Sunny was soft and precious as the petals of the rose, and her memory will be with us for years to come as we reach out to one another and to the wider Jewish and general communities.*
>
> *Rabbi Abraham Heschel left us an important insight when he wrote, "Judaism is a religion of time aiming at the sanctification of time." Yes, we can sanctify time. We can make every day holy if we choose to sanctify it. Time becomes holy when a part of it is given to others; when we share and care and listen. Time is sanctified when we remember that more important than counting time is making time count.*
>
> *Sunny made time count. She had an indomitable spirit and inner strength. She faced her year's struggle with cancer with a positive attitude and a smile on her face. She persevered as if she faced an endless future rather than giving in to her pain and self-pity. She drew even closer to her mother, who, at 92, traveled from Norfolk to take care of her. She treasured endless late night calls from her two sons, who tragically buried both of their parents in just 20 months. She changed her house over for Passover with great joy, since her granddaughters and her family surrounded her at this holiday just weeks ago.*
>
> *The Ahavath Achim Synagogue, The Hebrew Academy, The Bureau of Jewish Education, Hadassah and especially the National Council of Jewish Women were beneficiaries of her years of devoted volunteer service and leadership.*
>
> *Calls and letters have come to us from organizations including*

Planned Parenthood, ACLU, Rainbow Coalition, Timber Ridge Conference Center, where we held our Black/Jewish Coalition retreats, and from leaders in the religious and ethnic communities, from the person at Selig Enterprises who helped us find office space and the person who installed our telephone system. Everyone who had contact with Sunny was drawn to her in a special way.

Perhaps the most moving letter was from Ozell Sutton, U.S. Department of Justice, Community Relations Service and past co-chairman of the Black/Jewish Coalition. He wrote, "Sunny had nothing to say about when she was born, where she was born, nor what color she was born into. That was the will of God. Neither did she have a choice about when she died, where she died or how she died. That too was the prerogative of God. But that space between those two periods was hers to preside over. How she used her space in her time was her prerogative. What did she choose to do with her space in her time? She chose to 'Do justly, to Love Mercy, and to Walk Humbly' … Micah 6:8.

For over nine years, Sunny and I walked together as trusted friends as we worked to strengthen AJC's Atlanta Chapter and ACCESS. I feel blessed to have known her and shared this partnership with her. I will miss her always.

David Harris' memo to me following Sunny's death clearly showed how much she was valued on a national level.

I just had a chance to read your comments regarding Sunny at the Staff Seminar, and I want you to know that I was deeply moved.

As you know better than any of us, Sunny was a truly exceptional person. You were able to both capture and convey her essential being in a profoundly touching and personal way that could not have left a dry eye in the room.

Thank you so much for putting your remarks down on paper and, in doing so, creating such a fitting tribute to Sunny's memory.

Rosalind Penso Cohen

Black/Jewish Sisters Group at dedication of Barbara
Asher statue in downtown Atlanta,
(L-R) Johnnetta Cole, Spring Asher, Lois Frank, Dianne Harnell
Cohen, Myrtle Davis, Sherry Frank, Nancy Boxill, 1998

Coretta Scott King addressing AJC Annual Meeting honoring Cecil Alexander, 1982

Lillian Lewis and Sherry Frank with their sons Drew and John Miles, 1986

Sunny Stern and Sherry Frank preparing for an AJC meeting

# APPENDIX

―――――――――――――

## WOMEN'S ISSUES PROGRAMMING AND ADVOCACY

- January, 1979 – NCJW was influential in the formation of ERA Georgia. NCJW and AJC worked with numerous women's organizations in support of the Equal Rights Amendment.
- April, 1981 – AJC and NCJW co-sponsored a three-part series "Jewish Women in the 80s: Transition and Challenge." The topics were "Anti-Semitism in the Feminist Movement" featuring Susie Elson, Leah Janus and Georgia State Representative Cathey Steinberg; "Feminization of Poverty" featuring Fran Eizenstat, coordinator of Child Watch, Children's Defense Fund and Rona Schpeiser, Jewish Family Services, Inc.; "My Mother, My Daughter, My Son's Wife" featuring Dr. Elaine Levin, Associate Professor, Georgia State University.
- July, 1981 – I spoke at Atlanta Interfaith Broadcasters with Margaret Curtis, President of People of Faith for ERA Georgia
- November, 1981 – AJC and NCJW co-sponsored a forum, "Women's Issues in 1982," featuring Representative Steinberg and Margaret Curtis. Cathey introduced the ERA in the Georgia Legislature at the close of the 1981 Session so that it would come up in January, 1982. Margaret spoke about the Moral Majority's efforts to defeat the amendment and Jean Young's travels across the state to get black women involved.
- December, 1981-- AJC coordinated an event to enable ERA Georgia to buy TV ads.
- May 14, 1984 – AJC co-hosted a program with Professor

Richard L. Zweigenhaft, author of AJC's report "Who Gets to the Top? Executive Suite Discrimination in the 80s."

- March 20, 1985 – AJC hosted a program titled "Economic Empowerment – Is Comparable Worth the Answer?" featuring Lynn Hecht Schafran, national legal expert and member of AJC's National Pay Equity Task Force, and Ruth Gershon, Partner, Alston & Bird Law Firm and Chair, Atlanta Chapter Women's Issues Committee.

- February 10-12, 1988 – Rosalyn Carter, Betty Ford, Pat Nixon, and Ladybird Johnson were co-conveners of a major symposium in Atlanta titled "Women and the Constitution: A Bicentennial Perspective." Speakers included Supreme Court Justice Sandra Day O'Connor, former Texas Congresswoman Barbara Jordan, Coretta Scott King, and former Democratic nominee for Vice President, Geraldine Ferraro. Ronnie van Gelder, AJC's Assistant Area Director, co-chaired the volunteer recruitment effort. AJC was involved for nearly a year in the symposium, which drew 1,000 participants.

- September 6, 1990 – Elaine Alexander, Atlanta Chapter President, sent a letter to the editor to Durwood McAlister of the *Atlanta Constitution* stating "a woman's choice whether or not to abort should be based on her personal beliefs and religious traditions. The government should not enact legislation which interferes with or contravenes these deeply held and intimately private convictions." AJC and NCJW were active in Georgians for Choice, a statewide coalition of 44 pro-choice organizations.

- December 13, 1991 –I received a letter from U.S. Senator Wyche Fowler stating "knowing your interest in reproductive freedom and civil rights, I am writing to let you know of recent developments in Congress." He went on to say that he was a sponsor of the Freedom of Choice Act, which codified the Supreme Court's 1973 landmark *Roe V.*

*Wade* decision. He concluded with: "I am a co-sponsor of the Violence Against Women Act of 1991." This legislation included increased penalties for rape and aggravated assault, and triple funding for shelters for battered women.

- May 20, 1992 – AJC's ACCESS joined with the Atlanta Jewish Federation Business and Professional Women in co-sponsoring the program "Breaking the Glass Ceiling: Women in the Workplace."
- August 26, 1993 – Dianne Harnell Cohen, Atlanta Chapter Vice President, wrote a letter to the editor, *Atlanta Constitution*, urging Congress to support two reproductive freedom bills – the Freedom of Access to Clinic Entrances (FACE) and the Freedom of Choice Act (FOCA).
- March 7, 1994 – Lois Frank, Atlanta Chapter President, wrote to Lieutenant Governor Pierre Howard urging the retention of funding for Planned Parenthood's downtown facility and opposing all efforts to limit the counseling services they provide to their clients.

# LETTER FROM JUSTICE LEAH SEARS-COLLINS

*Supreme Court*
*of*
*Georgia*
*State Judicial Building*
*Atlanta, Georgia 30334*

AUG 5 1992

CHAMBERS OF
LEAH J. SEARS-COLLINS
JUSTICE

August 3, 1992

656-3474

Ms. Sherry Frank
The Atlanta Black/Jewish Coalition
One Securities Center, Suite 1310
3490 Piedmont Road, N.E.
Atlanta, GA 30305

Dear Sherry:

Thank you so much for supporting my election to the Supreme Court of Georgia. I am extremely grateful for all of your efforts.

My election to the Supreme Court is one of the proudest moments of my life. Your efforts made history in this state because never before has a woman won a contested state-wide election in Georgia. I am proud and grateful to be a Georgian.

Your assistance has worked to enhance a new era in our state by reaffirming the diversity that I represent. I commit to you that I will work hard to be one of the best justices that our state has ever known.

Although my campaign has come to a close, I will never forget those who offered me support. You have made a lasting impression on my mind and my heart.

Again, I thank you for your support.

Warmest regards.

Sincerely,

Justice Leah Sears-Collins

LSC/bjd

# ACCESS PROGRAMMING

## 1985

- *Jewish Perspective: Obstacles and Opportunities in the Arts, Politics, and Business*
- *Jews and Politics: Single Issue or Multi-Faceted?* featuring guest Howard Kohr, AJC's Assistant Washington Representative, and later director of AIPAC

## 1986

- Book discussion on *Love and Tradition: Marriage Between Jews and Christians* by Egon Mayer

## 1987

- *Wall Street Ambition: Greed and Ethics*
- *Election '88*
- *The Soviet Union under Gorbachev* – personal stories from AJC Chapter members' trip to meet with Refuseniks in Moscow, Leningrad (St. Petersburg), and Riga

## 1989

- *Israel and Palestine*
- *What Makes a Good Jew?*
- *White Supremacy and David Duke*

## 1990

- *The Rehnquist Court*
- *Immigration Trends*
- *Attitudes of Jewish Americans Towards Israel*
- *Atlanta Jewish History*
- *Is Judaism Reaching Out to Young Professionals and are They Reaching Back?*

1991

- *United Germany*
- *Bigotry in Politics*
- *Israel and Japan*

1992

- *Israel Update,* featuring guest Michael Oren, Director of AJC's Israel Office, later Israel's Ambassador to the U.S. and Knesset member
- *Ingredients for Bringing Jewish Holidays Home*
- *The Court's Eye Towards Religious Freedom and Individual Liberties*

1993

- *Entrepreneurs' Program* featuring Bernie Marcus, Co-founder and CEO of Home Depot
- *On the Capitol Steps: The Power Is in Your Hands, Learn How to Use It!* This advocacy training was held in the Georgia State Capital Chambers and was co-sponsored with Temple Young Professionals and Young Marrieds and AIPAC.
- *Why Be Jewish in the World Today?*
- *Israel and the Peace Process*

1994

- *Black-Jewish Relations*
- *Holocaust*
- *Extremism on College Campus*
- *Understanding the Different Movements in Judaism*
- *The Religious Right: Is It Wrong?* This event was held at the CNN Center as part of their *Talk Back Not Live* program series.
- *Peace in the Middle East and Its Effects on Israel and World Jewry* featuring former Knesset member, Michael Bar Zohar, visiting professor at Emory University
- Attended Chapter Shabbaton

**1995**

- *Success by 40* – topic of entrepreneurs' program hosted by The Coca-Cola Company featuring Barbara Babbitt Kaufman, Steve Koonin, Kent Alexander, and David Dubrof
- Tu B'shevat Seder
- *Purim Punchline*

**1996**

- Social Action became an additional part of the ACCESS agenda. They produced a guidebook for volunteer opportunities for young adults. Additional projects were added over the next decade. Projects included:
    - painting walls at Nicholas House
    - preparing meals for Project Open Hand
    - leading art projects for children at homeless shelters
- *What Makes Religion Front Page News?*
- *AJC's Role in Germany*, featuring guest Eugene DuBow, Director of AJC's Berlin Office

**1997**

- *I Can Get It For You Retail* – topic of entrepreneurs' program
- *Test Your Jewish IQ*

**1998**

- *Blacks and Jews in Music: Rhythm and Jews*
- Asian-Jewish Seder

**1999**

- *Skyscrapers and Super Highways: Metro Atlanta's Growth* – topic of entrepreneurs' program
- *Portrayal of Israel in the American Media*
- *Diversity in the Workplace* – co-sponsored with nine Asian and African-American organizations

2000

- *Then and Now: A Journey of the American Jewish Spirit* – topic of entrepreneurs' program, featuring Joel Babbit, Buck Goldstein, Steve Selig, and Chuck Wolf. Ten years earlier they had spoken at our first entrepreneurs' program.
- *Surfin' Jewish Style: Judaism on the Internet*
- Black and Jewish Comedy Night

2001

- *Shabbat Rocks in 3D: Davening, Dinner, and Discussion* - Ahavath Achim Synagogue, Temple Sinai, and Congregation Beth Jacob hosted this three-part series.
- *Hate on the Internet: Free Speech, Civil Rights, and Public Safety*

2002

- *December Dilemma*
- Traveled to Birmingham with 38 blacks and Jews
- *World after 9/11*
- *US-Israel Policy*

2003

- Entrepreneurs' program featuring Arthur Blank, Co-founder Home Depot and owner of NFL's Atlanta Falcons
- *Shaam-e-Shalom* Happy hour with Indian-American Young Professionals

ATLANTA BLACK/JEWISH COALITION 30TH ANNIVERSARY, 1982-2012

1982-1992

- Advocated for the renewal of the Voting Rights Act
- Supported legislation to create Martin Luther King, Jr., Holiday

- Opposed apartheid in South Africa and urged University of Georgia coach, Vince Dooley, to refrain from taking alumni group there
- Called upon Georgia Board of Pardons and Paroles to exonerate Leo Frank
- Held press conference to repudiate anti-Semitic remarks of Minister Louis Farrakhan
- Marched across Edmund Pettus Bridge in Selma, Alabama, for the 20th Anniversary of Selma to Montgomery March, which led to the Voting Rights Act of 1965
- Presented first Martin Luther King, Jr., Teach-In at Jewish day schools and City of Atlanta public schools: program continued for ten years
- Brought together teens from BBYO and NAACP
- Hosted Passover Seder led by Rabbi Alvin Sugarman, The Temple, and Mayor Andrew Young, co-sponsored by AJC, The Temple, NAACP, and Clergy and Laity Concerned: continued biennially with different clergy and co-sponsors until 2016
- Participated in March Against Fear and Intimidation in Forsyth County, Georgia, prior to first King Holiday observance
- Held reception at King Center with Coretta Scott King for Israel's first Arab Consul General, Muhamed Massarwa
- Traveled to Washington to commemorate 25th Anniversary of March on Washington and contributed support to sponsor student participants: returned for 30th Anniversary of the March
- Hosted Black and Jewish teen groups from Philadelphia and Washington: continued through the decades
- Planned memorial service to honor Congressman Mickey Leland of Texas: service led by Congressman John Lewis
- Held first of ten teen retreats for 10th and 11th graders
- Wrote to Georgia General Assembly members in support of Hate Crimes legislation

- Joined Atlanta Rabbinical Association in bus tour of black historic sites; Mayor Maynard Jackson served as tour guide

1992-2002
- Developed Project Understanding, a retreat for young Black and Jewish leaders; renamed in 1999, Marvin C. Goldstein Project Understanding Young Leaders Retreat, continues biennially
- Celebrated 10th Anniversary of Coalition with a luncheon at the King Center and dinner at Spelman College, hosted by college President Johnnetta Cole
- Created Black/Jewish Sisters Group
- Pushed for change on the Georgia State Flag; stayed with this issue until resolved
- Organized press conference at Atlanta City Hall at request of Mayor Maynard Jackson in response to violence in Los Angeles and Atlanta after Rodney King verdict
- Sponsored mayoral forum with candidates Myrtle Davis, Bill Campbell and Michael Lomax and later a series of lunches with mayoral candidates Robb Pitts, Shirley Franklin, and Gloria-Tinubu
- Traveled with Black/Jewish Sisters Group for day trips to U.S. Holocaust Memorial Museum in Washington, Harlem in New York and overseas tour in Israel
- Worked to pass Gun Control legislation in Georgia
- Hosted forum and book signing with authors Cornell West and Michael Lerner for their book, *Jews and Blacks: Let the Healing Begin,* and another with Congressman John Lewis and his book, *Walking With the Wind*
- Created retreat for Atlanta area black and Jewish college students
- Celebrated King Week at Atlanta Symphony with concert and private reception with Conductor Joel Levi, NPR's Martin Goldsmith, and Charlayne Hunter-Gault

- Launched home-hosted Dinners of Dialogue facilitating informal discussions for black and Jewish young leaders
- Participated in an interfaith service to reflect on black church bombings with Melissa Faye Green, author of *The Temple Bombing.*
- Helped rebuild the burned Gays Hill Baptist Church in Millen, Georgia
- Co-sponsored a Christmas, Hanukkah and Kwanzaa party and collected funds to donate black dolls from South Africa to children in homeless shelters

2002-2012
- Scheduled Goldstein Young Leaders Retreat and Passover Seder on alternating years
- Toured Birmingham Civil Rights Museum and repeated in later years
- Joined in Atlanta's march to commemorate the 40th anniversary of the March on Washington
- Remembered Mayor Maynard Jackson at memorial service at Atlanta City Hall
- Volunteered in community service project to observe Juneteenth, a celebration of the ending of slavery
- Co-sponsored event with National Black Arts Festival featuring Joshua Nelson, Jewish gospel singer and hosted luncheon at AJC office with him
- Drove residents of East Point and Toco Hills neighborhood to polls to vote
- Met with visiting Israeli young leaders in Atidim exchange program with AJC
- Opposed Voter I.D. Bill
- Volunteered at community service projects during King Day of Service

- Participated in inauguration of Morehouse College's Rabin-King Initiative at Martin Luther King, Jr., Crown Forum
- Promoted event to honor Reverend Dr. Gerald Durley and support Friends of the Arava Institute (Israel)
- Attended Rabin-King Initiative exhibit and forum on Helen Suzman and South Africa
- Celebrated the Coalition's 30th Anniversary at Passover Seder

Each decade was filled with programs to inform and educate and to build bridges of understanding among black and Jewish participants. Over the decades, Coalition members attended and often co-sponsored a wide array of cultural events and viewed exhibits at colleges and museums. Funding for Coalition activities came from voluntary donations from members as well as grant requests received from community organizations and foundations.

Celebrating 30 years of the Atlanta Black/Jewish Coalition,
Sherry Frank and Congressman John Lewis, 2012

1980/1981
- Created Ethnic Committee to explore coalition efforts with Greek, Hispanic, Black, and Arab Christian communities

1981/1982
- Hosted covered-dish dinner with AJC and Latin American Association (LAA)

1983/1984
- Participated in Georgia State University meeting to discuss immigration issues

1984/1985
- Assisted in the development of the Georgia State University conference on Acculturation and Assimilation

1985/1986
- Co-sponsored a forum on immigration with the Interdenominational Theological Center

1986/1987
- Worked with United Latin American Citizens to defeat "English Only" legislation

1988
- Attended a Chinese New Year Celebration
- Attended Organization of Chinese Americans national convention in Atlanta

1989/1990
- Attended ceremonial activities following Tiananmen Square violence

- Discussed Civil Rights Bill of 1990 with members of Asian, Hispanic, and Black organizations

1991/1992
- Brought together ethnic and religious agencies that work on immigration and resettlement issues regarding refugee funding
- Met with LAA to explore ways to work together
- Attended a dinner and dialogue hosted by Korean community leaders

1992/1993
- Featured a panel at summer board workshop with Hispanic, Black, and Korean leaders
- Initiated and chaired Shake Hands Atlanta, a one-day diversity and cultural festival, to foster positive intergroup relations

1993/1994
- Advocated against "English Only" bill at the Georgia Legislature
- Met for dinner with LAA to discuss issues of mutual concern and joint advocacy.
- Met with Indian-American leaders

1994/1995
- Opposed "English Only" bill
- Hosted an ethnic press briefing and presented an overview of the Jewish community

1995/1996
- Created the "Institute of Ethnic Awareness" for Jewish lay

and professional leaders, with a grant from the Atlanta Jewish Federation

- Met with Congressmen John Linder, Bob Barr, and John Lewis on anti-terrorism, immigration, and school prayer

## 1996/1997

- Held meetings on "The Changing Face of America" with ethnic communities
- Participated in the FIRM (Fair Immigration Reform Movement) Coalition, which worked to help legal immigrants receive their welfare reform benefits

## 1998/1999

- Shared materials and expertise of Jewish social service providers with representatives of agencies in the Asian, Hispanic, and Indian communities
- Co-sponsored a political forum with major Jewish, Chinese, Indian, Korean, and Hispanic organizations, featuring candidates for Governor, Lieutenant Governor, and U.S. Senate

## 2000/2001

- Hosted a luncheon with State Senator Sam Zamarippa discussing the Hispanic community
- Met with Josephine Tan, President, Chinese Community Center, regarding outreach to the Asian community

## 2001/2002

- Welcomed to Atlanta Mexican Consul General Remedios Gomez-Arnau at a reception with Jewish and Hispanic leaders hosted by Charles Ackerman

## 2002/2003

- Held screening of film "What's Cooking?" with numerous

ethnic organizations, which led to AJC initiating the Georgia Interethnic Coalition

- Hosted second ethnic press briefing
- Reached out to additional Hispanic organizations, Mexican American Legal Defense and Education Fund (MALDEF) and Georgia Association of Latino Elected Officials (GALEO)

## 2003/2004

- Co-sponsored with the Georgia Interethnic Coalition a voter registration training and hosted a family social with Harmony International Children's Choir
- Sponsored a series of programs with the Indian-American community
- Held a luncheon with the Indian Consul General
- Hosted an ACCESS-led panel of young ethnic leaders at the LAA offices for a program titled "Diversity in the City"

## 2004/2005

- Held a pre-Thanksgiving diversity luncheon at the LAA, using AJC's *America's Table®, A Thanksgiving Reader*
- Joined Rabbi Mario Karpuj in reaching out to the leader of Catholic Spanish-speaking priests at the Catholic Archdiocese of Atlanta

## 2005/2006

- Hosted a pre-Thanksgiving diversity luncheon with Congressman John Lewis and influential Hispanic organization professionals
- Co-sponsored a major program titled "Tapas and Topics in Entrepreneurship and Politics: Latino-Jewish Business and Public Policies Forum" with GALEO, Georgia Hispanic Network, and the National Society of Hispanic MBAs

Happy New Year! I am walking through the farmer's market and throwing things into the cart: apples, honey, fish, chicken, sweets – everything my New Year's spirit desires. A lot of us observe holidays with American Jewish families, volunteers who met us at the airport and helped us to arrange new housing and helped us through the tortuous process of learning English. These people became our friends and our mediators between the past and the present.

We sit at a holiday table at our friends' house. They all grew up here, but preserved the habits – as well as some fragments of the vocabularies – of their grandmothers who arrived at different times from Zhytomyr, Minsk, Kiev, Warsaw, Kishinev and other provinces. It's a noisy table, with praise for each new dish, a light licking of fingers, and a disorder that is pleasing to my eyes. Nobody is drunk. Everybody is happy and full and talking a lot. And, of course, they ask questions. Every year I give the same answers to the very same questions. Few of them have been to the country of their ancestors, and they know about it only through their grandmothers' reminiscences.

"Did you observe high holidays? Did you go to the synagogue? Did you light candles? Could you make a feast like this one? Tell us!"

"Our feasts were no worse than this one." That is the simplest and most truthful answer.

"The stores were empty, but not the dinner tables at our homes. I will tell you the truth about synagogues and lighting candles. I didn't go. I was a real Soviet citizen. I was afraid of everything."

They nod their heads. They understand everything. They want to know everything. How could we preserve our

Jewishness? What dishes did we fix on holidays? Did we put up with a lot of abuse?

"Did they insult you?" they ask.

"Just like everybody else."

I put a piece of cake in my mouth and squinted my eyes. They understand that at moments like these it is useless to ask questions.

As children, we divided all Jewish holidays into the really tasty, the tasty, and the so-so. In September my grandmother spoke those sibilant words: *Rosh Hashanah*. After that, food showed up on the table: gefilte fish, chicken, chicken soup, and most important, sweets. In a week she would say other words: *Yom Kippur*. After that, nothing at all showed up on the table. Grandmother lit candles, prayed, cried and asked for something. I wasn't especially inclined toward religion, but it was interesting to follow Grandmother. Grandmother was my favorite. All day she starved, and I tried to slip her a bite to eat. Not turning away, lightly swaying and without raising her voice she said, "Out!" and continued to whisper to the candle. No, *Yom Kippur* was only so-so for me.

My favorite holiday, and the one I waited for the longest, was *Hanukkah*. Friends and relatives walked in: "Where's the child?" and turned their pockets inside out looking for money. At that time the coins were still worth something. "What kind of people are you?" asked my Christian girlfriends. "People give you a pile of money, just because you're a kid?"

"We're that kind of people. Our children are very dear." I had no idea why they were paying me, but I was proud of my people.

My childhood was fantastic. I had my mama, my papa, my older brother, my grandmother and whole army of Russian, Ukrainian and Jewish neighbors. They all loved to reminisce, and the main themes of their memories were Nazi occupation, WWII, and liberation.

They recalled mostly to me since I was the only one who didn't witness these events. One by one, they set me on their shoulders and said, "Lucky thing! A post-war child!" I didn't understand my luck. On the contrary, I envied them, and felt like a second-class child.

I didn't sense my ethnic identity until I was six. One day our neighbors talked my mother into letting me stay for a week with their relatives in the country. It was a wonderful village: dairy cows, picking fruits and berries, the river and the pasture. They looked after me as their city guest. They gave me the best food, let me sleep all day and didn't let me get near the cows. Soon my wonderful week ended. Two days before I left, I was standing near the house waiting for the mailman to come on his horse. Away from my mother, I lost my look: my hair wasn't braided, my dress was on backwards, and my face was blue from mulberries from my mouth to my eyes.

The mailman's horse didn't come. Some women walked past. Their heads were wrapped in white scarves and they carried rakes and shovels. I nodded, having quickly picked up the rural custom of greeting everybody, they answered in a friendly way. "Who's that?" asked one of them in Ukrainian. "That's the little *kike* who came to see the Bartoshes." And they walked past. I went cold. Usually my tears pour out even before I've borne an insult, but here they stopped somewhere. I couldn't breathe. They didn't hit me, they weren't crude. They said the word almost tenderly. Why was I so ashamed? I ran home, packed my things, cried my eyes out to my hosts and they took me back to my mother that day.

"What did they say to you?" they asked.

"They said a word to me."

"What kind of word?"

But they couldn't make me repeat it. I had heard that word many times, thrown at me and those close to me, and even at my totally innocent Christian friends. Soon I got used to it. But at that time, one question tormented me: "Why? Why don't they like Jews?"

"Grandma, why don't they like us?"

"Hush!" she said. "The neighbors will hear. Some like us and some don't."

"But why is it some people don't like us?" She only sighed in response.

"Mama! Why don't they like Jews?"

"Hush!" Mama pointed at the door. "The neighbors!"

"What about the neighbors? They like us." But all of a sudden I switched to a whisper.

"Like us or don't like us. We're not daisies. Don't be a pest. You're too little. You'll grow up and then we'll talk."

"When will that be?"

"Let's say in ten years."

In ten years, I already had my diploma. I didn't ask stupid questions. Like most of my people, I possessed enough sense and vision to make out all the different kinds of hypocrisy. We knew where we could never get hired, what colleges would never accept us. We applied to universities that were located hundreds, if not thousands, of miles from our homes. And that unofficial quota in those places, we took as a quota of life.

I told my son only about the historical past of the Jews. He didn't ask questions about the present. We lived in a typical ten-story building. Children his age lived on almost every floor.

From the beginning, their strollers bumped into each

other, then they played in the sand box together, and, finally, they went off to the first grade. But after two weeks, my son came home from school, threw down his book-bag and made a declaration: "That's *it!* I'm not going to school anymore. Tomorrow I'm going to the housing committee and changing my nationality to Latvian."

"Latvian? And us? You'll be Latvian, and we'll be Jews?""Let's all be Latvian then," he shouted back.

"Well, no. We're not ready to be Latvians; we want to be Jews. And the housing committee only decide issues of living space. You change your nationality at another office, but you'll have to wait ten years."

"So, what should I do now?"

"Fight."

And I remembered my mother turning to whisper patience and humility. And I remembered my father, who fought and was wounded for his country, his empty right sleeve which earned him a card. When he showed that card, he could buy things without having to wait in line.

There was a peaceful line waiting for meat. Papa showed his card and pulled out his oversized bag, and the clerk threw in a brisket wrapped in newspaper. A young man said that word behind Papa's back. After his injury, Papa had poor hearing, and I placed my hope on that. Papa turned and slowly wound up the bag around his fist. The brisket poked out of the wet newspaper in places through holes in the bag. Papa walked up to the young man and, with his one hand, hit him in the face with the brisket right in front of those who stood quietly in line. A piece of meat stuck to the man's cheeks, and now the young man looked like an invalid, wounded in the face. No one said a word. "Next!" the clerk shouted, letting it be known that life would continue. I grabbed Papa by his empty sleeve and pulled it toward the street.

"Don't count on them." Papa motioned at the heavens, and I understood that he meant the government. "You have to fight."

I didn't know how to fight. But I didn't stand out for my silence, patience and humility either.

In the evening, I rang the doorbell of the first grader who insulted my son. He lived one floor above us. His sweet mother, with whom I sat at meetings behind the same desk, held her heart and asked her son, "How could you say that word?" "Everybody talks that way," the boy raised his eyes at me. I always liked him. After school he usually ate lunch, played and did his homework at our place. He was a future leader and a very attractive leader with a warlike last name of Orliuk (eaglet). On the floor stood his army of toy soldiers, and they waited for the attack. The little commander smiled at me and shrugged his shoulders as if with that he was excused for everything. It was time for him to begin battle – and for me too. I looked around his room: a writing desk, a bookshelf with children's encyclopedia, Pushkin Chukovsky, Marshak and Kassil (the famous Russian children's authors)

"Are these your favorite books?"

"Yes."

"And who is your favorite?"

"Kassil."

I walked to the bookshelf. "Help me," I said, holding out several volumes. "Let's go throw them out." I moved toward the window.

"What are you doing?" In excitement, he forgot my name.

"Just this. Your Samuel Marshak and your favorite Lev

Kassil are both Jews. Will you keep them, or should we take them to the dumpster?"

He stood with his books scattered around the room. His mother still held her hand to her heart. I walked toward the door.

During the next three years, I talked with teachers, spoke at meetings and led the whole class on an excursion to Babi Yar. (During World War II in Babi Yar, Nazis killed 100,000 Jews.)

Of course our name was not alone. There was Rabinovich, Burman, Pritzker in our ten-story building we lived in and still other tens of thousands of different-sounding surnames that bore the whole weight of everyday meanness toward our people. And everyone of them solved that problem in its own way.

We changed schools – to a school in the center of Ukraine's capital. After two weeks I came to talk to the homeroom teacher. An athletic boy smiled at me charmingly and politely opened the door into the classroom. A future leader, I thought. "Who is she?" the children asked him! "That's the mother of a future citizen of Israel," answered the boy expressively, not thinking whether I was listening or not. A true leader, I quickly changed my opinion. Papa was right. You do have to fight.

And we changed schools again, to a typical American school in the center of the capital of the state of Georgia. But the old question bothers me here, too. Do they like Jews or not?

Not really. But American Jews know that their religion, homes and families uphold the state that respects the law. You can always find offenders. So in American cities, large or small, there are always Jewish communities, federations and committees, where their members preserve their historical past and think of their future.

The year 5755 in the Jewish calendar has arrived. Some say that the count of years began with the creation of the world. How did we manage to preserve ourselves living apart in different countries, cities, in little towns in the strictly limited "Pale" and even in the ghetto? How did we manage to preserve ourselves after the Spanish Inquisition, after the pogroms in Eastern Europe and after six million perished in the Second World War? How did we manage to give the world Freud and Einstein? Oppenheimer and Landau? Mendelssohn and Marc Chagall? Franz Kafka and Heinrich Heine? It's a puzzle. But maybe our religion, tradition and culture, the sad dates in our history and our strong and loving families helped us preserve our unity.

The sounds of Jewish melodies uplift everybody, old men straighten up and join the circle of children and grandchildren. Shoulder to shoulder, we dance, holding tightly to each other and no one can break our circle or stop our *Hora*.

I am walking through the farmers market and throwing apples, honey and fish into the cart. Stop! I just remembered something.

In September, five years ago, we observed New Year's not long before our departure. We had already lost our Soviet citizenship, our apartment resembled a storage room, like everyone's apartments who took the same path. September is the best time in Kiev. Multicolored leaves fly all over. I wandered around my neighborhood and in my mind said goodbye to everything my eyes had gotten used to. It was easy to buy groceries at that time. Everything was there – carts stood on the streets full of fruits and vegetables. And almost every store was selling live fish. Silver carp was so cheap – it's unforgettable.

There was almost no one in line, just me and three old ladies. Under my arm I held a book "Teach Yourself to Speak English." I studied for three minutes or so and then started to follow the jumping fish. I have to remember this, I thought, saying goodbye in my mind to the fish too. My turn came around. I asked for three larger pieces. Then a woman behind me pushed slightly.

"What's wrong?" I said, turning.

"That's enough picking." Her eyes focused on my book. "Go to Israel! You can catch them yourself in your Dead Sea."

Should I hit her or not, I thought. An old lady? Never!

I took shiny fish, turned to the lady, and put my hand on her shoulder. Her unpleasant eyes turned frightened.

"My dear!" I said sadly. "Why? Why would you deprive me of my nostalgia?"

I went home quickly and lightly. My eyes didn't try to remember anything else. The fish flapped and opened its mouth.

"Today is New Year's. Forgive everybody," said its slippery lips.

"Of course, I forgive! Happy New Year!" Then I looked at my book, turned my face to the West and said, this time in English, "Happy New Year!"

Sasha and Dmitri Kodor, Russian immigrants

Me with
my eleven
grandchilren

With my
daughter
Jacque
Friedland's
family

With my son Drew
Frank's family

With my son Jake
Frank's family

With my
daughter
Laura
Barnard's
family

## ABOUT THE AUTHOR

Sherry Frank was born in Atlanta on November 11, 1942. She graduated from Henry Grady High School and attended Stephens College in Columbia, Missouri. She has served on major boards in the Atlanta Jewish community including the Ahavath Achim Synagogue, Congregation Or Hadash, Epstein School, Weber School, Jewish Family and Career Services, Jewish Federation of Greater Atlanta, Friends of the Israel Defense Forces, Birthright Israel Foundation Atlanta, and the Atlanta Jewish Film Society, Inc.

While Southeast Area Director for the American Jewish Committee, she was a community activist and intergroup relations specialist and was centrally involved in a wide array of interethnic and interfaith activities.

In the general community she has served on committees of United Way, the Atlanta Regional Commission, and the Community Foundation of Greater Atlanta and was appointed to the Georgia Human Relations Commission. Sherry Frank was a member of the 1983 class of Leadership Atlanta and the 1988 YWCA Academy of Women Achievers. In addition, she was on the National Boards of the National Council of Jewish Women and MAZON, A Jewish Response to Hunger.

She is the mother of four children and eleven grandchildren and resides in Atlanta, Georgia.